Reforms, Organizational Change and Performance in Higher Education

Rómulo Pinheiro • Lars Geschwind
Hanne Foss Hansen • Kirsi Pulkkinen
Editors

Reforms, Organizational Change and Performance in Higher Education

A Comparative Account from the Nordic Countries

palgrave
macmillan

Editors
Rómulo Pinheiro
Department of Political Science &
Management
University of Agder
Kristiansand, Norway

Lars Geschwind
School of Industrial Engineering and
Management
KTH Royal Institute of Technology
Stockholm, Sweden

Hanne Foss Hansen
Department of Political Science
University of Copenhagen
Copenhagen, Denmark

Kirsi Pulkkinen
Faculty of Social Sciences
University of Lapland
Rovaniemi, Finland

ISBN 978-3-030-11737-5   ISBN 978-3-030-11738-2   (eBook)
https://doi.org/10.1007/978-3-030-11738-2

Library of Congress Control Number: 2019935186

© The Editor(s) (if applicable) and The Author(s) 2019 This book is an open access publication
Open Access This book is licensed under the terms of the Creative Commons Attribution 4.0 International License (http://creativecommons.org/licenses/by/4.0/), which permits use, sharing, adaptation, distribution and reproduction in any medium or format, as long as you give appropriate credit to the original author(s) and the source, provide a link to the Creative Commons licence and indicate if changes were made.
The images or other third party material in this book are included in the book's Creative Commons licence, unless indicated otherwise in a credit line to the material. If material is not included in the book's Creative Commons licence and your intended use is not permitted by statutory regulation or exceeds the permitted use, you will need to obtain permission directly from the copyright holder.
The use of general descriptive names, registered names, trademarks, service marks, etc. in this publication does not imply, even in the absence of a specific statement, that such names are exempt from the relevant protective laws and regulations and therefore free for general use.
The publisher, the authors and the editors are safe to assume that the advice and information in this book are believed to be true and accurate at the date of publication. Neither the publisher nor the authors or the editors give a warranty, express or implied, with respect to the material contained herein or for any errors or omissions that may have been made. The publisher remains neutral with regard to jurisdictional claims in published maps and institutional affiliations.

Cover illustration: Björn Forenius / Getty Images

This Palgrave Macmillan imprint is published by the registered company Springer Nature Switzerland AG.
The registered company address is: Gewerbestrasse 11, 6330 Cham, Switzerland

For our dear colleague Helge Hernes (18.03.1946–06.09.2018), in memoriam

Acknowledgement

The data presented in the current volume and individual chapters emanate from a comparative study funded by the Norwegian Research Council under its FINNUT flagship program, a long-term program for research and innovation in the educational sector program. The project number was 237782, and the project was titled 'Does it matter? Assessing the performance effects of changes in leadership and management structures in Nordic Higher Education'.

Contents

Part I Setting the Stage 1

1 Does It Really Matter? Assessing the Performance Effects of Changes in Leadership and Management Structures in Nordic Higher Education 3
Kirsi Pulkkinen, Timo Aarrevaara, Laila Nordstrand Berg, Lars Geschwind, Hanne Foss Hansen, Helge Hernes, Jussi Kivistö, Jonas Krog Lind, Anu Lyytinen, Elias Pekkola, Rómulo Pinheiro, Bjørn Stensaker, and Johan Söderlind

2 Performance in Higher Education Institutions and Its Variations in Nordic Policy 37
Jussi Kivistö, Elias Pekkola, Laila Nordstrand Berg, Hanne Foss Hansen, Lars Geschwind, and Anu Lyytinen

3 Nordic Higher Education in Flux: System Evolution and Reform Trajectories 69
Rómulo Pinheiro, Timo Aarrevaara, Laila Nordstrand Berg, Tatiana Fumasoli, Lars Geschwind, Hanne Foss Hansen, Helge Hernes, Jussi Kivistö, Jonas Krog Lind, Anu Lyytinen, Elias Pekkola, Kirsi Pulkkinen, Bjørn Stensaker, and Johan Söderlind

Part II Cross Cutting Themes — 109

4 National Performance-Based Research Funding Systems: Constructing Local Perceptions of Research? — 111
Johan Söderlind, Laila Nordstrand Berg, Jonas Krog Lind, and Kirsi Pulkkinen

5 External Research Funding and Authority Relations — 145
Jonas Krog Lind, Helge Hernes, Kirsi Pulkkinen, and Johan Söderlind

6 The Changing Roles of Academic Leaders: Decision-Making, Power, and Performance — 181
Lars Geschwind, Timo Aarrevaara, Laila Nordstrand Berg, and Jonas Krog Lind

7 Strategy as Dialogue and Engagement — 211
Timo Aarrevaara, Rómulo Pinheiro, and Johan Söderlind

8 Evaluation Practices and Impact: Overload? — 235
Hanne Foss Hansen, Timo Aarrevaara, Lars Geschwind, and Bjørn Stensaker

Part III Taking Stock and Moving Forward — 267

9 Governing Performance in the Nordic Universities: Where Are We Heading and What Have We Learned? — 269
Lars Geschwind, Hanne Foss Hansen, Rómulo Pinheiro, and Kirsi Pulkkinen

Appendix A: FINNUT Interview Guide English — 301

Appendix B: FINNUT Survey Questions — 311

Index — 321

Notes on Contributors

Timo Aarrevaara is Professor of Public Management at the University of Lapland and has professional experience in public administration as well as in research and teaching. Aarrevaara has participated in and conducted several evaluating and auditing projects, and has acted as the principal investigator for a number of projects in higher education. Aarrevaara has strong international higher education research links and is a co-editor of Springer's 'The Changing Academy' Series and author and co-author of several papers and book chapters.

Laila Nordstrand Berg has a PhD in public policy and administration from the University of Bergen, Norway. She is working as an associate professor at Western Norway University of Applied Sciences. She is also an associate member of the Governance and Leadership in the Public Sector (GOLEP) research group at the University of Agder in Norway. She is doing research on management of universities and hospitals from public and private sector in a comparative perspective. Laila's interests are related to the intersection between public policy and administration, organisational studies, reforms, management and the influence of the market on management of the institutions from private and public sectors.

Tatiana Fumasoli is Associate Professor of Higher Education Studies at the University College London (UCL) Institute of Education (London, UK). She holds a PhD from the University of Lugano (Switzerland, 2011) with a thesis on university strategic management. She was before at ARENA Centre for European Studies and at the Department of Education at the University of Oslo, where she coordinated an international project comparing university managing practices across the continent. Her research interests lie at the intersection of management studies, organisation theory and sociology of professions and expertise. She has published with *Higher Education, Higher Education Policy, Minerva* and *Studies in Higher Education*, amongst others. Tatiana is co-editor of *Higher Education Quarterly* and is a member of the editorial board of several scientific journals on higher education studies.

Lars Geschwind is Professor of Engineering Education Policy and Management and coordinator of the research group HEOS (Higher Education Organization Studies at KTH Royal Institute of Technology, Sweden). His main research interests are higher education policy, institutional governance, academic leadership and management and academic work. He is involved in a number of projects focusing on change processes in higher education institutions, including, for example, governance and steering, quality assurance, academic careers and partnership with industry. Most studies include a comparative component and a historical perspective. He has published various scientific books, peer-reviewed journal articles and chapters in anthologies. Lars has professional experience from working on higher education and research from government agencies, private institutions and international consultancy. He has also worked as a researcher and senior lecturer at three different Swedish universities before joining KTH. Lars holds a PhD degree in history, a master of arts degree and a teacher training certificate (upper secondary school), all from Uppsala University.

Hanne Foss Hansen is Professor of Public Administration and Organisation at the Department of Political Science, the University of Copenhagen. Her main interests are public organisation and management, public sector reform, evaluation, evidence-based policy and practice, and higher education and research policy. Her recent publications include articles in *American Journal of Evaluation*, Evaluation, *European Journal of Higher Education, Science and Public Policy* and *Scandinavian Journal of Public Administration* as well as contributions to edited volumes published at Sage, Springer, Edward Elgar, Palgrave and Routledge.

Helge Hernes (1946–2018) was Emeritus Associate Professor of Public Administration at the University of Agder, Norway. Hernes holds a PhD from the Norwegian School of Economics in Bergen. He taught organisation theory and organisation behaviour, specialising in organisational bottom-up processes. Hernes has done research in the health and education systems. His research has been published in national book chapters and in international journals, for example, *International Public Management Journal*.

Jussi Kivistö is Professor at the Higher Education Group, Tampere University, Finland. Kivistö has over ten years of experience in teaching and coordination in higher education management programmes at the master's and PhD levels. He has served as consultant for the World Bank and acted as Principal Investigator/researcher in several national and international research and development projects. Kivistö is also a frequent keynote speaker or invited expert in events and projects related to Finnish higher education policy. Kivistö has authored around 75 publications, mainly in the field of higher education management and policy.

Jonas Krog Lind is a PhD student at the Department of Political Science, University of Copenhagen. His research interests cover science and university governance broadly and research funding, management and evaluation particularly. He has a professional background in science funding and policy from the Danish Agency for Science, Technology and Innovation.

Anu Lyytinen holds a PhD in administrative sciences and is working as a university lecturer (acting) at the Higher Education Group, Tampere University, Finland. She has several years' experience as a researcher and teacher in the field of higher education studies, higher education administration and management. Her main research interests include higher education institutions-society/stakeholder relationship and changes therein.

Elias Pekkola is Acting Professor of Administrative Science at the Faculty of Management, University of Tampere, Finland. Pekkola's publications include several articles and books on academic work, academic profession, careers and HR policy. Pekkola serves also as an academic coordinator of 'Nordic Master Programme in Innovative Governance and Public Management'. He has acted in various expert roles in Finland and in international projects on academic work, careers and higher education policy.

Rómulo Pinheiro is Professor of Public Policy and Administration at the University of Agder, Norway, where he co-heads the research group on public governance and leadership (GOLEP). His research interests are located at the intersection of public policy and administration, organisational theory, economic geography, innovation and higher education studies. Pinheiro has edited and co-edited a variety of books for major publishers like Springer, Palgrave and Emerald. His work has been published in scientific journals such as *Public Administration Review, Science and Public Policy, Higher Education, Studies in Higher Education, European Journal of Higher Education, Cambridge Journal of Regions, Economy and Society, Scandinavian Journal of Public Administration, Tertiary Education and Management*, and so on.

Kirsi Pulkkinen is a researcher at the Faculty of Social Sciences at the University of Lapland, Finland. She is finalising her doctoral thesis on the interaction between researchers and their societal counterparts, in particular the policy community. Kirsi is involved in a number of international projects studying the impact, public engagement and performance of research communities, and she is part of a consortium evaluating the research institutes and funding reform of Finland. Her research interests include the societal impact of research and the dynamics of knowledge production and utilisation between the scientific communities and their societal partners. Kirsi is particularly interested in the intricacies of the science-policy-practitioner interface and knowledge advocacy of universities. She has previously worked in managerial positions as an expert and advisor on higher education cooperation and civil society collaboration at the Ministry for Foreign Affairs of Finland, as well as advisor on co-creative methods and competitive research funding at the University of Helsinki. In addition to her scientific work, Kirsi works as a co-creation consultant and trains scientists on the methods of stakeholder engagement and collaboration.

Johan Söderlind is a PhD student at the School of Industrial Engineering and Management, KTH Royal Institute of Technology in Sweden. His research is focused on leadership and management of higher education and research, with a particular interest in the use of performance indicators. He holds an MSc in Political Science from Uppsala University. He has previous professional experience as a research-funding administrator and research assistant.

Bjørn Stensaker is Professor at the Department of Education, University of Oslo, Norway. He is also a Research Professor at the Nordic Institute for Studies in Innovation, Research, and Education (NIFU) in Oslo. Stensaker holds a PhD from the University of Twente, the Netherlands, and has a special research interest in reform, governance and organisational change in higher education. His work has been published widely in a range of international journals and books. Stensaker is the President of EAIR, the European Higher Education Society.

List of Figures

Fig. 1.1	The Nordic countries as the geographical focus of the book (excluding Iceland)	9
Fig. 3.1	University core funding and external research funding, 2003–2013	83
Fig. 5.1	Development in external funding as a percentage of the total funding for research at higher education institutions	151
Fig. 7.1	Participation in strategy formulation (percentage of those academics who agreed with values 4 and 5; scale ranged from 1 (*no participation*) to 5 (*strong participation*))	216
Fig. 7.2	Influence in strategy formulation (percentage of those who agreed with values of influence in strategy formulation, where 4 is *some influence* and 5 is *strong influence*)	221
Fig. 7.3	Respondents' views on how strategies affect resource allocation (percentage of those who agreed with values 4 and 5)	226
Fig. 9.1	Development in external funding as a percentage of total funding for research at Nordic HEIs	289

List of Tables

Table 1.1	Visions of the European university	15
Table 1.2	Survey population, sampling and response rate	25
Table 1.3	Comparative samples of managers and senior academics	26
Table 1.4	Number of interviewees per country	27
Table 1.5	Themes for primary data collection	27
Table 3.1	The Danish higher education university landscape, 2013	72
Table 3.2	University funding from 2007 to 2013, Thousand Danish Kroner-fixed prices	77
Table 3.3	Key policy initiatives within teaching	79
Table 3.4	Key policy initiatives within research	79
Table 3.5	Universities in Finland, 2013 (all figures are FTE)	81
Table 3.6	Key policy initiatives related to education	87
Table 3.7	Key policy initiatives related to research	87
Table 3.8	Universities in Norway, 2013 (all figures are FTE)	89
Table 3.9	Universities' core funding, selected years for the period 2003–2013 (in billion Norwegian Kroner or NOK, rounded figures)	94
Table 3.10	University research funding per source, 2003–2013 (in billion NOK, rounded figures)	94
Table 3.11	Key policy initiatives related to education	96
Table 3.12	Key policy initiatives related to research	96
Table 3.13	The Swedish university landscape, 2013 (all figures as FTE)	98
Table 3.14	University education and research funding per source, 2003–2013 (in million SEK)	101
Table 3.15	Key policy initiatives related to education	105
Table 3.16	Key policy initiatives related to research	105
Table 4.1	Analytical framework: the influence of metrics	118

Table 4.2	Main components of the PRFSs in Denmark, Sweden, Finland and Norway	124
Table 5.1	Autonomy in research topic, methods and project partners by country (the 'mean' is the mean score on a Likert scale from 1 'I strongly disagree' to 5 'I strongly agree')	156
Table 5.2	Tensions between managerial priorities and academic autonomy (the 'mean' is the mean score on a Likert scale from 1 'I strongly disagree' to 5 'I strongly agree')	157
Table 6.1	Managers' decision-making power represented as the percentage who responded with a 4 or 5 on a 5-point Likert scale	189
Table 7.1	Academics' views to meeting goals of strategies (percentage of those who agreed with values 4 and 5)	225
Table 7.2	Administrators' views to meet goals of strategies (percentage of those who agreed with values 4 and 5)	225
Table 8.1	A typology of evaluation models	238
Table 8.2	Overall pattern of evaluation practices at Danish universities	241
Table 8.3	Overall pattern of evaluation practices at Finnish universities	244
Table 8.4	Overall pattern of evaluation practices at Norwegian universities	247
Table 8.5	Overall pattern of evaluation practices at Swedish universities	250
Table 8.6	Evaluation models in use	255
Table 8.7	Respondents' views on the legitimacy of evaluation and measurement (percentage of those who answered 4 (*agree*) and 5 (*strongly agree*))	256
Table 8.8	Respondents' views on the impact of evaluation and measurement (percentage of those who answered 4 (*agree*) and 5 (*strongly agree*))	258
Table 9.1	Visions of the European university	274
Table 9.2	Evaluation models and procedures	282
Table 9.3	Main components of the performance-related research funding systems in Denmark, Sweden, Finland, and Norway	287

PART I

Setting the Stage

CHAPTER 1

Does It Really Matter? Assessing the Performance Effects of Changes in Leadership and Management Structures in Nordic Higher Education

*Kirsi Pulkkinen, Timo Aarrevaara,
Laila Nordstrand Berg, Lars Geschwind,
Hanne Foss Hansen, Helge Hernes, Jussi Kivistö,
Jonas Krog Lind, Anu Lyytinen, Elias Pekkola,
Rómulo Pinheiro, Bjørn Stensaker, and Johan Söderlind*

Helge Hernes passed away in the Fall of 2018.

K. Pulkkinen (✉) • T. Aarrevaara
Faculty of Social Sciences, University of Lapland, Rovaniemi, Finland
e-mail: kirsi.pulkkinen@ulapland.fi; timo.aarrevaara@ulapland.fi

L. N. Berg
Department of Social Science, Western Norway University of Applied Sciences, Sogndal, Norway
e-mail: laila.nordstrand.berg@hvl.no

L. Geschwind • J. Söderlind
School of Industrial Engineering and Management, KTH Royal Institute of Technology, Stockholm, Sweden
e-mail: larsges@kth.se; johanso2@kth.se

© The Author(s) 2019
R. Pinheiro et al. (eds.), *Reforms, Organizational Change and Performance in Higher Education*,
https://doi.org/10.1007/978-3-030-11738-2_1

Introduction: Rationalisation and Converging Higher Education Policies

As a sector of the economy, higher education has been the subject of substantial change in the last couple of decades, not least due to the exponential growth in the number of students and institutions, often seen as pertaining to the phenomena of massification (Trow and Burrage 2010). All over the world, organisational fields and their specific institutions, such as universities, have similarities in organisational design and activities. In many countries, universities have experienced a shift towards 'academic capitalism' (Slaughter and Leslie 1999) and are operating as 'entrepreneurial universities' (Clark 1998; Etzkowitz et al. 2008). Rationalisation of the universities as organisational actors has been done via the introduction of a more formal structure in terms of a stronger emphasis on quality assurance, evaluation, accountability measures and incentive systems. These can be considered a transnational process linked to the New Public Management (NPM) type of governance reforms (Ramirez and Christensen 2013; Seeber et al. 2015).

The social mechanisms of spreading ideas of rationalisation can be highlighted through the perspective of institutional isomorphism (DiMaggio and Powell 1983). Literature on isomorphism concentrates on the increasing similarity of organisational and institutional structures and

---

H. F. Hansen • J. K. Lind
Department of Political Science, University of Copenhagen,
Copenhagen, Denmark
e-mail: hfh@ifs.ku.dk; jkl@ifs.ku.dk

H. Hernes • R. Pinheiro
Department of Political Science & Management, University of Agder,
Kristiansand, Norway
e-mail: romulo.m.pinheiro@uia.no

J. Kivistö • A. Lyytinen • E. Pekkola
Faculty of Management and Business, Tampere University, Tampere, Finland
e-mail: jussi.kivisto@tuni.fi; anu.lyytinen@tuni.fi; elias.pekkola@tuni.fi

B. Stensaker
Department of Education, University of Oslo, Oslo, Norway
e-mail: bjorn.stensaker@iped.uio.no

cultures. Studies on policy convergence instead focus on changes in national policy characteristics. Policy convergence, that is, the development of similar or identical policies across countries over time (Knill 2005), seems to be particularly evident in Nordic countries. They show similar types of policy development in many significant areas of higher education policy, particularly those related to governance.

One of the most important reasons behind policy convergence is international policy promotion, where an actor with expertise in a policy field promotes certain policies. International (or supranational) organisations specialising in certain policy fields are the main actors for inducing the convergence of policies. This happens when they actively promote certain policies and define objectives and standards, as well as arguments, to support their case in an international setting. Countries diverging from promoted policy models may feel pressure to comply with the policies (Holzinger and Knill 2005; Knill 2005).

There are two overarching international political processes relating to higher education in Europe which presumably have a significant impact on the policy convergence: the higher education 'Modernisation Agenda' (European Commission 2006, 2011), promoted under the auspices of the EU institutions (European Commission, in particular), and the intergovernmental Bologna process (Moisio 2014). Many of the NPM ideals implemented in Nordic universities, such as promoting the accountability and autonomy of higher education institutions and improving the governance, funding, quality and relevance of higher education, are directly aligned with the Commission's Modernisation Agenda. Interestingly, the Modernisation Agenda presents the American higher education system and universities in particular as one of the important points of comparison in developing European higher education (Slaughter and Cantwell 2012; Slaughter and Taylor 2016).

Similarly, the Bologna process seems to increase policy convergence at the European level, even though research evidence for this is not yet entirely clear (Witte 2008). However, Voegtle et al. (2011) found that higher education policies of Bologna participants converge more strongly and that the Bologna process has made a crucial difference in increasing the similarity of higher education policies. Particularly in the area of quality assurance, the majority of Bologna signatories implemented most of the measures. They also included all the required actors into their quality assurance measures according to Bologna standards by 2008 (Voegtle et al. 2011).

Furthermore, international/intergovernmental organisations such as the Organisation for Economic Co-operation and Development (OECD), the World Bank and the United Nations Educational, Scientific and Cultural Organisation (UNESCO) are highly influential actors in higher education policy convergence (e.g. see Shahjahan and Madden 2015). At the European and Nordic level, the OECD has the most notably high level of impact on policy convergence. Nation states, including Nordic countries, often rely on the OECD to provide them with the latest data on trends, current issues and policy options. The OECD uses conferences, trend and review reports and the mediation of policy language to influence the thinking of national-level policymakers within and outside of its member countries (Shahjahan and Madden 2015). For instance, the OECD's thematic reviews can provide strong legitimisation or justification to national governments for initiating policy reforms, as has happened in Finland (Kallo 2009).

In addition to the influence of international organisations, cross-national policy convergence might simply be the result of similar but independent responses caused by the countries reacting to the same types of policy problems (Knill 2005; Bennett 1991). At the same time, convergence in policies is more likely in countries that are characterised by high institutional similarity. Policies tend to be implemented insofar as they fit with existing cultures, socio-economic structures and institutional arrangements. In their search for relevant policy models, states are expected to look to the experiences of those countries with which they share an especially close set of cultural similarities and ties (Knill 2005).

However, although policy convergence is clearly observable across the Nordic countries, it is important to note that similar policies are introduced at different points in time and with important variations in the details. For instance, all the Nordic countries have introduced performance-based funding systems linked to the distribution of resources for basic research. Yet, performance is measured using different indicators and redistribution potentials. The effects are also somewhat different. There seems to be more convergence in policy ideas and policy rhetoric than in actual policy implementation. Other examples of these dynamics are found in relation to the overall governance and management structures, as well as to the national quality assurance systems linked to education.

Reforms inspired by the NPM have had a profound effect on the internal structures and governance arrangements of public higher education institutions in the Nordic countries. The impact has been further strengthened by parallel calls for increasing accountability and efficiency (Pinheiro et al. 2014). Yet, few studies to date have systematically and comparatively investigated what types of effects the so-called modernisation efforts have had on teaching and research performance in publicly run and funded universities. This book responds to this gap in knowledge and brings forth new data and comparative analysis of universities in the Nordic countries.

The environmental conditions under which Nordic higher education institutions operate have changed dramatically in the last two decades. Policy efforts aimed at modernising the sector have paid considerable attention to the way in which public universities operate. A strong focus has been given to managerially inspired aspects, such as efficiency, effectiveness and accountability (de Boer and Enders 2017). In addition to managing their internal operations in more cost-efficient manners, public universities are increasingly expected to respond to the needs of various, rather different, external stakeholder groups. In light of the social contract that exists between the universities and society that, in essence, funds them, interacting with the surrounding society has become a task to be tackled actively (Fumasoli et al. 2014; de Jong et al. 2016). One of the many mechanisms being used to achieve these goals relies on enhancing the rationalisation of internal structures and activities by promoting professional management. As a result, most Nordic universities have developed extended administrative structures, ranging from central to unit levels. These structures have been designed to be capable of strategically supporting the primary activities of universities, that is, teaching and research (Amaral et al. 2003). Some have introduced changes in the nomination of formal leaders, that is, they are appointed rather than elected.

Reform efforts are both costly and demanding for the personnel. Therefore, it is necessary to monitor the extent to which they generate the expected results. Consideration should be given to the cost-efficient management of the universities as well as to the situations of the personnel whose task is to perform their duties according to the academic quality criteria in the midst of extensive reforms. As a key sector of the economy, it is necessary to take stock of the ways in which the higher education sector has changed performance-wise as a result of government-led and/or initiated reform efforts.

This is, in many ways, the case with Nordic countries, which are characterised by a welfare state ideology and development of the public sector within this framework. Moreover, they are relatively similar in terms of population size and geographical proximity and share the same type of political systems and political values. In terms of policy challenges, all Nordic countries have to deal with the financial, social and political sustainability of the Nordic welfare model which, in turn, as has been mentioned before, has triggered government-led reform efforts under the label of NPM, particularly in the higher education sector. In all countries, universities are expected to play an increasingly important role in local and national economic development and to spur innovation. Such expectations have further intensified government-led efforts to modernise the higher education sector in all Nordic countries but have also led to calls from the higher education sector to balance governmental funding and leeway regarding, for example, autonomy to better match with the growing demands for more diverse activities.

Before moving forward, we provide a brief note on the Nordic region, which is the geographical focus of this book. The Nordic region is situated in Northern Europe, and the Nordic countries are generally considered to include Denmark, Finland, Iceland, Norway and Sweden, including their associated territories (Greenland, the Faroe Islands and the Åland Islands) (Fig. 1.1). The region shares a strong cultural history and is known for its commitment to social-democratic values, equal opportunity and a generous but financially sustainable welfare state model (Hilson 2008). The Nordic region ranks rather high internationally across a multiplicity of comparative dimensions, ranging from innovation to trust in government to educational quality to quality of life. One of its great successes has been its ability to combine a strong safety net for its citizens, together with the adoption of market-based mechanisms (open economy) aimed at increasing its global competitiveness. When compared to other countries, and as a whole, the Nordics were able to withstand the pressures emanating from the 2008 financial crisis, despite being affected differently as a result of their economic profile and vulnerability to global export markets. That being said, as is the case elsewhere, the region faces a series of challenges, including but not limited to an ageing population, an over-reliance on particular industries (economic specialisation) and the need to reform the pension system (Norden 2014).

The next section provides information on the research project that provided the framework for the current volume.

Fig. 1.1 The Nordic countries as the geographical focus of the book (excluding Iceland). Source: Mapswire.com. This work is licensed under a Creative Commons Attribution 4.0 International License

The FINNUT-PERFACAD Study

Aim and Research Problem

This volume reports on the results emanating from a three-year (fall 2014–summer 2017) comparative, international research project entitled "Does It Really Matter? Assessing the Performance Effects of Changes in Leadership and Management Structures in Nordic Higher Education", funded by the Norwegian Research Council in the context of its FINNUT programme (Research and Innovation in the Educational Sector). The study's focus was on the relationship between changes in formal leadership structures and performance shifts and was substantiated around the following research problem:

- *To what extent are changes in leadership and management structures related to shifts in teaching and research performance in public universities across the Nordic countries (Norway, Sweden, Denmark and Finland) in the last decade?*

In doing so, it illuminated three key dimensions:

1. the *key drivers* promoting the rationalisation of academic activities in general and, specifically, the rise of managerialism within public universities,
2. the *roles* played by both internal (academics and administrators alike) and external actors in strengthening the managerial structures (central and unit levels) of universities and
3. the *effects* of changes in leadership/managerial structures in the (teaching and research) performance of individual subunits, as well as in the behaviours of internal actors.

In a nutshell, the study provided both a *quantitative* assessment of formal structures and a *qualitative* interpretation of the meanings held by social agents (central and unit levels) associated with those same structures, for example, on being 'modern', 'responsive', 'accountable', 'entrepreneurial' and so on. Rather than simply focusing on generating new sets of empirical data, the study aimed to advance new perspectives for theorising ongoing rationalisation processes on the basis of the various disciplinary traditions and competencies brought together in the multidisciplinary research team, the core of which was composed of the authors of the current volume.

Theoretical Foundation

Organisations have traditionally been conceived as either *instruments*, or tools to reach certain ends (goals), or as *institutions*, that is, having lives of their own (Scott 2008). Both views have merits and provide important insights on the dynamics facing modern organisations across the public and private sectors. The rational view of organisations (c.f. Scott 2003: 33–55) views internal behaviour as resulting from the purposeful actions of a set of coordinated social agents within a given local setting (Battilana 2006; Hay and Wincott 1998). Key elements like goal specificity and the formalisation of structures and procedures are seen as critical to the 'rationality of organizational action' (Scott 2003: 34), therefore ranking high on the managerial agenda. The general assumption in the literature is that, as a process, rationalisation is, first and foremost, substantiated around the formal structure of organisations (Thompson 2008; Pfeffer 1997):

> [...] in *rules* that assure participants will behave in ways calculated to achieve desired objectives, in *cognitive decision-premises* that guide individual decision making, in *control arrangements* that evaluate performance and detect deviance, in *reward systems* that motivate participants to carry out prescribed tasks, and in the set of criteria by which participants are *selected, replaced,* and *promoted*. (Scott 2003: 54; emphasis added)

The rational systems' view of organisations, vividly contested by many (March and Olsen 2006a), puts a preferential emphasis on the role of *formalised rules* (plans, strategies, programmes, etc.) and *normative structures* (roles, sanctions, regulations, etc.). In doing so, this view disregards more tacit dimensions, such as the effects of macro-level scripts (DiMaggio and Powell 1983) and the preferences and behavioural patterns of organisational participants (Powell and Colyvas 2008). Proponents of rational systems argue that structural (often hierarchical) arrangements play a critical role in the ways in which organisations interact with, and respond to, environmental demands (Selznick 1984). Leadership structures are celebrated, with the lower levels of the organisations primarily involved in the implementation, rather than problem assessment, of the key decisions undertaken at higher levels (Blau and Scott 2003).

In (continental) Europe, the basic structural features of academic organisations, that is, decentralisation of authority, loose-coupling of structures, multiplicity of tasks, unclear goals, complex technologies and so on (Pinheiro 2012; Clark 1983), have not traditionally been conducive to the implementation of centralised models of decision-making (Amaral et al. 2003). This is particularly the case when it comes to both the speed and scope of university responses to external demands (Hölttä and Karjalainen 1997). For example, Musselin (2007) contended that:

> [...] in universities, formal structures and procedures, even if numerous, rarely favor cooperation and coordination. They hardly define what to do and how to do it because of the specific characteristics of teaching and research [...] As a result, changing the formal structures most of the time has no effect [...] formal rules and structures weakly support hierarchical power. (Musselin 2007: 75)

Over the years and in many countries, including those within the Nordic region, the conception of traditional or classic research-intensive universities was that of 'ivory towers', that is, closed systems isolated from the dynamics of their surrounding environments (Etzkowitz et al. 2000). A key item in the policy agenda on national and supranational levels has been to institute a series of structural reforms in order to redesign universities. This is partly a result of the rise of a global knowledge-based society/economy (Maassen and Stensaker 2011) and partly due to the strategic imperatives surrounding the modernisation of the Nordic welfare state (Castells and Himanen 2004). This is particularly the case with those with a long historical record. The aim has been to make them more adaptive and responsive to external events and stakeholder demands (Maassen 2009; Etzkowitz 2001; Pinheiro and Stensaker 2013). In other words, ongoing reform processes aim at transforming public universities into organisational actors. There is a push towards becoming tightly integrated, goal-oriented and competitive entities which deliberately or strategically choose their own actions and are held accountable for their own behaviours (Krücken and Meier 2006; Ramirez 2010). In these circumstances, rationalisation measures such as the strengthening of managerial and leadership structures play an increasingly important role (Teichler 2005; Krücken 2011).

The view of universities as rational(ised) tools or *instruments* for reaching certain pre-determined goals or ends (Olsen 2007) pays considerable attention to the technical or material-resource features of the environment (c.f. Scott 2003: 133). These aspects are intrinsically related to the daily management and operations of universities, as well as their performance. In such circumstances, social agency is characterised by what March and Olsen (2006b) called the 'logic of consequences'. According to this logic, university actors behave in ways that are congruent with the successful realisation of strategic objectives either set internally by the central administration or emanating from the outside (government/funding agencies). For example, this is clearly visible in the prominence given to contractual arrangements (Gornitzka et al. 2004) and/or the rise of what Rip (2004) has termed 'strategic science regimes' in academia.

Yet, there are those who have convincingly argued that most organisations, universities included, are not simply instruments or tools at the mercy of certain internal (managers) or external (governments) social agents (Selznick 1966; Olsen 2007). They contended that internal rules, both formal and informal, and standard operating procedures like the allocation of academic power or authority (Tapper and Palfreyman 2011) cannot be changed arbitrarily (Maassen 2009; Maassen and Olsen 2007). Prior consent from academics at the unit level is similarly necessary for the definition of university strategic objectives (Zechlin 2010). Such limitations are seen to safeguard what Clark (1998) referred to as the academic heartland. This is the view held by most institutional scholars who, amongst other aspects, have argued against the limitations of 'means-ends rationality' while assessing change dynamics within organisations (Greenwood et al. 2008; Powell and DiMaggio 1991), universities included (Maassen and Olsen 2007; Pinheiro et al. 2012; Gornitzka 1999).

Regarding the rationalisation processes, it is worth bearing in mind that this is far from unique for the higher education sector. It follows the rationalisation of administrative structures across the entire public sector and even across the entire organisational landscape (Brunsson and Sahlin-Andersson 2000). Thus, studies shedding light on ongoing attempts at transforming public organisations along the lines of New Public Management reform regimes (Christensen and Lægreid 2007; Hood 1991, 1995) provided important insights for our study. We paid particular attention to the nature and degree of response to such transformative processes by social agents at the local (micro) level (Oliver 1991; Powell and Colyvas 2008) within the broad context of mimetic isomorphic processes/collective rationality (DiMaggio and Powell 1983) and the need for securing (internal and external) legitimacy (Deephouse and Suchman 2008). This includes, but is not limited to, the role played by such critical aspects as the *de-coupling* of structural arrangements (Bastedo 2007) and/or their contextualisation or local translation (Czarniawska-Joerges and Sevón 2005).

Conceptual Backdrop

Visions of the University

The study's conceptual framework is built on the work of Johan P. Olsen (2007) on the visions of the (European) university. Olsen made a distinction between an instrumental and institutional view of universities. In the former, the focus is on universities as means to achieve certain predetermined ends (e.g. policy goals or managerial aspirations); the latter sheds light on the university as a relatively independent fiduciary institution characterised by a life (norms, identity, inner dynamics) of its own. Following seminal work on formal organisations (Cohen and March 1974; March and Olsen 1979; Olsen 1988), Olsen advanced four stylised visions, or a typology (along two dimensions; autonomy vs. conflict), on the modern university. The typology was based on different assumptions about what the university is *for* as well as the circumstances under which it will operate appropriately. At the heart of Olsen's inquiry was this question: *what type of university for what type of society?* (Table 1.1).

The four visions represent key features of universities as organisations and institutions. They are thought to be complementary rather than mutually exclusive, that is, key features associated with the four visions are present at any moment in time, shaping dynamics within a given organisation:

> The four stylized visions are based on assumptions which make it unlikely that any of them alone can capture current university practices. As less than perfect approximations to the abstract visions, universities as practices show "a shocking diversity" (Neave 2003: 151), and the relations between universities, public authorities and society are characterized by a great variety of forms of interaction, intervention and control (Hood et al. 2004: Part III). (Olsen 2007: 33)

In the FINNUT-PERFACAD study, an issue of particular relevance was that of the interplay between different types of actors and their various roles in the broader higher education system. First, the interplay between internal and external dimensions of universities places pressure on the university governance systems. This reflects the instrumental view in Olsen's typology, as the interplay presumes that expectations exist between the external stakeholders and the internal university dynamics. It further implies that these expectations are mutual, that is, directed not only from

Table 1.1 Visions of the European university

Conflict: \ Autonomy:	University operations and dynamics are governed by internal factors	University operations and dynamics are governed by environmental factors
Actors have *shared* norms and objectives	**The University is a self-governing community of scholars** Constitutive logic: Free inquiry, truth finding, rationality and expertise. Criteria of assessment: Scientific quality. Reasons for autonomy: Constitutive principle of the University as an institution: authority to the best qualified. Change: Driven by the internal dynamics of science. Slow reinterpretation of institutional identity. Rapid and radical change only with performance crises.	**The University is an instrument for national political agendas** Constitutive logic: Administrative: Implementing predetermined political objectives. Criteria of assessment: Effective and efficient achievement of national purposes. Reasons for autonomy: Delegated and based on relative efficiency. Change: Political decisions, priorities, designs as a function of elections, coalition formation and breakdowns and changing political leadership.
Actors have *conflicting* norms and objectives	**The University is a representative democracy** Constitutive logic: Interest representation, elections, bargaining and majority decisions. Criteria of assessment: Who gets what: Accommodating internal interests. Reasons for autonomy: Mixed (work-place democracy, functional competence, *realpolitik*). Change: Depends on bargaining and conflict resolution and changes in power, interests, and alliances.	**The University is a service enterprise embedded in competitive markets** Constitutive logic: Community service. Part of a system of market exchange and price systems. Criteria of assessment: Meeting community demands. Economy, efficiency, flexibility, survival. Reasons for autonomy: Responsiveness to "stakeholders" and external exigencies, survival. Change: Competitive selection or rational learning. Entrepreneurship and adapting to changing circumstances and sovereign customers.

Source: Olsen (2007: 30). Figure used with permission from Springer.

the external inwards but also from the university towards the external players. The second interplay refers to the degree of internal conflict within the university institutions, which relates to the institutional view in Olsen's typology. It presumes that there is a shared foundation in the core values of the university institution. However, it accounts less for the differences in which the multiple professions in universities adapt to changes in the operational and working environment. In short, the university institution is seen to function in a constantly changing context in which a multiplicity of adaptive measures are necessary. Next, we inspect the different dimensions of interplay which formed a core qualifying factor for Olsen's typology and furthered the conceptual framework for our study.

Adaptation of University Governance Between Multiple Pressures
Higher education institutions are public organisations and operate in a highly institutionalised environment (laden with rules, regulations and procedures). They are heavily dependent on public resources to finance their core activities. As such, higher education institutions are susceptible to shifts in governance arrangements. Yet, these internal changes do not occur in a linear manner, and universities are far from being passive recipients of reform agendas. As institutions, universities have both a history and lives of their own. They are also characterised by multiple internal constituencies (academics, administrators, students, managers). Universities have traditionally been bottom heavy and loosely coupled organisations which change only through minor local adjustments and where academics have had a lot of autonomy to act and direct their own activities (Bleiklie et al. 2017; Clark 1983; Fumasoli and Stensaker 2013; Weick 1976). Internal factors have traditionally been essential in the governance of university dynamics, and a kind of vision of the university has been 'a self-governing community of scholars' (Olsen 2007).

Historically speaking, universities have proven to be rather resilient to shifts in political orientations and economic regimes. They are able to decouple themselves from short-term political imperatives (Bastedo 2007). However, due to globalisation, knowledge society development, changes in political thinking and financial stringency, universities are increasingly embedded in competitive markets, wider material resources and institutional environments. They have social connections, not only to internal academic constituencies and disciplines but also to policymakers and other external stakeholders (Bleiklie et al. 2017; Scott 2003; Williams and Kitaev 2005). This implies that universities are increasingly governed with external environmental demands and factors (Olsen 2007). All these aspects (and others) play an important role in the ways in which universities respond to shifts in government policy.

In looking at the reforms of public institutions' autonomy in general and university organisations in particular, assumptions regarding the rationale for autonomy appear. One key assumption is that reforms can be implemented only if administrative autonomy is strengthened. Such actions come tied to increased external result control, financial incentives and competitions (Fumasoli et al. 2014). This constitutes a double-edged sword: while input autonomy is granted to the public organisation, output control is kept tightly in the hands of the government (Verhoest et al. 2004). A second key assumption is the expectation that autonomy will semi-automatically strengthen competitiveness and specialisation, thus being beneficial to the public institution in comparison to other similar organisations acting in the same market (Fumasoli et al. 2014). Effectiveness, economic efficiency and a better competitive edge with regard to quality through prioritisation are expected to follow as a result of increased autonomy.

The interaction between the state and universities can be viewed as an interdependent principle–agent relationship (de Jong et al. 2016). Rational choice theory guides the thinking in which the institutional leadership of the agent is seen to lean on self-interest, while the principal requires control mechanisms as well as incentives to guide the action (Fumasoli et al. 2014). A social contract exists between the two actors in which the state provides funds to universities to perform research and teaching of the highest level. Policymakers need the information produced by the universities, not only for society at large but also, and in particular, to provide guidance on how to tackle complex and often ambiguous policy problems. Knowledge regimes, such as universities, act as sense-making apparatuses. In policy settings, sense-making includes power struggles as well as contestations and negotiation. Similarly, in universities, sense-making processes vary depending on how they are organised (Campbell and Pedersen 2014).

The policy guidance and control provided by the state (funder) to the universities in return for services rendered constitute a form of a social contract. Relevance of science to society is a central aspect of the contract. However, the meaning of *relevance* is not a constant; rather, it evolves in time and reflects the general societal development. Relevance changes over time in line with the ideas of what benefits science can bring to society

(Hessels et al. 2009). Knowledge regimes are fields of the policy research organisations and institutions that govern them. They are organisational and institutional machineries that generate data, research and policy recommendations, as well as other ideas that influence policy debate (Campbell and Pedersen 2014). The idea follows the same line of thought as Olsen's typology (2007), where the universities may be seen as instruments of national policies while also as leaning on a base of a community of scholars. In other words, universities are expertise-based institutions that simultaneously aim to influence policies proactively and respond to policy initiatives reactively.

The relationship between the state and the universities can be seen as based on highly different grounds. Universities have traditionally viewed themselves as communities of scholars where strong autonomy guarantees high quality and trustworthy research and teaching (Olsen 2007). As a result of this view, society is considered to benefit from a strong science basis without unnecessary middlemen. The state can be seen to sell the university free hands to manage its tasks in the way it sees fittest. In contrast—and juxtaposing this view with another classification of Olsen's typology—the university is an instrument of national policies. The state funds research and highest teaching with the condition that the university performs its duties in a transparent and cost-efficient manner (Olsen 2007). As a result, tax funds are used to support the development of society in ways that are deemed relevant. Activities are reported responsibly and in a way that demonstrates the accountability of the university institution towards the state funder and broader society. However, the autonomy of science is dependent on a non-autonomous economic and management system.

The concept of universities as specific kinds of organisations with limited rationality and loosely coupled has begun to change. The institutional form of universities lives in the midst of a socio-political (and economic) struggle characterised by pressures to reconsider their role, regulatory practices and funding arrangements, as well as the processes that link universities to other societal actors. Now, universities are increasingly transforming into penetrated hierarchies that are managed organisations with a central leadership and formalised rule systems (Bleiklie et al. 2015). Strategic actorhood has become a key aspect in this. Penetrated hierarchies balance between multiple pressures from a broad range of external actors and stakeholders who hold power in the funding and prestige of the universities. As such, this creates a dependence that affects the internal power structures, control mechanisms and working practices of universities. The academically focused pressures have been joined by managerial performance demands, not only from the government but also from other external actors who share an interest in how the university institution is managed. Yet, the ability of universities to respond to the external pressures to, for example, innovate and develop organisational strategies is dependent on the availability of resources from a number of actors (Whitley 2008).

The development of universities as particular types of strategic actors relies heavily on the policies of governments, in particular, regarding their role in steering. National politics and the governance of universities are strongly coupled through the implementation of policies, despite the formal autonomy of universities. The linkage has often been approached from a point of view of dichotomy, where the autonomy of universities and the external steering of them are seen as opposing poles (Stensaker 2014). In an attempt to move beyond a top-down/bottom-up dichotomy and a duel-based view of the governance model, Sabatier (2005) applied a more general policy implementation toolset for the analysis of university–state relationships. In this model, the study of policy implementation is approached with institutional learning as a central element. Though the top-down perspective allows the study of learning amongst proponents of a particular reform, it is ill-suited to similar studies amongst opponents of the reform. According to Sabatier, this lack can be rectified by looking at the strategies with which the bottom-uppers (the opponents) aim to strengthen the attainment of their goals. Sabatier called for the combination of the top-down and bottom-up approaches in the analysis to avoid a bias towards the proponents or opponents. In order to allow for the learning and systematic change (rather than ad hoc deviance from the norm), a period of at least a decade is necessary (Sabatier 2005).

Finally, the interplay between the university governance and political landscape can also be investigated based on the operational logics that are used. Universities work with a dynamic operational logic in their external relations and with an organic logic in the internal environments (Ståhle and Åberg 2012). The former outlines the conditions for the relationship between university actors and external stakeholders, while the latter defines the rationale for cooperation with actors outside academia. In a dynamic working environment, university actors network with other independent actors. The actors have a self-determined relationship with each other, and they can be seen to gain mutually from the interaction. Universities are not considered to simply react to changes in their surrounding environment and/or act as instruments for national political agendas (Olsen 2007), but are presumed to influence their working context themselves. Universities can, then, be seen as active elements of policy planning processes, provided they have the will and skills to act.

The way universities interact with the policy planning actors is, however, also linked to the *internal* working environment. In the modern context, universities function as a type of representative democracy (Olsen 2007) in the midst of managerial pressures. This democracy continues to rest on the ideals of academic freedom, broad interest representation, an open discussion culture and respect for the self-correcting mechanism of science—in essence, the academic heartland (Clark 1998). In the Nordic context, the democratic aspect includes an active organisation of student representation and involvement in the formal structures of the university. The systems have been built to be responsive to the needs of the groups whose work and study conditions are affected by collective decisions regarding the running and structure of the university. In such an organic working environment, dialogue and exchange of experiences and feedback are central building blocks in developing functions and academia (Ståhle and Åberg 2012). It can be argued that the core skills for dialogue exist in the conventional academic environment. Thus, the issue becomes whether these skills can be transferred and adapted for use in interaction with the university management and policy planning actors.

The interplay between shifts in governmental policy, university governance and internal university dynamics form a complex, continuously changing system. In the Nordic context the converging policies form a dimension that affects the way the national systems develop. These constitute a moulding tool that can either support system development or act as a hindrance to organisational learning.

Operationalisation of the Conceptual Framework
In order to operationalise the study, six organisational/management mechanisms related to organisational performance were identified (see later). A shared understanding of what performance means in an academic university context was formed in order to ensure a coherent approach to the major issue at hand. An in-depth discussion on the meaning of performance, as well as other central concepts such as accountability, are included

in Chap. 2 of this volume. Extant literature on organisations more generally, as well as on the nature of higher education systems and universities more specifically, was used to sketch these. These mechanisms are as follows:

- Strategy
- Decision-making structures
- Organisational structures
- Accountability measures
- Funding arrangements
- Cultural climate

The study acknowledged that modern universities are complex organisations, and that performance can be achieved in multiple ways. As such, 'NPM/modern reforms' is a messy concept; therefore, it was necessary to decompose what so-called new management structures imply for university performance. The six identified mechanisms were a way to acquire more knowledge about what the relationship is between management/governance structures and performance. The next step was to formulate the basic assumptions underpinning the study in light of the research problem following Olsen's work,[1] namely:

- there is a direct *positive* link between governance/management structures and performance (instrumental argument),
- there is a direct *negative* link between governance/management structures and performance (institutional argument) and
- there are a *number of contingencies* between governance/management structures and performance (matching instrumental and institutional views).

A series of core hypotheses for each of the six mechanisms were then identified, driving the development of the survey questionnaire and

---

[1] Analytically, Olsen's four stylised visions models can be reduced to two broad ideal types or archetypes, instrument and institutional or cultural views, with models being 'variants' of these archetypes. 'Market' models also assume a kind of rationality that build on the same mechanisms as the instrumental model. The 'democracy' model builds on a normative assumption about the legitimacy of participation, which connects back to the institutional or 'cultural' model.

interview guide.[2] These mechanisms are described in some detail later. It should be noted that while these hypotheses were not tested per se in the study, they were instrumental in developing the conceptual framework into a coherent structure. They played an important role as we designed the operationalisation for the gathering of quantitative and qualitative data. The hypotheses were used, for example, to ensure that the two sets of data corresponded with each other and could be utilised to study the same phenomena in a comparable and complementary manner. We return to these hypotheses in the concluding chapter of this book to reflect on their role and meaning in the empirical analysis of our data. The methodological considerations are discussed in more detail in the latter part of this chapter.

Strategy

- H0: an overarching and penetrating institutional strategy boosts performance
- H1: an overarching and penetrating institutional strategy alienates staff and negatively affects performance
- H2: strategies that are developed through participation boost performance

Decision-Making Structures

- H0: more hierarchical decision-making structures stimulate increased performance
- H1: more hierarchical decision-making structures negatively affect performance
- H2: participatory decision-making structures stimulate increased performance

---

[2] In order to operationalise the study empirically, a series of key questions were devised around eight key themes associated with each of the six mechanisms described above (consult Table 1.5 and interview guide and survey template in Appendix). The empirical evidence provided in Part II of this volume sheds light on key findings along selected core themes, emanating from the survey questionnaire and the interview data.

Organisational Structure

- H0: larger, more interdisciplinary structures boost performance
- H1: larger, more interdisciplinary structures negatively affect performance
- H2: diverse structures are best fitted to the diversity found in universities, and diversity boost performance

Accountability Measures

- H0: more systematic and regular (intense) reporting boost performance
- H1: more systematic and regular (intense) reporting negatively affects performance
- H2: it is the way and form of reporting that affect performance

Funding Arrangements

- H0: more incentive and result-oriented funding boosts performance
- H1: more incentive and result-oriented funding negatively affects performance
- H2: a mixed funding arrangement is the best way to boost performance

Cultural Climate

- H0: systematic training and competence building in the organisation boost performance
- H1: systematic training and competence building (takes time away from primary activities and) negatively affect performance
- H2: cultural change through participatory and trust-based processes drives performance

In addition to shedding light on the relationship between the identified mechanisms associated with new management structures and performance, the study also aimed at exploring:

- the linkages amongst the (six) mechanisms, for example, strategy is only effective if combined with hierarchical management and accountability measures;
- the possible tensions between the (six) mechanisms, for example, the existence of a strategy arguing for a particular profiling of the organisation may collide with pressure to achieve results in a shorter time frame; and
- the relative importance of institutional governance/management structures in relation to national steering frameworks, for example, whether national models override what single universities try to do and how they are organised.

Finally, the study aimed to provide new theoretical explanations for how changes in university governance can be interpreted in light of the extant literature and major organisational and public administration theories. Our interest was in the linkages between formal change and performance, although not in a strict causal sense.

Research Design and Methodological Considerations

This FINNUT project adopted a comparative research design and applied a mixed methods approach (Bryman 2006) comprising a desk-top analysis, surveys and interviews (see Appendix). While the time period 2000–2013 was set as the focus of study, some of the thematic analysis included developments until 2016 in order to respond to recent changes brought up in the empirical data, in particular, in the interviews. The desktop analysis consisted of major policy initiatives with national statistics and other official documentation on performance data related to education, research and management of the higher education sector. Such register-based and performance-related data can be compared across countries and institutions (Ragin and Rihoux 2009). The data provided background material for the further development of the study (in the form of a comprehensive database), and relevant information has been utilised in the individual chapters composing this volume. A large set of new empirical data was collected through surveys and interviews.

The target groups of the survey were full-time managerial staff and academics employed at the 54 publicly run universities in Denmark,

Finland, Norway and Sweden. The survey took place at the end of 2014 and the beginning of 2015. The sampling and the definition of the population was done differently in the four countries because of different national higher education systems, availability of sampling frames and also considering the different information needs of national research teams. Table 1.2 describes the study's population, sampling and response rate.

The national samples were planned in a manner that allowed for Nordic comparisons. The comparative international subsamples included the respondents working in senior positions (European career levels III and IV) in official management positions or in ordinary academic positions.

Table 1.2 Survey population, sampling and response rate

	Population	Sampling	Response rate	N
Denmark	Institutions: All	Managers	N/A	334
	Staff categories: II, III, IV (assistant, associate and professor levels, including post docs and managers)	Academics (census study)	17%	1989
Finland	Institutions: All	Managers: – (census)	44%	199
	Staff categories: III, IV			
	Managers: (deans, vice-deans, heads of departments, vice-heads of departments)	Academics: Systematic random sample (every second)	24%	757
	Academics: (University lecturers/researchers, associate professors, research directors, professors)			Total: 1038[a]
Norway	Institutions: All	– (census study)	10%	1300
	Staff categories: All			
Sweden	Institutions: 10 out of 16 public universities	Managers: – (census)	16%	700
	Staff categories: II, III, IV (all academics, including managers, excluding PhD candidates)	Academics: Stratified (Systematic random sampling (1/4). Small institutions (<800 academics) simple random sampling of 200)		

[a]Of the respondents, 73 did not report about their title, and 9 individuals worked primarily outside Finland

Table 1.3 Comparative samples of managers and senior academics[a]

	Seniors in official management positions	Seniors not holding official management positions
Denmark	319	1319
Finland	258	660
Norway	143	721
Sweden	215	289
Total	935	2989

[a]Question: 'Do you hold an official management position?'

The comparative samples are described in Table 1.3. Because the management positions differ from country to country, in comparative samples, the variable 'are you holding an official management position?' was used as a categorising variable. This means that the distinctions between academics and academic managers are based on the respondents' own reporting. The Nordic comparisons were made by using subsamples that best fit for the purpose. For instance, in some cases, it was better to compare only heads of departments and deans, whereas, in other cases, it was more suitable to work with the self-reported official management positions.

The most inevitable limitations of the data pertain to the fact that it describes subjective performance, that is, the performance as experienced and reported by the informants. During the research project, a large amount of statistical data on actual (objective) performance was also collected from each country. However, due to the long timescale of the academic performance, national differences in performance measurement and intervening variables, the connection between survey data and statistical data was statistically difficult to establish. Therefore, the survey findings described and explained the subjective performance (Kivistö et al. 2017).

For the interviews, we selected two case universities in each of the four countries. We chose to perform the interviews at one of the flagship universities in each country and one regional university. The case universities were multidisciplinary, and the inclusion criteria were that the universities have both natural (including medicine) and social sciences. Within the institutions, we selected participants strategically based on their official positions in the system. These positions were senior academics from the social and the natural sciences, managers from different levels who mainly had academic backgrounds and professionals in central administration dealing particularly with issues relating to research and teaching, as well as their development. Overall, a total of 93 interviews were conducted between the springs of 2015 and 2016 (Table 1.4).

A common interview guide was developed. As the selected participants were highly educated people and experts in their fields, we used the elite interviewing approach (Aberbach and Rockman 2002; Goldstein 2002). Such an approach puts an emphasis on giving room to the interviewees to talk freely on the presented themes while ensuring that the different themes are covered so as to be able to compare findings across the cases. A semi-structured interview approach was selected, and the questions were adjusted to the knowledge of the participants.

Since quantitative methods are more suitable for providing an overview from a larger audience, and the ability to dig deeper into a theme follows qualitative methodologies, different questions were posed in the survey and interviews. The questions evolved around similar themes (see Table 1.5) per the conceptual and analytical framework adopted in the study, as sketched out earlier. The qualitative data generated by the interviews aimed at shedding light on the main drivers of and reactions to

Table 1.4 Number of interviewees per country

	Denmark	Finland	Norway	Sweden	Total
Managers and administrators	17	14	18	9	58
Academics	11	10	8	6	35
Total	28	24	26	15	93

Table 1.5 Themes for primary data collection

Survey themes	Interview themes
Perceived performance	Goal specificity and degree of autonomy
Goal specificity and autonomy	Decision-making and strategy
Decision-making and strategy	Control and evaluation
Control and evaluation	Support structures
Support structures	External stakeholders
External stakeholders	Trust and accountability
Trust and accountability	Incentives/recognition
Incentives	

rationalisation processes. The data also helped identify qualitative effects across teaching and research activities. This way of collecting data increased the study's external validity (Denzin and Lincoln 2011). SPSS was used in the analysis of the statistical data. A systematic content analysis of the qualitative data was conducted using Nvivo.

Ethical guidelines were followed in the collection, publishing and the storing of data. We assured the anonymity of the participants in the data-collecting phase, and we referred to them in an anonymised manner related to the flagship/regional universities, positions and fields (consult Part II of the volume). The project was reported to and approved by the Norwegian Centre for Research Data, which also stored the anonymised quantitative data.

There were certain limitations which had to be accounted for through the analysis phase of the project. Due to different access requirements in administering surveys in the case countries, four individual approaches were applied. Some country teams sent the survey to all the academic staff, while others sent it to selected groups, as described earlier. This bias had to be addressed while selecting groups for the analysis of statistical data so that the same type of data were included in the comparisons. Another issue was the different organising structures of higher education institutions within the Nordic countries. This also had to be scrutinised, as we were comparing findings across cases and countries. A strategy to deal with these critical issues and to increase the reliability of the data was to include researchers with knowledge of the specific countries in each of the project's publications.[3] The semi-structured interview approach also made it more difficult to analyse the material when compared to fully structured interviews. This approach requires a more thorough reading and inductive approach to the data. The teams used a similar concept tree structure in the content analysis of the interview data to increase comparability between the countries.

---

[3] In the case of the current volume, each chapter (with the exception of Chap. 6) has at least one co-author from each of the four countries, and all the individual chapters have been peer reviewed by an editorial board composed of senior authors from the region who were also directly involved with the study, as either team leaders and/or members.

The Volume's Organisation and Individual Contributions

As indicated in section "Introduction: Rationalisation and Converging Higher Education Policies" of this chapter, the volume reports on the results of a comparative project that assesses the interplay between changes in leadership and management structures in public universities across the Nordic countries and shifts in teaching and research performance in the last decade and a half. The chapters included in this book illuminate the key aspects associated with some of the thematic areas presented earlier from a comparative perspective. However, each chapter stands on its own, both conceptually and empirically, and can be read separately. The overall results should, however, be assessed against the backdrop of the larger project that was undertaken.

This book is structured into three distinct Parts. In Part I, the first chapter sets the context and presents the rationale for and the design of the FINNUT-PERFACAD study and elaborates on the theoretical foundations and conceptual landscape underpinning it. Chapter 2 by Kivistö et al. provides clarification on the key terminology underpinning the study, including contextualisation within a Nordic setting. The book then moves on to Chap. 3 where Pinheiro et al. describe the system evolution, as well as the higher education systems of each of the four Nordic countries. Part II of the book is dedicated to thematically focused chapters. While all of them lean on the same conceptual backbone that encompasses the study as a whole, each of the chapters adopts its own theoretical approach to the question at hand. The chapters begin from the system level and move towards the institutional.

Part II begins with Chap. 4 by Söderlind, Berg, Lind and Pulkkinen on how research funding systems at the national level affect local perceptions of research as a core task. Chapter 5, by Lind, Hernes, Pulkkinen and Söderlind, elaborates on the role that increasing levels of external funding play on the experiences of autonomy and how the effects on academic freedom are felt in research work. In Chap. 6, Geschwind, Berg, Lind and Aarrevaara investigate the evolving roles of academic leaders and managers amidst reforms that emphasise performativity alongside academic virtues. Chapter 7, by Aarrevaara, Pinheiro and Söderlind, explore the various ways in which strategic processes play out within Finnish, Norwegian and Swedish universities. Chapter 8, by Hansen, Aarrevaara, Geschwind and Stensaker, undertakes a comprehensive approach to evaluation practices by bringing together some of the topics discussed in the other chapters composing Part II of the volume.

In Part III, we return to look at the results of the FINNUT-PERFACAD study as a whole. Led by Geschwind, the volume editors take a step back to reflect on where we started and what we have learnt on the journey this comparative study has taken us on. In closing the volume, the editors contemplate on next steps and potential new avenues for future research endeavours.

Acknowledgements The data presented in the current volume and individual chapters emanate from a comparative study funded by the Norwegian Research Council under its FINNUT flagship program, a long-term program for research and innovation in the educational sector program. The project number was 237782, and the project was titled 'Does it matter? Assessing the performance effects of changes in leadership and management structures in Nordic Higher Education'.

References

Aberbach, Joel D., and Bert A. Rockman. 2002. Conducting and Coding Elite Interviews. *Political Science & Politics* 35 (4): 673–676.

Amaral, A., V.L. Meek, and I.M. Larsen. 2003. *The Higher Education Managerial Revolution?* Dordrecht: Kluwer Academic Publishers.

Bastedo, M.N. 2007. Sociological Frameworks for Higher Education Policy Research. In *Sociology of Higher Education: Contributions and Their Contexts*, ed. P.J. Gumport, 295–318. Baltimore: The Johns Hopkins University Press.

Battilana, J. 2006. Agency and Institutions: The Enabling Role of Individuals' Social Position. *Organization* 13 (5): 653–676.

Bennett, C. 1991. What Is Policy Convergence and What Causes It? *British Journal of Political Science* 21 (2): 215–233. https://doi.org/10.1017/S0007123400006116.

Blau, P.M., and W.R. Scott. 2003. *Formal Organizations: A Comparative Approach*. Stanford: Stanford University Press.

Bleiklie, I., J. Enders, and B. Lepori. 2015. Organizations as Penetrated Hierarchies: Environmental Pressures and Control in Professional Organizations. *Organisation Studies* 36 (7): 873–896.

———. 2017. Organizational Configurations of Modern Universities, Institutional Logics and Public Policies – Towards an Integrative Framework. In *Managing Universities: Policy and Organizational Change from a Western European Comparative Perspective*, Palgrave Studies in Global Higher Education, ed. I. Bleiklie, J. Enders, and B. Lepori, 303–326. Cham: Springer International Publishing.

Brunsson, Nils, and Kerstin Sahlin-Andersson. 2000. Constructing Organizations: The Example of Public Sector Reform. *Organization Studies* 21 (4): 721–746. https://doi.org/10.1177/0170840600214003.

Bryman, Alan. 2006. Integrating Quantitative and Qualitative Research: How Is It Done? *Qualitative Research* 6 (1): 97–113. https://doi.org/10.1177/1468794106058877.

Campbell, J.L., and O.K. Pedersen. 2014. *The National Origins of Policy Ideas. Knowledge Regimes in the United States, France, Germany and Denmark.* Princeton: Princeton University Press.

Castells, M., and P. Himanen. 2004. *The Information Society and the Welfare State: The Finnish Model.* Oxford: Oxford University Press.

Christensen, T., and P. Lægreid. 2007. *Transcending New Public Management: The Transformation of Public Sector Reforms.* Aldershot: Ashgate.

———. 2017. Introduction. Accountability and Welfare State Reforms. In *The Routledge Handbook to Accountability and Welfare State Reforms in Europe*, ed. T. Christensen and P. Lægreid, 1–11. Oxon: Routledge.

Clark, B.R. 1983. *The Higher Education System: Academic Organization in Cross-National Perspective.* Los Angeles, CA: University of California Press.

———. 1998. *Creating Entrepreneurial Universities: Organizational Pathways of Transformation.* New York: Pergamon.

Cohen, M.D., and J.G. March. 1974. *Leadership and Ambiguity: The American College President.* Berkeley, CA: Carnegie Commission on Higher Education.

Czarniawska-Joerges, B., and G. Sevón. 2005. *Global Ideas: How Ideas, Objects and Practices Travel in a Global Economy.* Malmö: Liber & Copenhagen Business School Press.

de Boer, H., and J. Enders. 2017. Working in the Shadow of Hierarchy: Organisational Autonomy and Venues of External Influence in European Universities. In *Managing Universities. Policy and Organizational Change from a Western European Comparative Perspective*, ed. I. Bleiklie, J. Enders, and B. Lepori, 57–84. Cham: Palgrave Macmillan.

de Jong, S.P.L., J. Smit, and L. van Drooge. 2016. Scientists' Response to Societal Impact Policies. A Policy Paradox. *Science and Public Policy* 43 (1): 102–114.

Deephouse, D., and M. Suchman. 2008. Legitimacy in Organizational Institutionalism. In *The SAGE Handbook of Organizational Institutionalism*, ed. R. Greenwood, K. Sahlin Christine Oliver, and R. Suddaby, 49–77. London and Thousand Oaks: Sage.

Denzin, Norman K., and Yvonne S. Lincoln, eds. 2011. *Handbook of Qualitative Research.* 4th ed. Thousand Oaks: Sage Publisher.

DiMaggio, P., and W. Powell. 1983. The Iron Cage Revisited: Institutional Isomorphism and Collective Rationality in Organizational Fields. *American Sociological Review* 48 (2): 147–160.

Etzkowitz, Henry. 2001. The Second Academic Revolution and the Rise of Entrepreneurial Science. *Technology and Society Magazine* 20 (2): 18–29.

Etzkowitz, H., M. Ranga, M. Benner, L. Guaranys, A.M. Maculan, and R. Kneller. 2008. Pathways to the Entrepreneurial University: Towards a Global Convergence. *Science and Public Policy* 35 (9): 681–695. https://doi.org/10.3152/030234208x389701.

Etzkowitz, H., A. Webster, C. Gebhardt, and B.R.C. Terra. 2000. The Future of the University and the University of the Future: Evolution of Ivory Tower to Entrepreneurial Paradigm. *Research Policy* 29 (2): 313–330.

European Commission. 2006. *Delivering on the Modernisation Agenda for Universities: Education, Research and Innovation. COM (2006) 208 final*. Brussels: European Commission.

———. 2011. *Supporting Growth and Jobs – An Agenda for the Modernisation of Europe's Higher Education Systems. COM (2011) 567 final*. Brussels: European Commission.

Fumasoli, T., Å. Gornitzka, and P. Maassen. 2014. *University Autonomy and Organizational Change Dynamics*. ARENA Working Paper 8, July 2014.

Fumasoli, T., and B. Stensaker. 2013. Organizational Studies in Higher Education: A Reflection on Historical Themes and Prospective Trends. *Higher Education Policy* 26 (4): 479.

Goldstein, Kenneth. 2002. Getting in the Door: Sampling and Completing Elite Interviews. *Political Science & Politics* 35 (4): 669–672.

Gornitzka, Å. 1999. Governmental Policies and Organizational Change in Higher Education. *Higher Education* 38 (1999): 5–31.

Gornitzka, Å., B. Stensaker, J.-C. Smeby, and H. De Boer. 2004. Contract Arrangements in the Nordic Countries: Solving the Efficiency-Effectiveness Dilemma? *Higher Education in Europe* 29 (1): 87–101. https://doi.org/10.1080/03797720410001673319.

Greenwood, R., Christine Oliver, K. Sahlin, and R. Suddaby. 2008. *The SAGE Handbook of Organizational Institutionalism*. London: SAGE.

Hay, Colin, and Daniel Wincott. 1998. Structure, Agency and Historical Institutionalism. *Political Studies* 46 (5): 951–957. https://doi.org/10.1111/1467-9248.00177.

Hessels, L.K., H. van Lente, and R. Smits. 2009. In Search of Relevance: The Changing Contract Between Science and Society. *Science and Public Policy* 36 (5): 387–401.

Hilson, M. 2008. *The Nordic Model: Scandinavia Since 1945*. London: Reaktion Books.

Hölttä, S., and K. Karjalainen. 1997. Cybernetic Institutional Management Theory and Practice. *Tertiary Education and Management* 3 (3): 229–236.

Holzinger, K., and C. Knill. 2005. Causes and Conditions of Cross-National Policy Convergence. *Journal of European Public Policy* 12 (5): 775–796.

Hood, C. 1991. A Public Management for All Seasons? *Public Administration* 69 (1): 3–19. https://doi.org/10.1111/j.1467-9299.1991.tb00779.x.

———. 1995. The 'New Public Management' in the 1980s: Variations on a Theme. *Accounting, Organizations and Society* 20 (2–3): 93–109. https://doi.org/10.1016/0361-3682(93)e0001-w.
Hood, C., O. James, B.G. Peters, and C. Scott, eds. 2004. *Controlling Modern Government: Variety, Commonality and Change*. Cheltenham: Edward Elgar.
Kallo, J. 2009. *OECD Education Policy: A Comparative and Historical Study Focusing on the Thematic Reviews of Tertiary Education*. Helsinki: Finnish Educational Research Association.
Kivistö, Jussi, Elias Pekkola, and Anu Lyytinen. 2017. The Influence on Performance-Based Management on Teaching and Research Performance of Finnish Senior Academics. *Tertiary Education and Management* 23 (3): 260–275.
Knill, Christoph. 2005. Introduction: Cross-National Policy Convergence: Concepts, Approaches and Explanatory Factors. *Journal of European Public Policy* 12 (5): 764–774. https://doi.org/10.1080/13501760500161332.
Krücken, G. 2011. *A European Perspective on New Modes of University Governance and Actorhood*. Research & Occasional Paper Series: CSHE.17.11.
Krücken, G., and F. Meier. 2006. Turning the University into an Organizational Actor. In *Globalization and Organization: World Society and Organizational Change*, ed. G.S. Drori, J.W. Meyer, and H. Hwang, 241–257. Oxford: Oxford University Press.
Maassen, P. 2009. The Modernisation of European Higher Education: National Policy Dynamics. In *From Governance to Identity*, ed. Alberto Amaral, Ivar Bleiklie, and Christine Musselin, 95–112. Dordrecht: Springer.
Maassen, P., and J.P. Olsen. 2007. *University Dynamics and European Integration*. Dordrecht: Springer.
Maassen, Peter, and Bjørn Stensaker. 2011. The Knowledge Triangle, European Higher Education Policy Logics and Policy Implications. *Higher Education* 61 (6): 757–769. https://doi.org/10.1007/s10734-010-9360-4.
March, J.G., and J.P. Olsen. 1979. *Ambiguity and Choice in Organizations*. Bergen: Universitetsforlaget.
———. 2006a. Elaborating the 'New Institutionalism. In *The Oxford Handbook of Political Institutions*, ed. R.A. Rhodes, S.A. Binder, and B.A. Rockman, 3–22. Oxford: Oxford University Press.
———. 2006b. The Logic of Appropriateness. In *The Oxford Handbook of Public Policy*, ed. M. Moran, M. Rein, and R. Goodin, 689–708. Oxford: Oxford University Press.
Moisio, J. 2014. *Understanding the Significance of EU Higher Education Policy Cooperation in Finnish Higher Education Policy*. Doctoral Diss., School of Management, University of Tampere, Tampere University Press.
Musselin, C. 2007. Are Universities Specific Organisations? In *Towards a Multiversity? Universities Between Global Trends and National Traditions*, ed.

G. Krücken, A. Kosmützky, and M. Torka, 63–84. Bielefeld: Transaction Publishers.

Neave, G. 2003. The Bologna Declaration: Some of the Historic Dilemmas Posed by the Reconstruction of the Community in Europe's Systems of Higher Education. *Educational Policy* 17 (1): 141–164.

Norden. 2014. *The Nordic Model – Challenged but Capable of Reform*. Copenhagen: Nordic Council of Ministers.

Oliver, Christine. 1991. Strategic Responses to Institutional Processes. *Academy of Management Review* 16 (1): 145–179.

Olsen, J.P. 1988. Administrative Reform and Theories of Organization. In *Organizing Governance, Governing Organizations*, ed. C. Campbell and B.G. Peters, 233–254. Pittsburgh: University of Pittsburgh Press.

Olsen, J.P. 2007. The Institutional Dynamics of the European University. In *University Dynamics and European Integration*, ed. P. Maassen and J.P. Olsen, 25–54. Dordrecht: Springer.

Pfeffer, J. 1997. *New Directions for Organization Theory: Problems and Prospects*. Oxford: Oxford University Press.

Pinheiro, R. 2012. *In the Region, for the Region? A Comparative Study of the Institutionalisation of the Regional Mission of Universities*. PhD Diss., Faculty of Education, University of Oslo.

Pinheiro, R., P. Benneworth, and G.A. Jones, eds. 2012. *Universities and Regional Development: A Critical Assessment of Tensions and Contradictions*. Milton Park and New York: Routledge.

Pinheiro, R., L. Geschwind, and T. Aarrevaara. 2014. Nested Tensions and Interwoven Dilemmas in Higher Education: The View from the Nordic Countries. *Cambridge Journal of Regions, Economy and Society* 7 (2): 233–250. https://doi.org/10.1093/cjres/rsu002.

Pinheiro, R., and B. Stensaker. 2013. Designing the Entrepreneurial University: The Interpretation of a Global Idea. *Public Organization Review* 14 (4): 1–20. https://doi.org/10.1007/s11115-013-0241-z.

Powell, W., and J. Colyvas. 2008. Microfoundations of Institutional Theory. In *The SAGE Handbook of Organizational Institutionalism*, ed. R. Greenwood, K. Sahlin Christine Oliver, and R. Suddaby, 276–298. London: Sage.

Powell, W.W., and P. DiMaggio. 1991. *The New Institutionalism in Organizational Analysis*. Chicago: University of Chicago Press.

Ragin, Charles C., and Benoît Rihoux. 2009. *Configurational Comparative Methods*. Los Angeles: Sage.

Ramirez, F.O. 2010. Accounting for Excellence: Transforming Universities into Organizational Actors. In *Higher Education, Policy, and the Global Competition Phenomenon*, ed. Laura Portnoi, Val Rust, and Sylvia Bagely, 43–58. Basingstoke: Palgrave.

Ramirez, Francisco O., and T. Christensen. 2013. The Formalization of the University: Rules, Roots, and Routes. *Higher Education* 65 (6): 695–708.

Rip, Arie. 2004. Strategic Research, Post-modern Universities and Research Training. *Higher Education Policy* 17 (2): 153–166.

Sabatier, P. 2005. From Policy Implementation to Policy Change: A Personal Odyssey. In *Reform and Change in Higher Education. Higher Education Dynamics*, ed. Å. Gornitzka, M. Kogan, and A. Amaral, vol. 8. Dordrecht: Springer.

Scott, W.R. 2003. *Organizations: Rational, Natural, and Open Systems*. New York: Prentice Hall.

———. 2008. *Institutions and Organizations: Ideas and Interests*. London: Sage.

Seeber, Marco, Benedetto Lepori, Martina Montauti, Jürgen Enders, Harry De Boer, Elke Weyer, Ivar Bleiklie, Kristin Hope, Svein Michelsen, and Gigliola Nyhagen Mathisen. 2015. European Universities as Complete Organizations? Understanding Identity, Hierarchy and Rationality in Public Organizations. *Public Management Review* 17 (10): 1444–1474.

Selznick, Philip. 1966. *TVA and the Grass Roots: A Study in the Sociology of Formal Organization*. New York: Harper & Row.

Selznick, Philip. 1984. *Leadership in Administration: A Sociological Interpretation*. Berkeley, CA: University of California Press.

Shahjahan, R.A., and M. Madden. 2015. Uncovering the Images and Meanings of International Organizations (IOs) in Higher Education Research. *Higher Education* 69 (5): 705–717. https://doi.org/10.1007/s10734-014-9801-6.

Slaughter, Sheila, and Brendan Cantwell. 2012. Transatlantic Moves to the Market: The United States and the European Union. *Higher Education* 63 (5): 583–606. https://doi.org/10.1007/s10734-011-9460-9.

Slaughter, S., and L.L. Leslie. 1999. *Academic Capitalism: Politics, Policies, and the Entrepreneurial University*. Baltimore: Johns Hopkins University Press.

Slaughter, S., and B.J. Taylor, eds. 2016. *Competitive Advantage: Stratification, Privatization and Vocationalization of Higher Education in the US, EU, and Canada, Higher Education Dynamics*. Dordrecht: Springer.

Ståhle, P., and L. Åberg. 2012. Voiko yliopiston uudistumista johtaa? (Can the Renewal of Universities Be Managed?). In *Innostava yliopisto (An Inspiring University)*, ed. Pirjo Ståhle and Antti Ainamo. Gaudeamus.

Stensaker, B. 2014. Troublesome Institutional Autonomy: Governance and the Distribution of Authority in Norwegian Universities. In *International Trends in University Governance: Autonomy, Self-Government and the Distribution of Authority*, ed. M. Shattock, 34–48. New York: Routledge.

Tapper, T., and D. Palfreyman. 2011. *Oxford, the Collegiate University: Conflict, Consensus and Continuity*. Dordrecht: Springer.

Teichler, U. 2005. Research on Higher Education in Europe. *European Journal of Education* 40 (4): 447.

Thompson, J.D. 2008. *Organizations in Action: Social Science Bases of Administrative Theory*. 5th ed. New Brunswick: Transaction Publishers.

Trow, M., and M. Burrage. 2010. *Twentieth-Century Higher Education: Elite to Mass to Universal*. Baltimore: Johns Hopkins University Press.

Verhoest, K., B.G. Peters, G. Bouckaert, and B. Verschuere. 2004. The Study of Organisational Autonomy: A Conceptual Review. *Public Administration and Development* 24: 101–118. https://doi.org/10.1002/pad.316.

Voegtle, E.M., C. Knill, and M. Dobbins. 2011. To What Extent Does Transnational Communication Drive Cross-National Policy Convergence? The Impact of the Bologna-Process on Domestic Higher Education Policies. *Higher Education* 61: 77. https://doi.org/10.1007/s10734-010-9326-6.

Weick, K.E. 1976. Educational Organizations as Loosely Coupled Systems. *Administrative Science Quarterly* 21 (1): 1–19.

Whitley, R. 2008. Constructing Universities as Strategic Actors: Limitations and Variations. In *The University in the Market*, ed. L. Engwall and D. Weaire. London: Portland Press Ltd.

Williams, G., and I. Kitaev. 2005. Overview of National Policy Contexts for Entrepreneurialism in Higher Education Institutions. *Higher Education Management and Policy* 17 (3): 125–141.

Witte, Johanna. 2008. Aspired Convergence, Cherished Diversity: Dealing with the Contradictions of Bologna. *Tertiary Education and Management* 14 (2): 81–93. https://doi.org/10.1080/13583880802051840.

Zechlin, L. 2010. Strategic Planning in Higher Education. In *International Encyclopedia of Education*, ed. P. Peterson, E. Baker, and B. McGaw, 256–263. Amsterdam: Elsevier.

Open Access This chapter is licensed under the terms of the Creative Commons Attribution 4.0 International License (http://creativecommons.org/licenses/by/4.0/), which permits use, sharing, adaptation, distribution and reproduction in any medium or format, as long as you give appropriate credit to the original author(s) and the source, provide a link to the Creative Commons licence and indicate if changes were made.

The images or other third party material in this chapter are included in the chapter's Creative Commons licence, unless indicated otherwise in a credit line to the material. If material is not included in the chapter's Creative Commons licence and your intended use is not permitted by statutory regulation or exceeds the permitted use, you will need to obtain permission directly from the copyright holder.

CHAPTER 2

Performance in Higher Education Institutions and Its Variations in Nordic Policy

Jussi Kivistö, Elias Pekkola, Laila Nordstrand Berg, Hanne Foss Hansen, Lars Geschwind, and Anu Lyytinen

---

J. Kivistö (✉) • E. Pekkola • A. Lyytinen
Faculty of Management and Business, Tampere University, Tampere, Finland
e-mail: jussi.kivisto@tuni.fi; elias.pekkola@tuni.fi; anu.lyytinen@tuni.fi

L. N. Berg
Department of Social Science, Western Norway University of Applied Sciences, Sogndal, Norway
e-mail: laila.nordstrand.berg@hvl.no

H. F. Hansen
Department of Political Science, University of Copenhagen, Copenhagen, Denmark
e-mail: hfh@ifs.ku.dk

L. Geschwind
School of Industrial Engineering and Management, KTH Royal Institute of Technology, Stockholm, Sweden
e-mail: larsges@kth.se

© The Author(s) 2019
R. Pinheiro et al. (eds.), *Reforms, Organizational Change and Performance in Higher Education*,
https://doi.org/10.1007/978-3-030-11738-2_2

Introduction

Year after year, the higher education sector in Nordic countries continues to enjoy the highest level of public investments among all the OECD countries. Like in other European countries, these investments have put higher education institutions (HEIs) under increased scrutiny, with the obligation to explain their behaviour and performances. This trend is further intensified by the fact that the higher education sector competes with other sectors for public funds, namely primary and secondary education, public health, social services and defence. At the same time, Nordic HEIs are facing increasing expectations to become more 'entrepreneurial' and increase their abilities to compete in a more globalised market. All these mean that there is an increasing focus on cost efficiency and productivity, as well as quality.

The need for greater efficiency, productivity and quality in the higher education sector has triggered increased governmental interest towards different mechanisms of accountability, especially evaluation and performance measurement. This interest has developed over a relatively long period of time, but it has now reached its culmination point in many ways. For instance, advances in citation tracking, performance data collection and databases and the professionalisation of evaluative practices and methods have opened new avenues for verifying accountability.

This chapter offers definitions for the key concepts used throughout the book, which are as follows: accountability, evaluation and performance measurement and management. Each section is followed by a short contextualisation of the concept in Denmark, Finland, Norway and Sweden. The chapter ends with a short discussion about the policy convergence between Nordic countries and the reasons for it.

Accountability

The concept of accountability has always been a topical question in higher education. Over time, academics and their institutions have had relationships with various stakeholders (church, states and local communities) in which some sort of 'answerability' has continuously played an important role. In the modern world, such answerability relates to universities' accounting for public money spent, as well as academics explaining their professional work and its outcomes (Huisman 2018). The concept of accountability, however, is multifaceted and ambiguous, allowing a range of understandings and definitions (Christensen and Lægreid 2017). Often, the concept of accountability is used in a broad sense, making it difficult to maintain clear distinctions in terms of related concepts like transparency, responsiveness, responsibility, answerability and liability (Bovens 2007; Dubnick 2014). Essential questions for accountability are as follows: who is to be held accountable, for what, to whom, and through what means? (Huisman and Currie 2004; Trow 1996). However, in general, accountability can be considered a relational principle that attaches certain expectations of one party to the actions and performance of another, thereby making the performing party responsible for its actions. The concept can be studied according to a personal and a structural perspective (Sinclair 1995). The personal viewpoint relates to internal virtues that guide actors' actions, independently of formal rules, while the structural perspective is linked to mechanisms between an actor and a forum to justify actions (Bovens 2007). According to this latter view, accountability is a relational concept providing a link between those held accountable and those who have a right to claim the accountability of others (Bovens et al. 2014). For our analytical purposes, in defining accountability, we find Bovens' (2007, 450) definition especially useful, where accountability is generically seen as a 'relationship between an actor and a forum, in which the actor has an obligation to explain and to justify his or her conduct, the forum can pose questions and pass judgement, and the actor may face consequences'.

The main purposes behind the need for accountability vary. For instance, accountability is needed to discourage fraud and manipulation, strengthen the legitimacy of institutions and enhance the quality of performance and work as a regulatory device through the criteria made explicit in the various reports requested by the reporting institutions (Huisman and Currie 2004). As such, it can be understood as 'a constraint on arbitrary power, and on the corruptions of power, including fraud, manipulation, malfeasance and the like' (Trow 1996, 311). Much of the discussion on accountability is geared towards economic or financial aspects. In addition, in the context of higher education, discussion on accountability is often paired with discussion on efficiency, effectiveness and performance evaluation. In this sense, the process of verifying accountability calls for proving, by effective means, that higher education has attained the predetermined results and performance. Correspondingly, accountability in higher education includes elements such as the rational use of resources, provision of evidence, evaluation of evidence, attaching importance to costs and effectiveness and improving the education process (Dressel 1980; Kai 2009).

Accountability regimes in higher education systems still tend to be the combinations of types of accountability principles and processes (King 2015). Out of these perspectives, *professional* and *political* accountability are often considered, especially important in the context of higher education (cf. Huisman and Currie 2004; see also Bovens et al. 2014; Romzek 2000). The difference between these two factors is related to the source of standards for performance. Professional accountability involves a high degree of autonomy for individual academics, whose decisions are based on internalised norms of what is considered appropriate action and performance. Especially on the side of research, the professional accountability standards are formulated in the academic community based on internal professional norms, which are enforced by academics. Due to the strong emphasis on professional authority, they are also more difficult to steer or manage in formal organisational settings.

Political accountability refers to political expectations for HEIs' performance. In this sense, demands for accountability are a safeguard to protect the interests of various stakeholders and interest groups, as well as the public. In the widest sense, political accountability also includes an element of social accountability, which means HEIs' answerability to wider society, not just the constituencies and political actors involved in the governing of HEIs. In more narrow terms, political accountability illustrates the governance relationship between the state and state-funded universities. In this context, a further distinction can be made between legal and financial accountability on the one hand, and academic accountability on the other. Other equally important aspects of autonomy are *legal* and *financial* accountability (Trow 1996). Legal and financial accountability highlight the universities' obligation to report how state public resources have been used and to what effect. This side of accountability clarifies whether the university is doing what is required of it by law and whether its resources are being consumed for the purposes for which they were provided.

Discussion on accountability is often accompanied with discussion about the limits of the self-regulative capacity of institutions (autonomy) and individuals (academic freedom); the emergence of various accountability mechanisms can be interpreted as a signal of a lack of trust in academic work and the functioning of universities (Gornitzka et al. 2004; Kivistö 2007; Schmidtlein 2004). Institutions universally desire to uphold their rights and capacities of self-governance, maintain substantial autonomy, and exempt themselves from excessive interference from the government and other institution-external entities. However, accountability in its all forms implies outside interference, and intensification of accountability is often at odds, at least to some extent, with different aspects of institutional autonomy. As the notion of accountability seems to be highlighted more explicit on stakeholders' agendas than in the past, the balance between accountability and autonomy often tilts towards an overemphasis on accounting for performance (Huisman 2018; Kai 2009).

Contextualising Accountability in the Nordic Countries

Denmark

Universities in Denmark are met with several accountability requests. Professional accountability is important in relation to the quality of educational programmes, and especially, the quality of research. However, to some extent, professional accountability has been challenged by political accountability, especially in the wake of the mergers of former governmental research institutes into universities.

Not surprisingly, political accountability regimes are well developed in welfare states where higher education is fully funded through taxation and to a certain extent, research is too. Over the last 15 years, reforms as part of higher educational policy have aimed at enhancing not only political but also social accountability. External stakeholders have become members of advisory councils and university boards. A corporate-like governance structure, including boards with a majority of external members and a chairman who is politically approved, has been introduced. The former elected leaders have been replaced by top-down appointed leaders. All in all, political accountability has been enhanced through intensified managerial accountability, as well as through the introduction of New Public Management (NPM) instruments like contracts and performance-based funding. However, these instruments have come hand in hand with more traditional legal and bureaucratic forms of accountability in recent years, for example, the dimensioning of educational programmes not matching labour market demands.

Finland

Emphasising different aspects of accountability has played a substantial role in shaping the contents of the Finnish higher education policy over the past 25 years. After the introduction of block grants and the performance-based funding model in the mid-1990s, especially financial accountability has dominated the discussion about the accountability of universities. Currently, the Finnish university funding model is one of the most performance-oriented models in the world: over 70% of the core state funding is based on success in performance criteria (de Boer et al. 2015). At the same time, the role of legal accountability in Finnish higher education policy has weakened after the new Universities Act that came into effect in 2010. This legislative reform changed the legal status of universities from being part of the state administration to being independent legal entities. Legislative regulation on central aspects like staffing policies (especially, regulation on staff qualifications, recruitment and remuneration) and internal governance of universities was significantly changed; at present, Finnish universities enjoy a relatively high level of autonomy compared with universities in many other European countries, including other Nordic countries (see Bennetot Pruvot and Estermann 2017).

In Finland, the role of universities in developing the economy has been supported and actively managed by successive governments since the 1960s. This policy has continued to the present, when universities are seen as central actors in the Finnish knowledge-based economy and core parts of the Finnish innovation system expected to contribute to sustainable economic growth, employment and national competitiveness (Biggar Economics 2017). At the same time, Finnish higher education policy recognises the importance of higher education's social and civic responsibilities, for example, in reducing poverty, inequality and social exclusion. Year after year, among all the OECD countries, Finland is among the top three countries with the highest level of public expenditure (compared to the GDP) on HEIs (see, e.g. OECD 2017). This has kept political expectations, and therefore, political accountability, at a high level. Higher education in general and universities specifically continue to be at the core of educational policies, and thus, political interests. At the concrete level, this has been evident in the 'Government Programmes' and 'Action Plans' of the past ruling cabinets (see, e.g. Prime Minister's Office 2017). At the same time, important stakeholders, such as several trade unions, student unions and employer organisations (e.g. the Confederation of Finnish

Industries), have continued to keep universities and higher education high on their political agenda.

Professional accountability in Finland has remained strong alongside the other forms of accountability. For instance, various scientific associations operating under the Federation of Finnish Learned Societies are actively exercising their gatekeeping role, especially in publishing. Scientific associations are often responsible for publishing scientific journals and other publications, and they appoint the editorial boards and editors of these journals. In addition, the various trade unions, such as the Finnish Union of University Professors and Finnish Union of University Researchers and Teachers, continue to play a role in upholding and safeguarding professional norms and values of Finnish academic profession.

Norway
Accountability aspects have been in the focus of Norwegian higher education in the last three decades. The managerial structures have been changed through the 'Quality Reform' of 2003–2004, which involved an effort to enhance political and social accountability by including politically appointed stakeholders on the boards of the universities. The Ministry of Education introduced a model where the board appointed the chair, as well as the rector. This model replaced the traditional one where the rector was elected by the university and chaired the board (Gornitzka and Larsen 2004). Still, the individual institution could choose which model to follow, resulting in a hybrid version in many universities, with both appointed and elected leaders in the institutions. The aim in giving the universities the possibility of choosing the governance model was to increase autonomy (Stensaker 2014).

A performance-based funding system was introduced through the same reform, and this can be considered an important part of accountability programmes (Frølich 2011). Such a system offers a neutral framework for assigning funds between universities and scientific fields. The shares of funding related to performance-based indicators are much smaller than they are, for example, in the Finnish system. In Norway, 30% of the funding is assigned according to performance-based indicators from teaching and research, while the basic funding (70%) provides long-term and stable financing for the sector (Kvaal 2014). Most Norwegian HEIs are state owned, but private institutions are granted the same state funding as the public. As for professional autonomy, there has been an increased focus on quality of teaching and alignment in educational programmes, as well as on research quality and quantity. This focus on both quality and quantity has challenged the professional autonomy via a bureaucratic and political form of accountability.

Sweden
As in the other Nordic countries, Swedish universities are accountable to many stakeholders. The legal accountability in Sweden has changed in the last two decades. The country has a long tradition of central state steering based on planning. However, this changed during the 1980s and 1990s across many sectors, including higher education. During the 1990s, following a ground-breaking reform in 1993, the higher education sector was fundamentally deregulated, with a reduction in central laws and ordinances and an increased formal autonomy for HEIs. Although most universities remained state agencies, with the autonomy (or freedom) reform, two HEIs, namely University College Jönköping and Chalmers University of Technology, became private foundations upon applications to the government. The main differences were regarding the internal organisation and regulations of hiring academic staff. Academic positions had thus far been centrally regulated, but from then on, professorships could be initiated by each HEI.

An important aspect of the accountability context in Sweden is the funding system. The reform in 1993 also introduced performance-based funding in education. The system is based on the number of students starting education (input) and number of students graduating (output). The government also holds HEIs accountable in annual dialogues. Each year's 'production' is presented in appropriations laid out by the government. The main aspects of state accountability are within the realm of evaluation (details are given below). As in Denmark, external stakeholders are represented on university boards.

The professional accountability remains strong, both as a standalone aspect of academic work and as intertwined in political accountability. Like in Finland, university teachers' and researchers' unions are a strong voice for the academic profession. Peer review is an ever-growing activity, for example, in conferences, research proposals, academic publications and hiring and promotion of academic staff. Senior academics spend a significant amount of time assessing colleagues.

Evaluation
Evaluation is closely related to accountability, as it is often considered an action that is used to verify accountability. For this and other reasons, evaluation has been a key theme in the public policy and higher education literature for at least three decades. It is obvious that evaluation can be used for control, aiming at contributing to holding individuals, groups, departments and organisations accountable. However, evaluation can also be used for many other purposes, including further learning and enhancement and enlightenment purposes. Evaluation, therefore, is not limited to summative (retrospective) assessments, but it can be also formative (during the process) or diagnostic (prior to the process). Moreover, evaluation can be used in strategic and tactical ways when actors try to pursue specific interests, as well as in symbolic ways when they wish to signal aspects like novelty. A more recent discussion related to use is the discussion on constitutive effects of evaluation procedures and performance indicators (Dahler-Larsen 2014). The idea is that evaluation creates a new reality influencing and changing interpretations of the world, thereby enabling shifts in social relations and practices.

The literature is rich in defining the concept of 'evaluation'. The North American literature is mostly concerned with aspects related to programme evaluation. Michael Quinn Patton, for example, defines (programme) evaluation as involving 'the systematic collection of information about the activities, characteristics, and outcomes of programs to make judgements about the program, improve program effectiveness, and/or inform decisions about future programming' (Patton 1997, 23). In the Nordic context, evaluation has been defined in a much broader way, including evaluative procedures for assessing the effectiveness of public organisations. An example can be found in the work of Evert Vedung, who defines evaluation as 'careful retrospective assessment of the merit, worth and value of administration, output and outcome of government interventions (in Swedish: offentlig verksamhet), which is intended to play a role in future, practical action situations' (Vedung 1997, 3). This broader definition can be interpreted to resonate with the ideals of the Nordic institutional welfare state.

As evaluative thinking has increasingly become integrated into regulative and managerial practices, a distinction between evaluation on the one hand and other concepts, such as quality assurance, accreditation and performance measurement on the other, has become increasingly blurred. In the higher education sector, we find an array of evaluative systems and procedures performed at different levels and directed towards different activities, especially teaching and research (Geschwind 2016). At the national level, evaluative procedures are part and parcel of several accountability mechanisms by governments, such as performance-based funding and various external quality assurance instruments, most notably, accreditation and auditing systems (e.g. Gover and Loukkola 2018; Santiago et al. 2008). In the Nordic countries, these evaluative procedures are performed by national, autonomous organisations with their own boards, management and staff (Smeby and Stensaker 1999). Their various evaluation practices are typically based on peer review panels including members of academic staff, students and stakeholders from working life and supported by project managers from the evaluation body. These national bodies have an umbrella organisation called the European Association for Quality Assurance in Higher Education (ENQA). They have presented European standards and guidelines (ESG) to be followed by all national bodies. There is an ongoing and recurrent process of accreditation of quality assurance bodies (Stensaker et al. 2011).

Intra-institutional evaluative procedures play a critical role in shaping the teaching and research activities in universities. These procedures are built into educational programmes, for example, in monitoring student satisfaction, and at many universities, peer review–based evaluations of departments and programmes ('audits') are organised and carried through. Since the 1990s, HEIs in the Nordic countries have been expected to take responsibility for their own evaluation activities. Depending on the focus of the national systems, these institutional evaluations have either mirrored or complemented the national ones (Karlsson et al. 2014). This development of intra-institutional evaluation has also implied that HEIs invest in the internal evaluation capacity in the form of designated evaluation units and hiring professional staff with evaluation experience.

At the level of individual academics, peer review–based evaluative procedures are a standard precondition for scholars to be appointed and promoted, as well as having their research projects funded and findings published. Increasingly, conferences have become based on peer review. As a whole, higher education sectors in most European countries are saturated with aspects pertaining to evaluation to the extent that one can refer to 'evaluation overload'. For instance, a recent study showed that senior academics can spend around a month per year evaluating other researchers' work (Langfeldt and Kyvik 2010).

Evaluation focuses on assessing quality, comprising both education quality and research quality. The concept of quality is ambiguous, and both education quality and research quality are multifaceted and multidimensional phenomena. Quality can be judged, among other things, as exceptionality, consistency, fitness for purpose, value for money and transformation (Harvey and Green 1993). Originally, this traditional categorisation was an attempt to deconstruct the rather abstract concept of quality in the context of higher education, focussing on its various dimensions to reconcile different ways of thinking about quality (Santiago et al. 2008; Stensaker 2004). Over the years, it has undoubtedly become the most influential framework for understanding and discussing quality in the context of HEIs. Although almost 25 years old, its position remains unchallenged in the field of higher education research (Kivistö and Pekkola 2017).

In more concrete terms, quality in education can include aspects like preconditions (staff competence, talented student body and infrastructure), contents (relevant curriculum), process (pedagogical arrangements carried through by trained teachers) and the achievement of learning outcomes, retention and student employability (see, e.g. Gibbs 2010). Quality education can even be further contextualised, including the views and expectations of relevant stakeholders (Jongbloed and Benneworth 2010). The emphasis on the different phases of education differs over time, and evaluation systems are usually readjusted slightly according to the requirements of the operating environment. For example, in some systems, a great emphasis can be placed on teacher competences, whereas other systems can rely heavily on an assessment of the final thesis (Lindberg-Sand 2011).

Although it differs slightly across the scientific fields and methodologies used, the characteristics of research quality often relate to aspects like objectivity, validity (internal and external), reliability, open-mindedness, honesty and thorough reporting (e.g. Miles and Huberman 1994; Steinke 2004). As in education, not only has research output been under scrutiny, but so has the preconditions for undertaking research, that is, the research environments. Research quality evaluations have increasingly included assessments of the influence of the research, as shown both within academia and beyond, in the society at large. The latter could be evaluated by using patent and licensing data and counting the number of new companies, as well as by asking research environments to submit more qualitative 'impact cases' (Karlsson 2017).

The latest trend has been to evaluate the administrative operations at the institutional level as well. These 'administrative assessment exercises' have been undertaken with the same methodology as the evaluations of education and research, making use of panels of experts, both academics and professional support staff. The balance between central and local administrative support, digitalisation, efficiency and effectiveness and new roles and competency needs for administrative staff have been recurrent themes in these evaluations (Karlsson and Ryttberg 2016).

Contextualising Evaluation in the Nordic Countries

Denmark

Evaluative procedures are widespread in Danish higher education. External evaluation of educational programmes was adopted in the late 1980s and institutionalised in the 1990s, at first as a soft national system supporting local quality development, but from 2007 onwards, as a hard control-oriented accreditation system where every bachelor's and master's programme, new and established, had to be approved (Hansen 2011). Currently, the system is being changed into one based on approval of the internal quality systems at the institutions. If approval is refused, institutions are not allowed to establish new educational programmes, and existing programmes must be accredited. At the institutional level, student satisfaction evaluation is a routine exercise. Evaluations of educational programmes in the light of stakeholder and labour market requirements are carried out on an ad hoc basis.

Compared with education, research evaluation is less standardised. There is no national system for evaluation of departments, disciplines or scientific fields. Some universities have developed institutional procedures aiming at taking all departments through research evaluations based on international peer review, while others do evaluations on an ad hoc basis or organise with advisory councils giving advice on how to improve research quality. However, in connection with basic funding of research in universities, a performance-based funding system works as an evaluation tool for research. While this metrics-based evaluation tool is meant to be an accountability and quality improvement tool on a national level, giving universities incentives to improve research, the system has been used internally at universities in budget models and for setting performance demands (see Chap. 4). In addition, evaluation is also linked to competitive research funding. Funders of research, public and private, evaluate the quality of research proposals.

Finland

Finnish universities, units and academics are subject to several types of evaluative procedures. The most important of these are institutional audits (complying fully with previously mentioned ESG), which form the core of the national quality assurance system. The Finnish Education Evaluation Centre (FINEEC) and its predecessor the Finnish Higher Education Evaluation Council (FINHEEC) have conducted audits of the universities' internal quality assurance systems since 2005. According to legislation, all HEIs must regularly (every six years on average) participate in external audits of their operations and internal quality assurance systems (Eurydice 2018). The main emphasis of the audits is to secure that institutions have properly functioning internal quality assurance systems; however, they do not evaluate the quality of education, research, or other institutional activities per se. The nature of external audits is primarily enhancement and improvement rather than control; failing an audit does not result in any sanctions, but instead, only initiates a mandatory re-audit process. This development rather than control orientation in evaluation can partly be explained by the rather extensive use of performance-based funding in providing core funding to universities. Having an accreditation type of evaluation system could be considered to add another layer of control, thereby making quality improvement a process of mandatory compliment rather than actual development.

Compared with that of education, the evaluation of research in Finland is a more multifaceted process, and it is more driven by needs of securing accountability. The Academy of Finland, the national funding agency for research, is responsible for financing research, and therefore, evaluating the research quality (applications). In addition, most universities regularly conduct internal research assessment exercises based on international peer review. However, unlike in some other European countries, there is no national-level comprehensive and centralised evaluation procedure for research. The quality of research, however, is considered in the funding model based on the following: (1) a bibliometric indicator awarding universities for publications 'points' (13% weighting) based on their coefficient ('JUFO' levels 0–3), which is expected to reflect the quality of publication outlets, and (2) amount of competitive research funding (9% weighting).

Norway

According to legal rules, the individual Norwegian HEIs are responsible for maintaining the quality of the offered education through systematic evaluations of quality, but the institutions are allowed to choose how to organise this work. Such evaluations are supposed to cover quality aspects of education, learning processes for students and practical studies, as well as regarding relevance of the educations to society. In addition, the Norwegian Agency for Quality Assurance (NOKUT) supervises the institutions and evaluates how the quality assurance work is performed. NOKUT's mission is to supervise and provide information used to develop the quality of higher education in Norway, as well as evaluate and control the quality of study programmes and institutions. NOKUT performs periodic control of the accredited higher education programmes and institutions, but such controls are supposed to occur at least every eight years. The standards and guidelines recommended by NOKUT comply with ESG as far as possible.

The follow-up on research quality depends on several stakeholders acting as funders of the research. The Norwegian Research Council is a main actor in providing funding for research in Norway, but smaller public and private agencies also play a role. For accountability and competitive reasons, the quality of research applications is evaluated through peer-review processes. The Nordic Institute for Studies in Innovation, Research and Education (NIFU) is an independent research institute that aims to deliver data on how Norwegian research and innovation is developing and the importance for society. Another central actor is the Norwegian Centre for Research Data (NSD), which evaluates the quality of research projects prior to their initiating to secure anonymity of the participants; the NSD also acts as a national agent for securing and storing collected data. The Statistics on Higher Education (DBH) database information is also distributed by the NSD.

Several databases have been established in Norway to secure usable data to follow up on evaluations as actions to verify accountability. Data related to teaching, as well as research-related activities, are collected and publicly available at the NSD, DBH, NIFU and Statistics Norway (SSB). As one of the few countries offering this, a national and non-commercial bibliographical database named the 'Current Research Information System in Norway' (CRISTIN) is publicly available for recording scholarly and peer-reviewed literature. The individual researchers are supposed to report their publications, and data from CRISTIN are used as background material for assigning performance-based funding to the universities. According to the Norwegian Publication Indicator, publication points are separated at level 1 (lowest level) and level 2. The split of publication channels into two levels is due to peer reviews from academic associations, and the ratings of the different scientific journals and publishers are published on the webpage from NSD.

Sweden
Evaluation activities in Swedish higher education are performed at the national level, HEI level and by individuals. Starting with education, like in the other countries, a national system of evaluation has been in place since the 1990s, as part of the NPM-inspired reforms in the early 1990s. The first system can be described as a light-touch system, and it provided evaluations of each institution's quality assurance system. These so-called institutional audits were undertaken during two rounds, with small adjustments. The system that followed (2001–2006) included an emphasis on subject and programme reviews across the system. All subjects and programmes leading to a degree were included. Since the 1990s, accreditation of programmes, scientific areas and HEIs has also been implemented, as well as thematic evaluations. The emphasis has shifted over the years; currently, there is again more focus on institutional audits.

Evaluation of research has been the responsibility of several actors. Through the Swedish Research Council, the state has initiated comprehensive subject evaluations. All the funding bodies evaluate the research that is being funded. There has been a development from only ex ante assessments of proposals to mid-term and final evaluations of funded projects and programmes. Many HEIs have also initiated independent evaluations of research. They follow a similar basic model, including panels, bibliometrics, self-evaluations and site visits, with a slight variation regarding scope and emphasis (Geschwind 2017).

Performance Measurement and Management

As is the case with evaluation, performance measurement and management can be understood as instruments for exercising accountability. In the context of higher education, performance can refer to all actions, tasks and processes carried out in HEIs (teaching, research, and third mission activities), as well as outputs and outcomes resulting from these actions.

Given this high level of ambiguity, what is meant by performance is very much subject to different conceptions and definitions.

To determine its level (good vs. bad, low vs. high), performance needs to be measured somehow. As an activity, measurement requires objective 'measures' that can be utilised in the process of measurement to determine the performance (cf. Neely et al. 1995). In this sense, the selection of measures and the way in which they are utilised (weighting, measurement methodology, etc.) defines what is, at any point in time, considered performance. Thus, performance measurement is an evaluative act of quantification (of performance). By nature, performance measurement is always instrumental, as it is done for a certain purpose, whether symbolic or real. These purposes are often related to management and manifested around a set of instruments, such as 'management by objectives', 'total quality management', 'knowledge management', or 'strategic management', aimed at achieving organisational goals. Thus, performance management in higher education can be defined as an activity where universities use the information acquired through performance measurement to achieve and demonstrate progress towards a predetermined set of goals (e.g. Wholey 1999).

Performance measurement, however, is not only a tool to verify accountability; it is also a means of directing organisational attention and focus. This is done by translating the institutional strategy into a set of goals reflected in performance measures that make success (and failure) more concrete for everyone (Melnyk et al. 2004; Vasikainen 2014). The goal of this approach to management is shifting focus from input and focussing on bureaucratic rules and procedures, to the output with goal setting and use of performance information, where public organisations also focus on economic performance (Christensen et al. 2007; Hvidman and Andersen 2013). These techniques tend to be cyclical, incorporating the formulation of objectives, performance, evaluations and adjustments, and this information is used to make managerial decisions.

There is a generic assumption that 'management is management' (Hvidman and Andersen 2013, 37) and the same managerial techniques can be applied in both the private and public sector. Considering this, three organisational characteristics that differ between public and private organisations may theoretically mitigate the effectiveness of performance management in the sectors as follows: incentives, capacity and clarity. For incentives, managers in the public sector are presumably motivated less by pay and other financial incentives than managers in the private sector are, and they are steered by a public service motivation, where the value of doing something of importance for society is a personal incentive. Regarding capacity, public managers often have lower autonomy and higher levels of bureaucracy, and this affects their capacity to take advantage of the collected information, which can be used for decision-making. The clarity of goals is also more problematic in public organisations, as there are many stakeholders, multiple goals and different expectations of political responsiveness and social equity (see Boyne 2002).

Often, performance management is utilised simultaneously with performance-based funding, where funds are allocated by a formula or algorithm for achieving certain predefined measures of performance. In a higher education context, most of the performance indicators measure progression or completion of final outputs related to teaching and research, such as study credits, number of degrees awarded, publications, competitive research funding awarded, citations, patents, level of competitive/external research funding, or student satisfaction (Kivistö and Kohtamäki 2016). Performance-based funding is believed to incentivise institutions to improve or maintain their level of performance in exchange for higher revenue (Dougherty and Reddy 2011). By reformulating incentives so that institutions are rewarded or punished primarily according to actual performance, performance-based funding mechanisms stimulate a shift in institutional behaviour towards greater efficiency. However, whether this is accomplished in real terms is another matter (Kivistö and Kohtamäki 2016; Kivistö et al. 2017; Rutherford and Rabovsky 2014).

Performance management and performance-based funding are often associated with the use of performance contracts/agreements, both at the system level and in institution internal arrangements. Performance agreements are contracts (see Gornitzka et al. 2004) between the government and individual HEIs, which set out specific goals that institutions will seek to achieve in a given period. They specify intentions to accomplish given targets, measured against pre-set known standards (Claeys-Kulik and Estermann 2015; de Boer et al. 2015). Furthermore, performance management increasingly takes place at the level of the individual academics (Andersen and Pallesen 2008; Kivistö et al. 2017). This is especially the case when it comes to research performance, where measurement by publication points has become common place in Nordic countries, especially Norway, Denmark and Finland (see, e.g. Aagaard et al. 2015; Pölönen 2015). In some institutional contexts, direct financial rewards could even be allocated to individual academics for research achievements, for instance, in the form of publications in high-status journals (Opstrup 2014). These rewards can be paid as one-time bonuses, top ups of salaries and/or a maximum percentage of the individual's total salary (Arnhold et al. 2018).

Contextualising Performance Measurement and Management in Nordic Countries

Denmark

Performance measurement and performance management have been increasingly important principles in higher education governance in Denmark for more than 30 years. However, performance management has been criticised for encouraging production of quantity at the expense of quality. This criticism has recently been followed by a political request to incorporate quality criteria in the performance management approaches.

In the 1980s, performance management was introduced in educational funding. In today's funding system, educational programmes are funded solely according to a performance principle. Funding is based on the number of students passing exams, as well as on bonuses given if students accomplish their studies in due time. The system is based on a real-time principle implying that the universities do not know the exact amount of resources available for education in a given year until the autumn of the same year. The real-time principle can be said to have been an advantage for the universities in a period with considerable growth in student numbers, but uncertainty about budgets due to variations in student practice have posed challenges for the institutions. Recently, it has been decided to further develop the funding system, including employability criteria and quality aspects that are probably linked to student assessments. Over the years, the performance-based funding formula has thus become increasingly complex and still more tightly politically governed. Since 2009, an increasing part of the funding for basic research, currently amounting to 20%, has been performance based. The formula includes the number of graduates from master's and PhD programmes, the ability to attract external funding and the counting of publications. A quality aspect is included in counting publications, as publication channels are divided into two groups, one releasing more points and resources than the other.

Funding from the Ministry of Higher Education and Science is given to the institutions as a lump sum, meaning that the universities decide how to distribute the resources between faculties and departments. In relation to education, the performance-based principle is typically implemented all the way down in the hierarchy, whereas there are only a few examples of this in relation to funding for basic research. Universities also negotiate performance contracts with their parent Ministry. Hitherto, contracts have not been related to funding allocations, but the institutions must document goal attainment. Recently, it was decided to link goal attainment to funding from 2019. In Denmark, salaries are only marginally linked to performance, although this aspect is increasingly gaining importance.

Finland
In Finland, performance measurement and performance management have been guiding principles in higher education governance, both at the system and institutional levels, for over 20 years. Originally, performance management and measurement landed in the university sector within the general reform of state administration, which, to a large extent, was implemented following the ideals derived from NPM. Today, even after the reform of 2010, which made universities legally independent from the state hierarchy, the university sector can be considered one of the administrative sectors governed/financed by the state where the ideals of NPM are most comprehensively applied (see e.g. Kauko and Diogo 2011; Salminen 2003). Some of the recent empirical studies have also proven the effectiveness of using performance-based funding in the increasing performance of Finnish universities (see Seuri and Vartiainen 2018).

Although the execution of performance management on behalf of the Finnish Ministry of Education and Culture has been highly structured, its further application in individual universities in their internal management and strategies is not controlled by the Ministry. In fact, individual universities, and in many cases their subunits, like faculties, have developed their own internal variations of performance management (Kallio and Kallio 2014). The extensiveness of performance-based funding is mostly visible in allocation practices in providing resources to universities, in professionalisation of academic and administrative management positions, in the use of contractual arrangements (performance agreements), and in outsourcing and centralisation of support and administrative services in universities. Furthermore, as in many other European countries, old and new trends related to management, such as strategic management, quality management and knowledge management, have also been applied in universities.

One important aspect of performance measurement is the salary system for university personnel. Since 2008, the salary system of universities, comprising both academic and administrative staff, has been based on performance measurement, where a maximum of around one-third of the salary is performance based. Although the salary or other performance-based financial incentives have not proven to be the main motivation for Finnish academics to work harder (see Kivistö et al. 2017), they are applied as means of translating system- and institutional-level incentives to the individual level, thereby drawing attention to what is considered valuable (and what is not).

Norway

The funding system for HEI in Norway provides a more stable budget than that in the Danish system, as 70% of the funding is allocated as block grants. Still, the 30% of performance-based indicators increasingly function as a policy tool used to stimulate improvement in both teaching and research, as well as managerial tools in the institutions. Teaching indicators constitute the largest share (24%), focussing on throughput of students and internalisation. As for research indicators (the remaining 6%), these are related to the throughput of PhD students, external funding of research (e.g. from the EU and the Norwegian Research Council), and finally from the metrics related to publications. The Norwegian Publication Indicator as a measurement system was introduced in 2004. As a policy and performance management tool, such indicators from research are meant to stimulate excellence and productivity, as well as to increase the accountability of public research. Another important aspect is aligning research to societal and economic needs (Aagaard et al. 2015). Despite the broad objectives, the financial role of the indicator is marginal, as it only distributes 2% of the funding to the sector (Aagaard et al. 2015).

This funding system based on metrics and a market model has, on the one hand, increased the autonomy in the universities, as the boards are responsible for prioritising within the allocated financial frames and aligning their activities to meet the goals for the sector. On the other hand, ex post control has increased, and the contractual relationship between universities and the state based on performance metrics is replacing the trust-based foundational pact (Stensaker 2014). The increased autonomy is counteracted by controlling instruments, reporting systems and the financial incentive systems following students and research activities (Christensen 2011). The individual academics are still autonomous regarding teaching and research, but the autonomy is limited or steered by incentive and reporting systems; this can feel like a decrease in professional autonomy (Christensen 2011).

Sweden
Generally, performance and performance measurement have become ever more important over time in Sweden as well. These phenomena have also increasingly 'trickled down' and been reflected across organisational levels. The developments of education and research described below have affected HEIs significantly, and various responses have emerged.

As mentioned above, one of the most dramatic changes in Swedish higher education was the introduction of performance-based funding in education, based on the inflow of students and throughput. The previous system was criticised for being too rigid, based on central planning, and not driving quality enough. The latter argument has also been used against the current system. Since funding is so closely related to student success, there have been discussions about decreased demands for passing students. The system is based on the idea that different educational areas bear different costs. A student in the Humanities is supposed to cost far less than an Engineering student, for instance. Another effect of this system has been an increased marketing activity by HEIs. An important aspect of the system is the use of a 'ceiling' for the number of students recruited. Allocation of funds has a limit and it is linked to a maximum number of students. Throughput of students has been a controversial quality indicator. Whereas there have been occasional discussions on the risk of lowering demands on students, there are also examples where student throughput has been linked to incentives. Overall, this has not affected the individual academics but rather organisational units and HEIs.

In research, the traditional model was block funding based on historical principles rather than performance. Direct state funding was the bulk of the total funding for research. Lately, there has been a development towards more competitive external funding than direct state funding, and as of 2018, the external funding made up slightly more than half of the total funding. A milestone in Swedish research policy was the introduction of performance-based funding as part of the direct state funding. Since the introduction in 2009, 10–20% of the total funding has been allocated to

HEIs based on performance as shown in publications and external funding.

Converging Higher Education Policies

Organisational fields with their specific institutions, such as universities, have similarities in organisational design and activities all over the world. In many countries, universities have experienced a shift towards 'academic capitalism' (Slaughter and Leslie 1999) and operate as 'entrepreneurial universities' (Clark 1998; Etzkowitz et al. 2008). Rationalisation of the universities as organisational actors by the introduction of more formal structure, in terms of introducing a stronger emphasis on quality assurance, evaluation, accountability measures and incentive systems, can be considered a transnational process linked to the NPM type of governance reforms (Ramirez and Christensen 2013; Seeber et al. 2015). The social mechanisms of spreading the ideas of rationalisation can be highlighted from the perspective of institutional isomorphism (DiMaggio and Powell 1983). The literature on isomorphism concentrates on the increasing similarity of organisational and institutional structures and cultures, whereas studies on policy convergence focus on changes in national policy characteristics. Policy convergence, that is, the development of similar or identical policies across countries over time (Knill 2005), seems to be especially evident in Nordic countries, which show similar types of policy development in many significant areas of higher education policy, predominantly those related to governance.

One of the most important reasons behind policy convergence, although not the only one, is international policy promotion, where an actor with expertise in a policy field promotes certain policies. International (or supranational) organisations specialised in a certain policy field are the main actors for inducing the convergence of policies by actively promoting certain policies and defining objectives and standards in an international setting. Countries diverging from the promoted policy models may feel pressure to comply with the policies (Holzinger and Knill 2005; Knill 2005).

There are two overarching international political processes relating to higher education in Europe, which presumably have a significant effect on policy convergence, as follows: the higher education 'Modernisation Agenda' (European Commission 2006, 2011) promoted under the auspices of the EU institutions (especially the European Commission) and the intergovernmental Bologna Process (Moisio 2014). Many NPM ideals implemented in Nordic universities, such as promoting the accountability and autonomy of higher education institutions and improving the governance, funding, quality and relevance of higher education, are directly in line with the Commission's Modernisation Agenda. Interestingly, the Modernisation Agenda presents chiefly the American higher education system and universities as one of the important points of comparison in developing European higher education (see also Slaughter and Cantwell 2012; Slaughter and Taylor 2016).

The Bologna Process seems to increase policy convergence at the European level, although the research evidence for this is not yet entirely clear (see, e.g. Witte 2008). However, Voegtle et al. (2011) have found that the higher education policies of the Bologna participants converge more strongly and that the Bologna Process has made a crucial difference in increasing the similarity of higher education policies. Especially in the area of quality assurance, most Bologna countries implemented most of the measures and included all the required actors for quality assurance measures according to Bologna standards by 2008 (Voegtle et al. 2011).

International/intergovernmental organisations, such as the OECD, World Bank and UNESCO, are highly influential actors in higher education policy convergence (see, e.g. Shahjahan 2012; Shahjahan and Madden 2015). At the European and Nordic level, most notably, the OECD has had a high level of influence on policy convergence. Nation states, including Nordic countries, often rely on the OECD to provide them with the latest data on trends, current issues and policy options. The OECD uses conferences, trend and review reports and the mediation of policy language to influence the thinking of national-level policymakers within and outside of its member countries (Shahjahan and Madden 2015). For instance, the OECD's thematic reviews can provide a strong legitimisation or justification to national governments for initiating policy reforms, as has happened in Finland (Kallo 2009).

In addition to the influence of international organisations, cross-national policy convergence may simply be the result of similar but independent responses caused by the same type of policy problems to which countries are reacting (Bennett 1991; Knill 2005). At the same time, convergence in policies is more likely for countries that are characterised by high institutional similarity, as policies tend to be implemented insofar as they fit with the existing culture, socioeconomic structures and institutional arrangements. In the search for relevant policy models, states are expected to look to the experiences of those countries with which they share an especially close set of cultural similarities and ties (Knill 2005). In many ways, this is the case with Nordic countries, which are characterised by a welfare-state ideology and public-sector development in this framework. Moreover, they are relatively similar in population size and geographically proximate, and they share the same types of political systems and values. In terms of policy challenges, all Nordic countries have to deal with the financial, social and political sustainability of the Nordic welfare model, which in turn, as has been mentioned before, has triggered government-led reform efforts under the label of NPM, especially in the higher education sector. In all countries, universities are expected to play an increasingly important role in local and national economic development and innovation, which has further intensified government-led efforts to modernise the higher education sector in all Nordic countries.

Although policy convergence clearly is observable across the Nordic countries, however, it is important to observe that similar policies are introduced at different points in time and with important variations in the details. For instance, all the Nordic countries have introduced performance-based funding systems linked to the distribution of resources for basic research. However, performance in Nordic countries is measured using different indicators and redistribution potentials, and therefore, also the effects of the measurement are quite likely different. Other examples of divergence are found in relation to overall governance and management structures, as well as the national quality assurance systems linked to education. Overall, there seems to be more convergence in policy ideas and policy rhetoric than in actual policy implementation.

Acknowledgements The data presented in the current volume and individual chapters emanate from a comparative study funded by the Norwegian Research Council under its FINNUT flagship program, a long-term program for research and innovation in the educational sector program. The project number was 237782, and the project was titled 'Does it matter? Assessing the performance effects of changes in leadership and management structures in Nordic Higher Education'.

References

Aagaard, Kaare, Carter Bloch, and Jesper Schneider. 2015. Impacts of Performance-Based Research Funding Systems: The Case of the Norwegian Publication Indicator. *Research Evaluation* 24 (1): 106–117.

Andersen, Lotte B., and Thomas Pallesen. 2008. 'Not Just for the Money?' How Financial Incentives Affect the Number of Publications at Danish Research Institutions. *International Public Management Journal* 11: 28–47.

Arnhold, Nina, Elias Pekkola, Vitus Püttmann, and Andrée Sursock. 2018. *World Bank Support to Higher Education in Latvia: Volume 3. Academic Careers*. Washington: World Bank. https://openknowledge.worldbank.org/handle/10986/29738.

Bennetot Pruvot, Enora, and Thomas Estermann. 2017. *University Autonomy in Europe III. The Scorecard 2017*. Brussels: European University Association.

Bennett, Colin. 1991. What Is Policy Convergence and What Causes It? *British Journal of Political Science* 21: 215–233.

BiGGAR Economics. 2017. *Economic Contribution of the Finnish Universities*. Penicuik, Midlothian: BiGGAR Economics. http://www.unifi.fi/wp-content/uploads/2017/06/UNIFI_Economic_Impact_Final_Report.pdf.

Bovens, Mark. 2007. Analysing and Assessing Accountability: A Conceptual Framework. *European Law Journal* 13 (4): 447–468.

Bovens, Mark, Thomas Schillemans, and Robert Goodin. 2014. Public Accountability. In *The Oxford Handbook of Public Accountability*, ed. Mark Bovens, Thomas Schillemans, and Robert Goodin, 1–20. Oxford: Oxford University Press.

Boyne, George A. 2002. Public and Private Management: What's the Difference? *Journal of Management Studies* 39 (1): 97–122.

Christensen, Tom. 2011. University Governance Reforms: Potential Problems of More Autonomy? *Higher Education* 62 (4): 503–517.

Christensen, Tom, and Per Lægreid. 2017. Introduction. Accountability and Welfare State Reforms. In *The Routledge Handbook to Accountability and Welfare State Reforms in Europe*, ed. Tom Christensen and Per Lægreid, 1–11. Oxon: Routledge.

Christensen, Thomas, Per Lægreid, and Inger Marie Stigen. 2007. Performance Management and Public Sector Reform: The Norwegian Hospital Reform. *Public Management Journal* 9 (2): 113–139.

Claeys-Kulik, Anna-Lena, and Thomas Estermann. 2015. *DEFINE Thematic Report: Performance-Based Funding of Universities in Europe*. Brussels: European University Association.

Clark, Burton R. 1998. *Creating Entrepreneurial Universities: Organizational Pathways of Transformation*. Oxford: Pergamon.

Dahler-Larsen, Peter. 2014. Constitutive Effects of Performance Indicators: Getting Beyond Unintended Consequences. *Public Management Review* 16 (7): 969–986.

de Boer, Harry, Ben Jongbloed, Paul Benneworth, Leon Cremonini, Renze Kolster, Andrea Kottmann, and Hans Vossensteyn. 2015. *Performance-Based*

Funding and Performance Agreements in Fourteen Higher Education Systems. Enschede: Center for Higher Education Policy Studies, University of Twente.

DiMaggio, Paul J., and Walter W. Powell. 1983. The Iron Cage Revisited: Institutional Isomorphism and Collective Rationality in Organizational Fields. *American Sociological Review* 48 (2): 147–160.

Dougherty, Kevin, and Viskash Reddy. 2011. *The Impacts of State Performance Funding Systems on Higher Education Institutions: Research Literature Review and Policy Recommendations*. CCRC Working Paper No. 37, Teachers College, Columbia University, New York, NY.

Dressel, Paul L., ed. 1980. *The Autonomy of Public Colleges*. San Francisco: Jossey-Bass.

Dubnick, Melvin. 2014. Accountability as a Cultural Keyword. In *The Oxford Handbook of Public Accountability*, ed. Mark Bovens, Thomas Schillemans, and Robert E. Goodin, 23–28. Oxford: Oxford University Press.

Etzkowitz, Henry, Marina Ranga, Mats Benner, Lucia Guaranys, Anne Marie Maculan, and Robert Kneller. 2008. Pathways to the Entrepreneurial University: Towards a Global Convergence. *Science and Public Policy* 35 (9, November): 681–695. https://doi.org/10.3152/030234208X389701.

European Commission. 2006. *Delivering on the Modernisation Agenda for Universities: Education, Research and Innovation. Communication from the Commission to the Council and the European Parliament*. Brussels: European Commission.

———. 2011. *Communication from the Commission to the European Parliament, the Council, the European Economic and Social Committee and the Committee of the Regions on "Supporting Growth and Jobs—An Agenda for the Modernisation of Europe's Higher Education Systems"*. Brussels: European Commission.

Eurydice. 2018. *Finland. Quality Assurance in Higher Education.* https://eacea.ec.europa.eu/national-policies/eurydice/content/quality-assurance-higher-education-21_el.

Frølich, Nicoline. 2011. Multi-layered Accountability. Performance-Based Funding of Universities. *Public Administration* 89 (3): 840–859.

Geschwind, Lars. 2016. Academic Core Values and Quality: The Case of Teaching-Research Links. In *Att ta utbildningens komplexitet på allvar. En vänskrift till Eva Forsberg*, ed. Maja Elmgren, Maria Folke-Fichtelius, Stina Hallsén, Henrik Román, and Wieland Wermke, 227–238. Uppsala: Uppsala Studies in Education No. 138.

———. 2017. Reflections on Q&R17 by a Researcher on Research. In *KoF17 Quality and Renewal 2017. Research Environment Evaluation at Uppsala University*, ed. Anders Malmberg, Åsa Kettis, and Camilla Maandi, 34–38. Uppsala: Uppsala University.

Gibbs, Graham. 2010. *Dimensions of Quality*. Helsington, York: The Higher Education Academy. https://www.heacademy.ac.uk/system/files/dimensions_of_quality.pdf.

Gornitzka, Åsa, and I.M. Larsen. 2004. Towards Professionalization? Restructuring of Administrative Workforce in Universities. *Higher Education* 47: 455–471.

Gornitzka, Åsa, Bjørn Stensaker, Jens-Christian Smeby, and Harry de Boer. 2004. Contract Arrangements in the Nordic Countries: Solving the Efficiency–Effectiveness Dilemma? *Higher Education in Europe* 29 (1): 87–101. https://doi.org/10.1080/03797720410001673319.

Gover, Anna, and Tiia Loukkola. 2018. *Enhancing Quality: From Policy to Practice.* Brussels: EQUIP. http://www.eua.be/Libraries/publications-homepage-list/equip-publication_final.

Hansen, Hanne F. 2011. University Reforms in Denmark and the Challenges for Political Science. *European Political Science* 10: 235–247.

Harvey, Lee, and Diana Green. 1993. Defining Quality. *Assessment and Evaluation in Higher Education* 18 (1): 9–34.

Holzinger, Katharina, and Christoph Knill. 2005. Causes and Conditions of Cross-national Policy Convergence. *Journal of European Public Policy* 12 (5): 775–796. https://doi.org/10.1080/13501760500161357.

Huisman, Jeroen. 2018. Accountability in Higher Education. In *Encyclopedia of International Higher Education Systems and Institutions*, ed. Pedro Teixeira and Jung Cheol Shin. Dordrecht: Springer. https://doi.org/10.1007/978-94-017-9553-1_156-1.

Huisman, Jeroen, and Jan Currie. 2004. Accountability in Higher Education: Bridge over Troubled Water? *Higher Education* 48: 529–551.

Hvidman, Ulrik, and Simon Calmar Andersen. 2013. Impact of Performance Management and Private Organizations. *Journal of Performance Management in Public and Private Organizations* 24 (1): 35–58.

Jongbloed, Ben, and Paul Benneworth. 2010. Who Matters to Universities? A Stakeholder Perspective on Humanities, Arts and Social Sciences Valorization. *Higher Education* 59: 567–588. https://doi.org/10.1007/s10734-009-9265-2.

Kai, Jiang. 2009. A Critical Analysis of Accountability in Higher Education. *Chinese Education & Society* 42 (2): 39–51. https://doi.org/10.2753/CED1061-1932420204.

Kallio, Kirsi-Mari, and Tomi J. Kallio. 2014. Management-By-Results and Performance Measurement in Universities—Implications for Work Motivation. *Studies in Higher Education* 39 (4): 574–589.

Kallo, Johanna. 2009. *OECD Education Policy. A Comparative and Historical Study Focusing on the Thematic Reviews of Tertiary Education.* Doctoral diss., University of Turku, Jyväskylä, Fera.

Karlsson, Sara. 2017. Evaluation as a Travelling Idea: Assessing the Consequences of Research Assessment Exercises. *Research Evaluation* 26 (2): 55–65.

Karlsson, Sara, and Malin Ryttberg. 2016. Those Who Walk the Talk: The Role of Administrative Professionals in Transforming Universities into Strategic Actors.

Nordic Journal of Studies in Educational Policy 2016 (2–3): 315–337. https://doi.org/10.3402/nstep.v2.31537.

Karlsson, Sara, Karin Fogelberg, Åsa Kettis, Stefan Lindgren, Mette Sandoff, and Lars Geschwind. 2014. Not Just Another Evaluation: A Comparative Study of Four Educational Quality Projects at Swedish Universities. *Tertiary Education and Management* 20 (3): 239–251. https://doi.org/10.1080/13583883.2014.932832.

Kauko, Jaakko, and Sara Diogo. 2011. Comparing Higher Education Reforms in Finland and Portugal: Different Contexts, Same Solutions? *Higher Education Management and Policy* 23 (3): 115–133.

King, Roger. 2015. Institutional Autonomy and Accountability. In *The Palgrave International Handbook of Higher Education Policy and Governance*, ed. Jeroen Huisman, Harry de Boer, David D. Dill, and Manuel Souto-Otero, 485–505. Basingstoke: Palgrave.

Kivistö, Jussi. 2007. *Agency Theory as a Framework for the Government-University Relationship*. Doctoral diss., Higher Education Finance and Management Series, Tampere University Press, Tampere.

Kivistö, Jussi, and Vuokko Kohtamäki. 2016. Does Performance-Based Funding Work? Reviewing the Impacts of Performance-based Funding on Higher Education Institutions. In *Positioning Higher Education Institutions: From Here to There*, ed. Rosalin Pritchard, Attila Pausits, and James Williams, 215–226. Rotterdam: Sense Publishers.

Kivistö, Jussi, and Elias Pekkola. 2017. *Quality in Administration of Higher Education*. Stockholm: Sveriges universitets- och högskoleförbund (SUHF).

Kivistö, Jussi, Elias Pekkola, and Anu Lyytinen. 2017. The Influence of Performance-Based Management on Teaching and Research Performance of Finnish Senior Academics. *Tertiary Education and Management* 23 (3): 260–275.

Knill, Christoph. 2005. Introduction: Cross-National Policy Convergence: Concepts, Approaches and Explanatory Factors. *Journal of European Public Policy* 12 (5): 764–774. https://doi.org/10.1080/13501760500161332.

Kvaal, Torkel Nybakk. 2014. *Finansieringssystem for universiteter og høyskoler*. Oslo: Kunnskapsdepartementet.

Langfeldt, Liv, and Svein Kyvik. 2010. Researchers as Evaluators: Tasks, Tensions and Politics. *Higher Education* 62 (2): 199–212. https://doi.org/10.1007/s10734-010-9382-y.

Lindberg-Sand, Åsa. 2011. *Koloss på lerfötter? Utveckling av metodik för ett resultatbaserat nationellt kvalitetssystem i svensk högre utbildning*. Lund: Centre for Educational Development, Lunds universitet.

Melnyk, Steven, Douglas Stewart, and Morgan Swink. 2004. Metrics and Performance Measurement in Operations Management: Dealing with the Metrics Maze. *Journal of Operations Management* 22: 209–217.

Miles, Michael, and Matthew Huberman. 1994. *Qualitative Data Analysis: An Expanded Sourcebook*. 2nd ed. Thousand Oaks, CA: Sage Publications.

Moisio, Johanna. 2014. *Understanding the Significance of EU Higher Education Policy Cooperation in Finnish Higher Education Policy*. Doctoral diss., Tampere University Press, Tampere.

Neely, Andy, Mike Gregory, and Ken Platts. 1995. Performance Measurement System Design: A Literature Review and Research Agenda. *International Journal of Operations Management* 15 (4): 80–116.

OECD. 2017. *Education at a Glance 2017. OECD Indicators*. Paris: OECD.

Opstrup, Niels. 2014. *Causes and Consequences of Performance Management at Danish University Departments*. Doctoral diss., Syddansk Universitet, Det Samfundsvidenskabelige Fakultet.

Patton, Michael. 1997. *Utilization-Focused Evaluation*. 3rd ed. Thousand Oaks: Sage Publications.

Pölönen, Janne. 2015. Suomenkieliset kanavat ja julkaisut Julkaisufoorumissa [Finnish Language Publication Channels and Publications in the Publication Forum]. *Media & viestintä* 38 (4): 237–252. https://journal.fi/mediaviestinta/article/view/62073.

Prime Minister's Office. 2017. *Finland, A Land of Solutions. Mid-term Review: Government Action Plan 2017–2019*. https://valtioneuvosto.fi/documents/10184/321857/Government+action+plan+28092017+en.pdf.

Ramirez, Francisco, and Tom Christensen. 2013. The Formalization of University: Rules, Roots, and Routes. *Higher Education* 65 (6): 695–708.

Romzek, Barbara S. 2000. Dynamics of Public Sector Accountability in an Era of Reform. *International Review of Administrative Science* 66: 21–44.

Rutherford, Amanda, and Thomas Rabovsky. 2014. Evaluating Impacts of Performance Funding Policies on Student Outcomes in Higher Education. *Annals of the American Academy of Political and Social Science* 655: 185–208.

Salminen, Ari. 2003. New Public Management and Finnish Public Sector Organisations: The Case of Universities. In *The Higher Education Managerial Revolution?* ed. Alberto Amaral, Vincent L. Meek, and Ingvild M. Larsen, 55–69. Dordrecht: Kluwer Academic.

Santiago, Paulo, Karine Tremblay, Ester Basri, and Elena Arnal. 2008. *Tertiary Education for the Knowledge Society. Volume 1: Special Features: Governance, Funding, Quality*. Paris: OECD.

Schmidtlein, Frank A. 2004. Assumptions Commonly Underlying Government Quality Assessment Practices. *Tertiary Education and Management* 10 (4): 263–285.

Seeber, Marco, et al. 2015. European Universities as Complete Organizations? Understanding Identity, Hierarchy and Rationality in Public Organizations. *Public Management Review* 17 (10): 1444–1474. https://doi.org/10.1080/14719037.2014.943268.

Seuri, Allan, and Hannu Vartiainen. 2018. *Yliopistojen rahoitus, kannustimet ja rakennekehitys*. Talouspolitiikan arviointineuvosto: Helsinki. https://www.talouspolitiikanarviointineuvosto.fi/wordpress/wp-content/uploads/2018/01/Seuri_Vartiainen_2018-1.pdf.

Shahjahan, Riyad A. 2012. The Roles of International Organizations (IOs) in Globalizing Higher Education Policy. In *Higher Education: Handbook of Theory and Research 27*, ed. John C. Smart and Michael B. Paulsen, 369–407. Dordrecht: Springer.

Shahjahan, Riyad A., and Meggan Madden. 2015. Uncovering the Images and Meanings of International Organizations (IOs) in Higher Education Research. *Higher Education* 69: 705–717. https://doi.org/10.1007/s10734-014-9801-6.

Sinclair, Amanda. 1995. The Chameleon of Accountability: Forms and Discourses. *Accounting Organizations and Society* 20 (2–3): 219–237.

Slaughter, Sheila, and Brendan Cantwell. 2012. Transatlantic Moves to the Market: The United States and the European Union. *Higher Education* 63 (5): 583–606. https://doi.org/10.1007/s10734-011-9460-9.

Slaughter, Sheila, and Larry Leslie. 1999. *Academic Capitalism: Politics, Policies, and the Entrepreneurial University*. Baltimore: Johns Hopkins University Press.

Slaughter, Sheila, and Barret J. Taylor, eds. 2016. *Competitive Advantage: Stratification, Privatization and Vocationalization of Higher Education in the US, EU, and Canada*. Dordrecht: Springer.

Smeby, Jens-Christian, and Bjørn Stensaker. 1999. National Quality Assessment Systems in the Nordic Countries: Developing a Balance Between External and Internal Needs? *Higher Education Policy* 12 (1): 3–14.

Steinke, Ines. 2004. Quality Criteria in Qualitative Research. In *A Companion to Qualitative Research*, ed. Uwe Flick, Ernst von Kardorff, and Ines Steinke, 184–190. London: SAGE.

Stensaker, Bjørn. 2004. *The Transformation of Organisational Identities. Interpretations of Policies Concerning the Quality of Teaching and Learning in Norwegian Higher Education*. Doctoral thesis, CHEPS/University of Twente, Enschede.

———. 2014. Troublesome Institutional Autonomy: Governance and the Distribution of Authority in Norwegian Universities. In *International Trends in University Governance: Autonomy, Self-Government and the Distribution of Authority*, ed. Michael Shattock, 34–48. New York: Routledge.

Stensaker, Bjørn, Liv Langfeldt, Harvey Lee, Jeroen Huisman, and Don Westerheijden. 2011. An In-Depth Study on the Impact of External Quality Assurance. *Assessment & Evaluation in Higher Education* 36 (4): 465–478. https://doi.org/10.1080/02602930903432074.

Trow, Martin A. 1996. Trust, Markets and Accountability in Higher Education: A Comparative Perspective. *Higher Education Policy* 9 (4): 309–324.

Vasikainen, Soili. 2014. *Performance Management of the University Education Process.* Doctoral diss., University of Oulu, Oulu.

Vedung, Evert. 1997. *Public Policy and Program Evaluation.* New Brunswick: Transaction Publishers.

Voegtle, Eva M., Christoph Knill, and Michael Dobbins. 2011. To What Extent Does Transnational Communication Drive Cross-National Policy Convergence? The Impact of the Bologna-Process on Domestic Higher Education Policies. *Higher Education* 61: 77–94. https://doi.org/10.1007/s10734-010-9326-6.

Wholey, Joseph S. 1999. Performance-Based Management: Responding to the Challenges. *Public Productivity and Management Review* 22: 288–307.

Witte, Johanna. 2008. Aspired Convergence, Cherished Diversity: Dealing with the Contradictions of Bologna. *Tertiary Education and Management* 14 (2): 81–93. https://doi.org/10.1080/13583880802051840.

Open Access This chapter is licensed under the terms of the Creative Commons Attribution 4.0 International License (http://creativecommons.org/licenses/by/4.0/), which permits use, sharing, adaptation, distribution and reproduction in any medium or format, as long as you give appropriate credit to the original author(s) and the source, provide a link to the Creative Commons licence and indicate if changes were made.

The images or other third party material in this chapter are included in the chapter's Creative Commons licence, unless indicated otherwise in a credit line to the material. If material is not included in the chapter's Creative Commons licence and your intended use is not permitted by statutory regulation or exceeds the permitted use, you will need to obtain permission directly from the copyright holder.

CHAPTER 3

Nordic Higher Education in Flux: System Evolution and Reform Trajectories

*Rómulo Pinheiro, Timo Aarrevaara,
Laila Nordstrand Berg, Tatiana Fumasoli,
Lars Geschwind, Hanne Foss Hansen, Helge Hernes,
Jussi Kivistö, Jonas Krog Lind, Anu Lyytinen,
Elias Pekkola, Kirsi Pulkkinen, Bjørn Stensaker,
and Johan Söderlind*

Helge Hernes passed away in the Fall of 2018.

R. Pinheiro • H. Hernes
Department of Political Science & Management, University of Agder, Kristiansand, Norway
e-mail: romulo.m.pinheiro@uia.no

T. Aarrevaara • K. Pulkkinen (✉)
Faculty of Social Sciences, University of Lapland, Rovaniemi, Finland
e-mail: timo.aarrevaara@ulapland.fi; kirsi.pulkkinen@ulapland.fi

L. N. Berg
Department of Social Science, Western Norway University of Applied Sciences, Sogndal, Norway
e-mail: laila.nordstrand.berg@hvl.no

© The Author(s) 2019
R. Pinheiro et al. (eds.), *Reforms, Organizational Change and Performance in Higher Education*,
https://doi.org/10.1007/978-3-030-11738-2_3

Introduction

Higher education (HE) in the Nordic countries has experienced continuous change in the last three decades. This has partially been a result of the increased number of enrolled students, but it is also a result of the influence of larger societal trends, such as urbanisation, digitalisation, and the importance attributed to innovation and global competition. Governmental reforms have placed an emphasis on quality, excellence, efficiency, and accountability, and have led to significant changes in the internal fabric of publicly funded universities. At the system level, the traditional binary divide characterising higher education throughout the Nordic region has also been affected. In some countries, such as Norway, the general trend has been convergence towards a unitary model based on comprehensive research-intensive universities, whereas other countries (e.g., Finland) still exhibit policy commitments towards maintaining horizontal diversity, with different providers undertaking specific functions.

Given their geographical features, regional dimensions also play an important role; however, these have also been adapting to the new realities facing localities and regions beyond the largest urban areas. As is the case with other countries' higher education systems, the influence of market-based models has been felt in the Nordics, and new public management

---

T. Fumasoli
UCL Institute of Education, University College London,
London, United Kingdom
e-mail: t.fumasoli@ucl.ac.uk

L. Geschwind • J. Söderlind
School of Industrial Engineering and Management, KTH Royal Institute of Technology, Stockholm, Sweden
e-mail: larsges@kth.se; johanso2@kth.se

H. F. Hansen • J. K. Lind
Department of Political Science, University of Copenhagen,
Copenhagen, Denmark
e-mail: hfh@ifs.ku.dk; jkl@ifs.ku.dk

J. Kivistö • A. Lyytinen • E. Pekkola
Faculty of Management and Business, Tampere University, Tampere, Finland
e-mail: jussi.kivisto@tuni.fi; anu.lyytinen@tuni.fi; elias.pekkola@tuni.fi

B. Stensaker
Department of Education, University of Oslo, Oslo, Norway
e-mail: bjorn.stensaker@iped.uio.no

(NPM)-inspired reforms have resulted in the rise of managerialism focusing on efficiency, performance, and outcome-based assessments. The traditional social contract, which is based on trust between higher education institutions (HEI) and society and is brokered via the state, has gradually yet steadily been replaced by a contractual relationship in which providers are expected to deliver certain pre-determined outcomes in light of agreed-upon input factors (such as people and funding) and performance metrics (such as outputs).

Given their cultural similarities and their shared commitment towards public investments in the realm of welfare and education, the Nordic countries have often been grouped together to encompass the "Nordic model." Yet, beyond the surface, each Nordic country is unique in its own right, and this is reflected in the governance and organisation of their respective national higher education systems. Despite a considerable degree of policy convergence among the Nordic countries, important variations in terms of timing, content, and degree of change can be detected. These national specificities, described in some detail later in this chapter, provide the backdrop for assessing the results of the comparative study that comprise the bulk of this edited volume.

We start by describing how the four national systems included in this study—Denmark, Finland, Norway, and Sweden—are currently organised and structured, illuminating several specific features such as the types and sizes of the institutions, enrolment patterns, performance measures, and funding. The chapter then moves on by providing a snapshot of how higher education systems have evolved historically by shedding light on policy dynamics from the late 1990s to 2013, the baseline period for the comparative study. That being said, and when appropriate, the chapter reflects briefly on key policy developments in the last five years or so (2013–2018 period).

NATIONAL HIGHER EDUCATION SYSTEMS AND RECENT POLICY DYNAMICS

Denmark

Landscape
Higher education in Denmark is organised into three types of programmes offered by different types of institutions. Short-length programmes are

offered by business colleges (*erhvervsakademier*) responsible for vocational training, medium-length bachelor's programmes that train teachers, pedagogues, and social workers are offered by university colleges (*professionshøjskoler*), and long-length programmes (master's and PhD programmes) are, in addition to bachelor's programmes, offered by universities. Universities are also responsible for most of the sector's research activity. As indicated above, the empirical focus of this edited volume is solely on the university sector. In 2013, the Danish university landscape consisted of eight universities that enrolled 156,815 students and employed 33,446 staff, as shown in Table 3.1.

As the table shows, the higher education landscape is diverse. Denmark has very large institutions, such as the University of Copenhagen, small institutions, such as RUC, and even tiny institutions, such as ITU. The table also reveals that some institutions, such as CBS, have many students in comparison to the number of staff while other institutions, such as DTU and Aarhus University, have the opposite. Diversity has increased as a result of the merger reform in 2007 (described later) during

Table 3.1 The Danish higher education university landscape, 2013

Institution	Type	Number of enrolled students	Total number of staff (FTE[a])
University of Copenhagen	Multi-faculty	40,866	9652
Aarhus University	Multi-faculty	38,169	8216
University of Southern Denmark (SDU)	Multi-faculty	22,224	3626
Roskilde University (RUC)	Multi-faculty	7588	1020
Aalborg University	Multi-faculty	19,064	3379
Technical University of Denmark (DTU)	Mono-faculty	10,196	5721
Copenhagen Business School (CBS)	Mono-faculty	16,659	1526
IT University of Copenhagen (ITU)	Mono-faculty	1894	306
Total		156,660	33,446

Source: Statistics from Universities Denmark
[a]Full-time equivalent (FTE)

which most governmental research institutes were merged into the universities. Due to this reform, there are huge differences in the research intensiveness of these universities today.

System Governance
The main elements in the governance system of Denmark's university sector are legislation, development contracts (recently re-termed as strategic framework contracts), performance-based funding, accreditation, and dialogue. Universities are so-called self-owing institutions under the auspices of Denmark's Ministry of Higher Education and Science. Boards with external majorities have the overall responsibility of strategically managing the institutions and are accountable to the minister when it comes to the administration of economic resources. Furthermore, these boards appoint the vice-chancellors responsible for the daily management of the universities.

In the Danish university sector, reforms have become part of daily life. Looking back at the last 15 years, the most important policy developments and reforms related to governance have been: the introduction of contract steering in 2000, the governance reform in 2003, the merger reform in 2007, and the changes in output-based mechanisms for resource allocations in universities. Many of these developments can be traced back to a 2001 report that established a research policy reform agenda. This agenda was, first and foremost, geared towards the need to increase resources for public sector research, reform universities' management structures, strengthen evaluation and quality assurance, and boost PhD education. In addition, these changes were aimed towards securing critical mass through collaboration and mergers and developing the resource allocation system in a more results-based direction (Aagaard 2012; Hansen 2001; Research Commission 2001).

Since the year 2000, development contracts between Denmark's line ministry and the country's individual universities have been an important element in the governance of the sector. Contracts have lined up important goals and measurable results, but they have not been linked to resource allocations per se. Instead, they have been followed up by the documentation of results in the form of institutional annual reports. In 2015, "binding goals" were introduced, which line up political goals for the sector as such. The binding goals from 2015 to 2017 were to improve quality of education, increase relevance and collaboration, strengthen internationalisation, and increase social mobility. All Danish universities have been committed to helping achieve these goals. The aim of the contract regime is to ensure the responsiveness of the universities to societal political goals.

In 2003, a new university act was introduced. University leaders (vice-chancellors, deans, and heads of departments) who in the past had been elected from below (by their peers) were now being appointed from above. Boards with external majorities and elected chairmen among their external members were introduced. According to the law, nominated external board members require experience in the realms of education, research, leadership, organisation, and economics. Academic councils and study boards, in which the majority of members are elected by staff and students, remain important organisational elements. However, under the new governance regime, academic councils have become, primarily, advisory bodies for the deans. The overall intention behind the law was to turn universities into dynamic, strategic actors. In the wake of the reform, an intensive debate arose regarding the consequences of the reduced influence of staff on important decisions. An international evaluation in 2010 argued that the boards had to start taking responsibility to involve staff and students in decision-making processes (Ministry of Science, Technology and Innovation 2009). As a result, the law was changed in 2011, demanding public universities to adopt internal rules for enhancing staff and also demanding that students be directly involved in governance issues. The universities reacted accordingly by establishing more advisory bodies. With the 2003 act, public universities became self-owned institutions. The meaning of this, however, is unclear. Only a few universities own their buildings. Universities interested in becoming owners of their buildings have hitherto not been allowed to do so. This is one example of a significant restriction of Danish universities' autonomy. Universities were also made responsible for third mission activities. Tasks related to research communications were not new to universities, but the new law stressed the responsibilities of universities in this area.

In 2007, a merger reform was implemented in the university sector. This reform included both inter-university mergers as well as mergers between universities and governmental research institutes (GRIs). A total of 12 universities were reduced to eight, and nine GRIs were merged into the universities. An important overall argument for the mergers was economies of scale, namely, the pooling of finances, knowledge, technical facilities, and buildings to create increased competitiveness. In addition, economies of scale cover the possibilities of saving administrative and perhaps even teaching resources (Aagaard et al. 2016). A more specific argument was to strengthen the use of the GRI staff's competencies in the educational programmes of the universities. The merger reform process was politically initiated and coercive, but at the same time, it included a voluntary element. Universities and GRIs could choose with whom they would merge. In retrospect, governance reform can be interpreted as a precondition for merger reform. The new governance structure seemed to be more responsive than the old one. In addition, the new leaders were tempted by the promise of increased resources for research due to the globalisation agreement (as described later in the chapter). At the time of the mergers, the new universities were organised as federal structures, meaning that specific responsibilities remained within the participating institutions. In several Danish universities, post-merger reorganisation processes have been initiated with the aim to develop more unitary structures, whereas former participating institutions ceased to exist due to the adoption of new governance structures.

Funding Structures
Public resources for Danish universities are allocated through four channels: resources for education, basic resources for research, resources for carrying out tasks for ministries, and resources for research allocated through open competition via research councils and foundations. Over time, the system has become increasingly results-oriented. Resources for education have, since the 1980s, been linked to the number of students who pass their exams. Since 2009, this "taximeter system" has been supplemented by bonuses. Universities receive extra resources if students complete their studies in due time (Regeringen 2010). Among these universities, the allocation of most basic resources for research has been historically determined. Since 2010, however, the allocation of new basic resources for research has been results-based. New resources, which, in most years, have been generated through both cutting back 2% of the existing resources and using genuine, new, and politically prioritised resources, are allocated to universities according to each university's ability to generate educational resources. These abilities include the number of PhDs awarded by the university, the ability of the university to attract competitive research funds, and the bibliometric indicator measuring the total amount of research production in the university. The latter indicator, based on two quality levels, was developed upon inspiration from Norway. However, the Danish model only re-allocates resources across universities

within certain scientific fields, not across the main scientific fields as in Norway's model. Very different opinions exist regarding the bibliometric indicator (Dahler-Larsen 2012). Due to its limited re-allocation abilities, this indicator has been characterised as "a lot of fuss about nothing" (Schneider and Aagard 2012). Despite this fact, there is no doubt that the system influences researchers' behaviour, especially within fields where the introduction of the model is followed up by management demands about publication volume or wage bonuses.

Resources for education and basic resources for research are allocated to Danish universities as a lump sum, which gives these institutions strategic manoeuvring room. Danish universities have indeed taken a series of strategic initiatives; however, these are implemented in a context in which departments and faculties fight with one another to obtain their historically-gained resources. Since the merger reform, Danish universities have received additional resources for carrying out certain national tasks. These are allocated based on four-year contracts between specific universities and ministries. If a university does not fulfil its obligations, a ministry may enter into a contract with another actor, such as another university. There are several institutions responsible for allocating competitive resources for research. The most important are the Danish Council for Independent Research (recently renamed the Independent Research Fund Denmark), the Innovation Fund Denmark, which offers resources for strategic research, technology, and innovation, and the Danish National Research Foundation, which funds centres of excellence (for a comparative analysis of Nordic centres of excellence as a research policy initiative, consult Langfeldt et al. 2013). Apart from these main actors, there are several additional programmes within the ministries as well as private foundations, especially within the health sciences field. International research programmes, particularly within the EU (in the context of the European Research Council), are also highly important. In 2012, external research funding in Denmark totalled 28% of the total revenue for the university sector as a whole (Danske Universiteter 2013, 4). Table 3.2 breaks down the types of funding in the period 2007–2013.

The data shows considerable growth across the main categories. Funding allocations for education increased by 30%, and funding for both core research and external funding rose by 50% from 2007 to 2013. That being said, when it comes to the sharing of competitive funding emanating from the ministry (official tasks), the figures have been rather stable

Table 3.2 University funding from 2007 to 2013, Thousand Danish Kroner-fixed prices[a]

	2007	2008	2009	2010	2011	2012	2013
Core: education	6170.6	6269.3	6583.1	6944.1	7286.5	7621.1	8065.7
Core: research	6056.2	7374.7	8070.2	8330.8	8834.2	8868.9	9007.8
External	5385.5	5945.2	6282.7	6929.5	7188.7	7585.2	7950.6
Ministry tasks	536.9	508.8	541.1	505.9	517.3	489.2	488.7
Other	3738.4	2610.2	2759.6	2511.7	2339.4	2059.9	1917.8
Total	21,887.7	22,708.2	24,236.7	25,222.1	26,166.2	26,624.2	27,430.5

Source: Statistics from Universities Denmark

[a]Final figures have been rounded for simplicity. The year 2006 is not included, as its figures are not comparable due to the merger of GRIs into the universities. "Other" includes example revenues for other purposes, as well as financial revenues

over time. Overall, university funding allocations across all categories increased by 25% during the seven-year period.

As is the case with the introduction of governance through contracts, several key policy developments, including the merger reform and the development of an increasingly results-based resource allocation system, are very much in line with the more general trends in public sector reforms. Other development initiatives include more specific higher education policy initiatives. This can be seen particularly in the case of the governance of reform that has been discussed since the 1970s, during which time a very democratic governance structure was introduced. However, it also applies to some of the adjustments of the resource allocation system; for example, the introduction of bonuses for students who complete their studies in due time. The key policy developments reflect an ongoing discussion and a dilemma between, on the one hand, leveraging university autonomy (the idea of turning universities into dynamic strategic actors), and on the other, fostering universities' political (societal) responsiveness and state control. In a nutshell, the merger reform reduced the number of institutions, thus turning governance through contracts into a more manageable process, whereas the governance reform introduced hierarchical structures into universities, turning (some) leaders into very responsive actors in the eyes of the government.

Recent Policy Initiatives

In recent years, several policy initiatives have been developed that are aimed at boosting effectiveness and efficiency. On the teaching front, these initiatives have been geared towards increasing students' throughput, and on the research side, the bibliometric indicator may be interpreted as an initiative meant to increase research productivity as well as, to some extent, research quality. During the period between 2003 and 2014, the Danish government was concerned with both education and research-related issues; however, different governments attempted to balance the two sides of the system differently. For instance, the liberal government from 2001 to 2011 exhibited a very active research policy reform agenda, whereas the left-leaning government, which has been in power since 2011, has been more occupied with driving educational reforms. Towards the end of 2014, the political agenda shifted somewhat towards cutting back on educational programmes with high levels of graduate unemployment. Dimensioning initiatives have hit programmes within the humanities especially, but other areas have also been affected, for example, biology programmes. Below, we provide an overview of the key 2003–2014 policy initiatives aimed towards boosting performance in teaching, research, and doctoral education.

Historical Overview

Tables 3.3 and 3.4 outline a number of government-led initiatives in Denmark geared towards boosting the number of students in the higher education university system as well as initiatives for ensuring effectiveness and efficiency. The globalisation agreement increased the volume of the system in relation to research, especially with respect to PhD education. The increase in the number of youth applying to study at Danish universities (in 2011, marked by the political 25% goal for 2020), combined with the taximeter resource allocation system, has boosted the volume of the system in relation to teaching. System growth and the potentially problematic incentives of allowing students to pass their exams (due to the taximeter system) have raised concerns about whether quality problems exist in the sector. This has led to policy initiatives aimed at ensuring quality by further developing the accreditation system and, more recently, including a quality indicator in the funding system.

Table 3.3 Key policy initiatives within teaching

Year	Measures taken	Rationale	Reactions of higher education institutions
2007	Programme accreditation; all new and established programmes have to go through accreditation	Ensure quality and relevance of programmes	Negative; very resource- and time-consuming
2009	Bonus for students who complete their studies in due time	Improve throughput rates	Negative; universities did not find that they were able to influence student behaviour
2011	New government agreed that 25% of all youngsters in 2020 must obtain a master's degree		
2013	Fremdriftsreformen	Ensure that students study full time; improve throughput rates	Negative; see above
	Accreditation system changed to institutional accreditation, combined with administrative approval of new programmes	Ensure that universities have optimal procedures for ensuring the quality and relevance of their programmes	Rather positive; was seen as an improvement from the former system
2014	Reducing the number of students in programmes with graduate unemployment (dimensionering)	Enhance graduates' employability; cutting back on certain programmes	Overall positive, but sceptical towards the technical design of the system

Table 3.4 Key policy initiatives within research

Timeline	Measures taken	Rationale	Reactions of higher education institutions
2003–2005	Reform of the research council system	Separating strategic research initiatives from responsive mode funding and establishing a foundation for technology development	
2006	Globalisation agreement	Increased resources for research (2007–2012)	Positive
2010	Bibliometric indicator	Increased resources for PhD programmes (2007–2012)	Positive
	The Danish National Research Foundation evaluation increased resources and, some years later, cutbacks		Varied; some used it actively, and others mostly ignored it
2014	Innovation Fund Denmark		

Finland

Landscape

The Finnish higher education system consists of two complementary sectors: universities and universities of applied sciences. Both sectors have their own distinct profiles and missions. As specified in Finnish legislation, the mission of universities is to conduct scientific research and provide undergraduate and postgraduate education based on this research. Universities must promote free research and scientific and artistic education, provide higher education based on research, and educate students so that they can serve their country and humanity. While carrying out this mission, universities must interact with the surrounding society and strengthen the influence of research findings and artistic activities on society (Universities Act 558/2009). In contrast, the mission of universities of applied sciences is to train professionals in response to labour market needs and to conduct applied research, development and innovation activities which supports instruction and promotes regional development in particular (Finnish Ministry of Education and Culture n.d.).

In 2013, there were altogether 14 universities operating under the auspices of Finland's Ministry of Education and Culture (see Table 3.5). All these universities offer bachelor's, master's, licentiate, and doctoral degrees. The standard degree obtained by students at Finnish universities is the master's degree. The bachelor's/master's distinction is more or less a formality introduced to align with the two-cycle Bologna system, as the bachelor's degree is not widely regarded as a degree with which one can enter the labour market.

System Governance

Finland's university sector is steered through legislation, performance-based funding, performance agreements, and quality assurance measures, as well as through national mid-term (five years) development plans before their abolishment in 2015. National legislation (acts and decrees) has a particularly strong influence on the structure of the Finnish university sector. Legislation determines the number of universities, the missions and tasks of the universities, the governance and administrative structures and bodies of the universities, the regulations related to studies and studying, the number of academic staff, and so on.

Table 3.5 Universities in Finland, 2013 (all figures are FTE)

University	Type	Number of students	Number of academic staff	Number of non-academic staff
Aalto University	Multidisciplinary	12,772	2845	1886
Hanken School of Economics	Business (Swedish-speaking)	1696	130	109
Lappeenranta University of Technology	Technical	3270	588	351
Tampere University of Technology	Technical	6147	1175	664
University of Eastern Finland	Multidisciplinary	10,798	1497	979
University of Helsinki	Multidisciplinary	23,505	4186	3493
University of Jyväskylä	Multidisciplinary	9718	1512	917
University of Lapland	Multidisciplinary	3193	304	273
University of Oulu	Multidisciplinary	10,374	1645	989
University of the Arts Helsinki	Art	1577	386	298
University of Tampere	Multidisciplinary	10,045	1055	842
University of Turku	Multidisciplinary	12,716	1758	1350
University of Vaasa	Multidisciplinary	3622	285	196
Åbo Akademi University	Multidisciplinary (Swedish-speaking)	4187	729	464
Total		113,620	18,095	12,811

Source: Vipunen database

Finland's university admissions system has been highly decentralised in contrast to other European countries. Finnish universities are free to establish their own criteria for the admission of students. Entrance examinations, in the majority of cases, differ from one university to another. Unlike many other countries, all fields of study in Finnish universities apply numerous clauses to their admission policies. Universities are not allowed to initiate degree-based training in new disciplinary fields (e.g., engineering, medical science, or law) without the approval of the Ministry of Education and Culture. The purpose of this restriction is to ensure national coordination and the quality of the programmes within the scope of the higher education institutions' educational responsibilities, as well as the (public) resources available to them (Kivistö and Pekkola 2013). Otherwise universities have high levels of autonomy in developing their programme portfolios. This policy choice is based on the welfare state ideology in which forecasting labour (market) demands plays an important role due to the qualification requirements for many (public) professions, whereas university degrees have traditionally functioned as screening devices. Admission and degree targets for each field of education are agreed upon between them and contained in each higher education institution's performance agreement with the Ministry of Education and Culture. In 2015, the government decided to bring an end to all mid-term policy planning and concentrate more on strategic planning. Thus, the development plans are part of administrative history—for the time being (Kivistö and Pekkola 2013).

The national authorities that are primarily responsible for science and technology policy in Finland are the Ministry of Education and Culture and the Ministry of Employment and the Economy. The former is in charge of matters related to researcher training and science policy, as well as the Academy of Finland. The latter deals with matters related to industrial and technology policies, the National Technology Agency (TEKES) (renamed Business Finland as of 2018), and the Technical Research Centre of Finland (VTT). The bulk of public R&D funding is channelled through these two ministries (cf. Ministry of Education 2005). Finnish national science, technology, and innovation policies are formulated by the Science and Technology Policy Council (1987–2008) and the Research and Innovation Council (since 2009), which were and are chaired by the Finnish Prime Minister. The role of these councils was and is to advise the government on the strategic development and coordination of Finnish science and technology policy as well as the national innovation system.

Funding Structures
From 2003 to 2013, state funding allocated through the funding model (core funding) was relatively stable and covered approximately 72–75% of total university funding, depending on the year (consult Fig. 3.1). The differences between the years, therefore, were no greater than 3%.

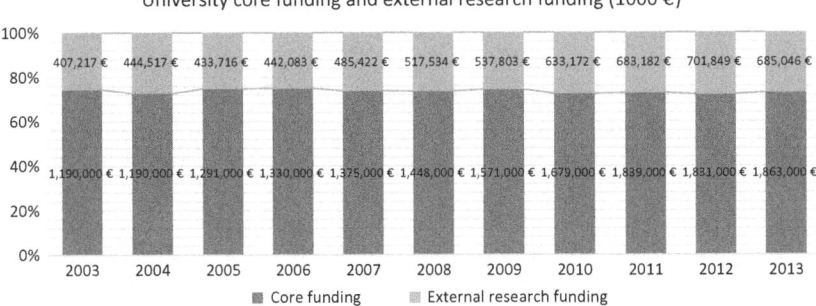

Fig. 3.1 University core funding and external research funding, 2003–2013. Source: Statistics Finland

Throughout the period between 2003 and 2013, the greatest share of external research funding was allocated by the Academy of Finland, in which the proportion of all research funding ranged between 31% and 39%. Notably, during this decade, the share of the Academy of Finland's funding increased from 33% to 39%. TEKES' share of total external research funding has been more stable; it ranged from 20% to 22%, depending on the year. Similarly, the share of funding from the EU fluctuated between only 8% and 11%, depending on the year. However, the relative share of domestic companies steadily decreased from 2008 (13%) to 2013 (8%), in both relative and absolute terms.

Recent Policy Developments
In 2010, the Finnish university system witnessed a profound reform that encompassed the implementation of a totally new legislation (Universities Act 558/2009) accompanied by a series of reform acts and policies known as the "structural development" of the entire higher education system. Consequently, universities became independent legal and economic entities, separate from state financial administration. Universities became either foundations under private law (Aalto University and the Tampere University of Technology) or corporations under public law (all the other universities). This meant that these universities assumed full financial liability for both their operations and their properties.

The change in legal status also meant a change in the status of the university staff, who were no longer employees of the state. Thus, civil service employment relationships were changed to contractual employment relationships. This change permitted the universities to exercise more independent human resource policies, including staffing and the transfer of all related employer responsibilities (e.g., insurance and collective bargaining) to universities (Pekkola and Kivistö 2012). The New Universities Act pushed the universities towards a more professional model of management, with the board as the supreme decision-making body. One of the new responsibilities of the board was to appoint a rector. Previously, rectors had been elected by an election collegium. Moreover, in contrast to the previous situation in which the rector acted as the chairperson of the board, under the new act, the chairperson was to be elected among external board members. Universities were allowed to charge tuition fees for international master's programmes from non-EU/EEC students on a trial basis (2010–2014).

In 2008, as part of the reform of Finland's salary system, the salary system in the state's universities was also changed. The new salary system replaced the old system with salary categories and experience (age) bonuses. The new system was composed of two components: the task's requirement level (fixed) and individual performance level (0–46, 3%). The reform of the salary system introduced a biannual evaluation of individual performance (including teaching, research, and other tasks) and an institutional two-partite mechanism to define the requirement levels in all departments and disciplines. In addition to the performance component in the salary, many universities introduced performance bonus systems.

From 2003 to 2013, the core funding for Finnish universities was allocated as a lump sum, primarily through a performance-based funding formula that covered approximately 70–90% of the total core state funding. The performance agreements between the Ministry of Education and Culture and each university set operational and qualitative goals and determined the resources required to reach these targets over a three- to four-year period. However, the actual influence of these agreements has somewhat diminished due to the indicator-driven, performance-based funding system.

Thematic system-based evaluations form the basis of Finland's national evaluation and quality assurance system. The main actor pertaining to these evaluations has been the semi-autonomous Finnish Higher Education Evaluation Council (FINHEEC), which is responsible for conducting external quality assurance activities (though as of 2014, it is now the Finnish Education Evaluation Centre [FINEEC]). Finland does not have a higher education accreditation system per se; however, each institution is mandated by the Universities Act (in both the 1997 and the 2009 versions) to take part in external evaluation of their activities and quality assurance systems on a regular basis. In line with this requirement, Finnish universities were first audited by FINHEEC/FINEEC during the period between 2005 and 2012. The second round of audits, with a slightly revised auditing scheme, began in 2013. Contrary to the systems that evaluate all degree programmes in the same disciplinary field, each university established its own quality assurance system. Universities also became responsible for the quality and continuous development of their educational programmes and other operations. The evaluations are developmental in nature and are aimed towards helping institutions improve their operations (cf. Melin et al. 2015).

The Ministry of Education and Culture's policy of upgrading its university funding model every three years has been aligned with standard period of performance agreements between the Ministry and the universities from 2003 to 2013. In the period between 2013 and 2015, the allocation (funding) model with regard to universities was completely restructured. The number of indicators incorporated into the new model was significantly lower compared to the model in the period 2010–2012. The rationale behind the restructuring was to further increase the clarity and transparency of the model and, at the same time, offer fewer but stronger incentives for universities to reach their expected outputs and outcomes. In addition to reducing the number of indicators, the 2013–2015 model introduced some new ones. The new teaching-related indicators included: the number of students who gained more than 55 study credits European Credit Transfer System (ECTS) within one academic year, the number of students who gained study credits in open university and non-degree programmes, the number of employed graduates, and the number of master's degrees awarded to foreign nationals. In the research component of the model, the new indicators included a revised way of calculating scientific publications, which were now linked to national classification scheme ("publication forum") levels based on impact assessment, "international teaching and research personnel," and "PhD degrees awarded to foreign nationals." As in the 2010–2012 model, the teaching and research components together comprised 75% of the core funding allocated through the model.

In terms of politics, the goal of increasing the share of private revenue (from sources other than tuition fees) has, in most cases, been considered favourably throughout the period 2003–2009. Finland's constitution guarantees tuition-free education for all students (apart from student union membership fees), based on the idea of higher education as a right rather than a privilege and a generous student support system supported by a progressive tax structure (Melin et al. 2015). Private contributions to higher education are limited to industry and foundation funding. Before passing the new Universities Act (558/2009), changes in comprehensive government policies that encouraged the generation of private revenue have been minor or nonexistent. In terms of the development of new approaches to cost-sharing, the 2009 Universities Act encouraged universities to compete for international research funding and donations and to increase revenues from business ventures to diversify their funding bases. Due to its strong welfare state ideology, the practice of giving and donating in Finland is weak.

The most pressing policy concerns with respect to university education have been the policies' delayed entry into higher education, the long study durations, and problems associated with completion rates (cf. Melin et al. 2015). Between 2003 and 2013, several policy measures have been taken to tackle these challenges, namely, the introduction in 2005 of an ECTS system as part of the implementation of Bologna's policy in Finland and a transition period between 2005 and 2008 to the two-cycle degree system in all university degree programmes. In September 2008, all the degrees (with a few exceptions) granted by Finnish universities were Bologna-compatible, and the normative study durations for lower and higher level university degrees were set according to the Universities Act (1997, 2009).

Historical Overview

Tables 3.6 and 3.7 shed some light on the importance of Bologna's process in promoting efficiency and harmonisation within teaching (from 2005) as well as the mixed receptions such measures entail. On the research front, the policies pointed towards the effort to integrate policy streams across governmental portfolios. They also pointed towards a series of structural reforms aimed at enhancing the global competitiveness of higher education institutions as well as the social influence by promoting interdisciplinary collaborations across the board.

Table 3.6 Key policy initiatives related to education

Timeline	Measures taken	Rationale	Reactions of higher education institutions
2005–the present	ECTS	European harmonisation/efficiency	Mixed; more administrative work, but promotes the accomplishment of European higher education
2005–2008	Two-cycle degrees	European harmonisation/efficiency	Mixed; more administrative work, but promotes the accomplishment of European higher education
2005	Restrictions for the duration of study	Efficiency	Mainly positive due to the performance-based funding model
2005	Changes in study-related benefits; better conditions for loans	Efficiency	Mainly positive due to the performance-based funding model

Table 3.7 Key policy initiatives related to research

Timeline	Measures taken	Rationale	Reactions of higher education institutions
2005–present	Strengthened the role of the Science and Technology Council	To integrate science, technology, higher education, and innovation policy	Mixed to positive; more emphasis placed on competitive research funding and additional funding
2007–2013	Strategic Centres for Science, Technology and Innovation (SHOKS)	To create globally competitive innovation clusters	Mixed; no major impact on universities or their funding
post-2013	Research institute and funding reform	To promote mergers for larger and stronger entities, multidisciplinary research, and social significance	Mixed to positive; new funding instruments and more competition in the research sector as a whole

Norway

Landscape

The Norwegian higher education system consists of universities, specialised university institutions, and university colleges. All three of these institution types are regulated in the framework of the 2005 Act relating to universities and university colleges. The mission of higher education institutions is articulated around teaching, international high-quality research, and the dissemination of knowledge for public administration, cultural life, businesses, and industries (Act 2005, 1–1). Norwegian public higher education institutions are owned by the state and belong to the public sector and administration. However, they are granted academic and artistic freedom with respect to the academic content of their teaching and research activities, individual appointments, and organisational structures within the limits of the framework regulations (Act 2005, 1–5). Higher education and research in Norway are the responsibility of the Ministry of Education and Research. In 2013, a total of eight universities operated in Norway offering bachelor's (three years), master's (two years), and combined five-year programmes (e.g., teacher training), professional programmes, and doctoral degrees (three to four years). Our analyses also include the Norwegian School of Economics (NHH), which belongs to the category of specialised university institutions owned by the Norwegian state. Overall, close to 110,000 students enrolled in Norwegian universities in 2013, as shown in Table 3.8.

The Ministry of Education and Research determines the admission criteria for the education sector and carries the ultimate responsibility for state educational institutions, student welfare, and student financial support. There are no student fees in public universities. Universities and university colleges are also responsible for the student learning environment; they are usually connected to a student union that takes care of student welfare needs. The student unions are established by the Ministry of Education and Research but are not administered by a central government. The student welfare organisations are independent organisations, as stipulated in relevant legislation and regulations, and receive state funding, tuition fees, and access to office space and basic equipment (provided through educational institutions at no cost) in order to offer high-quality, reasonably priced services to students. The Norwegian Universities and Colleges Admission Service (NUCAS) is responsible for determining admission to most programmes at Norwegian universities; that said, some

Table 3.8   Universities in Norway, 2013 (all figures are FTE)

	Type	Number of enrolled students	Number of academic staff	Total number of staff
Norwegian School of Economics (NHH)	Specialised, business	3370	260	398
Norwegian University of Science and Technology (NTNU)	Technical, comprehensive (research-intensive)	22,935	2965	5029
University of Agder	Comprehensive, vocational[a]	10,470	571	960
University of Bergen	Comprehensive, research-based	14,895	2082	3463
University of Nordland	Comprehensive, vocational	6015	319	558
University of Stavanger	Comprehensive, vocational	9680	684	1144
University of Oslo	Comprehensive, research-based	27,360	3394	6067
University of Tromsø—The Norwegian Arctic University	Comprehensive, research-based	10,400	1445	2613
Norwegian University of Life Sciences	Specialised, natural sciences	4595	582	1045
Total		109,720	12,302	21,277

Source: NSD, database for statistics in higher education

[a]"Comprehensive-vocational," refers to its origin as former university-college and stronger vocational profile (professional training)

institutions have their own admission systems. This applies to several private university colleges as well as university colleges that have entrance examinations or auditions.

The national government plays an important role in the Norwegian Research and Development (R&D) system. At the political level, the responsibility for research is organised according to the "sector principle." Several ministries allocate sizable resources to research projects that are related to sectors within their respective domains. Research appropriations are widely distributed among several ministries. The Ministry of Education and Research is the largest source of governmental research funding and is responsible for the inter-ministerial coordination of national research policies and the government's overall research funding. At the operational level, three agencies are largely accountable for implementing the government's research and innovation policies. The Research Council of Norway (RCN), acts as the only operational research policy agency in Norway. In addition to funding research, the RCN has a mandate to advise the government on research policy and to create communication and coordination arenas for actors in research, industry, and government. The Ministry of Research and Education and the Ministry of Trade, Industry, and Fisheries are the most important contributors to the RCN's budget, which was approximately NOK 7.67 billion in 2013. The other two, Innovation Norway and the Industrial Development Corporation of Norway (SIVA), are the primary public institutions which support innovation. Innovation Norway offers programmes and services to promote innovation at the regional and national levels, giving a particular focus to small- and medium-sized companies. SIVA is involved in the provision of science parks, incubators, and services (mainly to start-up firms).

The Norwegian higher education system was traditionally divided into a university sector and a college sector (Kyvik 2009), the latter established as part of an expansion of the educational system in the late 1960s and 1970s. Traditionally, university degree programmes were inspired by the continental university model, with a four-year first degree and a two-year second degree. Some professional degrees have differed from this structure (e.g., teaching programmes, medicine programmes, etc.). The system has changed dramatically in the last two decades, mainly as a result of the so-called Quality Reform (St. Meld. 27, 2000–2001). This reform, initiated by a conservative government in the late 1990s and further developed by a social–democratic government in a 2001 white paper and implemented within higher education institutions starting in 2003 (a regulation established by yet another conservative government), was an attempt to address several challenges in higher education. These issues involved the following needs:

- The need for improved efficiency in higher education and research (by the early 2000s Norwegian higher education experienced a high level of student dropout and delayed graduation).
- The need to enhance the quality of higher education (it was seen as problematic that students had little contact with teachers, old-fashioned teaching methods emphasised traditional lectures, and little emphasis was given to student learning).

- The need to adjust Norwegian higher education to the ongoing Bologna Process and Norway's related obligations.
- The need to find a system of governing the higher education sector that would enable it to respond to the challenges listed above (Ministry of Education 2005).

As part of the Quality Reform, governance structures at the institutional level allowed universities full autonomy in relation to organisational and management issues below the board/rector level. In essence, this autonomy implied that individual institutions were to decide their own internal organisation and governance systems. However, at the institutional level, only two main models of institutional leadership could be chosen by the universities' boards. The standard model—seen as a continuation of existing governance arrangements—saw a rector elected by the staff of the individual institution. This model implied that the rector also became the board chairperson. However, if this model was chosen, the institution also had to establish dual leadership at the institutional level and had to appoint a director responsible for all administrative matters (Stensaker 2014). The alternative governance model was one where the rector was appointed by the board for a limited time. An external member of the board then had to become the chairperson. If the rector was appointed, he/she had full academic and administrative responsibility, and the law did not demand the appointment of a director. A two-thirds majority among board members was required for an institution to opt for this alternative model. Following the standard rule, a board consisted of 11 members.

Following the Quality Reform, a new funding scheme for higher education was also introduced in 2004. The development of this scheme can be said to represent a continuation of earlier changes in funding, emphasising an output and performance system orientation. The most important change in the system was that a greater part of the budget became dependent on results, and several new "performance indicators" were therefore introduced. In 2017, the funding system was adjusted to include a performance indicator that incentivises universities to become more entrepreneurial in the acquisition of external funds, further incentives to improve students' throughput rates, and adjustments to the publishing indicator to ensure that all subject areas counted equally and that both national and international research cooperation are stimulated.

As part of the budgeting process, the Ministry requires an annual report from every higher education institution on its results, achievements, and future plans. This report is also used as the foundation for consultative annual meetings between representatives of the Ministry and of the individual institution. The reports and meetings are important for monitoring and for setting targets and objectives for the coming years. This form of dialogue-based approach between the Ministry and public higher education institutions has a long tradition in Norwegian higher education (Bleiklie et al. 2000), and in recent years, it has been formalised as the standard procedure. As part of the Quality Reform, a new scheme for student financial support, aimed at providing more incentives for students to graduate on time, was also introduced.

In the 2003 quality reform, accreditation of all institutions within the Norwegian higher education system was introduced alongside systematic evaluations of institutional quality assurance systems. This accreditation system can be said to represent a new way to categorise the institutions within the Norwegian higher education landscape, where institutional autonomy is conditioned by an institution's status within the accreditation system. For example, if an institution is accredited as a university, it is given full rights regarding the establishment and cessation of degree programmes at all levels.

The establishment of a national database for higher education (called the DBH-NSB) has also been an important step towards improving both the system's accountability and information about its performance. The DBH-NSB was established prior to the Quality Reform but has received much more attention in the last decade. This database, which is accessible to everyone and is frequently used by newspapers and other media, contains information on staff, students, and student mobility, as well as financial data; it is mainly used by the Ministry of Education and Research for planning, monitoring, and budgetary purposes.

As a result of participating in the Bologna Process, a new degree structure was also launched through the 2003 Quality Reform. Restructured bachelor's, master's, and doctorate degrees (according to the three-year bachelor, two-year master, and three-year doctorate degree model) and a new grading system based on the ECTS were introduced. The new degree structure could be considered a rather dramatic change to the system, as it involved the establishment of a series of shorter modules with examinations for each within a given study programme (Michelsen and Aamodt 2006). In addition to the structural change at the programme level, new forms of student guidance were also introduced, with evaluation and assessment systems aimed at improving student feedback, reducing dropout and study interruption, and encouraging students to complete their programmes on time.

Funding Structures
Approximately 80% of governmental funding for R&D in higher education institutions is channelled directly from the Ministry of Education and Research, mainly as institutional funding. Most of these funds are given through block funding as a lump sum. The rest is distributed based on reported student performance, research performance, and strategic research considerations. Since 2003, resulting from the Quality Reform, a new institutional funding structure has been in place. It consists of three core components:

- *Basic funds*, which are block funds without detailed use specifications. This component originally accounted for about 60% of institutional funding (on average for all universities) but has decreased somewhat.
- A *teaching component*, by which funds are distributed on the basis of reported student performance; this component initially amounted to approximately 25% of institutional funding and has increased somewhat.
- A *research component*, which amounts to approximately 15% of institutional funding. This component is subdivided into two parts, a performance-based part and a strategic part, within which earmarked funds are allocated to specific institutions for hiring PhD students and for acquiring/maintenance of scientific equipment.

From 2008 to 2013, state subsidies allocated to universities increased by 79%, while total revenues in the decade 2003–2013 more than doubled after a 129% increase (Table 3.9). The ratio of core funding to competitive funding has remained largely constant in recent years. However, the changes in the structure of core funds indicate a greater recent emphasis on performance- and strategy-based core research funding. Competitive funding is mainly channelled through the RCN. Central RCN funding schemes involve a competitive national arena for researcher-initiated basic research projects (FRIPRO) and so-called large-scale programmes covering strategic areas of national research policies. The FRIPRO scheme is

Table 3.9 Universities' core funding, selected years for the period 2003–2013 (in billion Norwegian Kroner or NOK, rounded figures)

	2003	2005	2008	2010	2011	2012	2013
State subsidies	NA	NA	108.4	167.8	182.8	185.9	193.8
Revenue	110.9	122.5	103.7	220.3	239.7	242.7	253.8

Source: DBH-NSB

Table 3.10 University research funding per source, 2003–2013 (in billion NOK, rounded figures)

	Lump sum (state grant)	Total external	Industry	Public sector	RCN	Overseas total	EU
2003	48.8	26.1	3.7	17.2	13.8	2.2	NA
2005	58.3	32.3	4.3	21.8	16.7	2.8	NA
2007	75.8	41.5	4.7	29.6	19.8	2.9	1.5
2009	89.6	44.9	5.1	31.9	23.7	3.3	1.8
2011	94.4	48.2	5.7	34.8	25.2	2.7	2.4
2013	108.2	51.2	6.6	35.2	20.2	3.3	2.6

Source: DBH-NSD and NIFU database

funded by appropriations from the Ministry of Research and Education and corresponds to about 15% of the RCN's annual budget. Over the years, state funding allocated through core funding has regularly increased by an average of 5% per year, as shown in Table 3.10. The greatest share of external research funding has been allocated by the RCN at around 4–5%. EU framework programmes have accounted for, on average, around 1%.

Recent Policy Developments
In 2014, the then new centre-right government put forward a reform agenda for the entire higher education sector, aiming to build strong academic environments capable of carrying out research and addressing important social challenges. This occurred despite the presence of strong research environments in select areas (most notably, within the life sciences and biomedical research) and improvements in international research aspects (Gornitzka and Langfeldt 2008). In comparison with other Nordic countries, Norwegian research lags somewhat. Among other concerns, the government worries that universities do not assert themselves com-

petitively for EU funding, despite Norway's generous contributions to the EU's financial mechanism, most notably within the programmes run by the European Research Council (ERC).

A series of evaluations conducted in recent years point to academic environments without critical mass, lacking sufficient stability, and facing efficiency issues. As a result, a new wave of mergers and restructuring has been taking place as part of a reorganisation process, initiated in 2014, that focuses on a structural reform of the entire sector (Kyvik and Stensaker 2013). The current policy moves away from the traditional binary of universities and non-university institutions and instead focuses on smaller, but more robust and competitive, universities with distinctive teaching and research profiles. That said, there are serious concerns with respect to the growing homogenisation (in the convergence of structures, strategies, and programmes) that has resulted from these mergers (Pinheiro et al. 2016) and the resulting erosion of diversity that has historically characterised the domestic higher education system (Pinheiro and Stensaker 2018; Skodvin and Lid 2018).

Quality development and specialisation have become cornerstones of recent policy initiatives, resulting in a 2016–2017 white paper on higher education quality (St. Meld. 16 2016–2017). In addition to the use of merging, quality and specialisation is to be achieved in the following ways:

- Channelling a considerable amount of result-based public funding via student graduation or throughput rates;
- Developing fit-for-purpose performance indicators for quality measures;
- Enacting new incentives, for institutions and academics alike, to prioritise high-quality education, as has been the case regarding research excellence (Skodvin and Lid 2018, 408).

Other key priorities of the ongoing reform process include an update of the long-term strategy for higher education and research (for the period 2015–2024), a revamping of teaching education (as the foundation for a "knowledge society"), and a revision of the working conditions of academic staff, including recruitment, employment, and career structure. A process is currently underway to improve the attractiveness of the academic profession, with a focus on the recruitment and retention of talented individuals. This includes a future revamping of the tenure-based career track that has traditionally been composed of only two stages:

associate and full professorships. A new third category of "senior professors," focussing on top achievers, is being considered.

Historical Overview

Table 3.11 below demonstrate the major changes from 2002 to 2013 relating to the implementation of the Quality Reform and the policy efforts put towards European compatibility, efficiency, and accountability (within the teaching realm). Measures to promote scientific excellence and the global competitiveness of the domestic research environment within universities are also considered (Table 3.12).

Table 3.11 Key policy initiatives related to education

	Measures taken	*Rationale*	*Reactions by higher education institutions*
2002/2003	New degree structure	Efficiency European harmonisation (Bologna Process)	Implemented without major resistance
2002/2003	New funding system	Performance-orientation; student graduation and credit production	Implemented without major resistance despite critics of the "market" (including student groups)
2002/2003	Quality assurance agency ("NOKUT")	Provide oversight and international comparison	Relatively uncontroversial, given that universities were given more autonomy
2002/2003	Strengthening managerial autonomy	Improve accountability and efficiency	Positively, despite some academic criticism of managerialism

Table 3.12 Key policy initiatives related to research

	Specific measures taken	*Rationale*	*Reactions by higher education institutions*
2003	Establishment of the Centres of Excellence scheme	Excellence and global competitiveness	Positively
2003	Bibliometric system (based on two levels)	Incentive to research productivity	Positively for the most part, despite some criticisms on the process for determining the publication levels (levels 1 and 2/highest) in certain fields.

Sweden

Landscape
All higher education is offered by public institutions or independent education providers granted degree-awarding powers by the government. Third-cycle courses and programmes are offered by universities or university colleges that have been granted the entitlement to award third-cycle qualifications. There are 14 public universities and 17 public university colleges in Sweden. In addition, there are three independent institutions that are entitled to award either all or some third-cycle qualifications: Chalmers University of Technology, the Stockholm School of Economics, and Jönköping University. In addition, there are nine independent education providers entitled to award first-cycle and, in some cases, second-cycle qualifications; four independent course providers are also entitled to award qualifications in psychotherapy (Table 3.13).

To be able to award a specific qualification, each institution offering a programme—whether it is accountable to the state or is independent—is required to have degree-awarding powers (i.e., special permission to award particular qualifications). Universities are entitled to award first-, second-, and third-cycle general qualifications. Public university colleges have a general entitlement to award diplomas, bachelor's degrees, and 60-credit master's degrees. Those granted the ability to award third-cycle qualifications within one or more specified fields, according to new regulations from 2010, are also entitled to award 120-credit master's degrees in specified fields. The Higher Education Act stipulates, however, that each higher education institution has the right to apply to the Swedish Higher Education Authority for the entitlement to award 120-credit master's degrees in one or more fields of study. In other cases, the government or SHEA determine institutional entitlement to award general qualifications. In the case of first- and second-cycle professional qualifications and all cycle qualifications in the fine, applied, and performing arts, both universities and university colleges must apply to SHEA for degree-awarding powers. In addition, university colleges must apply to SHEA for the entitlement to award third-cycle qualifications. Independent education providers must apply to the government for degree-awarding powers. This is also the case for the Swedish University of Agricultural Sciences and the National Defence College.

Table 3.13 The Swedish university landscape, 2013 (all figures as FTE)

	University type	Total number of students	Total number of academic staff	Total number of staff
Uppsala University	Comprehensive	24,621	3017	6237
Lund University	Comprehensive	27,702	2997	7166
University of Gothenburg	Comprehensive	24,781	2491	5192
Stockholm University	Comprehensive	29,555	2227	4578
Umeå University	Comprehensive	16,015	1935	3897
Linköping University	Comprehensive	17,716	1633	3432
Karolinska Institute	Specialised, medical	6027	2097	4791
KTH Royal Institute of Technology	Specialised, technical	12,000	1533	3875
Luleå University of Technology	Specialised, technical	7823	632	1510
Swedish University of Agricultural Sciences	Specialised, agricultural	3835	1381	3015
Karlstad University	Comprehensive	7994	593	1047
Linnaeus University	Comprehensive	13,817	952	1704
Mid Sweden University	Comprehensive	6840	467	864
Örebro University	Comprehensive	8615	542	1048
Chalmers University of Technology	Specialised, technical	8926	1173	2863
Stockholm School of Economics	Specialised, business	1804	105	224
Total		218,071	23,775	51,443

Source: UKÄ (Annual report 2014)

System Governance

In Sweden, the overall responsibility for higher education and research rests with the Riksdag (the Swedish parliament) and the government, which decide on the regulations that apply to higher education. The Riksdag decides which public higher education institutions may be established. The government determines whether an institution has university status and outlines the objectives, guidelines, and the allocation of resources for higher education and research. The Ministry of Education and Research handles issues relating to schooling, higher education institutions, research, adult education, public education, and student finance. Public higher education institutions are accountable to the Ministry of Education and Research. One exception is Sveriges Lantbruksuniversitet (the Swedish University of Agricultural Sciences), which is accountable to the Ministry for Rural Affairs.

In Sweden, public higher education institutions are agencies in their own right that report directly to the government. The operations of higher education institutions are regulated by laws and statutes. Higher education institutions are also subject to administrative and labour-market legislation and the provisions of the Instrument of Government. Operations are also governed by the parameters and funding determined by the Riksdag and the government. The mission of the higher education institutions is to offer education based on an academic or artistic foundation and proven experience. They must also undertake developmental work, including research and artistic development. In addition, higher education institutions must co-operate with their surrounding communities, provide information about their operations, and act to ensure that benefits are derived from the findings of their research.

Higher education in Sweden is governed by the Higher Education Act and the Higher Education Ordinance. The Higher Education Act was enacted by the Riksdag and contains regulation on the operations of higher education institutions, which are often supplemented by the provisions laid down in the Higher Education Ordinance. The Higher Education Act's regulations focus on the courses and programmes offered by higher education institutions. For instance, the Act characterises courses and programmes at different levels and stipulates the freedom of research. It also provides a framework for the organisation and governance of higher education institutions and states that every institution must have a board of governors and a vice-chancellor. Additionally, the Act regulates the duties of teachers and contains provisions on student influence. It requires that higher education institutions foster equal opportunity and broaden their recruitment.

The Higher Education Ordinance was enacted by the government and is linked to the provisions of the Higher Education Act; for instance, the Ordinance states that students must be able to influence their courses and programmes. It also contains regulations on entrance qualifications, the selection of courses and programmes, and the appointment of teachers and doctoral students. In addition, it regulates course and programme syllabi, grades, and qualifications.

Annex 2 to the Higher Education Ordinance and the annexes to the Ordinance on the Swedish University of Agricultural Sciences and the Ordinance on the Swedish National Defence College are qualifications ordinances that contain the descriptors for all institutions. Within these parameters, higher education institutions are relatively free to decide their own organisation, allocation of resources, and course offerings. The system is based on the principle of management by objectives. The government lays down the directives for operations of higher education institutions in annual public service agreements. The Swedish Higher Education Authority, a government agency responsible for quality assurance, legal supervision and for monitoring efficiency, supervises these institutions to ensure their compliance with the relevant statutes and regulations and also reviews the quality of higher education and the efficiency and effectiveness of resources and public funding within it.

Funding Structures

The Riksdag determines the funding for higher education institutions. Resources are allocated to institutions for first- and second-cycle courses and programmes according to the number of students enrolled in each cycle, expressed in terms of full-time equivalents (FTEs) and the number of credits attained (which are annual performance equivalents). Every year, the government determines an institutional funding cap—the maximum amount that can be given to each institution. In June 2010, the Riksdag decided that resources for first- and second-cycle programmes are also to be allocated according to the results of the Higher Education Authority's quality evaluations. This meant that institutions with the highest ratings are incentivised with additional funding (a measure called "quality funding"). Quality-based resource allocation applies to public higher education institutions as well as the Chalmers University of Technology and the Jönköping University Foundation; this type of allocation was effective as of 2013. Direct funding for research and third-cycle courses and programmes is based mainly on past allocations, but since 2009, about 10% of funding and new resources have been allocated on the basis of two quality indicators: reported publications and citations and the amount of research funding from external sources. The Swedish University of Agricultural Sciences has a special budgeting and reporting system by which funding for research, courses, and programmes is allocated for three-year periods alongside educational targets for the same periods (Table 3.14).

Table 3.14 University education and research funding per source, 2003–2013 (in million SEK)

	2003	2004	2005	2006	2007	2008	2009	2010	2011	2012	2013
Total research income	3175	3106	3282	3240	3448	3717	3975	4130	4306	4672	4874
Research income (external)	1781	1662	1799	1717	1862	2029	2274	2094	2239	2481	2666
Research income (other)	1394	1444	1483	1523	1586	1688	1701	2036	2067	2191	2208
Income for first and second cycle education	1698	1705	1713	1919	1875	1962	2216	2271	2247	2281	2357
Direct state funding as a share of income (%)	65.2	64.6	65.7	62.8	64.8	65.5	64.2	64.5	65.7	67.2	67.4
Share of external research funding (%)	56.1	53.5	54.8	53.0	54.0	54.6	57.2	50.7	52.0	53.1	54.7

Source: Högskoleverket and UKÄ (annual reports from 2004, 2006, 2008, 2010, 2012, and 2014)

Recent Policy Developments

Turning now to the evolution of the system, an important reform in Swedish higher education was launched in the early 1990s when the current funding and governance system was introduced (Geschwind 2017). In June 2005, the Swedish government presented proposals to reform its higher education system according to the Bologna Process (Swedish Govt. Bill 2004/2005, 162). The bill was adopted by the parliament in February 2006; changes to the Higher Education Act and the Higher Education Ordinance commenced on 1 July 2007. In 2009, the bill for greater autonomy in higher education institutions (Swedish Govt. Bill 2009/2010, 149) created additional opportunities to transform domestic providers. Faculty boards were no longer mandatory or regulated by the Higher Education Ordinance, as was the case before. In brief, the bill stated the following:

- Higher education institutions shall have a board and a president, but are otherwise free to develop their own organisation.
- Decisions requiring a particular, qualified assessment must be made by people with scientific or artistic qualifications.
- Students have the right to representation when decisions are taken or preparations are made that significantly affect their education or situations.
- Staff in the categories of "Professor" and "Senior Lecturer" will continuously be regulated by the Higher Education Ordinance. Otherwise, higher education institutions can choose their own career structures and staff categories. They can also recruit staff to professorships without the need for the traditional open competition.
- Education will be less governmentally regulated, and some state-regulated examination goals shall be abolished.

The bill "A Reformed Constitution" (Swedish Govt. Bill 2009/2010, 80) also included two amendments to increase the freedom of higher education institutions. The amendments came into effect on 1 January 2011 and introduced new provisions to protect the freedom of research. Furthermore, the stipulation that heads of government agencies and members of government agency boards must be Swedish citizens was removed from the instrument of government but can instead be included in an act of primary legislation. The bill also emphasised the continued importance of collegial bodies at colleges and universities and increased their freedom in organising their internal affairs. In particular, it abolished the regulation requiring there be a faculty board at every institution, resulting in a debate on whether collegiality is at risk of elimination at Swedish universities.

According to a 2000–2001 bill (Swedish Govt. Bill 2000/2001), strong research environments were to be established through funding from the then new Swedish Research Council (Vetenskapsrådet). Its belief is that "…to sustain the position as a leading research nation, a mobilisation is needed in Swedish research" (Swedish Govt. Bill 2000/2001, 12). From its foundation, the Research Council has funded "basic research of highest quality," initially by primarily funding individuals or small teams of researchers. As a response to competition from the initiatives of private foundations and pressure from the Swedish government, which pushed for such schemes, Centre of Excellence schemes were eventually introduced despite some hesitation from the Council.

In the following research bill (Swedish Govt. Bill 2004/2005), a new type of large-scale funding programme was launched, inspired by international developments. Consequently, a number of schemes were established from 2005 onwards, including one with scientific excellence as the overall objective (the Linnaeus Environments), another focussed on economic rationales and innovation (the VINN Excellence Centres), and several other schemes with multiple objectives. These other schemes included the FAS Centers (aiming at scientific excellence, social challenges, and strategic objectives), the Berzelii Centres (aiming at scientific excellence, economic rationales, and innovation), and the Strategic Research Centres (aiming at social challenges, strategic objectives, economic rationales, and innovation). The latter scheme was funded by a private foundation. The total number of centres funded by the schemes mentioned above is nearly 100, of which 20 were hosted by the dominating institution, Lund University.

The implementation of these excellence centres was delegated to the funding bodies (i.e., the research councils and the innovation agency VINNOVA). In the following 2008 bill (Swedish Govt. Bill 2008/2009), the further concentration and prioritisation of resources was at the policy forefront. In line with previous bills, the government criticised earlier allocation models based on historical criteria (i.e., head counts) rather than excellence, per se. Instead of allocating direct state funding as block grants, more high-profile institutions and prioritisation were now desired. The policy solution to this was termed "Strategic Research Areas" (SROs) and involved long-term funding for designated areas based on an institution's publications, citations, and ability to attract external funding (Benner 2008).

In the 2012–2013 research and innovation bill (Swedish Govt. Bill 2012/2013), the quality target was further developed. Compared to earlier bills, a stronger emphasis was put on the role of direct state funding as a precondition for breakthrough research: "…it is the government's opinion that it is natural to let a bigger share of the funding than before be allocated according the quality measures introduced in the previous research and innovation bill" (Swedish Govt. Bill 2012/2013, 17). Notably, the earlier focus on "big environments" had shifted to one on "excellent individuals," including both researchers early in their careers and internationally recognised scholars. Additionally, a new system for resource allocation based on peer review (inspired by the British

Research Excellence Framework, among other models) was investigated and a proposal was submitted to the government. Currently, a government inquiry is investigating the governance and funding structures of the Swedish higher education system (Strut 2019).

Regarding education quality and accreditation, Sweden introduced a national quality assurance system in the early 1990s. Initially, its focus was on accreditation and institutional audits. From 2001 to 2006, a comprehensive evaluation of all programmes and subjects culminating in a degree was undertaken by peer review teams. After the round of reviews completed in 2014, excellence could be rewarded financially. The current system has changed its focus again, now evaluating quality assurance systems at the institutional level and, by doing so, returning to the concept of higher education institutions being responsible for their own quality assurance. Furthermore, the Swedish Higher Education Authority (UKÄ) has been entrusted with the task of evaluating research (again at the quality system level).

Additionally, according to the Higher Education Ordinance, higher education institutions since 2010 have had the right to summon and appoint a staff member as a full professor if he/she is of significant importance to the academic environment. This procedure (known as Kallelseförfarandet) should be used restrictively and per the decisions of the vice-chancellor. Since its launch, 40 people (as of the autumn of 2013) have been summoned, of which 30 were men and 10 were women.

Historical Development
The tables below demonstrate that policy efforts focussing on revamping the governance and funding systems and on teaching quality span more than two decades. In the last decade, policy focus has shifted to deregulation and efficiency imperatives—measures that received little resistance at the system level. When it comes to research, as seen in the other three countries (policy convergence), the policy focus has been on incentive systems and structural changes aimed at promoting excellence and global competitiveness (Tables 3.15 and 3.16).

Acknowledgements The data presented in the current volume and individual chapters emanate from a comparative study funded by the Norwegian Research Council under its FINNUT flagship program, a long-term program for research and innovation in the educational sector program. The project number was 237782, and the project was titled 'Does it matter? Assessing the performance effects of changes in leadership and management structures in Nordic Higher Education'.

Table 3.15 Key policy initiatives related to education

Timeline	Measures taken	Rationale	Reactions by Higher Education Institutions (HEIs)
1993	New governance and funding systems	Performance-orientation; student graduation and credit production Deregulation of academic positions and educational programmes	Implemented without major resistance
1995	New quality assurance agency (Högskoleverket)	To undertake accreditation, evaluations, and institutional audits	Implemented without major resistance
2001	Strengthened institutional autonomy	Deregulation of organisational units and academic positions	Implemented without major resistance
2005	New degree structure	Efficiency European harmonisation (Bologna)	Implemented without major resistance

Table 3.16 Key policy initiatives related to research

Timeline	Measures taken	Rationale	Reactions by Higher Education Institutions (HEIs)
2004/2005	Establishment of Centre of Excellence schemes	Excellence and global competitiveness	Positively
2009	Performance-based funding based on metrics	Incentive to research productivity	Positively

REFERENCES

Aagaard, Kaare. 2012. Reformbølgen Tager Form. In *Dansk forskningspolitik efter årtusindeskiftet*, ed. K. Aagard and N. Mejlgaard, 37–57. Aarhus: Aarhus Universitetsforlag.

Aagaard, Kaare., Hanne Foss Hansen, and Jørgen Gulddahl Rasmussen. 2016. Mergers in Danish Higher Education: An Overview Over the Changing Landscape. In *Mergers in Higher Education: The Experience from Northern Europe*, ed. Rómulo Pinheiro, Lars Geschwind, and Timo Aarrevaara, 73–88. Heidelberg: Springer.

Act. 2005. *Act Relating to Universities and University Colleges*. Oslo: Ministry of Education and Research. www.regjeringen.no/no/dep/kd/.

Benner, Mats. 2008. *Kunskapsnation i kris? Politik, pengar och makt in svensk forskning.* Lund: Nya Doxa.

Bleiklie, Ivar., Roar Høstaker, and Agnete Vabø. 2000. *Policy and Practices in Higher Education: Reforming Norwegian Universities.* London: Jessica-Kingsley Publishers.

Dahler-Larsen, Peter 2012. Betydningen af bibliometriske indikatorer. In *Hvordan styres videnssamfundet? Demokrati, ledelse og organisering,* ed. Jan Faye and David Budtz Pedersen. København, 337–357. Frederiksberg: Nyt fra Samfundsvidenskaberne.

Danske Universiteter. 2013. *Tal om de danske universiteter.* Copenhagen: Danske Universiteter.

DBH-NSB. *Database for Statistics on Norwegian Higher Education.* https://dbh.nsd.uib.no/.

Geschwind, Lars. 2017. Higher Education Systems and Institutions, Sweden. In *Encyclopedia of International Higher Education Systems and Institutions,* ed. Jung Cheol Shin and Pedro Nuno Teixeira. Dordrecht: Springer.

Gornitzka, Åse and Liv Langfeldt. 2008. *Borderless Knowledge: Understanding the "New" Internationalisation of Research and Higher Education in Norway.* Dordrecht: Springer.

Hansen, Hanne Foss. 2001. Forskningspolitik i vidensamfundet: Styrker og svagheder i Forskningskommissionens betænkning. *Samfundsøkonomen* (8): 11–18.

Kivistö, Jussi and Elias Pekkola. 2013. *Qualitative Data Finland.* Unpublished Background Report for Orr, D., Wespel, J., and Usher, A. 2014. Do Changes in Cost-Sharing Have an Impact on the Behaviour of Students and Higher Education Institutions? *Evidence from Nine Case Studies.* Volume II: National Reports. Brussels: European Commission.

Kyvik, Svein. 2009. *The Dynamics of Change in Higher Education: Expansion and Contraction in an Organisational Field.* Dordrecht: Springer.

Kyvik, Svein and Bjørn Stensaker. 2013. Factors Affecting the Decision to Merge: The Case of Strategic Mergers in Norwegian Higher Education. *Tertiary Education and Management* 19 (4): 323–337. https://doi.org/10.1080/13583883.2013.805424.

Langfeldt, Liv, Siri Borlaug, Dag Aksnes, Mats Benner, Hanne Foss Hansen, Egil Kallerud, Ernst Kristiansen, Anti Pelkonen, and Gunnar Sivertsen. 2013. *Excellence Initiatives in Nordic Research Policies: Policy Issues – Tensions and Options.* NIFU Working Paper 10/2013, Oslo.

Melin, Goran; Zuijdam, Frank; Good, Barbara; Angelis, Jelena; Enberg, Johanna; Fikkers, Derek Jan; Puukka, Jaana; Swenning, AnnaKarin; Kosk, Kristel; Lastunen, Jesse; Zegel, Stijn. 2015. *Towards a Future Proof System for Higher Education and Research in Finland.* Report of the Ministry of Education and Culture, Finland 2015:11, Ministry of Education and Culture, Helsinki.

Michelsen, Svein and Peter Åmodt. 2006. *Kvalitetsreformen møter virkeligheten. Delrapport 1 [The Quality Reform Meets Reality. Evaluation Report 1].* Oslo: Norsk forskningsråd.

Ministry of Education. 2005. *OECD Thematic Review of Tertiary Education: Country Background Report for Norway.* Oslo: The Norwegian Ministry of Education and Research.

Ministry of Science, Technology and Innovation. 2009. *The University Evaluation 2009.* Evaluation Report, Copenhagen, p. 105.

Pekkola, Elias and Jussi Kivistö. 2012. Reforming the Finnish University System: Policies and Institutional Responses. In *Leadership and Governance in Higher Education: Handbook for Decision-Makers and Administrators,* ed. Bergan Sjur, Eva Egron-Polak, Jürgen Kohler, Lewis Purser, and Martina Vukasović, 87–105. Berlin: Raabe.

Pinheiro, Rómulo., Lars Geschwind, and Timo Aarrevaara, eds. 2016. *Mergers in Higher Education: The Experience from Northern Europe.* Vol. 46. Cham/ Heidelberg/New York/Dordrecht and London: Springer.

Pinheiro, Rómulo and Bjørn Stensaker. 2018. Balancing Efficiency and Equity in a Welfare State Setting: High Participation Higher Education in Norway. In *High Participation Systems of Higher Education,* ed. Brendan Cantwell, Simon Marginson, and Anna Smolentseva, 386–417. Oxford: Oxford University Press.

Regeringen. 2010. *SU, der skaber vækst og beskæftigelse. Bedre brug af SU-midlerne.* Copenhagen: Regeringen.

Research Commission. 2001. *The Research Commission's Report, B 1 and 2.* Report No. 1406, Research Commission, Copenhagen.

Schneider, Jesper and Kare Aagaard. 2012. Stor ståhej for ingenting. Den danske bibliometriske indicator. In *Dansk forskningspolitik efter årtusindeskiftet,* ed. Kare Aagaard and Nils Mejlgaard, 229–260. Aarhus: Aarhus Universitetsforlag.

Skodvin, Ole-Jacob, and Stein Erik Lid. 2018. Governance Tools to Increase Quality and Diversity in Higher Education: Emerging Trends in Norway. In *Quality, Performance and Accountability in Higher Education,* ed. E. Hazelkorn, H. Coates, and A. McCormick, 487–497. Cheltenham and Northampton: Edward Elgar.

St. Meld. 16 (2016–2017). *Kultur for kvalitet i høyere utdanning: Melding til Stortinget.* Oslo: Det Kongelige Kunnskapsdepartementet. Online. https://www.regjeringen.no/no/dokumenter/meld.-st.-16-20162017/id2536007/.

St. Meld. 27 (2000–2001). *Gjør din plikt – Krev din rett: Kvalitetsreform av høyere utdanning.* Oslo: Det Kongelige Kirke-, utdannings- og forskningsdepartementet. Online. https://www.regjeringen.no/no/dokumenter/stmeld-nr-27-2000-2001-/id194247/.

Statistics Finland. Online. https://www.stat.fi/index_en.html.

Statistics from Universities Denmark. Online. https://dkuni.dk/tal-og-fakta/beredskab/.

Stensaker, Bjørn. 2014. Troublesome Institutional Autonomy: Governance and the Distribution of Authority in Norwegian Universities. In *International Trends in University Governance: Autonomy, Self-Government and the Distribution of Authority,* ed. Michael Shattock, 34–48. New York: Routledge.

Strut 2019. U 2017:05 Styrning för starka och ansvarsfulla lärosäten. http://www.sou.gov.se/utredningen-om-styrning-for-starka-och-ansvarsfulla-larosaten/.
Swedish Govt. Bill 2000/2001. Swedish Government. 2000. *Forskning och förnyelse (Research and Renewal), Prop, 3.* Vol. 01. Stockholm: Ministry of Education.
Swedish Govt. Bill 2004/2005. Swedish Government. 2005. *Forskning för ett bättre liv (Research for a Better Life), Prop, 80.* Vol. 05. Stockholm: Ministry of Education.
Swedish Govt. Bill 2008/2009. Swedish Government. 2008. *Ett lyft för forskning och innovation (A Boost for Research and Innovation), Prop, 50.* Vol. 09. Stockholm: Ministry of Education.
Swedish Govt. Bill 2009/2010:80. *En reformerad konstitution (A Reformed Constitution).* Stockholm: Ministry of Education.
Swedish Govt. Bill 2012/2013. Swedish Government. 2012. *Forskning och innovation (Research and Innovation), Prop, 30.* Vol. 13. Stockholm: Ministry of Education.
The Ministry of Education and Culture. https://minedu.fi/en/frontpage.
UKÄ. Swedish Higher Education Authority. http://english.uka.se/.
Universities Act, 165/1997. Finnish Ministry of Education and Culture. Accessed September 27, 2018. https://www.finlex.fi/fi/laki/kaannokset/1997/en19970645.pdf.
Universities Act, 558/2009. Finnish Ministry of Education and Culture. Accessed September 27, 2018. https://www.finlex.fi/en/laki/kaannokset/2009/en20090558.

Open Access This chapter is licensed under the terms of the Creative Commons Attribution 4.0 International License (http://creativecommons.org/licenses/by/4.0/), which permits use, sharing, adaptation, distribution and reproduction in any medium or format, as long as you give appropriate credit to the original author(s) and the source, provide a link to the Creative Commons licence and indicate if changes were made.

The images or other third party material in this chapter are included in the chapter's Creative Commons licence, unless indicated otherwise in a credit line to the material. If material is not included in the chapter's Creative Commons licence and your intended use is not permitted by statutory regulation or exceeds the permitted use, you will need to obtain permission directly from the copyright holder.

PART II

Cross Cutting Themes

CHAPTER 4

National Performance-Based Research Funding Systems: Constructing Local Perceptions of Research?

Johan Söderlind, Laila Nordstrand Berg, Jonas Krog Lind, and Kirsi Pulkkinen

---

Laila Nordstrand Berg, Jonas Krog Lind, and Kirsi Pulkkinen contributed equally to this work.

J. Söderlind (✉)
School of Industrial Engineering and Management, KTH Royal Institute of Technology, Stockholm, Sweden
e-mail: johanso2@kth.se

L. N. Berg
Department of Social Science, Western Norway University of Applied Sciences, Sogndal, Norway
e-mail: laila.nordstrand.berg@hvl.no

J. K. Lind
Department of Political Science, University of Copenhagen, Copenhagen, Denmark
e-mail: jkl@ifs.ku.dk

K. Pulkkinen
Faculty of Social Sciences, University of Lapland, Rovaniemi, Finland
e-mail: kirsi.pulkkinen@ulapland.fi

© The Author(s) 2019
R. Pinheiro et al. (eds.), *Reforms, Organizational Change and Performance in Higher Education*,
https://doi.org/10.1007/978-3-030-11738-2_4

INTRODUCTION

In this chapter, we explore how the introduction of performance-based research funding systems (PRFSs) in Denmark, Sweden, Norway and Finland is influencing the perception of research within universities. Here, performance-based resource allocation constitutes a new way of distributing institutional research funding, and its establishment is related to the general development of the increasing quantification of the higher education sector (Hicks 2012). Various performance measures are currently used to inform internal and external actors about organisational activities and to govern and control higher education institutions (HEIs) (see Chap. 2; de Rijcke et al. 2016). On the one hand, this has been propelled by demands from within the education sector. Academics have always been keen on evaluating and comparing the work of colleagues, and the development of quantitative tools to describe academic work has a long history (Garfield 1955; Nelhans 2013). With advances in information technology, quantification and performance indicators have become more refined, precise and complex but also more accessible to, and used by, professionals and amateurs alike (Gläser and Laudel 2007; Leydesdorff et al. 2016; van Raan 2005).

On the other hand, there are also a number of external pressures that have been suggested as ways to induce the increasing quantification of academic work. According to Portnoi, Rust and Bagley (2010), there is a clear trend towards global competition in the higher education sector. This is related to the advent of academic capitalism (Slaughter and Leslie 1997) but also to a global knowledge economy and a neoliberal paradigm in higher education governance (Olssen and Peters 2005). The increasing size and costs of the sector during the twentieth century have also created demands for increasing efficiency, transparency and accountability. Responses have often comprised the introduction of new public management reforms, including marketisation, a strengthening of management structures and a focus on performance measurement (Paradeise et al. 2009). Thus, performance measures are used in various ways to assess institutional activities but also to incentivise universities and academics to increase their performance.

Although similar in many ways, the Nordic countries display considerable differences in university governance policies (Gornitzka and Maassen 2012, 124; Pinheiro et al. 2014). This also includes how metrics are used to assess, evaluate and award academic work. Although all the Nordic countries have implemented PRFSs in recent years, the design of these systems varies. The systems have furthermore come to influence institutional resource allocation practices because local PRFSs often are established at institutional or subinstitutional levels. However, recent research has found that local implementations of PRFSs vary greatly and rarely reflect the configuration of national systems (Aagaard 2015; Hammarfelt et al. 2016). Aagaard (2015, 736) suggests that these findings 'only can be explained by including local conditions and personal perceptions at lower levels of the institutions'. Therefore, it is imperative to study not only the local resource allocation systems but also the nonsystematic and informal use of metrics in the organisation and execution of research activities.

This is the aim of the present chapter; we study how the varying use of performance indicators in the national PRFSs of four Nordic countries is reflected within universities. Our intention is to explore how national performance metrics affect local perceptions of research as organisational actors make sense of these novel forms of resource allocation. As suggested by Weick (1995), an organisation is not only a formal structure, but it also includes the way people interpret and categorise their daily experiences to make sense of a more or less disorderly reality. How the metrics that are used in national PRFSs are understood and acted upon within universities is thus likely to be of major importance for the local organisation of research. An investigation of these issues allows for a deeper comparative analysis of the qualitative aspects of the ways in which indicators influence research practices. It also contributes to the ongoing debate of the design, use and effects of performance-based funding of university research (e.g., European Commission 2018). Thus, taking a closer look at the perceptions and uses of research metrics within universities may provide important insights into how external performance measures structure everyday thought and action.

Because national PRFSs vary regarding their design, we expect the influence of research metrics at the institutional level to vary as well. Therefore, we compare the national PRFSs in four Nordic countries and ask how they affect the way university actors perceive and make sense of research activities at the institutional level. To study this, we conduct a comparative study between the four countries to explore how the link between national macro-states affects organisational behaviour within the universities. We identify three factors highlighted in previous research on performance metrics that have been suggested as being instrumental in influencing organisational action. Through interviews with academics and managers at eight universities in Sweden, Norway, Denmark and Finland, we explore how these factors inform the perception of research in Nordic universities.

The chapter is structured as follows: first, we review previous studies that analysed the effects of performance measures. Based on this, we develop our analytical framework. The framework identifies three major ways in which research metrics influence HEIs; their ability to enable action, to enhance legitimacy and to solidify taken-for-granted representations of reality. Second, we describe the methods used for the analysis in the present study. We then turn to the design of the national PRFSs in Denmark, Finland, Norway and Sweden. Next, we present the empirical analysis of our interview data. The final section contains a comparative discussion of the results.

The Roles and Effects of Performance-Based Funding Systems

Performance measures are tools that describe organisational activity and are constructed and applied with the intention to direct organisational attention (see Chap. 2). When introduced to incentivise actors, to support and facilitate decision-making and to enhance accountability, they perform these functions in new ways, thus complementing or replacing previous practices (Dahler-Larsen 2014; Espeland and Stevens 1998). As incentives, they measure and monitor everyday work in very precise and compartmentalised ways, neglecting undefined aspects and introducing the risk of displacing holistic assessments. As support for decision-making, they may constitute a transparent basis for decisions, counteracting personal biases and fraudulent behaviour, but they may also substitute for qualitative assessments, peer review and professional judgement. To account for organisational activities, indicators easily replace trust between people and may cause a myopic concern for numerical comparisons (Porter 1995). In some respects, metrics are superior to alternative ways of describing organisational activity, but in other ways, they are inadequate. The most immediate benefit of metrics is their ability to enable clear comparisons and induce action, but some notable side effects are that they decontextualise the measured phenomenon and structure reality in ways that may not always be desirable (Dahler-Larsen 2014; Espeland and Stevens 1998; Rottenburg et al. 2015). Thus, research on the role and effect of performance measures points out several ways in which metrics may influence organisational action. Drawing on these insights, we identify three factors that cause metrics to affect organisations: *actionability*, *legitimacy* and *institutionalisation*.

Actionability

Actionability refers to the ability of indicators to induce an action. This may occur either in decision-making processes, where indicators arbitrate between alternative routes of action or in the case where incentives are tied to the indicators, making the subjects of measurement motivated to act in certain ways. Regarding decision-making, actionability is a reason behind the popularity of rankings because they transform the differences in raw scores that may be negligible to clearly ordered alternatives that range from less to more or best to worse, thus facilitating decision-making (Espeland and Sauder 2007). Actionability is a factor that has been identified in several studies as being important when it comes to the influence of indicators. Aagaard (2015, 735), for example, shows how a publication indicator 'functions as a potent instrument of managerial decision-making'. Even when the accuracy of indicators is questioned, they may be seen as useful. For instance, this has been shown to be the case for citation metrics (Aksnes and Rip 2009), the journal impact factor (Rushforth and de Rijcke 2015), journal lists (Mingers and Willmott 2013) and business school rankings (Wedlin 2007).

As noted by Espeland and Sauder (2007), measurement also alters the behaviour of the individuals being measured. Incentives combined with performance indicators are powerful tools to structure action because measurement causes reactivity from the subjects being measured. Incentives may be remunerative or normative, they may be positive or negative and they may be more or less formalised. Remunerative incentives imply the conditioning of material resources in relation to some indicator. Here, PRFSs are instructive because funding is allocated based on performance, which is often measured using quantitative indicators. Normative incentives, however, include the symbolic gains and losses that are related to an indicator. Institutional reputation is an example because it is a critical resource for universities that often is thought to be related to various indicators, such as university rankings. Also, PRFSs have been suggested as contributing heavily to the gains and losses of institutional reputation (Hicks 2012).

Legitimacy

Legitimacy is another factor that has been suggested to be important for the ability of performance measures to exert influence over organisations. Because metrics highlight the various aspects of organisations and their activities, they also can impart legitimacy to the organisation because its performances are demonstrated to internal and external actors. Whether metrics can perform this function depends on the legitimacy of the indicators because they must be accepted as valid. Here, we can distinguish between *technical* and *normative* legitimacy, where the former is conferred because of a perceived correspondence between the indicator and object, while the latter occurs as an indicator and is seen as appropriate to use. Regarding technical legitimacy, Bowker and Star (2000, 245) demonstrate the importance of designing indicators that resonate with people's idea of the described phenomenon. Without a reasonable correspondence between the indicator and object, there is a risk that people will reject the indicator as a valid representation of reality, making the indicator unable to affect the organisation. This has been a major concern for research metrics, and the debate has continued about the validity of research metrics (Donovan 2007; Gläser and Laudel 2007; van Raan 2005).

However, normative legitimacy may be conferred to an indicator even though it has low technical legitimacy. Here, it is instead a matter of the perceived appropriateness to measure at all, even though accurate metrics may be missing. Power (2004, 769) notes that 'specific measurement systems may be defective and fail, but they also constantly reproduce and reinvent an institutional demand for numbers'. The desire to measure, hence, trumps the ability to accurately do so. A prominent example may be university rankings, which have been criticised for being invalid measures of scientific excellence (Harvey 2008; van Raan 2005; van Vught and Westerheijden 2010). External actors may, however, consider the limited information provided by rankings better than the alternative, which often is overwhelming and impervious. The rankings thus gain normative legitimacy and provide an ostensible transparency of university excellence. In a similar way, Rushforth and de Rijcke (2015) show that researchers see the journal impact factor as useful for various purposes, despite having knowledge of its limitations. Aksnes and Rip (2009) also note that researchers doubt the ability of citation metrics to indicate scientific quality, but the metrics are seen as useful because they convey academic prestige. The normative legitimacy of these metrics thus makes them influential, even though they may represent reality in a unidimensional or inaccurate manner.

Institutionalisation

While actionability and legitimacy are effects that organisational actors are more or less conscious of, institutionalisation refers to the process where metrics are taken for granted (Scott 1987; Zucker 1987). When indicators solidify and become firmly established, people come to accept the general agreement of the indicator as representative of reality. Being accepted as real, the metrics' limitations and flaws are easily forgotten, and they become more likely to influence decision-making and organisational activity. The institutionalisation of indicators may occur through a number of processes, including habituation, reification and reconstitution. Habituation implies that an indicator may gain increasing acceptance over time as people get used to it. Sauder and Espeland (2009) note how the novelty of rankings initially made universities dismiss them, but, in due time, these rankings came to be very influential. Reification implies the solidification of an indicator as it is built into the practical organisation of labour and resources. This may take place as offices are established to handle issues relating to the indicator, where an example includes bibliometric offices dealing with rankings (Espeland and Stevens 1998). Finally, reconstitution occurs as indicators alter the notion of the indicated objects. Dahler-Larsen (2014) describes this as the constitutive effects of indicators, and Woolgar (1991, 319) notes how 'the very system of measuring and manipulating citations redefines the phenomenon it is supposed to measure'. Because bibliometrics emphasise publication in international peer-reviewed journals, this may alter the perception of publication quality to the detriment of publications in alternative outlets. How quality in research is understood may thus change to align with the indicator. The constitutive effects of the indicator cause institutional lock-in as the indicator and object converge.

The Analytical Framework

Summarising these insights, performance measures have been noted as influencing organisational action in three ways. First, metrics *induce action* because numerical indicators are able to rank and clearly order alternatives for decision-makers; this also occurs because the subjects of measurement adapt their behaviour as they are being measured. Second, performance measures can *impart organisational legitimacy*. This is contingent on the technical and the normative legitimacy of the metrics, which reflects the accuracy of the measures and the perceived usefulness of measuring performances. Third, performance measures can influence the organisation as they become *institutionalised* and are taken for granted as valid descriptions of reality. This occurs over time when people grow accustomed to indicators, when indicators are built into the practical organisation of activities and when people alter their idea of the measured object to better fit with the indicator. These three ways in which performance measures can influence universities are summarised in Table 4.1. They compose the analytical framework applied in the current study as we explore how the metrics used in national PRFSs influence Nordic universities and how this in turn affects the way academics make sense of research activities.

A caveat to note is that performance measures are not seen as unambiguously imposing actionability, legitimacy or institutionalisation. Instead, these effects may emerge as academics interpret performance measures in relation to the measured activities. Therefore, the influence of indicators depends on the perception and understanding of organisational actors. As academics experience performance measures as novel tools to describe research, they may then use these tools to reconstruct the meaning of research. It is the *perception and interpretation* of performance measures made by university actors that enables the metrics to be actionable, enhance legitimacy or become institutionalised.

Table 4.1 Analytical framework: the influence of metrics

Actionability
  Decision making
  Incentives
Legitimacy
  Technical legitimacy
  Normative legitimacy
Institutionalisation
  Habituation
  Reification
  Reconstitution

Methods

In this chapter, we address how university actors perceive research activities in light of the performance measures used in national PRFSs. Because the purpose of the chapter is to reach a deeper understanding of these processes, we adopt a qualitative approach and apply a comparative case study method (Yin 2009). The study may furthermore be described as a mix of a congruence analysis and causal process tracing (Blatter and Haverland 2012). In our efforts to explore the influence of PRFSs on local perceptions of research, we utilise previous theoretical insights into our theoretical framework. Some of these insights are likely to be more influential than others and hence may provide more explanatory power. The current study will perform a congruence analysis, where the applicability of earlier theoretical accounts is tested. With the analytical focus on the influence of performance measures on university actors, however, there is also a large interest in the causal configurations of these processes. Thus, the analysis will contain a significant portion of causal process tracing because we want to analyse the way national PRFSs influence local perceptions of research.

A desktop study was conducted to map the national PRFSs. The sources include earlier research, as well as official reports from governments and government agencies. To study how research metrics implemented in national PRFSs affect perceptions of research at the institutional level, we conducted 93 semi-structured interviews with academics, managers and administrators at eight Nordic universities. The universities chosen include one flagship and one regional university per country. The interviews sought to illuminate organisational reactions as numerical indicators are used to describe and incentivise organisational action through national PRFSs. Although the perspectives varied among the respondents, they were all interviewed regarding their role as academic professionals and considered to represent their respective organisation and culture in which they were situated.

To perform the analysis, the interviews were recorded and transcribed verbatim with the approval of the respondents. The transcriptions were systematically analysed with the aid of computer software to code the data and structure the findings. Initially, the analysis was inductive and attentive to the material, exploring how performance measures influence perceptions of academic work. In later stages of the analysis, a refined coding was made to categorise the findings according to the analytical framework, where we explored whether national PRFSs create actionability, legitimacy and institutionalisation that in turn affects how the informants understand research activities. The results have subsequently been analysed and compared across the countries.

Before moving on, some terminology will be discussed to enable an informed comparison between the countries. The funding system terminology used has been adopted from the EU report 'Performance-Based Funding of University Research' (European Commission 2018, 27–29). The term *institutional funding* is used to denote government resources provided to universities, which they may spend more or less as they wish. However, a notable exception is that institutional funding in some countries is provided separately for teaching and research. In these cases, the term *institutional research funding* will be used to specifically indicate the institutional funding allocated for research activities. Institutional funding is furthermore separated into block grants and performance-based funding. Performance-based funding is allocated depending on the outcome of various performance measures, which may be related to teaching, research, societal interaction or other activities. A *block grant* denotes the rest of the institutional funding and is often contingent on historical allocations. *External funding* denotes revenue from public and private organisations that normally is designated for particular purposes and won by individual researchers in a competition with others. Some countries use *performance contracts* between HEIs and the government's ministry. As long as these do not contain a funding formula, such as those found in a PRFS, these contracts are considered to inform the allocation of the block grant.

The Nordic Performance-Based Research Funding Systems

Although the four Nordic countries in the current study have implemented PRFSs in recent years, the systems differ in their configurations. The PRFSs are designed in different ways and include different indicators. In the following, the four PRFSs are presented and compared.

Denmark

In Denmark, a PRFS has been in place since the end of the 1990s, and it has distributed a small part of the institutional research funding based on student throughput, external research funding and PhD production, while the larger part has been constituted by block grants. Because of dissatisfaction with the absence of output measures of research quality, a fourth indicator was added to the Danish PRFS in 2010: the Bibliometric Research Indicator (BRI). The BRI took its inspiration from the Norwegian bibliometric indicator, measuring the publication activity in peer-reviewed journals and books, and awarding points to universities depending on their relative performance in a zero-sum game. Hence, the BRI covers the breadth of publishing patterns across scientific areas, including monographs, conference proceedings and so forth, to be relevant for all the disciplines.

Panels in each scientific discipline evaluate the journals and book publishers in their field and place them on either level 1 or level 2 (Schneider and Aagaard 2012). The evaluation of journals is done according to a quality criterion (originality and novelty) and a relevance criterion (that the journals are of interest to, and accessible to, Danish researchers). However, other than these very basic guidelines, it is very much up to the panels to decide how the assessment is conducted. All Danish researchers can suggest changes to the list that the panels will have to consider. Every year, the results of the panels' work on placing journals on the authorised list are made publicly available.

The total funding distributed from the PRFS depends on how much new money is put into the system from year to year. In 2010, the PRFS distributed 4 per cent of the institutional research funding of Danish HEIs, but this amount increased to 19 per cent in 2017 (Aagaard 2016).

Finland

The Finnish funding system changed in the early 1990s when the first performance-based elements were introduced in the form of performance agreement negotiations. The new system was intended to offer incentives for increased efficiency and effectiveness, but it remained very input oriented. It was not until 2010 that performance-based funding was introduced, which is now used to allocate resources to universities in a zero-sum game. Currently, roughly 70 per cent of the institutional funding of universities is performance based. The current PRFS consists of a model where education performance accounts for 39 per cent, research performance for 33 per cent and other education and science policy considerations for 28 per cent. The research indicators used include doctoral degrees, scientific publications and external funding, which are about equally weighted. In addition, universities have strategy-based funding that is agreed upon between the university and the government as part of their negotiations. The funding scheme aims at strengthening the quality, impact and performance of universities. The institutional funding is thus largely performance based because the funding is allocated according to the performance results of the previous four years (for a current analysis, see Seuri and Vartiainen 2018).

For the bibliometric indicator, scientific outlets are given a rating by the publication forum, a classification system created by the Federation of Finnish Learned Societies. The evaluation of publication outlets is conducted by expert panels that consider the typical publication practices of the specific research fields, the existing appreciation of the particular publication channel within the scientific community and the balance presence of various disciplines at higher quality levels. In this system, each scientific outlet is placed on a level between 1 and 3. Also, nonrefereed journals are included at level 0, and publication in these outlets provide very low rewards.

Norway

In Norway, a PRFS was introduced in 2005, allocating institutional funding based on both teaching and research indicators. The purpose of the PRFS has been to provide a neutral framework for assigning funds between universities and scientific fields but also to stimulate better performance and reward successful research environments. In 2014, 24 per cent of the funds were distributed based on teaching indicators and 6 per cent based on research indicators (Kvaal 2014).

There are four research indicators: number of PhDs awarded, allocation of EU funding for research, allocation of funding from the Norwegian Research Council and bibliometrics. Regarding the bibliometric indicator, a national, non-commercial bibliographical database has been established to classify different types of scholarly and peer-reviewed literature from the whole sector, including journal articles, book chapters and monographs. Scientific outlets are classified at two levels, and publications in these outlets are rewarded with publication points fractionalised according to the number of authors. The data are used to allocate funding but also enhance transparency across institutions. This transparency is also supposed to increase the quality of research in the sector. The database is available online and is open to the public.

Sweden

In 2009, a performance-based dimension was introduced to the institutional research funding of Swedish HEIs, sending a clear signal from decision-makers of their desire to increase the quality of research performed at Swedish HEIs (Swedish Government Bill 2008/09:50). By conditioning part of the institutional research funding on performance indicators, incentives were created for the HEIs to increase their research output, but this system has changed several times in its short lifespan.

The system reallocates 20 per cent of the institutional research funds based on the outcome of two indicators: bibliometrics, which is composed of publication counts and citation counts, and the amount of external funding acquired. The resources are allocated based on the relative performance of each HEI compared with the others in a zero-sum game. Any new research funds granted by the government from one year to another are also allocated according to the model. The bibliometric data are collected from Thomson Reuters and are field normalised and fractionalised according to the number of authors. External funding is measured as a running three-year average and is weighted by discipline. The effects of the model have been moderated by various decisions throughout its existence. The continuous increase of the total institutional research funds has also left the worst performers with at least as much institutional research funding as the previous year. In a few cases, special allocations have been made to guarantee that no HEI experiences decreasing institutional research funding, with the result being that the redistributive effects of the model are modest (Universitetskanslersämbetet 2015, 2017, 19f.).

Similarities and Differences in the Nordic Performance-Based Research Funding Systems

Table 4.2 summarises the main components of the PRFSs in the four countries, showing a number of similarities but also some notable differences. The introduction of the systems all occurred at the same time, with the exception of Norway as a forerunner and acting as an inspiration for the Danish BRI and the Finnish bibliometric model. The Swedish system, however, utilises data from an already existing infrastructure, while the other three countries established completely new databases. Furthermore, the reasons behind implementing the PRFSs have been similar across the four countries. Allocating research funds through a PRFS in a zero-sum game is intended to provide universities with incentives to increase their performance. Higher competition is supposed to enhance both research quality and productivity. In Norway, the PRFS is also noted to improve the equity of the resource allocation system.

The amount of funds allocated through the PRFSs is similar in Denmark and Sweden, where about 20 per cent of the institutional research funds are performance based. Because HEIs in Denmark and Sweden receive separate institutional funding for teaching and research, the percentages of the amount of resources allocated by the PRFSs are not directly comparable

Table 4.2 Main components of the PRFSs in Denmark, Sweden, Finland and Norway

	Denmark	*Finland*	*Norway*	*Sweden*
Introduced	2010	2010	2005	2009
Size	19% of institutional research funding and increasing every year	33% of total institutional funding	6% of total institutional funding	20% of institutional research funding and annual additions
Indicators	– Publications (fractionalised) – External research funding – PhD production – Student throughput	– Publications – External research funding – PhD production	– Publications (fractionalised) – External research funding – EU research funding – PhD production	– Publications (fractionalised) – Citations – External research funding

with those in Norway (6 per cent) and Finland (33 per cent), where institutional funding also includes teaching funds. However, as noted in the EU report 'Performance-Based Funding of University Research' (European Commission 2018, 37), the use of PRFSs and external funding from the state affects whether research funding is more or less contested. The report notes that Norway and Sweden are restrained in their use of performance-based funding and rely heavier on external funding. Finland, on the other hand, has high competition for funds, where the PRFS is an integral component, thus creating strong incentives for universities to perform.

The indicators used differ somewhat between the countries. All countries use publication counts, but Finland differs somewhat because the PRFS do not fractionalise the publication counts. This makes it beneficial for researchers to coauthor their publications because the number of authors does not dilute the publication points awarded. This also imply a bias towards fields such as the natural and health sciences, where the tradition of copublication is strong, and the number of coauthors is high compared with the social sciences (Muhonen and Pölönen 2016). Sweden also includes a measure of citation counts that enables an assessment of the impact of individual publications. In the other three countries, publication outlets are given different weightings, giving all publications in the same outlet the same value in the PRFS. Denmark, Finland and Norway are not using citation counts because they have opted for systems with their own bibliometric databases, while Sweden relies on the already existing database of Thomson Reuters. The latter bibliometric database includes citations but does not have the same coverage of publication outlets as the databases created in Denmark, Finland and Norway.

Furthermore, all countries have indicators for external research funding, though what is counted differs somewhat. Although Norway also has a specific indicator for EU funding, this is accounted for in the measures of external funding in the other countries. Additionally, it can be noted that in Norway and Denmark, non-competitive funding is included as well (European Commission 2018, 50). All countries except Sweden have indicators for the number of PhDs awarded. In Denmark, there is also a connection to teaching performance because the use of student throughput informs the institutional research funding. Teaching metrics are, however, also used in Norway and Finland, though the connection to research

The Influence of Metrics on the Perceptions of Research

Actionability

For all four countries, the research metrics utilised in the national PRFSs are clearly actionable. Primarily, they facilitate managerial decision-making at different levels of the universities, but the formalisation in the use of metrics for this purpose differs. The perceived incentives provided by the PRFSs also differ. In some cases, the PRFSs provide clear and substantial incentives for universities and individual researchers, while the incentives in other cases are perceived as weaker or not directly related to the PRFSs.

In Denmark, the BRI has affected both the organisation of academic practices and the academic practices themselves. The most prominent example of changes in the organisation of academic practices is how the BRI has been used locally by universities in their budget models for allocating resources to lower organisational levels. It does, however, depend greatly on the context in what way, if at all, the BRI has been used. At the flagship university, the BRI has not been used in the budget model at the university level because international publishing was already seen as the norm. This was different at the regional university where they interpreted the BRI as very actionable because it could be used as a management tool for boosting performance. Thus, the regional university implemented the national PRFS locally for allocating funding to the faculty members and even made it apply to all the funding for research, in contrast to the approximately 20 per cent at the national level. Therefore, the PRFS, and especially the BRI, is seen as an extremely disciplining remunerative incentive at the lower-levels, affecting such things as publication practices. A manager stated, 'What has pushed the publication activities mostly is the BRI system' (Flagship, manager, DK).

The inclusion of the BRI in the budget models has also spurred changes in academic practices. Hence, it is mostly at the regional university that we see researchers reacting to the BRI. In the sociology department, the budget model was experienced as extremely disciplining: 'There was money on each BRI point earned, and you could see it directly on the budget of the department' (Regional, manager, DK). Therefore, management started to demand that in a period of two years, researchers produce BRI points. The researchers reacted by putting much more emphasis on making sure their outlets were on the sanctioned BRI list. Some reported that this led to less Danish language research outputs, less broad dissemination and more stress among faculty.

Also, in Finland, we note how the PRFS affects decision-making and provides incentives for the universities and individual researchers. At an institutional level, the PRFS has provided an action-induced and predictable way of improving the chances of receiving the required resources. The PRFS has pushed universities to make strategic choices regarding how they allocate funding internally and prioritise scientific fields. Seen from a manager's point of view, the PRFS is also a way to provide support to the academic work and to the development of science within the university more broadly. The incentives of the PRFS also clearly affect research practices: 'The publication forum classification has steered our publication activities in social sciences and the humanities towards more international fora' (Regional, manager, FI). The PRFS is thus seen as enhancing the pressure on academics to strive for high-quality and impactful science. Many academics have seen this resulting in positive career developments at personal levels and hence have come to accept these changes as something that drives science forward.

In the previous Finnish system, where performance was tracked to a much lesser degree, problems of academic units and departments could, according to the interviewees, also be overlooked. In the current PRFS, this is no longer the case because universities now have the ability to see problems before they become too large to manage. Issues behind low performance are becoming visible, which encourages managers to provide the necessary academic leadership to overcome the situation; this provides managers with the support they need to bring out the best in their staff: 'Once a year we have a performance discussion with the rector and go through the main indicators of how well the faculty has done. We look at the state of the faculty and its development prospects' (Regional, manager, FI). As such, the PRFS aids managerial decision-making because it highlights underlying problems, such as poor human resources management, weak leadership and favouritism, which in a more transparent system will be a call for action.

In Norway, the PRFS is also seen as a potent instrument, providing actionability at both the organisational and individual level. Organisationally, it facilitates decision-making, for instance, because universities have implemented local variations of performance-based funding. These local systems also provide incentives for the researchers, though their influence often is considered to be limited. Examples of these incentives include how some departments have established systems to reward researchers with a type of bonus that is earmarked for attending international conferences. These rewards are awarded for publications at levels 1 and 2 but also popular science publications in addition to the completion of a master thesis, PhD dissertation and external funding. Those who are working in units where metrics result in the allocation of bonuses find this to be an important part of the freedom to attend international conferences. Still, the amount of money is not large, so the influence on motivation is limited, as exemplified by a researcher: 'It is clear, there are other things that drive what you are doing than money. It is ... kind of not the reason why you are sitting down to write your articles, to get 5000 NOK' (Regional, academic, NO). However, regardless of the connection to rewards or not, publication points and citations are highly valued by many academics. Also, other types of metrics are important to academics, such as citation indexes and journal impact factors, despite the fact that these metrics are unrelated to direct financial rewards. The metrics are instead regarded as symbols of success, and this is interpreted to be important for being invited to networks and research projects and obtaining new positions.

Performance metrics are also used to assign (and refuse) sabbaticals, a practice that is used at both case universities in Norway: '[Publication points] are presented as statistics to all of us ... and this is used to assign sabbaticals, so this is a strong guiding principle for our institution' (Regional, manager, NO). Metrics can also be used by managers to inspire and motivate academics and are often brought up in the annual appraisal meetings. Publication points are used to follow up on academics who are not publishing very much, not to punish, but rather to offer support and facilitation. A manager explains, 'Actually, it is more like I am saying; "Is there anything we can do?" It is not like; "We are expecting you to publish five articles next year." It is not on that level, we are not a factory' (Flagship, manager, NO).

In Sweden, there is less emphasis on the actionability of performance measures compared with the other countries. There is broad agreement that performance measures are to some extent necessary to enable decision-making, but also that they are inevitable as others use them. Academics do, for instance, acknowledge the accountability relationship between the university and ministry and how this results in requirements to report organisational activities in standardised ways. Also, the dependence on external funders and other stakeholders is evident, and that they sometimes prefer simplified metrics to assess research. Thus, the actionability created by metrics is appreciated and accepted because it enables necessary accountability relations and resource allocation flows.

As incentives, the PRFS is most notable within the social sciences, where the increasing emphasis on bibliometrics has implied a shift in publication patterns. As explained by a manager, 'Everyone is moving towards scientific articles. Not exclusively, but it is what people talk about and what we are supposed to aim for' (Regional, Manager, SE). In the natural sciences, publications and citation counts are instead described as traditional measures of research performance. For researchers, the incentives provided by research metrics are, however, rarely related to the national PRFS. Instead, these indicators are important for other reasons. External funding is essential because it provides resources for the individual researchers, and bibliometrics are vital because of the reputational gains for researchers being well published and well cited. Whether research metrics are effective motivational tools is an issue where opinions vary. Some express the notion that they make researchers increase their output: 'If you measure things, if you look at things and take notice of things, more things happen' (Regional, Manager, SE). However, others doubt the necessity of creating stronger incentives because academia already is rife with incentives, emphasising that academics primarily are motivated by their own initiatives. The establishment of local PRFSs is thus challenged: 'The question is whether we need to make yet another assessment to distribute the government grant' (Flagship, Manager, SE). This also emphasises the transparency that indicators create because metrics may provide clear and indisputable grounds for decision-making. Although neither of the two Swedish case universities uses a PRFS at the institutional level, these systems exist at both universities at the faculty level. However, the local PRFSs are rarely strict implementations of the national system but often include a variety of components, such as PhDs awarded and teaching performance. The indicators of the national PRFS are thus applied in the local PRFS because they are seen as useful to allocate resources between organisational units, but they are not the only metrics used here.

Legitimacy

Research metrics are largely seen as important for legitimising organisations and their activities. It is generally acknowledged that metrics are important in demonstrating performance to external actors in simple and understandable ways. Also, equity issues are brought forward because metrics enhance transparency and thwart arbitrary decision-making. Although some critique may be noted against the necessity to measure research so closely, it is mostly seen as just and appropriate. Regarding the technical legitimacy of the PRFSs, there is more variation. In particular, we note how academics primarily from the natural sciences are sceptical of the PRFSs. They often perceive these systems as crude and unable to accurately gauge the value of scientific publications.

In Denmark, the BRI is a new measure of publication performance; it has, to varying degrees, challenged the status quo of the existing methods for assessing the value of different kinds of scholarly publications and outlets. Within the social sciences, the BRI constitutes a new indicator that reflects the publication patterns of the social sciences. For the faculty members of natural sciences, it was a different case. Here, the impact factor of what journal the research was published in had for decades been the standard to measure the quality of a journal. Hence, the BRI was seen as a crude measure because it only differentiated between two levels. In the eyes of natural science scholars, the BRI had low technical legitimacy and was competing against a well-institutionalised and entrenched measurement system. A similar logic differentiates the flagship university from the regional university. Although the BRI was understood as an appropriate tool to boost performances at the regional university, this was seen as unnecessary at the flagship university, where researchers were already publishing in international fora. Therefore, the BRI has never been fully accepted as a proper measurement tool by various groups and universities, thus suffering in both technical and normative legitimacy. This is especially the case in the natural sciences, where researchers simply do not know the BRI or reject it as faulty. As one researcher replied when asked if they take notice of the BRI, 'No, I don't think so. Because it is a bit wrong' (Flagship, academic, DK).

In Finland, on the other hand, the PRFS generally enjoys high normative legitimacy but suffers from a somewhat lower technical legitimacy. Although there is some concern over how well the PRFS actually increases the quality of research, most academics and managers see it as a constructive, forward-looking system. Measuring academic performance is perceived to be an inseparable part of a modern university. However, the normative legitimacy is strongly coupled with the transparency of the indicators: 'The more there is fair competition where rules are open, the better we do. But if there is competition where the rules of the game are not known by those who compete, it is simply an arbitrary use of power' (Flagship, manager, FI). From a managerial perspective, measuring performance is a tool used for the smooth running of a complex expert organisation but also for ensuring the fair treatment of personnel. For the academics, the situation is more complex. They value the openness and transparency of the PRFS but do not necessarily feel they can trust the administration in upholding these standards because university managers adopt and use these metrics. In the eyes of academics, the legitimacy of the system is, hence, coupled with a fair and open application of the performance measures throughout.

Regarding the technical legitimacy of the metrics included in the PRFS, they are largely seen as established indicators of research performance and hence as technically legitimate. The use of bibliometric indicators is perceived to follow the logic of academia and is seen to align well with academic conventions. However, a concern is that the system is not seen as meeting or serving the interests of high-quality research: 'Measuring performance can have a side effect that if the demands are too low or too quantitative we start to count how many publications to do, and so you start to produce lower quality publications because their quality is not measured, only quantity' (Flagship, academic, FI). How much is published is considered to be stressed at the expense of quality, posing a threat to scientific integrity. This is the main reason for the mistrust towards the use of metrics in the evaluation of academic performance.

In Norway, performance measures are used to increase transparency between and within universities. However, there are large variations within the universities on how this is practised. In some departments, they share the information on an individual level to all employees, while others use the data to compare at the department and faculty level. The practice of sharing data at the individual level raises critical voices among both academics and managers because of the shaming of academics with few publications: 'I believe it feels personally more uncomfortable, because it is so visible now. It is more apparent' (Regional, academic, NO).

Generally, research metrics may be said to hold normative legitimacy as tools to indicate success. However, there seems to be differences in the legitimacy of the national PRFS among the academic fields. Within the natural sciences, the system of quantification was not questioned, but it was noted that it provided an increased focus. As illustrated by a researcher: 'There is a larger focus on symbols, for instance in relation to highly ranked journals. To get an article in Nature of Science or others has larger significance now. This is almost immediately reported to the rector and on the web site. The flagging and use of status symbols ... have changed dramatically, I think' (Regional, academic, NO). Research performance, as indicated by metrics, is thus used more often to demonstrate achievements and acquire legitimacy for the university as an organisation.

There are also critical voices, mainly within the social sciences, where academics emphasise the problem of turning values of research into measurable points, problems related to quality versus quantity and highlighting that not everything is countable. Furthermore, these voices question how the role of the university as an independent research institution would be affected by the close connection between funding and metrics. The social scientists were also highly critical towards what they perceived as the new public management influence in the sector, as one academic expressed: 'We are a kind of counter culture ... many of the most prominent critics to the leadership of the university come from our department' (Flagship, academic, NO).

In Sweden, the various components of the PRFS are fairly well established as indicators of research performance and may be considered to have a high level of technical validity. External funding is 'the accepted method of measurement when it comes to research performances' (Flagship, administrator, SE). It aligns well with the idea that external research grants are awarded to the most prominent applicants after a rigorous peer-review process; therefore, the acquisition of grants is an acknowledgement of academic merit. This is also a notion that is well represented within Swedish universities: 'If you are rewarded and get a lot of grants you will be perceived as successful' (Flagship, administrator, SE). Also, the bibliometric indicators used in the PRFS align well with academic conventions, though differences exist between the disciplines. Although some sections of academia are more familiar with bibliometrics and the publication practices it refers to, others have been less so. However, a shift is underway, making research metrics increasingly common within the social sciences.

Although generally accepted, the metrics of the PRFS are not exempt from critique. On the contrary, both researchers and managers emphasise the difficulties of measuring research. The critique is, however, mostly levelled towards measurement in general rather than focusing on specific problems with the existing indicators. An example is provided by a manager who states that fulfilling performance criteria 'does not necessarily imply that the performance has high quality' (Flagship, Manager, SE). There is a general awareness about the limitations of performance measures, and that academic work often produces benefits that are not easily captured by performance metrics. Also, the level where metrics are applicable is noted. Here, a manager states that most metrics are unfit to assess individual performance: 'Your performance is not a result of your own efforts alone, it is largely collective' (Flagship, manager, SE).

The research metrics of the Swedish PRFS are generally seen as normatively legitimate because they legitimise research activities. Still, this is contingent on the relatively high technical legitimacy. It is, however, generally stressed that the research metrics will not benefit the universities if these metrics come to define and control academic work internally. As expressed by a manager, 'We need to make room for the fact that research can occur in various ways' (Regional, manager, SE). Swedish academics are thus holding a quite pragmatic view of these research metrics, one where their benefits and limitations are acknowledged.

Institutionalisation

The research metrics of the national PRFSs have been variously institutionalised in the four studied countries. In some ways, they are now deeply institutionalised because they have been reified in organisational structures, and people are becoming increasingly habituated to them. On the other hand, there is variation regarding how much they are taken for granted. In some cases, they clearly affect how people make sense of the research activities. However, there are also findings indicating that these metrics are not internalised and taken for granted, yet people relate to them in attentive and deliberate ways.

In Denmark, the BRI is by far the element in the PRFS with the largest but also the most differentiated effects on the organisation and practice of academic work. Because the other elements of the PRFS (external funding, student throughput and PhD production) have been in use for almost two decades, they are already institutionalised in the organisation of academic work. Furthermore, they are also important measures in themselves outside of the PRFS. Hence, the importance of securing external funding is not tied so much to its inclusion in the PRFS but rather stems from the necessity to acquire external funding to enable research activities. Although researchers emphasise that the acquisition of external funding has become increasingly important and that they experience pressure from management, no one ties this specifically to external funding being included in the PRFS. However, it cannot be ruled out that the processes of reification and habituation have made external funding even more important because of its inclusion in the PRFS.

On the other hand, the BRI is clearly being institutionalised. We have already described how it is reified in the budget models at the regional university. Its effects on how research results are disseminated are also noted. As a manager states, 'Another perverse effect is what we have felt strongly for, because we originally were created by the surrounding society: To disseminate to the surrounding society [...]. You stopped doing that' (Regional, manager, DK). Introducing the BRI has thus led to a reconstitution of what 'quality publication' is. However, despite the BRI leaving its mark on various places, it has not been broadly institutionalised as a taken-for-granted measure of research performance. This is related to the low legitimacy of the BRI among some groups within Danish universities, preventing the full acceptance of metrics. Moreover, most actors at the university level act under the impression that the BRI is only distributing a small fraction of the total funding for research. As one top manager notes, 'If you look at how much it [the PRFS] has redistributed, then I think you will see that it has redistributed next to nothing' (Regional, manager, DK). Hence, it seems that some institutionalisation of the BRI has taken place, though a very general and taken-for-granted type of lock-in effect is lacking.

In contrast, in Finnish universities, the performance measurement is becoming well institutionalised. It is now perceived as a control mechanism both for the purpose of keeping track and ensuring the accountability of academic staff, as well as being a transparency instrument allowing those who perform well to be rewarded. The internal application of PRFSs to allocate funding also indicates an increasing institutionalisation of the national PRFS. With institutional funding being highly performance based and as the competition for external funding increases, it has become sensible for universities to focus on strong and rising fields of research and to build incentive systems to reward high-achieving departments. Therefore, the logic of the PRFS has been internalised within Finnish universities. A manager exemplifies this when stating that 'our revenue generation logic leans clearly on performance [...] and results have to be somehow measurable' (Regional, manager, FI). Although there is criticism against performance indicators and the way they are designed, the indicators have also influenced the way people understand research activities: 'Also in research, people have started to speak that way, that research activities need to be effective and efficient, that they must be measurable and that the system is a kind of steering mechanism for how good research is' (Regional, manager, FI). This indicates that reconstitution has started to occur because research indicators have influenced how academics perceive the meaning of everyday activities.

Also, in Norway, there is general agreement on the influence metrics have over the organisation of research. In particular, it is noted that the performance measures of the PRFS are institutionalised in several ways. The local use of performance measures derived from the national PRFS constitutes an institutionalisation of these metrics, both as they are reified in organisational decision-making structures and as people become habituated to an increasing measurement of academic performance. There are also signs of reconstitution: an increasing measurement of performance alters the notion of research activities among academics. There is now an increasingly widespread notion that research needs to be measurable so that academics can demonstrate their performance quantitatively. A manager notes how this influences the notion of sabbaticals as a reward rather than preconditions for research achievements: 'Of course, there is more focus on that people have to deserve sabbaticals' (Flagship, manager, NO). Thus, the use of metrics is influential as an organisational principle, and it affects the way people think about research:

> It [publication metrics] means a lot today, even... It is almost comical, right? I can see what it does to my head. I mean, there are far too many journals, too much focus on publication points, because it is not saying anything about the quality, either this is level 1 or 2. Still, it messes with your head as you are measured and weighed, so you are in a way searching for... It means a lot. Therefore, this is an incredibly strong organisational principle. (Regional, manager, NO)

In Sweden, the metrics of the PRFS are quite well institutionalised. Although academics within the natural sciences are more familiar with them, social scientists are now well acquainted with these measures, making the habituation ubiquitous. The measures are, along with other measures of academic work, reified in the decision-making structures at various places in the two universities, albeit not at the highest level.

The reconstitution of the research metrics is relatively weak in Sweden. Although a general acceptance of the indicators of the PRFS has implications for the way university actors perceive research activities, this does not seem to stem from the PRFS. Mainly, the PRFS is not understood to be of particular importance to academics in organising their research activities when compared with other instances where research metrics appear. The way academics describe the relation between performance indicators and research activities instead alludes to a wider context where these metrics are seen as important. That the PRFS does not have a major influence on the way academics perceive research can be explained by the fact that the construction of the PRFS has proceeded from measures already institutionalised as indicators of research performance. However, the specific measures included in the PRFS are often the ones that academics refer to when describing research and the ways in which it is measured. A manager states, 'We measure performance in external funding, publication and citations; those are the tools we have' (Flagship, manager, SE). This indicates that the metrics included in the PRFS are institutionalised and that the PRFS aligns well with established conventions of how to measure research. Although the PRFS is not the origin of these metrics, its implementation creates yet another source of pressure on universities, reinforcing the power of these research indicators. A reconstitution of research in line with prevailing performance measures does seem to be absent, something that can be explained by the relatively weak actionability and incentives of the PRFS when compared with the other three countries.

Concluding Discussion: What Role Do Performance Metrics Play in Research?

In the present study, we have sought to illuminate how the PRFSs of Sweden, Norway, Denmark and Finland affect the way university actors understand research activities at the institutional level. The PRFSs have all been introduced in recent years, but the ways in which they are configured differ somewhat. This is true for the indicators used, as well as for the amount of funds the systems are distributing. Our results indicate that the establishment of these PRFSs has had notable effects within Nordic universities. The performance measures of the PRFSs are implemented as formal structures for resource allocation and decision-making, but they are also used informally and in nonsystematic ways to organise and perform research activities. In particular, they contribute subtly to the institutionalisation and consolidation of research metrics as the descriptions and organising principles of research and to the notion that all scientific contributions can be compared with each other.

However, it is not only the metrics of the four PRFSs that are used within the universities. A number of performance measures are applied by university actors to make sense of research activities and to navigate in a context where there is evermore measurement, evaluation and competition. The PRFSs should therefore be seen in this wider context, where the PRFSs may be understood as expressions of government intentions to promote quantitative evaluation that allows for measurable evidence to be used to describe and compare a complex situation. Even though questions are raised within the universities against the various uses of performance measures, the metrics are generally accepted and often appreciated as valuable tools for enhancing transparency. The introduction of the PRFSs can thus be seen as an important contribution to the quantification of research and as effective in establishing an all-encompassing research evaluation regime.

Analysing the empirical findings against our analytical framework, the different ways in which performance measures have been noted to influence organisations in previous studies all possess explanatory power in the present study. Regarding the actionability of the performance measures (Espeland and Sauder 2007), they are instrumental in supporting decision-making within the universities. This is emphasised in all the studied countries, though the ways in which metrics are used for this purpose differ somewhat. Although there are examples of local PRFSs in all countries at the institutional or subinstitutional level, our results indicate that the metrics in Norway are also used to allocate funding for conferences or sabbaticals. In Denmark, there is a large variation between universities depending on the presence of local PRFSs, which are used at regional universities to improve organisational performance. This is also the main use of the metrics, as emphasised in Finland, where metrics are seen as enhancing transparency and thus the general development of Finnish universities. Therefore, performance measures are used to assist universities in making priorities and to aid managers in providing support to researchers. In Sweden, the metrics are described to aid decision-making at a higher level, where the actionability is mostly related to external accountability relationships and resource allocation flows.

Regarding the incentives, the picture is more consistent across the countries, despite the fact that the preconditions differ among the countries and universities. Most notably, perhaps, is that publication practices are perceived to be heavily influenced in all four countries, at least within the social sciences. Researchers are considering the implications of where they choose to publish their research, as defined by the prevailing performance measures. However, even when remunerative rewards are coupled with the achievement of measurable performances, it is mainly the symbolic rewards—such as reputational gains—that researchers desire. The reason is that the motivation of researchers to perform is commonly found elsewhere: in respect of peers and more traditional academic merits. Thus, the introduction of remunerative incentives is seen as superfluous. Instead, it is the visibility of performance created by the metrics that operates as a motivational tool because metrics allow researchers to transparently show evidence of their labour. There are, however, some differences regarding the importance of the remunerative incentives. At the regional university in Denmark, it is observed that the remunerative incentives are extremely disciplining, and in Finland, it is noted that the PRFS increases the pressure on academics to produce impactful, high-quality research.

We have seen several examples of metrics that are perceived as important, even though they are not tied to remunerative rewards. Our interpretation is that the establishment of national PRFSs contributes to the legitimisation of metrics as indicators of research performances, which then can be used to convey success. Examples of this include the findings from Norway, where publications in prestigious journals immediately are reported to the rector and are published on the university website. This brings us to the next concept in our analytical framework: the legitimacy that indicators can imbue to researchers and universities. Previous research has indicated that this process is contingent, in part, on the technical legitimacy of the performance measures (Bowker and Star 2000), as well as the normative legitimacy of measuring performances (Power 2004). Our results indicate that the technical legitimacy of the various performance measures of the four PRFSs is generally high because the metrics are largely seen as capturing research performance in an accurate manner. There are some differences between the countries, but primarily, we can see that the interviewees from the natural sciences often are sceptical towards bibliometric measures. Their critique is often levelled against the crudeness of the measures, as with the ones used in Norway, Denmark and Finland, where publications are categorised on a scale that has just a few levels. This is also understood as a risk to high-quality research because it is seen as promoting the production of more publications of lesser quality. This is not experienced as a problem in Sweden, where citations are also included to define the value of publications.

Although there are some concerns about the ability of performance measures to capture the relevant aspects of research, as well as the necessity to measure research performance as it is currently done, there is a general acceptance of performance measurement. This may be most strongly emphasised in Finland, where it is understood to be part and parcel of a modern university organisation and an important tool to promote transparency and a better (human resources) management of the university. In Finland, it is also understood as an essential tool for university managers to identify and handle internal issues, as well as to hold academics accountable. In contrast, the Swedish results indicate that the performance measures acquire normative legitimacy because of their ability to facilitate relations with external actors. The strongest criticism against performance measurement is found in Norway, where it is considered to challenge the independence of the universities.

The measures of the PRFSs have also been more or less institutionalised (Scott 1987; Zucker 1987). As already noted, bibliometrics have been used for quite some time within the natural sciences, but this has been less so in the social sciences. Although some opposition has been noted, our results indicate that, within the social sciences, people are getting more habituated to the performance measures and come to act in accordance with the incentives provided by them. There are also clear signs of reification (Espeland and Stevens 1998) because the measures of the PRFSs are used locally in various ways to make decisions and allocate resources. Our results indicate that reification occurs mainly where performance measures are less institutionalised. As noted in Denmark, the PRFS was thoroughly implemented at the regional university, but in the flagship university bibliometrics were already institutionalised, which made the PRFS seem superfluous.

Perhaps most interesting are the differences regarding the reconstitution of research (Dahler-Larsen 2014; Woolgar 1991) as a result of the PRFSs. There are clear examples of this in Norway, where the interviewees mention the importance of the publication outlet levels and how this affects the way they make sense of research. It also shows in the way that sabbaticals are perceived as something a person deserves rather than have a right to. Also, in the Finnish interviews, there are indications that the measurement logic as embodied by the PRFS has reconstituted the perception of research activities within universities. The efficiency and measurability of results are now considered to be important aspects of research. Finally, the Danish case shows that the PRFS has led to less Danish publications, indicating a reconstitution of what quality publications are. These aspects are not as prevalent in the Swedish case. In Sweden, we have instead noted scattered voices of criticism against the implementation of local PRFSs, pointing mainly to the homogenising force of metrics and their inability to measure individual-level performance. This opposition seems to prevent reconstitution, while a pragmatic approach accepts the use of metrics for other purposes, such as external relations.

Taken together, it appears that the reactions from Sweden differ somewhat from the other three countries. In general, the Swedish interviewees display less concern about the use of PRFSs compared with the interviewees from Denmark, Finland and Norway. A possible explanation for this finding is that the bibliometric models used in the other three countries are experienced as more actionable than the one used in Sweden. The Danish, Finnish and Norwegian systems create clear incentives for researchers and enable decision-making based on publication points. The inclusion of citations in the Swedish system does, however, make it harder to assess the value of individual performance before some time has passed and the work has been cited. It is also clear that the novelty of the metrics is greater in Denmark, Finland and Norway, where completely new databases have been constructed. These have been large endeavours for the scientific communities in these countries and have also made a large impact on the researchers measured by the systems. The Swedish PRFS though, is built on an already existing database, which includes well-known metrics that many researchers were already relating to.

Going back to the original question of this chapter, we have sought to illuminate how the varying use of performance-based research funding is reflected within universities across the Nordic countries. We have looked at the formal resource allocation systems at the national level and studied the effects they have had on the perceptions of research at local levels. All of the studied countries have adopted PRFSs, and over the course of roughly two decades, they have modified their PRFSs to suit the national context and their role in the changing global working environment. The increasingly competitive environment and the systems put in place to monitor the research performance of Nordic universities have been internalised locally to varying degrees, partly based on differences in disciplinary practices and divergence between the traditions of flagship and regional universities.

In the current study, actionability, legitimacy and institutionalisation have functioned as valid factors to analyse how metrics affect university organisations. According to our analysis, an additional temporal dimension could be taken into account when looking deeper into the ways in which these three factors influence the use of metrics. As we look at the case universities, it seems that aspects of actionability, decision-making and incentive systems have been somewhat more straightforward to implement as managerial tools because their use is more under the control of formal management structures. Legitimacy and institutionalisation, however, require a longer temporal perspective because their success depends more on gaining trust and showing appreciation mutually between the academic, managerial and administrative professions.

Acknowledgements The data presented in the current volume and individual chapters emanate from a comparative study funded by the Norwegian Research Council under its FINNUT flagship program, a long-term program for research and innovation in the educational sector program. The project number was 237782, and the project was titled 'Does it matter? Assessing the performance effects of changes in leadership and management structures in Nordic Higher Education'.

References

Aagaard, Kaare. 2015. How Incentives Trickle Down: Local Use of a National Bibliometric Indicator System. *Science and Public Policy* 42 (5): 725–737.

———. 2016. Manglende Debat om Stigende Præstationsbaseret Finansiering af Dansk Forskning. *Forskningspolitikk* 2016 (4): 14–15.

Aksnes, Dag W., and Arie Rip. 2009. Researchers' Perceptions of Citations. *Research Policy* 38 (6): 895–905.

Blatter, Joachim, and Markus Haverland. 2012. *Designing Case Studies. Explanatory Approaches in Small-N Research*. Basingstoke: Palgrave Macmillan.

Bowker, Geoffrey C., and Susan Leigh Star. 2000. *Sorting Things Out: Classification and Its Consequences*. Cambridge: MIT Press.

Dahler-Larsen, Peter. 2014. Constitutive Effects of Performance Indicators: Getting Beyond Unintended Consequences. *Public Management Review* 16 (7): 969–986.

Donovan, Claire. 2007. The Qualitative Future of Research Evaluation. *Science and Public Policy* 34 (8): 585–597.

Espeland, Wendy Nelson, and Michael Sauder. 2007. Rankings and Reactivity: How Public Measures Recreate Social Worlds. *American Journal of Sociology* 113 (1): 1–40.

Espeland, Wendy Nelson, and Mitchell L. Stevens. 1998. Commensuration as a Social Process. *Annual Review of Sociology* 24 (1): 313–343.

European Commission. 2018. *Performance-Based Funding of University Research*. Brussels: European Commission.

Garfield, Eugene. 1955. Citation Indexes for Science. *Science, New Series* 122 (3159): 108–111.

Gläser, Jochen, and Grit Laudel. 2007. The Social Construction of Bibliometric Evaluations. In *The Changing Governance of the Sciences: The Advent of Research Evaluation Systems*, ed. Richard Whitley and Jochen Gläser, 101–123. Dordrecht: Springer.

Gornitzka, Åse, and Peter Maassen. 2012. University Reform and the Nordic Model. In *National Higher Education Reforms in a European Context: Comparative Reflections on Poland and Norway*, ed. Marek Kwiek and Peter Maassen, 111–126. Frankfurt: Peter Lang.

Hammarfelt, Björn, Gustaf Nelhans, Pieta Eklund, and Fredrik Åström. 2016. The Heterogeneous Landscape of Bibliometric Indicators: Evaluating Models for Allocating Resources at Swedish Universities. *Research Evaluation* 25 (3): 292–305.

Harvey, Lee. 2008. Rankings of Higher Education Institutions: A Critical Review. *Quality in Higher Education* 14 (3): 187–207.

Hicks, Diana. 2012. Performance-based University Research Funding Systems. *Research Policy* 41 (2): 251–261.

Kvaal, Torkel Nybakk. 2014. "Finansieringssystemet for universitetet og hoyskoler. Kunnskapsdepartementet. Regjeringen. no." https://www.regjeringen.no/contentassets/2af5e2be144c431886f900f9f3432961/finansieringssystemet_universiteter_og_hoyskoler.pdf.

Leydesdorff, Loet, Paul Wouters, and Lutz Bornmann. 2016. Professional and Citizen Bibliometrics: Complementarities and Ambivalences in the Development and Use of Indicators—A State-of-the-art Report. *Scientometrics* 109 (3): 2129–2150.

Mingers, John, and Hugh Willmott. 2013. Taylorizing Business School Research: On the 'One Best Way' Performative Effects of Journal Ranking Lists. *Human Relations* 66 (8): 1051–1073.

Muhonen, Reetta, and Janne Pölönen. 2016. Paljonko on Paljon? Bibliometrisen Tutkimuksen Näkökulmia Yhteiskunta- Ja Humanististen Tieteiden Julkaisukäytäntöihin. *Tieteessä Tapahtuu* 2016 (5): 11–19.

Nelhans, Gustaf. 2013. *Citeringens praktiker: Det vetenskapliga publicerandet som teori, metod och forskningspolitik*. PhD diss., Göteborgs universitet. Humanistiska fakulteten. Institutionen för filosofi, lingvistik och vetenskapsteori.

Olssen, Mark, and Michael Peters. 2005. Neoliberalism, Higher Education and the Knowledge Economy: From the Free Market to Knowledge Capitalism. *Journal of Education Policy* 20 (3): 313–345.

Paradeise, Catherine, Emanuela Reale, Ivar Bleiklie, and Ewan Ferlie, eds. 2009. *University Governance. Western European Comparative Perspectives*. Dordrecht: Springer.

Pinheiro, Rómulo, Lars Geschwind, and Timo Aarrevaara. 2014. Nested Tensions and Interwoven Dilemmas in Higher Education: The View from the Nordic Countries. *Cambridge Journal of Regions, Economy and Society* 7 (2): 233–250.

Porter, Theodore. 1995. *Trust in Numbers. The Search for Objectivity in Science and Public Life*. Princeton: Princeton University Press.

Portnoi, Laura, Val Rust, and Sylvia Bagley, eds. 2010. *Higher Education, Policy, and the Global Competition Phenomenon*. New York: Palgrave Macmillan.

Power, Michael. 2004. Counting, Control and Calculation: Reflections on Measuring and Management. *Human Relations* 57 (6): 765–783.

Rijcke, de, Paul F. Wouters Sarah, Alexander D. Rushforth, Thomas P. Franssen, and Björn Hammarfelt. 2016. Evaluation Practices and Effects of Indicator Use—A Literature Review. *Research Evaluation* 25 (2): 161–169.

Rottenburg, Richard, Sally E. Merry, Sung-Joon Park, and Johanna Mugler. 2015. *The World of Indicators. The Making of Governmental Knowledge through Quantification*. Cambridge: Cambridge University Press.

Rushforth, Alexander, and Sarah de Rijcke. 2015. Accounting for Impact? The Journal Impact Factor and the Making of Biomedical Research in the Netherlands. *Minerva* 53 (2): 117–139.

Sauder, Michael, and Wendy Nelson Espeland. 2009. The Discipline of Rankings: Tight Coupling and Organizational Change. *American Sociological Review* 74 (1): 63–82.

Schneider, Jesper, and Kaare Aagaard. 2012. Den Danske Bibliometriske Indikator. In *Dansk Forskningspolitik efter Årtusindskiftet*, ed. Kaare Aagaard and Niels Mejlgaard, 229–260. Aarhus: Aarhus Universitetsforlag.

Scott, Richard W. 1987. The Adolescence of Institutional Theory. *Administrative Science Quarterly* 32 (4): 493–511.

Seuri, Allan, and Hannu Vartiainen. 2018. *Yliopistojen Rahoitus, Kannustimet ja Rakennekehitys. Talouspolitiikan Arviointineuvoston Taustaraportti. Talouspolitiikan Arviointineuvosto 2018*. Universities' Funding, Incentives and Structural Development. A Background Report to the Economic Policy Council 2018. Helsinki: VATT Institute for Economic Research.

Slaughter, Sheila, and Larry L. Leslie. 1997. *Academic Capitalism: Politics, Policies, and the Entrepreneurial University*. Baltimore: The Johns Hopkins University Press.

Swedish Government Bill 2008/09:50. "Ett lyft för forskning och innovation." Accessed 20 January 2018. http://www.regeringen.se/rattsdokument/proposition/2008/10/prop.-20080950/.

Universitetskanslersämbetet. 2015. *Forskningsresurser baserade på prestation. Tilldelning och omfördelning av basanslag till forskning och utbildning på forskarnivå baserat på indikatorer 2009–2014.* Rapport 2015:15. Stockholm: Universitetskanslersämbetet.

———. 2017. *Forskningsfinansieringen vid svenska universitet och högskolor. Intäkter till forskning och utbildning på forskarnivå 2005–2015.* Rapport 2017:1. Stockholm: Universitetskanslersämbetet.

van Raan, Anthony F. 2005. Fatal Attraction: Conceptual and Methodological Problems in the Ranking of Universities by Bibliometric Methods. *Scientometrics* 62 (1): 133–143.

van Vught, Frans, and Don F. Westerheijden. 2010. Multidimensional Ranking: A New Transparency Tool for Higher Education and Research. *Higher Education Management and Policy* 22 (3): 1–26.

Wedlin, Linda. 2007. The Role of Rankings in Codifying a Business School Template: Classifications, Diffusion and Mediated Isomorphism in Organizational Fields. *European Management Review* 4 (1): 24–39.

Weick, Karl E. 1995. *Sensemaking in Organizations.* Thousand Oaks: Sage Publications.

Woolgar, Steve. 1991. Beyond the Citation Debate: Towards a Sociology of Measurement Technologies and Their Use in Science Policy. *Science and Public Policy* 18 (5): 319–326.

Yin, Robert K. 2009. *Case Study Research: Design and Methods.* London: SAGE.

Zucker, Lynne G. 1987. Institutional Theories of Organization. *Annual Review of Sociology* 13: 443–464.

Open Access This chapter is licensed under the terms of the Creative Commons Attribution 4.0 International License (http://creativecommons.org/licenses/by/4.0/), which permits use, sharing, adaptation, distribution and reproduction in any medium or format, as long as you give appropriate credit to the original author(s) and the source, provide a link to the Creative Commons licence and indicate if changes were made.

The images or other third party material in this chapter are included in the chapter's Creative Commons licence, unless indicated otherwise in a credit line to the material. If material is not included in the chapter's Creative Commons licence and your intended use is not permitted by statutory regulation or exceeds the permitted use, you will need to obtain permission directly from the copyright holder.

CHAPTER 5

External Research Funding and Authority Relations

Jonas Krog Lind, Helge Hernes, Kirsi Pulkkinen, and Johan Söderlind

---

Helge Hernes passed away in the Fall of 2018.
Helge Hernes, Kirsi Pulkkinen, and Johan Söderlind contributed equally to this work.

J. K. Lind (✉)
Department of Political Science, University of Copenhagen, Copenhagen, Denmark
e-mail: jkl@ifs.ku.dk

H. Hernes
Department of Political Science & Management, University of Agder, Kristiansand, Norway
e-mail: romulo.m.pinheiro@uia.no

K. Pulkkinen
Faculty of Social Sciences, University of Lapland, Rovaniemi, Finland
e-mail: kirsi.pulkkinen@ulapland.fi

J. Söderlind
School of Industrial Engineering and Management, KTH Royal Institute of Technology, Stockholm, Sweden
e-mail: johanso2@kth.se

© The Author(s) 2019
R. Pinheiro et al. (eds.), *Reforms, Organizational Change and Performance in Higher Education*,
https://doi.org/10.1007/978-3-030-11738-2_5

Introduction

Over the last three decades, universities have undergone massive transformations (Ferlie et al. 2009). To make universities more productive and attentive to society's needs, governments have introduced new public-management-inspired reforms in most European countries. Although the aims and scope of these reforms and their actual implementation have varied between countries, they all share the same repertoire of reform elements: strengthened management, accountability measures, performance management, and increased competition (Paradeise et al. 2009). One of the central aims of these efforts has been to create more unified and hierarchical organisational actors that are better able to compete in the global market of higher education (HE), which could especially be carried out by strengthening management at universities (Brunsson and Sahlin-Andersson 2000; Krucken and Meier 2006; Seeber et al. 2015).

However, not all of the reform elements necessarily point in this direction. As pointed out by Richard Whitley and Jochen Gläser (2014), some trends in the state's attempt at steering the research within universities might go against the trend of strengthening the formal hierarchy. Developments in the funding of research, especially the proliferation of external project funding for research, could have contradictory effects because they are likely to increase the authority of external funding agencies, while decreasing the authority of managers in universities (Whitley 2011; Whitley and Gläser 2014): 'As universities became more concerned to compete for scientific reputations on the basis of their employees' contribution to knowledge, though, and researchers were more able to raise project money from external sources such as state research foundations, the ability of managers to control academics' behaviour has declined' (Whitley and Gläser 2014, 34).

Although Whitley and Gläser state this development as a fact, it should rather be seen as a hypothesis in need of empirical testing, since the authors do not base their conclusions on an empirical investigation of how authority relations play out in a specific empirical context. We intend to explore this hypothesis in a Nordic context by answering the following research question:

How does increasing external research project funding affect the authority over research for managers and researchers in Nordic universities?

In answering this research question, we draw on the concept of *authority relations*, which was also first developed by Whitley and Gläser. Authority relations are defined as the 'legitimate power of actors' and address the issue of governance, focusing on the actors involved in the decisions concerning research. In this chapter, we focus specifically on the effect of external research project funding on the authority over research that managers and researchers have.

The chapter is structured as follows: first, we develop the theoretical framework in section "Theory: Authority Relations", presenting and further developing the authority relations concept. Then, we present the methods and data in section "Methods and Data". In section "Changes in External Funding", we explore the policy developments concerning external funding in the case countries. In section "Analysis", we conduct an analysis of the survey results, which is followed by an analysis of the qualitative data on a country basis. In section "Comparison and Discussion", we comparatively discuss the similarities and differences concerning how external funding has affected the authority over research for managers and academics. In section "Conclusion", we conclude the findings of the chapter.

Theory: Authority Relations

Authority relations are defined as the 'legitimate power of actors' and revolve around analysing 'the relative authority of a set of interdependent actors' (Gläser 2010, 359); this concept is closely related to the concept of governance. Although governance has been defined in various ways in the literature, a central concern has been how '… different activities and interests are coordinated and regulated' (Whitley 2011, 360). The governance perspective focuses on the systems or modes of governance and hence focuses more on the processes of regulating activities and less so on the specific actors who attempt to exercise authority. The authority relations perspective is both more specific and more inclusive than the governance perspective. As Gläser (2010) states:

> It is more specific insofar as it focuses on actors (authoritative agencies) and uses institutional structures and processes of governance as 'background information' on how authority is produced and exercised. At the same time, it is more inclusive because it always includes all actors who have authority concerning a specific decision process regardless of their inclusion in particular governance instruments. (359)

In the case of this chapter, and in the works of Whitley and Gläser, the specific decision process is about the conduct of research (which we specify further below). One of the central governance mechanisms that has affected authority relations in this area is the proliferation of external project funding in universities, which will be the focus of this chapter.

As defined above, authority is about the legitimate power of actors. However, Whitley and Gläser (2010) do not explicitly define how one should approach and understand power. We will develop an understanding of power that is grounded in the institutional theory as a foundation for the authority relations concept. In the institutional theory, power and authority are not commodities or something an individual can possess; rather, they are a relational phenomenon (Clegg 1989; Lawrence 2008). Therefore, we will not confine our analysis to looking at how authority is formally distributed, but rather, we will focus on how different actors experience the authority relations they find themselves in. According to Thomas Lawrence (2008), power comes in two forms: *episodic power*, which is 'relatively discrete, strategic acts of mobilization initiated by self-interested actors' (6), and *systemic power*, which is the taken-for-granted routines and practices rooted in cultural systems (Lawrence et al. 2012). Hence, episodic power covers all kinds of exercise of power where an individual—or a collective of individuals—purposefully attempts to further his or her interests. This could be accomplished through controlling critical resources (Pfeffer and Salancik 1978) or through having privileged access to knowledge (Clark 1979). However, it could also be engaging in struggles to define what is to be seen as appropriate and true. Hence, episodic power can be used to change institutions and is therefore related to systemic power (Lawrence 2008). Systemic power, though, is when cultural systems and practices become taken for granted and work in less obvious ways. Hence, the exercise of systemic power cannot be attributed to specific actors but still holds power over them.

However, exercising authority over research plays out quite differently for the studied actors in this chapter, and therefore, the concept of authority relations requires some operationalisation. It is likely—and indeed what we partly find in this chapter—that different actors do not want to have authority over the same aspects of research. The researcher wants authority over the actual conduct of research, while managers are interested in authority over the broader direction of research and, as we shall see, are more focused on the authority over research related to resource generation and management in their unit. Furthermore, the studied actors in this chapter have to exercise authority in different ways. Although managers (and other actors—in the case of this chapter, the external funders of research especially) will have to exercise their authority over research through others (mainly by affecting researchers' choices or affecting who is allowed to do research), researchers will exercise authority over research by limiting the authority of other actors. This asymmetry comes from the professional knowledge and skills that only researchers have and the basic unpredictability of the scientific endeavour (Clark 1979; Whitley and Gläser 2014). Hence, for researchers, it becomes a question of protecting their research freedom. There is much discussion—yet no agreement—on what research freedom and the broader concept of academic freedom entails (Akerlind and Kayrooz 2003; Altbach 2001). Furthermore, there are different notions of academic freedom among different cultural spheres and countries (Neave 1988). Therefore, we have chosen to use an inductive approach to increase our understanding of what authority over research means for the studied actors in this chapter. More specifically, we focus on the way actors exercise authority over *content* (research themes and methods used), *time* (actual time to, and time frames for, doing research), and *people* (who gets involved in the research). These themes are based mainly on how researchers define the important areas of research authority and will structure the current analysis. Managers also find these themes relevant but emphasise other aspects of them as important to have authority over when compared with researchers. In addition, managers emphasise additional themes that do not fit with the three themes of *content*, *time*, and *people*. Nevertheless, because these themes are more diverse between countries, they will not be subject to an initial categorisation that will structure the analysis. Instead, in the discussion section, we will sum up these and discuss how manager authority in these areas has changed.

Methods and Data

The chapter uses both the interviews and the survey conducted as part of the FINNUT project (see Chap. 1 of this volume for an in-depth description of the methods used in the FINNUT project). Regarding the interviews, the analysis relied on the FINNUT coding scheme. This chapter mainly draws on two questions in the interview guide that are relevant for this study. For researchers, the question was how much freedom they have in research. For managers, the question was how much freedom they have in making strategic choices regarding the research profile of the unit.

These questions were purposely phrased to be open, allowing the participants to define their degrees of freedom. In doing so, the interviewees inevitably elaborated on the authority relations they found themselves in.

In the survey, we use the part that relates to autonomy. We use quantitative data to obtain a general understanding of how academics experience their autonomy in research. The qualitative data are used to qualify and make sense of the findings in the quantitative date, which, at first glance, seems to reveal somewhat contradicting findings.

Changes in External Funding

The overall development in external funding can be seen in Fig. 5.1. The country sections describe the national tendency in more detail. Although the largest percentage of external funding comes from national sources—mostly research councils and foundations—in recent years, an increasing percentage is coming from the EU. Denmark and Finland have the highest percentage (Denmark had 9.6% in 1999 and 10.2% in 2013, while Finland had 6.7% in 1999 and 13.0% in 2013) and Norway and Sweden the lowest (Norway had 5.8% in 1999 and 6% in 2013, while Sweden had 4.6% in 1999 and 7.8% in 2013).[1] Hence, although their contribution to the increase in external funding is rising, it is still rather marginal, especially in Norway and Sweden.

Denmark

The spending on research at Danish universities has increased substantially over the years. Since around the year 2000, spending on research has tripled. Likewise, the percentage of external funding of research has been—more or less—steadily increasing over the past decades (see Fig. 5.1). The development gained speed during the 1980s, where the percentage more than doubled in a decade, from about 15% to 30% of the total research funding. After a period of stagnation during the 1990s and first part of the 2000s, the development took off with the Globalisation Agreement in

---

[1] Organisation for Economic Co-operation and Development (OECD), gross domestic expenditure on research and development (R&D) by sector of performance and source of funds: https://stats.oecd.org/Index.aspx?DataSetCode=GERD_FUNDS. The most recent data on EU funding on all four countries are from 2013.

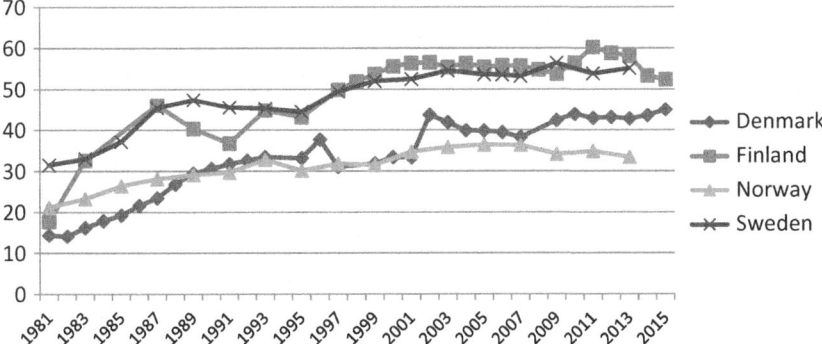

Fig. 5.1 Development in external funding as a percentage of the total funding for research at higher education institutions. Source: Own figure, based on OECD data. To have comparable data, we use OECD data (gross domestic expenditure on R&D by sector of performance and source of funds): https://stats.oecd.org/Index.aspx?DataSetCode=GERD_FUNDS. These are for all higher education institutions (HEIs) and are impossible to break down to only universities. However, they should still indicate the general trend because universities by far conduct the most research among higher education institutions. The Organisation for Economic Co-operation and Development (OECD) data were cross-checked with the national available data, which revealed only minor discrepancies for Sweden, Finland and Norway. However, for Denmark, the numbers differ substantially in the years up to 2007. The national data reveal a large jump in the percentage of external funding in 2007. This makes sense because a large number of governmental research institutions with a high percentage of external funding merged with universities, and the globalisation strategy boosted the external funding of universities. However, this jump does not occur in the OECD data. However, the percentages in recent years match well, and therefore, we have, for reasons of comparability, used the OECD data for all countries

2006, which significantly increased the total funding for research, especially external funding (Aagaard 2012).

Organisationally, most competitive funding up until the 2000s was managed by the state research councils (one for each scientific area). In 1992, the Danish National Research Foundation was established, whose aim was to fund centres of excellence (CoEs). Funding was decided by recognised researchers and given to basic research. Hence, the external funding system was still very much in the hands of the academic elite. However, after recommendations from a research committee in 2001, a range of reforms, introducing new, more innovation-oriented councils and foundations, changed the organisational landscape for public external funding (e.g., the Council for Technology and Innovation was established, along with the Foundation for High Technology). All these organisational innovations were established to move research more towards applied science and business collaboration (Aagaard and Ravn 2012). In addition to the public funding of research, private foundations slowly developed, especially in recent years, as an important source of research funding. Funding from these sources is, however, problematic from a university management point of view because they do not come with overheads. All in all, the Danish system for external funding is very diverse, with a lot of funders coming in different sizes, with different purposes, and oriented towards different scientific disciplines.

Finland

The general level of research funding has seen a steady increase for decades, culminating with a doubling of funds between 2000 and 2012, when the levels slightly dropped. The level of external funding grew substantially in the beginning of the 1980s and then again after a few years of decline during the 1990s (see Fig. 5.1). Here, external funding reached levels above 50% of the total funding for research. In 2009, external funding increased again as a reaction to the new university legislation that took effect on 1 January 2010. The total value of external funding nearly doubled between 2000 and 2016. The general picture is one where the levels of external funding have been more than 50% for two decades.[2]

With the levels of lump-sum funding increasing only moderately compared with the rising level of demands, the pressure for universities to increase their research funding through external funding grew. To boost the utilisation of research in broader society (including business) more effectively, the government has founded a number of new strategically oriented funding instruments. Organisationally, the shift towards more strategically oriented, competitive funding has increased the role of the Academy of Finland and, to a lesser degree, Business Finland (formerly Tekes, the national innovation agency).

---

[2] Because universities of applied sciences are included in the OECD data, the shift to external funding as the dominating source appears earlier than if numbers were for universities only (Statistics Finland).

Norway

Funding for research at Norwegian universities has increased substantially in the past few decades, especially since around the year 2000. The level of external funding has also risen steadily but at a slower pace than the other Nordic countries (see Fig. 5.1). The development took off during the 1980s and then again at the end of the 1990s and beginning of the new millennium, after which the development stagnated. The level of external funding is now significantly lower than that of Finland and Sweden.

Among the domestic external funding organisations, the Research Council of Norway is the most important. It was established in 1993 as a merger of five discipline-based councils and has an annual budget of about NOK 9 billion, which is allocated based on discipline, as well as to CoEs and to topic-based research. In 2014, coming up with a long-term plan for research and higher education (Norwegian Ministry of Education 2015), the government announced an increase in research and development appropriations to 1% of the gross domestic product and to scale up appropriations to research and higher education within six long-term priority areas: seas and oceans; climate, environment, and clean energy; public sector renewal, better and more effective welfare and health, and care services; enabling technologies; innovative and adaptable industry; and world's leading academic groups. Although there is one dominating research council, the funding programmes are quite diverse, and there are regional councils supporting research that has local relevance. Therefore, the system seems as diverse as the other Nordic countries in terms of the types of funding available.

Sweden

Research funding for Swedish higher education institutions (HEIs) has seen a continuous increase in recent decades, doubling since the year 2000. The percentage of external funding for research has also risen substantially since the early 1980s (see Fig. 5.1). Earlier, external funding was mainly provided by the national research councils and the sectorial research boards, which were established in the post-war era. The research councils operated as an inter-institutional faculty board where researchers could apply for funding. This was also the case for the sectorial research boards, which emphasised societal utility and impact as important criteria (Askling 2012, 57).

In 1993, the government introduced a major reform that entailed substantive deregulation and decentralisation. Simultaneously, it also established a number of research foundations. These foundations have various strategic missions and support initiatives such as environmental research and cultural research but also internationalisation and cooperation with industry. In 2001, the Swedish Research Council was established as a new government agency, taking over the activities of the earlier research councils. The trend of an increasing share of external research funds for university research thus continued, reaching levels over 50%, where it has remained since around the year 2000.

During the years that followed, the national research policy has emphasised quality and excellence. Regarding resource allocation, a number of initiatives have been taken up to effectively concentrate resources for research, often to areas of particular concern for decision-makers (Geschwind and Pinheiro 2017).

The Nordic Countries in Comparison

Although we can identify some differences in the policy development on external funding, there is substantial congruence in the general trends.

First, the organisation of research funding seems somewhat similar across countries although there are variations. In all countries, there is a variety of different funding opportunities, where some lean towards basic or blue-sky research, and others are more application or innovation oriented. Even the Norwegian and Finnish systems, which both have one dominating research council, are, in reality, diverse systems with many subprogrammes that support research in a variety of ways.

Concerning the development in the level of external funding (see Fig. 5.1), this has at least one common general feature for all countries, namely, the rise of external funding. In the 1990s, a clear picture emerges, one where Sweden and Finland generally lie at 10% (or more) above Denmark and Norway. However, although Denmark and Norway follow a very similar development from the 1980s and onward, Denmark increases the percentage of external funding substantially from around 2007. Hence, for almost ten years, the picture has been one where Sweden and Finland are at the top, with Denmark following close, and Norway at a level substantially lower than the other Nordic countries.

Hence, the policy development in the four countries has been very similar in terms of the organisational arrangement of research funding (great diversity) and of growing external funding. This seems to have followed a European script for research policy, where initiatives such as the Lisbon Strategy have pushed for more competition (also in funding) and for research policy being embedded in innovation policy to support economic development in a globalised world (Olsen 2007). The biggest difference between the countries seems to be the level of external funding, where there are substantial differences. The question is how these developments have been interpreted by managers and researchers in the four countries. We will explore this in the next section.

Analysis

We will begin the analysis by looking at some of the survey data from the FINNUT project. We asked researchers (associate and full professors) in the studied Nordic universities whether they had autonomy regarding the research topic, methods and project partners.[3] In the context of this chapter, autonomy should be seen as a measure of authority over research. If academics experience high autonomy, we interpret this as others having a low authority over research. The results (see Table 5.1) show that on average, researchers report having fairly large autonomy over research (or authority over research). It is also interesting to note that the differences between countries are not large. On average, the autonomy level is slightly higher across countries for research methods (4.46). This could indicate that research funding mostly affects the topics covered (4.27) and the people who are involved (4.23). This would be consistent with the way external funding usually is managed, where there are often topic restrictions or demands in terms of who should be involved as partners in projects. Requirements in terms of methods are rare. However, it should be noted that the autonomy in research, as measured in this survey item, is of course also determined by factors other than external funding.

However, we also asked researchers whether they experienced any tension between managerial priorities and academic autonomy (Table 5.2). Somewhat contradictory to the high scores on research autonomy, they also score quite high on experiencing these tensions. Although there are variations between countries, they are quite small. It should be kept in

[3] We do not have suitable survey data on the experiences of managers in terms of their authority over research.

Table 5.1 Autonomy in research topic, methods and project partners by country (the 'mean' is the mean score on a Likert scale from 1 'I strongly disagree' to 5 'I strongly agree')

The country in which you work (for your primary job):		I have autonomy in research topic.	I have autonomy in research methods.	I have autonomy in choosing partners for research projects.
Denmark	Mean	4.18	4.44	4.21
	N	1616	1620	1586
	Std. deviation	0.969	0.809	0.977
Finland	Mean	4.46	4.57	4.38
	N	558	557	552
	Std. deviation	0.829	0.785	0.904
Norway	Mean	4,29	4.42	4.13
	N	809	806	781
	Std. deviation	0.923	0.864	1.098
Sweden	Mean	4.39	4.50	4.31
	N	357	357	347
	Std. deviation	0.857	0.756	0.929
Other, please specify	Mean	4.55	4.55	4.64
	N	11	11	11
	Std. deviation	0.522	0.688	0.674
Total	Mean	4.27	4.46	4.23
	N	3351	3351	3277
	Std. deviation	0.929	0.814	0.993

mind that we did not ask specifically about research autonomy but rather about academic autonomy in general. Also, the numbers do not reflect whether researchers experience a tension between the priorities of external funders and their academic autonomy.

Looking at the survey results, a rather murky picture appears where academics, on the one hand, experience quite large autonomy in research but, on the other hand, experience tensions between manager priorities and their academic autonomy. In the qualitative part of the analysis, we will shed light on these seemingly contradictory findings.

In the following sections, using the qualitative data, we will analyse the authority relations regarding research for managers and researchers seen in

Table 5.2 Tensions between managerial priorities and academic autonomy (the 'mean' is the mean score on a Likert scale from 1 'I strongly disagree' to 5 'I strongly agree')

The country in which you work (for your primary job):		There is a tension between managerial priorities and academic autonomy.
Denmark	Mean	3.70
	N	1739
	Std. deviation	1.192
Finland	Mean	3.70
	N	773
	Std. deviation	1.184
Norway	Mean	3.56
	N	847
	Std. deviation	1.225
Sweden	Mean	3.60
	N	530
	Std. deviation	1.182
Other, please specify	Mean	3.55
	N	11
	Std. deviation	1.036
Total	Mean	3.66
	N	3900
	Std. deviation	1.197

relation to the growing share of external project funding. First, we will conduct an analysis for each country separately. The analysis will focus on, and be structured around, the authority over research regarding *content*, *time*, and *people*.

Denmark

External funding plays a huge role in researchers' authority over research. In fact, although especially salient in the natural sciences, external funding is almost the sine qua non in contemporary research. On the other hand, researchers generally experience little direct steering of their research. The following quote exemplifies this paradox well: 'On the research side, I have quite big freedom. But what determines what I can do research in is very much controlled by what I can apply and get funding for' (regional, researcher, natural sciences). Managers, on the other hand, experience very little authority over the research being conducted in their units. Even though they formally have the final authority over the applications being sent out, the actual authority is confined to budgetary concerns linked to the research. The general perception is that the competition over external funding has only increased in time.

Danish researchers experience a large amount of freedom in choosing the *content* of their research.[4] Most researchers do not experience pressure from managers to change the content of their research. As one researcher puts it, here, commenting on a general lack of academic influence, 'However, it is not that I think our research freedom is suffering. There are no one at the rector or dean level who interferes with which research projects we propose or write or anything' (regional, researcher, social sciences). Managers confirm that they are not directly able to affect content by instructing researchers on the conduct of research, and some state that this is by no means desirable. They see recruiting new staff as the main way to exercise authority over the content and direction of research. Although in some cases there are procedures for the internal evaluation of applications, this is more seen as supporting the creation of good applications, and no one has experienced a situation where managers would reject an application on the grounds of the content (or even quality). However, funders do exercise indirect authority over the content of research. Because of the pressure to obtain funding, some researchers try to align their content with the wishes of funders. This is done in subtle ways, though, as one researcher explains that he tries to read what potential partners in ministries think is interesting at the moment and then tries to make his own research interests fit into this agenda. This kind of influence is, however, the most noticeable when funding comes from private sources or public, non-funding agency funders (e.g., ministries, regions, municipalities, etc.). However, researchers are often able to target their applications to funders who are more suitable for their kind of research to avoid this influence. For example, one researcher mostly acquired funding from hospitals

---

[4] Researchers from former governmental research institutes (GRI) were not included in the qualitative part of the study. These researchers have research assignments more tightly connected to, and often regulated by, contracts with agencies within the central administration. If included, we would perhaps have found other results.

and avoided the national research councils (because it was hard to get funding for cross-disciplinary research), and quite oppositely, another researcher mostly applied to the national research councils because his research was more fundamental and less applied. Hence, because there is a range of different funding options available in the Danish system, better chances for funding can be obtained through some strategic thinking on the part of the researchers.

One of the biggest obstacles to actually doing research is *time*. First, many researchers complain about a lack of time to do research because they increasingly have other assignments. Writing applications for external funding is one of those tasks—although it differs whether researchers see this as a waste of time or as a part of the research process of refining their ideas (or recognise both). Further enhanced by these developments, it is generally felt that external funding is needed for actually having time to do research. Danish researchers do not automatically have a sabbatical semester where they are free from teaching. Hence, getting funding to be 'bought free' from teaching is important. However, in one case, even though a researcher was 'bought free' from teaching, the researcher still had to teach anyway because of the big teaching load at the department. Of course, managers could, in principle, choose to give sabbaticals to their researchers. However, this would mean more teaching for all staff when they are not on sabbatical. Hence, the authority over research concerning time also has to do with the ministry or state authority over general funding for education.

External funding also affects who gets involved in research. Some funders make explicit that certain types of partners should be included in applications (e.g., businesses, certain public research institutions, stakeholders, etc.). In one case, the funders themselves had so much at stake in the research that they wanted to have carried out that they pushed for a specific person to be included in the project. However, it seems that most researchers actually are able to set the research team and partners in their projects themselves. Managers typically do not have any authority over who gets to apply. However, in cases where a foundation intends to invest heavily in a university, for instance, by granting large donations or donating or cofunding new buildings, the top management is very important, even though the investment is in a specific faculty. Hence, the authority of managers seems to be somewhat related to the size and scope of the external funding that enters the university.

Both researchers and managers experience pressure to get funding. This means that on the part of the managers, most are willing to accept all types of funding. This includes what one manager calls 'money from hell' (regional, manager), which is funding with no overhead, high cofunding, and a lot of paperwork. These are problematic and diminish the authority of managers because they bind core funding to the (under)funded projects. Researchers, likewise, experience pressure from managers to get funding. Even if a researcher would accept researching only in his or her spare time (when not teaching), without any external funding, this can be very hard because there is an implicit expectation from management that the researcher should acquire external funding (or at least try to). One interviewee explained how this pressure to secure external funding was also linked to the merit system. In this case, it was made clear that the researcher needed to obtain more funding from prestigious sources, such as the national research councils, to advance to the full professor level.

A problem specific to the natural science faculties and departments is that there is less laboratory assistance available. This is a development that has happened because of increasing external funding. It is now expected that a researcher gets the laboratory assistance needed through external funding. Hence, researchers in the hard sciences almost cannot do research without external funding. However, this goes for all units and universities: it is hard to get internal funding for any activities, and external funding often is important to fund hosting conferences, going on field work, going to international conferences, and so forth.

Finland

The increasing importance of external funding plays a significant role in the ways researchers and managers perceive their authority over research. Acquiring competitive external funding is strongly emphasised in the Finnish higher education system in general, especially regarding research activities. There is a strong consensus across disciplines and universities that researchers' authority over research has steadily decreased. This development is linked to the rise of external funding, as well as performance-based funding and result-oriented management. The enhanced focus on requiring external funding, which has been pushed by internal performance management, is seen to be problematic when research work is valued first and foremost through the economic output, reflecting an attitude of 'If you cannot eat it tomorrow, it is not worth doing' (flagship, researcher, natural sciences). For researchers, this represents a move from science being in the centre of the university to being moved into a periphery position. Strategic thinking has become an irremovable part of academic work, and when planning a research project, researchers must now weigh the risks and consider the possibilities for publication and meeting performance requirements more strategically than before.

For the discussion on Finland, we will begin by focusing on the authority of researchers and managers over the *content* of the research. Academic staff see the acquisition of external competitive funding as a way to simultaneously secure and risk their freedom: freedom from the management decisions of the university because their work is secured by their external funding, yet a risk to freedom through potentially steered funding. Regarding the latter, the Finnish informants agree that funders have taken a more active role and are increasingly opening thematically focused calls or setting parameters for research areas through participatory processes. Rather than allocating fairly open funding, they now steer the funding more specifically to particular (often societally relevant) fields, for example, around the so-called wicked problems, such as climate change or the ageing society. Through these actions, funders are seen by the academic staff to knowingly limit researchers' authority over research and the space for scientific curiosity. A researcher explains how this is experienced: 'Although we, in principle, have freedom of research and you can choose your areas, the preconditions of today's world define what is wise to do and what is not' (regional, researcher, natural sciences). This development, as well as the more general push from managers to be more strategic thinking, as described above, is drawing the attention of researchers away from the content of research and towards the production of knowledge itself. When requiring external funding becomes an important goal in and of itself, the content of the research is one of the parameters where one can choose to compromise. Yet in general, most Finnish informants agree that a strategic touch is a positive and built-in mechanism in research because it increases quality: 'In research it is automatically so that we don't get the grants to fund research projects if the research is not of high quality and published in good international journals. It's a built-in mechanism in our type of research' (flagship, researcher, natural sciences). Hence, although the increasing push to acquire external funding and the need to think more strategically to some extent limit the authority of researchers over their research, it is also seen as an important quality assurance mechanism. Managers have very little direct authority over the content of the research.

However, like in the Danish case, their authority is indirect—carried out through the process of hiring researchers that they think match their strategic priorities.

Second, we will now turn to the authority over *time*. The increasing role of external funding is reflected in the time span that academics have for their work. There is a trend towards results being wanted quicker, leading to academics having to find new ways of working, as seen in the following quote: 'Applied research is emphasised strongly and research has become much more short-sighted. You need to get results at a faster pace. We should be given some time to think a little' (regional, researcher, social sciences). Time has also been coupled with an increase in workloads because researchers are required to allocate more time to the writing of funding proposals. Although being frustrated by the situation, the Finnish informants also see the development as positive, in that it pushes academic professionals to be more strategic in their planning. Drafting competitive proposals for the much-wanted European Research Council funds, for example, is not only time-consuming but also highly demanding. It requires the goal-oriented tapping of their scientific creativity and, in practice, more cooperation with colleagues that can provide valuable input and support. In other words, as the role of external funding has risen, so has a new form of collegiality that can balance competition with support.

Third, we now turn to the authority over research concerning *people*. Managers have, as in the other cases in Nordic countries, very little authority over who gets involved in the specific projects that researchers bring in through external funding. However, the rising role of external funding affects recruitment practices in another way. Instead of having authority over the people involved in specific research projects, managers exercise authority over the kinds of external funding that are being applied for by hiring faculty staff they believe will get external funding in areas that the managers prioritise. External funding is viewed as an instrument for getting the necessary resources for doing societally significant and scientifically interesting research, as one manager states, 'In many units recruiting is directed so that we can get certain kinds of personnel, we can't have researchers all from the same field, there needs to be diversity' (regional, manager, social sciences). A diverse academic staff within reasonably focused research fields strengthens the chances of building strong institutional research profiles and research consortia that are able to acquire competitive funding.

Norway

The growing governmental pressures for increasing externally funded research in Norway over the last decade have brought about important changes in the authority over research for different actors. In the Norwegian higher education system, acquiring external funding has become highly relevant, giving this issue very high legitimacy. This reinforces the tendencies described below, increasing the efforts by researchers to obtain external funding and giving successful universities an enhanced reputation.

First, we will focus on the authority of managers and academics over the content of the research. External funders have demands for the research they are funding: 'You must do something that people are interested in. And you have to do a good research job' (flagship, researcher, natural sciences). However, there seems to be a low degree of direct attempts from external actors to influence the research content: '... and the external actors with whom we cooperate, they have been very professional to understand that they can't interfere in the research processes' (regional, manager).

The relationship between university strategies and authority over research concerning content is a quite complicated one. The informants in the Norwegian study quite consistently report that the university and faculty strategies in recent years have become more specific and operationalised, indicating that managers might exercise authority over research through these strategies. Although the strategies are still characterised by compromises and rhetoric, to a great extent, they emphasise renewed strategic effort to: (a) give direction to the entire institutions; (b) encourage the faculties and departments to collaborate and facilitate more internationalisation; and (c) establish CoEs and similar units, which can be seen as 'soft' attempts at steering research. However, within these frames, there are substantial possibilities for initiatives and interpretations at the faculty, department, research group, and down to the individual researcher level: 'The five strategic fields are considerably wide, so you should be quite unfortunate if you are not included.... But strategies are always used when we argue for priorities' (regional, manager). There are also examples of initiatives that have materialised without being mentioned in the formal strategies: 'Our first project within the (mentioning the specific area of commitment) at the university, for example, was in (mentioning the discipline) which was not according to the university's strategy' (flagship, researcher, natural sciences). Such phenomena are, among other things, because of external funding opportunities that in turn may enable enhanced competence, for example, through the recruitment of new scholars.

We will now touch upon how external funding affects managers' and academics' authority over *time* to do research. Time is the most crucial resource in higher education institutions; the demands for scholars' time are manifold. The pressure towards and within higher education institutions to emphasise external funding both increases and changes these demands. For one thing, a substantial part of scholars' and managers' available time is allocated to write research project applications. When these applications are successful, researchers are expected to conduct this research in addition to their other tasks. In other cases, funding may enable scholars to reduce their teaching load—they are 'bought free'. Because the outcome of the application processes is a crucial factor and is decided upon by actors external to the seeking institutions, the allocation of time is, to a substantial degree, beyond the managers' control, meaning that successful scholars prosper while the situation of others is more challenging. This trend might reinforce a tendency found in some universities where a sharper divide between academics who only teach and academics who only do research is found (Geschwind and Broström 2015). Therefore, the increasing amount of external funding for research seems to increase the authority over research regarding time for academics who are successful in attracting external project funding for research. However, in contrast to the situation in the other Nordic countries, many Norwegian researchers are granted sabbaticals on a periodic basis (although this practice varies between universities and even the units within them). Although the granting of these sabbaticals might depend on one's performance in scientific publishing, thereby indirectly being affected by the ability to attract external funding, sabbaticals will supply researchers with more concentrated time for research.

Finally, we now turn to the authority over research concerning the people involved in the research. Because of different opportunities and traditions between the academic disciplines, a lack of competence, too fragmented research foci, and other factors, there are substantial variations in external funding between faculties, departments, research groups, and individual scholars. These variations generate interesting intraorganisational processes. The researcher informants in the Norwegian study who have succeeded in raising external funding report a high degree of congruence between the university and unit strategies and their own academic work. Rather than complaining about the recent developments in the university's managerial systems, these informants seem to take advantage of these processes, especially that they facilitate external funding for them. Thus, these processes are perceived more as possibilities for the scholars and less as threats to the researchers' authority over research. Neither do the informants in our study who do not benefit from substantial external funding seem to make any serious complaints or protests about the developments in the university managerial systems. They do considerable research within the limits of governmental funding, and they report some degree of resignation and rely on universities as loosely coupled entities and the subsequent freedom that follows: 'There is a low degree of leadership. If one withdraws, one is to a high degree able to micromanage one's own working day' (flagship, researcher, social sciences). However, these differences point to external funding as a differentiating mechanism that privileges some groups of researchers over others.

The organisational effects of external funding concerning the people involved in the research thus seem to be subtler, such as when researchers become less dependent on the basic budget and, importantly, even more dependent than before on collaborating with scholars at domestic and international institutions. Managers may be somewhat marginalised in this system of increasing external funding. According to the Norwegian interviews, however, managers do not necessarily perceive these developments as challenging; managers, instead, tend to overemphasise the impact of their managerial roles in other areas and focus on the importance of strategic plans. Additionally, managers may be important facilitators of external funding and may participate in external projects. Following also the strategies of Norwegian universities, CoEs have been established as semi-autonomous organisational entities that rely heavily on external funding. Although this is often a strategic ambition that managers have decided to pursue themselves, CoEs paradoxically also represent a challenge for the established university managerial systems, which have very limited authority over whom and in which areas these are established. Hence, external funding seems to reinforce existing patterns among and within higher education institutions; high-performing institutions, centres, and researchers become even more able to provide external funding, while others may fall behind, pointing to the Mathew effect commonly found in the sciences (Kwiek 2016).

Sweden

A clear result from the Swedish interviews is that funding is the most important factor when it comes to authority over research. Funding is essential in enabling any research, and because external actors are allocating a larger share of the resources for research, they are also gaining more authority over research.

We will begin by focusing on the authority of researchers and managers over the *content* of the research. The most salient way in which influence is exerted over the research process is that researchers adapt to the conditions set by the funders. At times, this may not amount to more than changing the rhetorical framing of the proposed research, which in fact might be seen as a defence strategy known as 'window dressing' (Laudel 2006), but in other instances, it includes major adjustments and compromises to secure funding. One example is a professor at the technical faculty saying that 'you have to try to adapt to whatever is popular to fund at a specific time' (flagship, researcher, engineering science). More severe influences may, for instance, be noted in collaborative research projects, where the goal of companies to develop a product takes precedence over the researchers' desire to produce and disseminate new knowledge. It is also clear how funders may influence research at an institutional level above the individual researcher. Examples primarily include large infrastructural investments that may allow the university to develop their research substantially within particular areas. An example is provided by a research office manager who recalls how a large sum of money was donated to the university for the construction of a house dedicated to design studies. The manager says, 'Of course, you get large effects, since you invest a lot in areas where someone has allocated some hundred million' (flagship, administrator).

Generally, however, there is agreement that the integrity of researchers is quite robust and has not yet been severely challenged by the increase in external funding. Although academics may voice a desire for more authority over research, they also express confidence in their own, as well as their colleagues', ability to maintain their integrity in relation to external actors. A social scientist says, 'You know where to draw the limit, how to dispose your time, and you very often keep in mind what really is important' (flagship, researcher, social sciences). Several informants also emphasise the institutional safeguards against the risk of being co-opted by external interests. Because a main incentive for academics is to acquire academic qualifications, it is fundamental to pose scientifically interesting questions and publish the results. According to a top manager, it is therefore 'somewhat suicidal' (flagship, manager) to enter too many projects that do not award academic merits, and the system is thus 'to a large extent self-regulating' (flagship, manager). As a further precaution, this manager states that the university has established support structures to ensure that collaboration agreements with external actors are reviewed by lawyers to guarantee the freedom of the researchers to publish their findings. A trend among funders is also the increasing focus on societal expectations, needs, and impact. To some extent, this is appreciated by academics and managers alike in Swedish universities. As expressed by a sociologist, 'If sociology does not matter for society, what then is the point of sociology?' (flagship, manager, social sciences).

We now turn to the authority of managers and researchers over *time* to do research. Researchers point out that fewer applications are granted funding today and that 'we have to write more applications now' (flagship, researcher, engineering science). Low success rates and general pressure to obtain external funding have thus led to a situation where the process of applying for external funding is more time-consuming than ever before. These new obligations come on top of the other tasks a researcher has, putting pressure on the time to actually do research: 'You feel as an individual researcher that there is a need to have control over all this [calls for external funding] and at the same time do your research, that is tough' (flagship, manager, engineering science). To alleviate some of this pressure, and as a response to the general pressure that managers also experience when it comes to boosting external funding, a strategic priority of universities today is to support researchers in their attempt to acquire external funding. Currently, most universities have a research office that aids in identifying potential funders and in writing applications. At the subinstitutional level, initiatives are also taken to support researchers to acquire funding, as reported by a head of department: 'At the faculty, we have calls, for instance for writing support, article support or application support' (regional, manager, social sciences). These efforts also tie into managing the general insecurity that the increasing share of external funding has created. A top manager notes, 'If large projects end for our researchers, and they cannot find new funding, we have a problem' (regional, manager). Fluctuations in revenues from external actors must be balanced by internal funding to maintain the workforce. When a university increases its research activity and when a larger share of this activity is funded by external resources, the risk also increases for the organisation because, to a large extent, this funding is temporary. Working actively to support researchers in their pursuit of external funding is an attempt to manage this risk.

Finally, we now turn to the authority of managers and researchers over the *people* involved in research. As the share of external funding has increased, managers at various levels note that they now have little influence over the people employed to do research at universities, faculties, and departments. Deciding on projects to fund, and thereby people to promote, is very much in the hands of funders. This also affects the ability of universities to promote quality in research and, in particular, to support up-and-coming researchers, as noted by a top manager. Although successful researchers are rewarded through the acquisition of external funding, researchers with great but yet unrealised potential are often in need of financial support. With scarce resources, however, this is difficult for universities to provide. A final example of how external funding affects the *people* involved in research is tied more directly to how external funders make concrete demands. A research office manager notes that all external funders demand an impact strategy to make sure that the researchers consider the societal implications of their work. However, some funders do also require active participation from industry and stakeholders, as exemplified in the following quote: 'And of course, that is a huge opportunity to influence the project. And that obviously also affects our research profile' (regional, administrator).

Another trend that reinforces the managers' lack of authority over research, one that cuts across the themes of *content*, *time*, and *people*, is the increasing demands from external funders for cofunding. Because cofunding is required, many internal resources become tied up in research projects, which effectively diminishes the ability of departments to make their own prioritisations. A head of department notes that cofunding deprives researchers of a base resource for research, and a dean points out how this trend undermines the faculty's performance-based resource allocation model (the more cofunding given, the less funding is available to distribute according to the chosen model). Others do, however, state that the less money available to the university management, the more they need to prioritise: 'It forces us to take a strategic stand' (flagship, manager).

A notable difference in the experiences of managers and academics is that the managers see the consequences of external funding from a broader perspective. Although academics may express a need to frame their research proposals to fit the desires of the funders, managers also reflect on how this affects their authority over research in terms of the ability to prioritise, maintain a healthy working environment, and enhance the quality of the research conducted.

Comparison and Discussion

The analysis of the influence of external funding on authority over research reveals both many similarities and some differences across the studied countries. However, we should be careful when trying to explain these similarities and (especially) differences by the overall policy development concerning external funding. As the country analyses have also shown—and which is an important point in its own right—many other factors interfere with how external funding affects the authority of different actors over research, including, for instance, how much de facto authority managers generally have, how many time constraints there are that can limit research, how Performance-based Research Funding Systems (PRFSs) affect some of the same issues, how important universities strategies are, and so forth. Therefore, how external funding affects authority over research is an intricate matter to analyse. In this section, we will comparatively discuss the country cases and survey data analysed in the previous sections.

One of the broad conclusions we can draw when comparing the country cases is that external funding has become increasingly important for conducting research and has changed the authority of different actors over research. Applying for external funding has become an indispensable part of academic life. The pressure to acquire funding and the competition to obtain these funding sources have increased according to the experiences of both managers and academics. The Finnish, Danish, and Swedish data especially indicate that it is increasingly hard to do research without external funding. Researchers need funding to do what is required of research today, where international cooperation is a necessity, where there is less internal funding for laboratory assistance, and where funding is often necessary to go abroad—on field work or to conferences. But managers also need funding to 'keep the shop running' and experience a huge pressure to increase revenue through external funding. In fact, it seems that obtaining external funding has become a goal in and of itself for some managers; thus, a *budget-maximisation logic* seems to have become prevalent. Hence, external funding has become an important general condition for the management and conduct of research.

In the following, we focus on the authority over research for the two analysed groups: managers and researchers. We begin by focusing on the researchers. When taking a first look at the qualitative data, these seem to, in some ways, mirror the somewhat contradictory findings in the survey. When asked directly, researchers generally stress that they have quite large freedom when it comes to research. As the Swedish case shows, the integrity of researchers has not been broken. The same goes for the Norwegian and Danish cases (while the Finnish case stresses the decline of academic freedom to some extent although this is more related to the importance of the strategic priorities of managers). However, when researchers elaborate on the way external funding affects the conditions for research, nuances appear. We find that both the *content* of the research, the *time* to do research, and the *people* involved in doing the research are affected by the increasing amount of external funding.

Regarding *content*, the Danish, Finnish, and Swedish cases especially show that, at times, researchers adjust the content of their research to meet the demands of funders or to improve their chances of getting funded. Typically, this is done when researchers try to guess what is popular to fund. The Finnish interviews stressed that researchers are learning 'what is wise to do and what is not'. In some cases, university strategies contribute to this effect by pointing out areas where there is more support available. This is especially salient in the Finnish case. Also, the general pressure from managers to obtain external funding further pushes the need to bend to the wishes of external funders.

Regarding *time*, external funding is increasingly necessary simply to have the time to conduct research. In addition, sometimes, as in the Danish case, there are still time pressures even after a researcher has been 'bought free' in a project. Both the Danish and Swedish cases show how writing applications for external funding are sometimes viewed as a waste of time, preventing researchers from actually doing research. However, some also view this process as an integrated part of the scientific process. The Finnish interviewees especially stressed that time frames have shortened because of external funding and demands for quick results in projects with short deadlines. Management clearly contributes to this process. This calls for more strategic behaviour from researchers. In Sweden, Denmark, and Finland, external funding is usually necessary to have the concentrated time required to do research, while at least a proportion of the Norwegian researchers have better opportunities because of regular research sabbaticals that are not directly dependent on external funding. Although the *time* to do research is probably to a large extent equal between the scientific disciplines, the actual *possibility* to do research might depend even more on project funding in the natural sciences because researchers in this field usually depend more on external funding to carry out research (with experiments requiring laboratory assistance, expensive equipment, etc.).

Regarding *people*, the rise of external funding has generally made cooperation between researchers necessary. Most national funders demand cooperation in the project funding they offer. To obtain international funding, as from the EU frame programme HORIZON 2020, international cooperation is often mandatory. However, as the Finnish and Norwegian cases show, this is seen as a natural development in line with how academic norms have developed. However, sometimes, funders are more specific about the partners that will be involved in research projects, as the Swedish and Danish cases illustrate, which limits the authority over research in terms of project partners.

It is important to note that the ways external funding affects the authority over research for researchers are more systemic than episodic in nature. Instead of episodic power, for instance, which would be in the form of direct instruction from managers, the increasing amount of external funding sets up incentives that direct action in more subtle ways through systemic power. A global script pushing for more competition, more industry cooperation to support innovation, demands for societal impact, and so forth has materialised in new funding schemes and in increased competitive funding. The systemic nature of the power exercised by research funders might be one of the explanations for why the survey reveals relatively high research autonomy and why, when asked directly, researchers report great freedom in research: systemic power works in ways that, to a lesser extent, are felt like intrusions into one's agency. Hence, the depth of the qualitative interviews helps uncover the nuances in this authority over research.

However, researchers are not defenceless against these systemic powers. Across the cases, one can identify a range of 'defence mechanisms': first, the academic value of integrity is a systemic power that prevents total surrender to the incentives of funding opportunities. Researchers 'know where to draw the limit', as expressed by a Swedish interviewee. It seems that some of the traditional academic values, as made explicit by Robert

Merton (1973), are still very much alive. Second, a strategy is to only apply to funders and funding programmes that fit the research agenda of the researcher. Although most clearly expressed in the Danish case, this strategy is likely an option in all the Nordic countries because the funding opportunities are diverse, as the national descriptions of the funding systems have shown. This seems to offer some support for the conclusion found in an article by Richard Whitley and Jochen Gläser (2014), where they hypothesised that high funding flexibility (i.e., diversity in funding opportunities) would lead to more protected space for researchers to conduct research. Third, the Swedish results point to the rhetorical framing of projects, also known as 'window dressing' (Laudel 2006), as a possible defence mechanism. Fourth, as highlighted by the Swedish results, there are also institutional safeguards against being co-opted by external interests in the form of legal advice on collaboration agreements. Hence, safeguarding against external interests is not just a matter for individual researchers but also is sometimes supported by managers.

Looking at the qualitative data, in Finland, the authority over research for researchers seems mostly restricted by the development in external funding, with a little less in Denmark and Sweden, and the least so in Norway. However, it is hard to assess the differences precisely. Although the survey results point only to small differences across countries, there are reasons to believe, as has been argued above, that the qualitative data are better suited for capturing the subtler effects of external funding on the authority over research. This adds to the likelihood that, in reality, there are more differences between countries than the survey results indicate.

We now turn to the authority of managers over research. The national cases mostly point to external funding as a factor that limits the authority of managers over research, at least if focusing on the three themes of *content*, *time*, and *people*. Managers cannot directly affect the *content* of research, which the Swedish, Danish, and Finnish cases emphasise. Even though they have the formal authority to do so, because managers have to approve applications for external project funding, no one seems to take advantage of this option (or find it appropriate). In this case, it seems that the professional authority of researchers, stemming from the knowledge and skills only they possess, offers researchers a degree of authority over research that limits managers in their use of formal authority. Although this is a structural factor, based on the basic asymmetry between managers and researchers in terms of knowledge, there is also an institutional and cultural factor. The fact that managers do not find direct intervention in research appropriate might reflect that the values of academic freedom are also salient among managers. Instead, the authority over the *content* of research being conducted is exercised mainly through hiring tenured faculty staff. The same is the case regarding *people*. Managers have little authority over who gets involved in research projects based on external funding; instead, it is through hiring tenured faculty that they exert their influence. In terms of *time*, managers have a role in setting the basic conditions for time to do research although the opportunities for doing so are heavily circumscribed by the general teaching loads in the specific university or unit. However, because external funding is increasingly necessary to have time for research, the authority of managers in this regard is rather limited.

Instead of trying to affect the conduct of research through the themes of *content*, *time*, and *people*, managers generally seek another type of influence, namely, maximising and securing a steady stream of income. This points to the possibility mentioned in the theory section that managers and researchers might have different priorities concerning the aspects of research that they see as important to exercise authority over.

First, managers attempt to boost their research income by pressuring researchers to obtain funding. In most cases, this pressure is something researchers feel is more implicit than explicit, being an indirect but still unequivocal expectation. However, in the Finnish case, setting targets for units in terms of getting external funding is an example of more explicit measures to increase the pressure to obtain external funding. In this case, but also in the Danish case, linking the success of getting funding to the merit system increases this pressure. This finding might be one of the explanations for why researchers, as shown in the survey data, experience tensions between managerial priorities and academic autonomy. Second, managers also try to increase external funding by setting up offices for research support, offering support for writing funding applications and so forth. Although this can be seen as a strategic choice, it can also be seen as the only choice in a more competitive environment where there are powerful isomorphic pressures (Dimaggio and Powell 1983) to do as other universities have done. Funding has become so important that managers will accept almost all kinds of funding, including funding with no overhead and demands for cofunding. Paradoxically, this is pointed out as problematic, especially in the Danish and Swedish cases, because it hampers the ability of managers to make strategic prioritisations and because internal funding is tied to these projects. The work of Mats Benner and

Gunnar Öquist (2012) partly explains the low level of breakthrough research in Sweden—which is defined as the percentage of articles within the world being in the top 10% most cited articles—with the high levels of external funding: 'The universities' own priorities are therefore overshadowed and emphasis is laid on how to obtain funding rather than which research priorities to select' (11). Although we offer some credence to the hypothesis that external funding hampers strategic priorities of managers, it is out of the scope of this chapter to assess whether this could be an explanation for lower performance. However, it does seem as though getting external funding has become so important that it has become a goal in and of itself. This finding is consistent with the well-known mechanism that certain activities become institutionalised and thereby infused with value beyond the technical requirements of the task at hand (e.g., of improving the quality of research in universities) (Selznick 1957).

Another theme that cuts across the themes of *content*, *time*, and *people* is the effects of external funding being concentrated in specific units or specific researchers, also known as the Matthew effect (Kwiek 2016; Langfeldt et al. 2015), which, in turn, affects the authority over research for both managers and researchers. As found in the Norwegian and Finnish cases, this seems to reinforce existing patterns: the talented and well-funded researchers receive even more funding. An example in the Norwegian case is how CoEs give authority to local centre leaders at the expense of other units (which also diminishes the authority of the upper management, hence weakening the organisational hierarchy). A similar effect is also seen in the Swedish case, where large infrastructure investments in one area affect other areas. However, in this case, as in the Danish case of very large external funding donations, the authority of the upper management seems strengthened because top managers in universities need to be involved in these huge donations. These examples of the concentration of resources mean that external funding also creates distinctions within the groups of managers, on the one hand, and among researchers, on the other hand. Furthermore, there are examples of external funding empowering either low-level managers (mostly project funding) or top-level managers (large donations). As others also have found (Kwiek 2016; Langfeldt et al. 2015), a layer of very well-funded researchers and research leaders—who are less dependent on being in the fields of strategic priority for the university—also seems to have been developed, along with a layer of less well-funded researchers who live a more precarious existence. Furthermore, when success in funding acquisition is also connected to career advancements, these divisions of 'winners and losers' become even more pronounced.

Conclusion

We will now return to our research question in which we asked how the increasing amount of external funding affects the authority over research for managers and researchers in Nordic universities.

When focusing on the managers, the first answer is that the external funding of research negatively affects their authority over research; they have very little authority over research within all three themes of *content*, *time*, and *people*. At least, though, their authority is indirect and confined to signalling through strategies and setting broad conditions for research that indirectly affect the research being carried out. Some managers, especially in Sweden, see this as problematic. However, there is another dimension to the authority over research, one where managers exert a stronger influence: the effort to maximise and secure a steady stream of income (a budget-maximisation logic). Although this could be seen as an 'authority dimension' that is two steps away from more substantial directing of research efforts, in terms of the strategic ambitions a manager might have for the type of research being conducted in his or her unit, it is seen by managers as an important avenue for authority over research. This view on what kind of 'authority dimension' to emphasise might also itself be a result of the increasing amount of external funding. When a substantial share of the funding available for research comes from external sources, managing this income becomes more important than the more substantial directing of research efforts.

To assess the consequences of more external funding on managerial authority, one also needs to consider how the counterfactual situation, in which more or all the resources were controlled by managers (external funding being converted to basic funding for universities), would look like. In this situation, managers would be better able to control the direction of research through hiring researchers who fit the local strategies for research. Therefore, in another funding reality, managers' views on what dimensions of research it is important to control might be a different one. The question of whether or not the authority over research for managers has declined, as Whitley and Gläser (2014) have hypothesised, then depends on how this authority is defined. However, the findings do indicate—which was certainly expected—that the authority of funders has increased.

Whether the authority of researchers over research has declined or increased as a consequence of the rise of external project funding is also hard to make any firm conclusions about. Although they do, as the survey results indicate, experience quite high general authority over research, a range of mechanisms related to funders and managers reduce this authority. Generally, funders are the most important source of influence over *content*, *time*, and *people*, and the role of managers seems mostly to be a pushing factor for the conditions set by the funders (by pushing for the acquisition of funding, for instance, by linking success to the merit system). However, especially in Finland, managers' influence is so forceful that researchers generally experience a decline in their authority over research. In all countries, the authority of researchers over research seems to vary between successful and less successful researchers. Those who are able to attract large grants generally hold much more authority over research and can create a type of local autonomy from managers. Those with less fortune live a more precarious existence. However, all researchers have at their disposal a range of 'defence mechanisms' that especially balances the authority of the funders.

Obviously, an important question arising from these findings is whether the appropriate balance between external funding and internal funding has been struck in each country. Regarding managers, the Danish, Finnish, and Norwegian results do not show the participants wishing for less external funding. Although they have expressed the troubles emphasised above, most think that competitive external funding is a necessary, basic condition, and they instead focus on the authority dimension related to boosting external funding, as mentioned above. In the case of researchers, most also do not wish for a smaller share of external funding (although the Danish case shows that the researchers in the natural sciences might think more internal funding is needed to have more lab assistance). Quite oppositely, in most cases, researchers think there is too *little* external funding in the sense that success rates, when applying for external project funding, are too low. That both managers and researchers do not wish for less external funding indicates how institutionalised the current funding allocation system has become. Here, the systemic power of reforms over the last decades has been successful in convincing both managers and researchers that competitive funding is a natural part of science. One explanation for this success could be that the competitive nature of the science system (in securing tenure and getting published) aligns well with increasing competitive funding. One can only speculate how another funding situation would affect the authority relations between managers and researchers. However, it is likely that less external funding would lead to less emphasis on the budget-maximisation logic, which is currently strong in the analysed countries—and probably also beyond.

Acknowledgements The data presented in the current volume and individual chapters emanate from a comparative study funded by the Norwegian Research Council under its FINNUT flagship program, a long-term program for research and innovation in the educational sector program. The project number was 237782, and the project was titled 'Does it matter? Assessing the performance effects of changes in leadership and management structures in Nordic Higher Education'.

REFERENCES

Aagaard, Kaare. 2012. Reformbølgen Tager Form. In *Dansk Forskningspolitik Efter Årtusindskiftet*, ed. Kaare Aagaard and Niels Mejlgaard, 37–58. Aarhus: Aarhus Universitetsforlag.

Aagaard, Kaare, and Tina Ravn. 2012. Forskningsrådssystemet: Tilføjelser Og Forskydninger. In *Dansk Forskningspolitik Efter Årtusindskiftet*, ed. Kaare Aagaard and Niels Mejlgaard, 159–194. Aarhus: Aarhus Universitetsforlag.

Akerlind, Gerlese, and Carole Kayrooz. 2003. Understanding Academic Freedom: The Views of Social Scientists. *Higher Education Research & Development* 22 (3): 327–344. https://doi.org/10.1080/758482627.

Altbach, Philip G. 2001. Academic Freedom: International Realities and Challenges. *Higher Education* 41 (1–2): 205–219. https://doi.org/10.1023/a:1026791518365.

Askling, Berit. 2012. *Expansion, Självständighet, Konkurrens. Vart Är Den Högre Utbildningen På Väg?* Göteborg: Göteborgs Universitet.

Benner, Mats, and Gunnar Öquist. 2012. *Fostering Breakthrough Research: A Comparative Study*. Stockholm: The Royal Swedish Academy of Sciences.

Brunsson, Nils, and Kerstin Sahlin-Andersson. 2000. Constructing Organizations: The Example of Public Sector Reform. *Organization Studies* 21 (4): 721–746. https://doi.org/10.1177/0170840600214003.

Clark, Burton R. 1979. The Many Pathways of Academic Coordination. *Higher Education* 8 (3): 251–267. https://doi.org/10.1007/BF00137211.

Clegg, Stewart. 1989. *Frameworks of Power*. London: SAGE Publications Ltd.

Dimaggio, Paul J., and Walter W. Powell. 1983. The Iron Cage Revisited: Institutional and Collective Rationality in Organizational Fields. *American Sociological Review* 48 (2): 147–160. https://doi.org/10.2307/2095101.

Ferlie, Ewan, Christine Musselin, and Gianluca Andresani. 2009. The Steering of Higher Education Systems: A Public Management Perspective. In *University Governance - Western European Comparative Perspectives*, ed. Catherine Paradeise, Emanuela Reale, Ivar Bleiklie, and Ewan Ferlie, 1–19. Dordrecht: Springer. https://doi.org/10.1007/sl0734-008-9125-5.

Geschwind, Lars, and Anders Broström. 2015. Managing the Teaching–Research Nexus: Ideals and Practice in Research-Oriented Universities. *Higher Education Research and Development* 34 (1): 60–73. https://doi.org/10.1080/072943 60.2014.934332.

Geschwind, Lars, and Rómulo M. Pinheiro. 2017. Raising the Summit or Flattening the Agora? The Elitist Turn in Science Policy in Northern Europe. *Journal of Baltic Studies* 48 (4): 513–528. https://doi.org/10.1080/016297 78.2017.1305178.

Gläser, Jochen. 2010. From Governance to Authority Relations? In *Reconfiguring Knowledge Production: Changing Authority Relationships in the Sciences and Their Consequences for Intellectual Innovation*, ed. Richard Whitley, Jochen Gläser, and Lars Engwall, 358–370. Oxford: Oxford University Press. https://doi.org/10.1093/acprof:oso/9780199590193.003.0012.

Krucken, George, and Frank Meier. 2006. Turning the University into an Organizational Actor. In *Globalisation and Organisation: World Society and Organisational Change*, ed. Gili S. Drori, John W. Meyer, and Hokyu Hwang, 241–257. Oxford: Oxford University Press. https://doi.org/10.1017/CBO9781107415324.004.

Kwiek, Marek. 2016. The European Research Elite: A Cross-National Study of Highly Productive Academics in 11 Countries. *Higher Education* 71 (1): 379–397. https://doi.org/10.1007/s10734-015-9910-x.

Langfeldt, Liv, Mats Benner, Gunnar Sivertsen, Ernst H. Kristiansen, Dag W. Aksnes, Siri Brorstad Borlaug, Hanne Foss Hansen, Egil Kallerud, and Antti Pelkonen. 2015. Excellence and Growth Dynamics: A Comparative Study of the Matthew Effect. *Science and Public Policy* 42 (5): 661–675. https://doi.org/10.1093/scipol/scu083.

Laudel, Grit. 2006. The Art of Getting Funded: How Scientists Adapt to Their Funding Conditions. *Science and Public Policy* 33 (7): 489–504. https://doi.org/10.3152/147154306781778777.

Lawrence, Thomas B. 2008. Power, Institutions and Organizations. In *The SAGE Handbook of Organizational Institutionalism*, ed. Royston Greenwood, Christine Oliver, Roy Suddaby, and Kerstin Sahlin, 170–197. London: SAGE Publications Ltd.

Lawrence, Thomas B., Namrata Malhotra, and Tim Morris. 2012. Episodic and Systemic Power in the Transformation of Professional Service Firms. *Journal of Management Studies* 49 (1): 102–143. https://doi.org/10.1111/j.1467-6486.2011.01031.x.

Merton, Robert. 1973. *The Sociology of Science: Theoretical and Empirical Investigations.* Chicago: The University of Chicago Press.

Neave, Guy. 1988. On Being Economical with University Autonomy: Being an Account of the Retrospective Joys of a Written Constitution. In *Academic Freedom and Responsibility*, ed. Malcolm Tight, 31–48. Buckingham: Open University Press.

Norwegian Ministry of Education. 2015. *Long-Term Plan for Research and Higher Education.* Report.

Olsen, Johan P. 2007. The Institutional Dynamics of the European University. In *University Dynamics and European Integration*, ed. Peter Maassen and Johan P. Olsen, 25–54. Dordrecht: Springer. https://doi.org/10.1007/978-1-4020-5971-1_2.

Paradeise, Catherine, Emanuela Reale, and Gaële Goastellec. 2009. A Comparative Approach to Higher Education Reforms in Western European Countries. In *University Governance: Western European Comparative Perspectives*, ed. Catherine Paradeise, Emanuela Reale, Ivar Bleiklie, and Ewan Ferlie, 197–225. Dordrecht: Springer Netherlands. https://doi.org/10.1007/978-1-4020-9515-3_9.

Pfeffer, Jeffrey, and Gerald R. Salancik. 1978. *The External Control of Organizations: A Resource Dependence Perspective.* New York: Harper and Row. https://doi.org/10.2307/2231527.

Seeber, Marco, Benedetto Lepori, Martina Montauti, Jürgen Enders, Harry de Boer, Elke Weyer, Ivar Bleiklie, et al. 2015. European Universities as Complete Organizations? Understanding Identity, Hierarchy and Rationality in Public Organizations. *Public Management Review* 17 (10): 1444–1474. https://doi.org/10.1080/14719037.2014.943268.

Selznick, Philip. 1957. *Leadership in Administration: A Sociological Interpretation.* New York: Harper & Row.

Whitley, Richard. 2011. Changing Governance and Authority Relations in the Public Sciences. *Minerva* 49 (4): 359–385. https://doi.org/10.1007/s11024-011-9182-2.

Whitley, Richard, and Jochen Gläser. 2014. The Impact of Institutional Reforms on the Nature of Universities as Organisations. In *Organizational Transformation and Scientific Change: The Impact of Institutional Restructuring on Universities and Intellectual Innovation*, ed. Richard Whitley and Jochen Gläser, 19–49. Bingley, UK: Emerald Group Publishing Limited. https://doi.org/10.1108/S0733-558X20140000042000.

Open Access This chapter is licensed under the terms of the Creative Commons Attribution 4.0 International License (http://creativecommons.org/licenses/by/4.0/), which permits use, sharing, adaptation, distribution and reproduction in any medium or format, as long as you give appropriate credit to the original author(s) and the source, provide a link to the Creative Commons licence and indicate if changes were made.

The images or other third party material in this chapter are included in the chapter's Creative Commons licence, unless indicated otherwise in a credit line to the material. If material is not included in the chapter's Creative Commons licence and your intended use is not permitted by statutory regulation or exceeds the permitted use, you will need to obtain permission directly from the copyright holder.

CHAPTER 6

The Changing Roles of Academic Leaders: Decision-Making, Power, and Performance

Lars Geschwind, Timo Aarrevaara, Laila Nordstrand Berg, and Jonas Krog Lind

INTRODUCTION

Most chapters in this book focus on specific aspects of organisational life, governance, and management and thus follow the famous recommendation by sociologist Howard S. Becker, to study activities rather than people

---

L. Geschwind (✉)
School of Industrial Engineering and Management, KTH Royal Institute of Technology, Stockholm, Sweden
e-mail: larsges@kth.se

T. Aarrevaara
Faculty of Social Sciences, University of Lapland, Rovaniemi, Finland
e-mail: timo.aarrevaara@ulapland.fi

L. N. Berg
Department of Social Science, Western Norway University of Applied Sciences, Sogndal, Norway
e-mail: laila.nordstrand.berg@hvl.no

J. K. Lind
Department of Political Science, University of Copenhagen, Copenhagen, Denmark
e-mail: jkl@ifs.ku.dk

© The Author(s) 2019
R. Pinheiro et al. (eds.), *Reforms, Organizational Change and Performance in Higher Education*,
https://doi.org/10.1007/978-3-030-11738-2_6

(Becker 2008). The contribution of this chapter, though, is to complement the other themes in the book by focusing on academic leaders in relation to these activities. Following the lines of New Public Management (NPM; Pollitt and Bouckaert 2011), there is now high pressure for there to be strategic action (Thoenig and Paradeise 2016), accountability, and performance in academia. With more formal autonomy, higher education institutions (HEIs) have become strategic actors competing for reputation and resources in a global market (Krücken and Meier 2006). This development has also put more focus on academic management and leadership (Paradeise et al. 2009), and extensive earlier research has shown that the power, responsibilities, as well as expectations of leaders have increased in the last decades. This has been described as a 'managerial revolution' (Amaral et al. 2003) or a 'managerial turn' (Krücken et al. 2013).

But what do we actually mean when we talk about academic leadership? Much of the earlier research has focused on formal leaders and their personal traits, experiences, and qualifications: vice-chancellors (Goodall 2009), deans, and middle managers such as heads of department (Meek et al. 2010). Traditionally, disciplinary-based departments were chaired by the leading professor (or one of the leading professors; (Pechar 2010). This model has now, in many HEIs, been replaced by professional managers who are not primarily in these positions based on their academic credentials but rather based on their management skills and experiences. There has also been a transition from the classic rotating system—where the members of the 'community of scholars' (Nybom 2007) took turns in office, elected by their colleagues—to organisations with line management—where managers, from the unit level to deans and vice-chancellors, are appointed (Haake 2004). This has transformed how we think about academic leadership in a fundamental way (Degn 2018).

Furthermore, there are also a number of other positions without line management responsibilities but potentially have great influence on everyday academics' lives, including but not limited to directors of studies, programme directors, and research leaders. Evermore structured education programmes with demands on coherence, progression, and constructive alignment have proliferated in the last decade, not least since the implementation of the Bologna Process (Witte 2006). Programme directors have become key individuals in this development with large responsibilities for staff, students, and quality in the provided courses. On the research side, we have experienced a development towards bigger programmes, centres, platforms, and other initiatives that require leadership and management skills (Hansson and Mønsted 2008). In both education and research, external stakeholders also play important roles whilst holding universities accountable for their actions (Benneworth and Jongbloed 2010). Last but not least, new professional support staff have been hired in order to tackle all the demands of and opportunities from the university management and from external stakeholders (Karlsson and Ryttberg 2016). This complexity in terms of responsibilities, reporting, accountability, power relations, and line management has become part and parcel of academic life. These complexities seem to have been strengthened in many countries due to NPM, and with many other leadership roles that have emerged as well. In the PERFACAD project, all these leadership roles have been discussed and recognised.

In this chapter, we study to what extent higher education reforms over the last decades have changed academic leadership. The following main research question is asked: how can the roles of academic leaders be understood in the light of recent reforms? Our analysis is based on classic aspects of management and leadership, all reflected in the themes of the rest of the volume: notions of power and responsibilities, strategy formulation and follow-ups, and the evaluation and assessment of performance. Before turning to our findings, we discuss our key concepts.

ACADEMIC LEADERS BETWEEN PROFESSIONALISM AND MANAGERIALISM

The dominant critique paving the way for NPM reforms stressed the idea that equity, freedom of choice, and the ability to prioritise in the interest of society instead of one's own individual interests, to produce expected results and to accept external control, were not met through professional bureaucracies in universities (Carvalho and Santiago 2016). Following this criticism, the assumption was that collegial and professional bureaucratic structures should be replaced by new types of decision-making structures to make public organisations more flexible. By altering these sectors through reforms, universities were expected to become 'complete' organisations through decentralisation, delegated autonomy, and the unification of structures and decision-making channels (Krücken and Meier 2006). Consequently, one core aspect of NPM is managerialism, or 'new' managerialism (Deem and Brehony 2005), emphasising the management of public sector organisations through rational structures, standardised procedures, and clearly defined responsibility and accountability.

Earlier research has shown how practices from the private sector have challenged and transformed the public sector (Flynn 2002). In studies of the higher education sector, this development has been contrasted with professional, collegial ideas of leadership (Deem 1998). Lately, a growing discussion on 'leaderism' has developed, described by O'Reilly and Reed (2010, 960) as 'the belief that many core aspects of social life can and should be co-ordinated by one or more individuals who give direction and/or purpose to social activity conducted by themselves and others'. There are indeed differences between managerialism and leadership related to the concepts of 'management' and 'leadership', respectively, where the latter is more positively connoted, but it is common for these NPM-related trends to place an increased emphasis on individuals in management positions. This has also fuelled critical management studies, questioning ideas of a 'strong leader' with masculine features (Alvesson and Spicer 2012). A recent example of this research is an article by Ekman and colleagues who have shown how managerialism and leaderism discourses have played out in Swedish state inquiries on higher education. The state committees have continuously questioned the current status of academic leadership, and there are frequent calls for stronger leadership and more managerial power in a deregulated higher education sector (Ekman et al. 2017).

A way to explore the different connotations of academic leadership is to apply the approach of institutional logics with a focus on the symbols and practices that guide actions in organisations (Thornton et al. 2012). Such practices and symbols are institutionalised and taken for granted. Different logics can work side by side in an organisation and bind the work of different professionals together, yet logics are often conflicting and competitive (Greenwood et al. 2011). The traditional logic in the university sector has been professional logic based on collegiality. Professional logic is rooted in the platform of knowledge acquired from education and training in the actual profession or academia (Abbott 1988). The work of professionals relies on discretion, trust, autonomy, and collegiality, and decision-making is consensus-oriented, collegial, and bottom-up. The criteria of selection are based on professional skills, and the best amongst peers are selected (Sahlin and Eriksson-Zetterquist 2016). Different types of professionals advocate distinct ideas on how to practice management (Abbott 1988; Freidson 1994). There is a strong focus on preserving the interests of the profession that cohere with the priorities, identities, and values of the professional group.

As a means to change the perceived ineffectiveness of this professional logic, 'managerialism', inspired by market logic, was introduced by NPM-inspired reforms, and the idea was to strengthen the managerial role. A role is viewed as an external attribute and is linked to social positions within the social structure, and there is an expectation that the role will influence the identity of the academics. The identity is viewed as internal, consisting of 'internalized meanings and expectations associated with a role' (Stryker and Burke 2000, 289). The strengthening of the managerial role is done by altering managerial structures and by introducing new institutional logics with more focus on efficiency, budgetary discipline, and cost reduction. Following this, there is more attention on the management of resources and performance, and therefore different types of controlling systems as assessment, metrics, and management by objectives have been introduced (Christensen and Lægreid 2011; Pollitt and Bouckaert 2011; Flynn 2002).

In this new role, there is an emphasis on the division of labour and hierarchical relations (Rost 1993). Rational planning and the distribution of tasks from the leader to the follower are seen as crucial processes (O'Reilly and Reed 2010, 2012). The manager is loyal to the organisational objectives and has to be able to develop new strategies accordingly as well as adapt to changes in the environment. Managerialism is system-oriented in the sense that the managers try to influence the followers by formalised controlling systems (Ladegård and Vabo 2010). Decision-making is top-down with an emphasis on hierarchy and line management. Managers show loyalty and identify with the organisation. Increased accountability is one of the solutions to achieve improvements (Christensen and Lægreid 2011; Pollitt and Bouckaert 2011) along with a strengthening of the managerial role. Technologies, such as metrics and assessments, that discipline the behaviour of actors, are also a means to direct the organisational attention and focus (Cantwell and Taylor 2013). This could be done by translating the institutional strategy into a set of goals reflected in performance measures that make success (but also failure) more concrete for everyone (Melnyk et al. 2004). In this way of managing, the aim is to shift focus from input and bureaucratic rules and procedures to the output through goal-setting and the use of performance information (Hvidman and Andersen 2013; Christensen et al. 2007). Performance-based funding is believed to incentivise institutions (and individuals) to improve or maintain their level of performance in exchange for higher revenue (Dougherty and Reddy 2011).

Based on the discussion earlier, we analyse cases in relation to how perceptions of the managerial logics co-exist with, complement, or come into conflict with the professional logic. The consequences of university reforms, made with the aim to make universities in these four countries more 'manageable' or 'well managed', will then hopefully come to the fore.

Method

The chapter is primarily based on qualitative data in the form of semi-structured interviews and quantitative survey data from Denmark, Finland, Norway, and Sweden (a more detailed description of the methodology and data is found in Chap. 1). The interviews and the survey included the following themes:

- Goal specificity and the degree of autonomy
- Decision-making and strategy
- Control and evaluation
- Support structures
- External stakeholders
- Trust/accountability
- Incentives/recognition (career, HR, dialogue, etc.)

These broad themes were addressed in all interviews (total number 93) with academic staff, administrators, and managers. The themes were also useful concepts for analysing the data using the NVivo software. The interviews included at the top level, senior leaders from central university management; from the mid-level, deans, or their equivalent; and lastly, at the academic level, units, departments, groups, or programmes. The interviews were undertaken at two universities in the respective countries, one of which is referred to as the 'flagship university' and the other as the 'regional university'.

The Role of Managers: Decision-Making, Power, and Performance

National Reforms and Systems

We start with a short description of the current systems and regulations in the four respective countries. In Denmark, the reform introduced in 2003 led to dramatic changes. Following earlier attempts at strengthening the management at universities, the government finally gained support for radical changes that effectively abolished the collegial governance model. The aim was to make universities more competitive, among other things, by strengthening the power of managers at various levels. The reform had two key elements: the first was the establishment of a board of directors with an external majority and where the chairman also had to be from outside the universities. The second was replacing the former elected managers with appointed ones. This introduced a line management model, where the board hired the vice chancellor, the vice chancellor hired the deans, and the deans hired the head of departments (Degn and Sørensen 2015).

In the early 2000s, there was an increased autonomy implemented in Finland by the performance agreements between the universities and the Ministry of Education. These agreements also emphasised efficiency, effectiveness, and performance management. By 2006, university-steering reforms were implemented with defined performance-management systems using data from national university databases and financial statements. These steering instruments increased the need for internal university performance management. The Finnish universities of the 2010s have a strong administrative and financial autonomy. The level of institutional autonomy has become more complicated with more focus on external funding, institutional profiling, and less collegiality in university governance. This has strengthened the role of line managers in performance-management issues. At the same time, lower-level leader roles maintain strong in setting academic priorities (Aarrevaara et al. 2011). However, their role in these universities is not strong in performance management, as academic units, such as research groups and educational programmes, are not performance units. This role is reserved for appointed middle managers at the faculty level.

A central reform regarding the governance of the Norwegian higher education sector was introduced in 2003 (St meld nr 27 2000–2001). The aim of this reform was to increase university autonomy (Stensaker 2014) but also to increase the capacity to react to external changes by centralising and speeding up decision-making (Torjesen et al. 2017). As for leadership, the universities were allowed full autonomy in how to organise and govern at the level below the rector/board, and two leadership models could be chosen (Stensaker 2014). The 'standard model', with a vice-chancellor elected by the staff, could continue, but now it would be supplemented by an appointed director responsible for administrative matters in a dual leadership model (Gornitzka and Larsen 2004). In this model, the vice-chancellor was the chair of the board. A model referred to as the unitary leadership model (Berg and Pinheiro 2016) was also offered as an alternative model (this was preferred by the government). In this model, the vice-chancellor was appointed by the board for a certain period and had the full responsibility for both academic and administrative matters, and the law did not demand an administrative director in this model. The appointed vice-chancellor could not be the chair of the board, but an external member of the board would be appointed by the Ministry of Education for that role. The board would consist of 11 members: four elected by academic staff, one elected by administrative staff, two elected by students, and the remaining four appointed by the Ministry of Education. The autonomy in choice of leadership structures has resulted in a hybrid system within many institutions, as there might be both elected and appointed leaders—still most vice-chancellors are elected (Stensaker 2014).

An important reform in Swedish higher education is the so-called Freedom Reform from 1993, which increased the formal autonomy of HEIs in a fundamental way. A new funding system was introduced based on the admission of students (input) and graduation (output), and university managers were also made more autonomous in issues regarding the hiring of academic staff and which programmes to provide. The increased freedom for HEIs was accompanied by a national evaluation system developed during the 1990s. Strong academic leadership was requested, and the ultimate role of the vice-chancellor as the institutional leader was emphasised. The government strengthened academic individual leadership by explicitly pointing to the vice-chancellor as the institutional leader, and, without directly arguing against the traditional collegiate model, the government expected a more corporate management-like style of internal governance (Askling et al. 1999). The idea with external stakeholders in the university boards has a long history in Sweden, emanating from the great higher education reform in 1977. In 1997, it was decided that there should be an external person acting as chair rather than vice-chancellor (Benner and Geschwind 2016).

The next reform affecting leadership and management specifically was the so-called Autonomy Reform introduced in 2011. One of the main novelties introduced was the increased freedom to create academic positions and career tracks, apart from senior lecturer and professors, whose positions remained centrally regulated. Also, the governance and steering regulations changed. Collegial bodies like the faculty board were deregulated and made non-mandatory. As a consequence, many HEIs have made collegial bodies advisory rather than decision-making organisations. As in Norway, the reforms have not been compulsive and mandatory, which means there is significant variety in terms of, for instance, appointed or elected leaders and recruitment patterns. An overall pattern is that the older HEIs harness the collegiality and traditional primus inter pares model, but there is variation also within universities (Engwall 2014).

Results from the Survey

In the survey, we asked managers a general question regarding decision-making power in relation to four themes: budgetary matters, staff recruitment, strategies, and performance indicators. The results are summarised in Table 6.1.

Question: Does your current position include decision-making in the areas stated below?

As we see from the table, strategy is the area in which managers' decision-making power seems most prevalent, with Sweden on top with as much as 88% of managers responding positively. In some categories, there are significant differences across countries, most notably for budgetary

Table 6.1 Managers' decision-making power represented as the percentage who responded with a 4 or 5 on a 5-point Likert scale

	Budgetary matters	*Staff recruitment*	*Strategies*	*Performance indicators*
Denmark	48	50	78	61
Finland	66	69	79	69
Norway	47	57	84	58
Sweden	76	71	88	62

matters, where three-thirds of the Swedish managers and two-thirds of the Finnish managers report having decision-making power, whereas not even half of the managers in Denmark (48) and Norway agree or strongly agree that they have decision-making power. Also, regarding staff recruitment, the differences are remarkable: only half of the Danish respondents indicated a 4 or 5 on the 5-point scale, whereas in Finland (69) and Sweden (71), this was more common. Generally, a comparison across the four countries shows that the Danish managers responded that they have little power in these categories. In contrast, Swedish managers' responses included the options 'agree' or 'strongly agree' to a much higher degree.

Results from the Interviews

Denmark

It was a general experience among the Danish interviewees that the hierarchical steering from roles such as vice-chancellors and department heads has been strengthened significantly. Reflecting on the difference from the old system before the 2003 reform, one top manager said, 'One of the negative aspects of the old system was that it was hard to do strategic initiatives on the university level. Actually, almost impossible' (Flagship, manager, DK). This has proven to be easier after the reform, especially in terms of being able to attract extremely large private donations, which was only possible with central institutional support. The hierarchical model of steering is felt all the way down at the bottom level, where there is a concern about the lack of employee influence on decisions. However, at this level, collegiality is also still alive. As one academic said:

> Well, everybody in these systems [universities] has this knowledge that, if we [the academic staff] won't bother, then nothing will happen [...]. That is, we need to feel up for it. We will accept being pressured and many other things, but if there is something we really don't want, then nothing is going to happen. (Flagship, academic, DK)

However, the degree of real hierarchical steering is quite different between universities. In the regional university, the hierarchical model seems very ingrained and (sometimes reluctantly) accepted. However, in the flagship university, some of the collegial culture seems to have survived (as the quote above indicates). It is harder to get things done if there is opposition from below (be it subordinate managers or academics) and decisions, once taken, are also easier to revisit and change.

Managers have quite strong authority over resources and budgetary matters, at least on paper. General university funds can be spent rather freely. However, most of these funds are invested in the salaries of steadily employed professors, making a change in priority somewhat difficult. In addition, there is the growing amount of external funding. Managers have very little means of influencing research based on external funding, which means that directing through external funding is very much delegated to the academics themselves, who decide what they want to apply for funding for, and to funding agencies and other funders, who make decisions on funding based on own criteria (see Chap. 5 in this volume). Finally, performance-based funding systems also pressure managers in budgetary matters since these models pressure managers into following the national model internally—to some degree at least (see Chap. 4 in this volume). These conditions could be part of the explanation for why the Danish managers scored low in the survey, compared to the other countries, on decision-making power over budgetary matters. This means that one of the most effective ways of steering performance is by hiring and firing.

Although there are assessment and hiring committees involved in the process, managers generally feel that they have substantial influence on who is hired. This is the way managers can most easily enact the strategy for research they have for the department—not by steering research directly. As one line manager put it:

> Well, I cannot control what people want to do research on. And you should not. People need to be engaged in what they do. If they do not, forget it. But I do get some [researchers] who knock on the door and say: Could you hire me? I would like to go to [the regional university]. And then I will look at their research profile. So, we have actually gotten, I guess, 3–4 people in this way. Because they are strong researchers, and they have a research profile that I can see fits. (Regional, manager, DK)

Hence, hiring is one of the most important instruments for managers who want to manage performance. It is more mixed when it comes to firing. In one department, at the regional university, management fired several people who were not performing well on research (this was phrased as 'cleaning up'). Here, firing was seen as an effective performance management tool. In the flagship university, this was more unusual. Hiring new staff was most often only possible when someone resigned or if there was new funding—not by firing.

As the survey results suggest, managers feel they have quite substantial decision-making power over strategies. Managers generally feel that strategies are important. They spend considerable time on planning the processes for shaping strategies. Sometimes they are quite top-down, at other times they are organised to involve a range of internal and external stakeholders. Lower-level managers generally do not feel too restricted by upper-level strategies. A typical quote on the question of the coupling between strategies was 'They are coupled [everybody laughs]. They [the strategies] are not integrated, yet they are not completely free-floating in the sense that I have looked at the faculty strategy' (Flagship, manager, DK). As a managerial tool, though, most researchers do not find that the strategies mattered much for work 'on the ground'. Here, performance-management instruments, like performance indicators, are much more important.

Managing performance is practised by all managers to some degree. It does, however, depend on local conditions if the management is mostly 'soft' (i.e., no or small incentives, hiring new personnel only when natural vacancies occur, managing by employer development conversations, etc.) or 'hard' (i.e., firing researchers who do not perform, using bibliometric research indicator [BRI] metrics as a goal-setting tool, giving bonuses for publications, etc.). Managers were given a new performance management tool when the BRI was introduced in 2010. Although it only distributed a small fraction of total funding for research, management at the regional university viewed it as a powerful tool for improving the research performance of the university. Managers used it as a tool by demanding that researchers within a two-year period scored points on the BRI scale (which means publishing in at least one of the journals on an authorised list). Hence, introducing the indicator in the budget model had a very disciplining effect all the way down to the researcher level (although mostly in the social sciences faculty). However, at the flagship university, the BRI was not used as extensively as a performance-management tool, and when it was used, researchers did not see it as very disciplining. Instead, managers use mandatory employee development conversations (which are also mandatory in other public sector workplaces) to talk about goals, achievements, and so on. But these mostly feel like conversations to help the individual progress, and less like a method for controlling the performance of individuals. These are also used at the regional university. Monetary incentives were not used in any of the departments among our cases. However, there are departments in Denmark that have linked BRI publication directly to bonuses. Although we do not know the full extent of this practice, it is not merely a curiosity (Opstrup 2014).

Finland
In the two case universities analysed in this chapter, academic leaders are still most often selected internally, although some recruitment of academic leaders from other universities has also occurred. The expectations for academic leaders are still collegial, although practices of performance management have strengthened the status of leaders since the University Act of 2010:

> At this moment, the power system is still the same in that our department head is really far from us. This is a large social institution, I do not even assume that the department head will know about the work of 300 staff, or by no means can you expect to get congratulations when you get on a rampage. (Flagship, academic, FI)

> [The academic] leaders have to work more than before, and leadership work has probably tripled over the last ten years. I've been here almost ten years in this job, so I've seen the entire chain. (Regional, academic, FI)

> We used to have about 200 academic leaders in this university, and now the number is less than 30—of course, this group has become smaller and each one has had more power than in the previous time. (Flagship, academic leader, FI)

> The management thinking is different from what it used to be, very different from the traditional academic leader. This is also reflected in the reform of university regulations, and more power is concentrated in a particular leader. (Flagship, academic leader, FI)

Tools for strengthening this position have also come from other reforms, such as the salary system reform, which has provided managers with performance-management tools. However, managers with performance-management tools only exist at the faculty level and at the institutional level since academic leaders lack these tools at the academic level of research groups or educational programmes. This means that performance management and the responsibility for achieving results are to be found at the top level. At the academic level, in turn, it is quite hard for academics to define how they are evaluated in terms of performance management and how they can influence work conditions. Managerialism in the 2010s seems to mean more centralised management systems, and that the division of labour between academics with performance-management tools is not successful:

> Of course, we, as researchers, are hoping for different performance evaluations to better know how to allocate resources, but it is a bit of a slight step forward with a little impact. (Flagship, academic leader, FI)

Academic leaders at the two Finnish universities have a dualistic attitude towards performance management. Some interviewed leaders see the tools as clearly supportive of work and as valuable tools to enhance transparency. Performance management was also seen in some of the interviews as an essential tool to combine institutional-level strategy and academic activities: 'Performance is a realisation of a strategy' (Regional, academic leader, FI). For the leaders of the academic units, however, there is a lack of performance-management incentives for the unit-level functions comparing to the mid- or top levels. In the academic units, incentives are often directed at individuals, and decisions are confirmed at institutional levels. This has changed the nature of academic leaders' work:

> Units are not rewarded, and our reward is that we are doing a good job, and we still have a prospect on the balance sheet. But individuals are rewarded. (Flagship, academic leader, FI)

A change seems to have taken place in the 2010s in Finnish universities as the institutional-level indicators have begun to direct work in academic units. These indicators are not chosen by academics, but leaders play a key role in tracking indicators. The indicators monitor the conversion of results, above all in terms of education and research. Tracking is focused on the results of the work, such as qualifications, the accumulation of credits, and manager discussions on these factors. Similarly, research is an indicator of performance, and, in particular, performance is measured by the number of publications according to the national publication forum. When there is a lack of performance-management tools, key indicators are of great importance. In this chapter, indicators are found first of all as management tools, but they can also be valuable for the academic staff to define the content of work. The indicators do not cover all dimensions of work, as indicated in following quotes:

> In my opinion, there are clear indicators for degrees and graduates, and in my own work, I think first of all about the quality of the research. (Flagship, academic leader, FI)

> For me, effectiveness is things like that, that I'm pretty moderate and waiting for if all this work, and I wait to see if all this work will be done, and I always say yes to all interview requests and lectures. I have never refused. That is probably part of performance. (Flagship, academic, FI)

While there is a lot of criticism for the performance indicators, the interviewees also stressed the indicators' benefits in academic work. This is reflected in how academics determine performance and how they describe their relationship with the indicators. Some of the interviewees considered a very positive starting point to be measuring performance by when their work becomes visible and can be compared to other academic units. This starting point is reflected in two quotations, which also describe the interviewees' estimates of the most valuable indicators:

> I always found [that performance is] performing as well as possible as well as possible all the tasks you received, and sometimes [you] fail, and sometimes [you] succeed, but the goal is to produce according to your promises. (Flagship, academic leader, FI)

> The result [of performance] is scientific publishing and competitive international research. (Flagship, academic, FI)

Norway
The managerial role has been strengthened over the last few years in the Norwegian HEIs hierarchically, not least by the use of strategies and action plans. Still, it seems like the role of the head of a department has been weakened (hence the term 'facilitator'). This could be tied to the fact that this role is seldom attractive for senior professors, and attending professors often see this as their duty for a few years. The role is thereby often undertaken by junior academics with a temporary contract and as a part-time job. The department head position works as a stepping stone into academia for juniors who do not have the same legitimacy as a professor.

Findings from the Norwegian part of the survey shows that only around one-third of the managers have a high degree of influence over budgetary matters, staff recruitment, and performance indicators. It seems like they have the most influence over strategies, as more than half of the managers reported this. Many findings from the interviews also revolve around the development of strategies, and it seems like this is an important tool for the managers. One expressed:

> The strategies have a four- to six-year range and are operationalised into yearly action plans within the hierarchical units. These strategies seem to have gained increased importance the last years and are a tool for the daily work of managers. (Flagship, administrator, NO)

There is a general trend that suggestions for overall strategies at the universities are developed by the vice-chancellor, who is thereafter open for hearings and the broad involvement of all employees. The chosen strategy is expected to be reflected in the strategies within the hierarchy. At the faculty level, the process to develop strategies seems to be the same, while at the levels of departments, there are more variations. Some leaders use the same approach—to shield the academics from administrative tasks—while others use a more democratic and collegial approach and collect input at an early stage of strategy development.

The agenda setting in strategies relates both to signals in steering documents from the Ministry of Education and from initiatives within the universities:

> We had strategies earlier also, but they were often put on the backburner[...] Now, it is expected that we use the strategy. When we make action plans for next year, there is an expectation from the Ministry of Education, which permeates the action plans within the university. But, we consider these according to our strategic goals, and we try to make it as adherent as possible. (Flagship, manager, NO)

The strategies seem to be used as an overall framework for academic work, but leaders across levels do not severely interfere with the work of individual academics. A department manager described the leadership role as minimal and more like a facilitator:

> The influence from the managerial role is tiny—management is totally overrated. My task is more like a facilitator. That means, first of all, to protect the

academics from all kinds of administrative bull and nonsense and reporting issues, to structure teaching, research. (Regional, manager, NO)

The leaders also had low impact on the content of the teaching curriculum, as this had to be aligned with a programme. Still, the individual academic has the freedom to influence curriculum and teaching methods. Managers and academics from the social sciences were critical towards new managerial tools regarding teaching quality, and they expressed their frustration from dealing with such systems:

> You have this definition of quality that is cut out of New Public Management ... student satisfaction, primary applicants. Things like that, it isn't about quality at all! It is all about the labour market ... blah, blah, blah. (Flagship, manager, NO)

Managers do not interfere with the research of the individual academics, who have considerable freedom to choose whether they want to apply for internal or external funding in addition to the amount of research time they have available in their position. Still, the close ties between strategies and funding seem to be an organising principle that steers the focus of the academics too, as one manager illustrates: 'The researchers are opportunistic, so when the money and incentives are tied in one direction, the researchers head that way' (Regional, manager, NO). Another leader discussed academic freedom and the risk for dilution as the professional work has to adjust to plans and strategies but also pointed to the advantages that follow: 'At the same time, I can see that those who actually chose to fit into the profile are getting a boost, so it seems like there are two answers out there' (Flagship, manager, NO).

A manager from the administrative hierarchy pointed to the tension of logics between academics and the administrators. One example was a professor who had not filled up the classroom and had room for more students, and the administrators who wanted to follow the procedures of admittance: 'They do not quite understand why we are doing things this way' (Flagship, administrator, NO). Conflicting demands not only came from within the institutions but also from external stakeholders regarding content in research, financial issues, and, particularly, ownership of the product: 'There are still discussions in each project agreement regarding the ownership of rights and what time you are allowed to start publishing.

The postponement of publications is always up for discussion' (Regional, manager, NO).

Strategies are also used to guide the recruitment of new employees. A manager told how they use their discretion to strengthen areas important for them: 'As to be expected, recruitment must be done according to the strategies. And this means that we are trying to enhance our strengths or areas we find worthy to continue' (Regional, manager, NO).

Performance indicators have become an important tool to assess performance within the universities and to follow up with managers. Yet, performance indicators are still employed to a low degree at the individual level in assessing academics. Annual appraisal meetings between the leader and the employees were used to follow up on progress in their work and plans for the year to come, and most professors in managerial positions implement such meetings. Some of the departments were publishing publication points at an individual level, while others just kept track at the unit level. The metrics were not used to punish academics with low publication rates, and so on, but discussing this was a theme in the annual meetings. Such metrics were sometimes connected to an incentive system, where extra funding could follow from finalising master or PhD students or popular science disseminations. The extra funding could, for example, be used for sabbaticals or going to conferences. The Norwegian managers were careful not to use the data in an offending way, particularly towards academics with few publications. Instead, they use the information from the metrics to map what to facilitate for a higher level of publication from those who needed help or a push:

> We can see that there are things we can facilitate, and we have been able to make people publish who have not done that before. But of course, people are different. Some of them are publishing regularly, while others are like a bottle of ketchup: They have a project and nothing and nothing and nothing is coming, and then suddenly it is flushing out. And we have a couple who are at the point of not getting a sabbatical, and then they just need a small push. (Regional, manager, NO)

Sweden

More than half of the managers in Sweden noted in the survey that their current position includes a high degree of decision-making powers about strategies, budgetary matters, and staff recruitment (Table 6.1). Their power to make decisions about performance indicators is a bit more limited. As in Norway, strategy is the area over which the managers seem to have most influence, where 88% of the managers claimed to have a degree of decision-making power 4 or 5 on a Likert scale.

More generally, it is noticeable from interviews that it is important who is in charge. Many interviewees, at both universities, discussed changes that occurred when a new vice-chancellor took office. It seems like the vice-chancellor has become increasingly important, and that employees notice large differences between vice-chancellors, although it is not really clear what the effect will be on the everyday operations of the academics:

> Every time there is a new vice-chancellor, there is kind of a new agenda. [...] And, in particular, in a smaller place, it is more obvious than at a big university. (Regional, manager, SE)

Reflecting upon the role of the vice-chancellor, one interviewee stressed the power the position now is characterised by:

> Well, [there are] those who think the leader is unimportant because [they are] pinioned and only a pencil pusher; no, a vice-chancellor has a lot of formal and informal power. And if the vice-chancellor wants to use that formal or informal power and the power over money, a lot can be influenced in the current system. (Flagship, manager, SE)

More emphasis on management and an increased focus on management roles were also more generally discussed in the interviews. Ever higher demands require designated management skills in the higher education sector. The pool of potential recruits needs to be as big as possible since the role has become so challenging and demanding, in particular, due to the trend towards bigger multidisciplinary departments:

> But, I think we work a lot with leader development. I am curious about leadership. It is so important when we have big departments to get the right people as well. Because they affect employees, and one should engage people, so I think there should be more focus on those issues. (Regional, manager, SE)

As for budgetary matters, it has become increasingly common that the vice-chancellor sets aside strategic funds in education and research. This money could be used for strategic recruitments or research programmes, for instance. This is usually done in close dialogue with deans and faculty:

> And then the vice-chancellor has strategic funds in education and research, and faculties know that money is not supposed to pile up but rather be used for strategic efforts jointly agreed. These are usually a professor programme, more female professors, more post docs etc. (Regional, academic, SE)

Some of the interviewed managers also thought they needed more discretion over decision-making and resources:

> In regard to research, we would want discretion over money, so to say. When I say 'we', I mean the management, not necessarily university management, but also faculty or department management, someone who can steer funding, so to say. (Flagship, manager, SE)

The tension between line managers and research leaders also came to the fore in the interviews. One department head discussed how power over money is crucial for everyday business:

> Because, if you look at research, it is rather those who are referred to as research leaders who have the greatest influence; i.e., the professors and disciplinary leaders who have the possibility to steer. What I can do is a kind of steering by management, steering by money. To steer what I decide to fund. Now, the research budget is not exactly expanding and gigantic but rather very scarce, and most of it is locked in fixed expenditures like doctoral students and supervision. Mostly that. So, the means with which I can steer is not particularly much. Having said that, I can also govern indirectly because we discuss this a lot in the Head of Department group together with the dean. [...] So, I can't steer by making orders, but I am around, that's how I would put it. (Regional, manager, SE)

One senior manager referred to the then-recently presented Leadership Inquiry (SOU 2015: 92), proposing more power to managers and stronger universities:

> I think a lot is in line with what's written in the Leadership Inquiry, that academic leadership needs to be strengthened. You need management who dares to make decisions, prioritise decisions and so. And it has been a bit problematic sometimes because of the character of these assignments. They are fixed term, and perhaps you have an academic position as a base, which

makes it difficult to make hard decisions and so on. But it feels like it increasingly resembles the private sector. [It] goes in that direction, that one dares make tough decisions and prioritise. And you also have to—well, it is really important with leadership, it affects so much. It affects the work environment; it affects many issues. (Regional, manager, SE)

The same interviewee also discussed the complex character of academic leadership, in comparison to other kinds of organisations:

You can't run things like that in a university. You might do that in a private company, what do I know. Because, I mean, you have pretty simple goals in a private company. They are a bit more complicated in a university. (Flagship, manager, SE)

In particular, at the flagship university, a collegial way of leadership was referred to:

And the current management is very much into [the idea] that this is a collegial issue, everything needs to be anchored in academic leadership, and we have a particular body, which is, in a way, the core in these decisions, the strategic decisions. And that is the vice-chancellor's leadership council, comprising the vice-chancellor, the pro vice-chancellors and so on, and all the deans. (Flagship, manager, SE)

The more general discussion about the allocation of funding above is also closely related to performance when it comes to deliveries. Again, one of the interviewed managers thought that current managers were not tough enough:

OK, we have all the others making priorities for us, research councils and others, but we cannot escape from the fact that we ourselves set priorities. But then, we also need to be a bit tough, to dare to say that this type of activity is not good enough because nothing has been produced. And that is related to performance: you haven't published anything, you haven't done anything in two years, now this will be closed down. And I think we need to improve regarding this. We haven't been particularly good at that historically. (Regional, manager, SE)

What roles do managers play when it comes to following up on individual performances? Swedish universities, as state agencies, are supposed to undertake annual review dialogues with all employees. One of the managers reflected upon the character of those dialogues:

> Well, I do have those dialogues at my department, and it is more or less [the case] that individual goals are followed up, if they have reached the goals. And that can be everything from becoming a docent or writing three articles or that my two doctoral students should finish or [that] I get funding for this exciting project. So, yes, there is absolutely a follow-up like that, but it never leaves those two people. (Flagship, manager, SE)

An important issue is whether performance is related to consequences. Are high performers rewarded and low performers punished? Interestingly, salary development does not seem to be related at all to performance:

> So, I wouldn't say that salaries are based on performance. Deciding salaries is a complicated matter as such. (Flagship, manager, SE)

> Well, we don't assess performance directly, that is, publications, if you have done this or that. We don't do that at that level. (Flagship, manager, SE)

There are discussions at both universities whether, for instance, bibliometric measures should affect salaries. According to one interviewee, this is primarily advocated by those who can show good bibliometric data for themselves. However, it is also mentioned that too much of a focus on publications could have a negative effect on other parts of academic work: 'We cannot have a workplace where everybody sits at home and splashes out papers, but no one is in the office. [...] From my perspective, it is very important to have people who can collaborate, but we don't measure that'. (Flagship, manager, SE) Performance is therefore a broader concept than research output only. Bibliometric data are a basis for the discussion rather than a 'hard' criterion related to rewards.

The increasing focus on performance is also related to the whole idea of an academic career ladder. One consequence for managers is an increasing demand for career counselling young academics who want advice and clarity when it comes to performance expectations—for example, how to interpret promotion criteria. The role as a manager is to mobilise support in order to fulfil the goals:

> Yes, as department head I have felt that it is my responsibility to find support in order to achieve the goals, if I find them so important. [If] it is perhaps a

doctoral student who hasn't completed [their] studies, then we have to think of why and address it. (Regional, manager, SE)

The relation between strategic plans and goals at various levels and for individual academics are discussed by managers. The same interviewee also stressed that all goals at the institutional level are not relevant at the department level and even less so at the individual level. All interviewees at the Swedish universities argued against following up on performance at the individual level in a 'hard' way:

> I think it's a dramatic difference from, say, 10 years ago. But I have a feeling it's still the way to go. Then, I think we should never strive for this corporate model, this stone-hard…, because we need to remember that this is, like, an educating and researching environment, and there has to be room for detours and stuff like that. So, it can't be too tough either. But I do think there are still things to do. (Flagship, academic, SE)

At the flagship university, there are differences between different faculties. One of the faculties recently introduced the individual measurement of academic staff performance. This has been controversial and was met with deep scepticism by the other faculty members according to the interviewees.

Concluding Discussion

The aim of this chapter has been to shed light on the role of managers in higher education institutions. Major reforms in the Nordic countries have transformed HEI systems in a profound way (see Chap. 3). They have increased the formal autonomy of HEIs to make decisions over their own activities, both academic core tasks and managerial/administrative activities. The preceding, more state-regulated system meant detailed centralised decision-making about, for instance, hiring of professors and the introduction of new educational programmes. The new autonomy has led to the introduction of new managerial practices in HEIs in line with NPM and inspired by private firms: strategy-making, strict budgetary management, performance measurements, and so on. The issue addressed in this chapter is how these changes have affected the role of the academic leader.

Drawing on earlier research on managerialism and leaderism in higher education (O'Reilly and Reed 2010; Ekman et al. 2017), we see clear signs of change regarding academic leadership in these four Nordic countries. Overall, we see an interesting mix of institutional logics in the interviews: the professional, collegial traditional academic leadership, which is based on rotating systems, election among peers, and collegial decision-making has been complemented with, and in some places replaced by, a managerial logic with top-down order-giving, performance measurement and appointed managers as a new competitive academic profession (Thornton et al. 2012). Many interviewees mentioned the increased focus on these kind of management practices. Another related trend is the greater focus on individual managers. This is the case in all four countries albeit with slight differences in emphases. There are also mixed feelings regarding this managerialist/leaderist trend. For some of the interviewed academics, the development was deeply worrying and a major concern. This is particularly the case in Denmark. For others, particularly in the Finnish interviews, it seems that, for instance, increased transparency in reporting and communicating performance could be considered positive. The analysis also shows that Denmark and Finland are the countries that lead the way when it comes to increasing the formal authority of managers. The introduction of appointed managers rather than elected ones has altered the way HEIs operate in these two countries. However, as this chapter has shed light on, management reform has not been implemented in the same depth and with the same pace across and within universities. Hence, the ability and willingness to follow a strict, more corporate-like management style are unevenly distributed, although some commonalities can be found (Lind and Aagaard 2017).

The role of individual leaders has also increased in other countries, as shown in the interviews from Sweden in which the vice-chancellor's role at both HEIs was considered big and increasing over time. A similar pattern is appearing in Norway, where the strategising process was initiated from the vice-chancellor at one of the HEIs. There are also indications in the interviews that power has been centralised—that is, a strengthened steering core of HEIs. However, this increased power of managers, which appears clearly in the interviews, is still compromised, and the complex matrices of organisations that universities make up are still challenging to lead. Some of the interviewed Swedish managers even discussed what they perceived as a need for more managerial power over resources at various levels. They aired a frustration when it came to making priorities and to launching strategic initiatives. This partly reflects the national debate on the balance between external funding and direct state funding. A prerequisite for more managerial power is more money directly allocated to HEIs rather than external competitive funding, which strengthens individual researchers and research leaders rather than managers.

Another theme is performance management—that is, identifying, recognising, and rewarding academic staff in relation to their efforts in education and research. Across countries, it seems that there is more focus on performance and performance management. In Denmark, and to a certain level in Norway, the BRI has become a new managerial tool and is also used to some extent at the individual level for performance follow-ups. Performance is not followed up at the individual level in most places in Sweden and Finland. Annual staff appraisals are not based on performance data, but salaries are rarely affected by the level of performance. The increasing awareness of performance measurement among academic staff also affects managerial roles. In Sweden and Denmark, the role of the manager seems to include coaching and career counselling more than controlling. Early career academics are highly aware of career demands regarding performance and want guidance when it comes to making priorities. Also, the interviews from Norway indicate that the publication indicator affects individual researchers to a high degree.

The topic of management and leadership has been related to different kinds of HEIs in earlier research. Older, research-intensive, comprehensive universities have typically held on to elected leaders, and collegial bodies have been maintained in national systems where this has been possible (i.e., Sweden and Norway). In contrast, younger institutions have introduced a stricter line management structure with more emphasis on professional management skills rather than academic merits for holders of management positions (Engwall 2014). Sweden, and particularly Denmark, reveal some interesting albeit expected differences between the older flagship university and the regional university. The line management is stronger, the collegial bodies are downplayed, and decision-making is more top-down in the younger institutions. It also seems that resistance is stronger at the older universities, in particular, at the Danish flagship university.

The final conclusion is that there has been a convergence in reform initiatives, and many ideas have indeed been used in all four countries with deep consequences for academic leadership and management. However, the implementation of the reforms differs significantly across and within countries and institutions. There is a consistent, complex interplay between the two co-existing logics of managerialism and collegiality (Greenwood et al. 2011), a balancing act for managers whose power has increased to a degree that seems to frighten their co-workers but, nevertheless, for some, is frustratingly compromised.

Acknowledgements The data presented in the current volume and individual chapters emanate from a comparative study funded by the Norwegian Research Council under its FINNUT flagship program, a long-term program for research and innovation in the educational sector program. The project number was 237782, and the project was titled 'Does it matter? Assessing the performance effects of changes in leadership and management structures in Nordic Higher Education'.

REFERENCES

Aarrevaara, T., Ian R. Dobson, and E. Elias Pekkola. 2011. Finland – Captive Academics – An Examination of the Binary Divide. In *Changing Governance and Management in Higher Education. The Perspectives of the Academy*, ed. William Locke, William K. Cummings, and Donald Fisher, 243–262. Dordrecht: Springer.

Abbott, Andrew. 1988. *The System of Professions*. Chicago: University of Chicago.

Alvesson, Mats, and André Spicer. 2012. Critical Leadership Studies: The Case for Critical Performativity. *Human Relations* 65 (3): 367–390.

Amaral, Alberto, Oliver Fulton, and Ingvild M. Larsen. 2003. A Managerial Revolution? In *The Higher Education Managerial Revolution?* 275–296. Dordrecht: Kluwer Academic Publishers.

Askling, Berit, Marianne Bauer, and Susan Marton. 1999. Swedish Universities Towards Self-regulation: A New Look at Institutional Autonomy. *Tertiary Education & Management* 5 (2): 175–195.

Becker, Howard S. 2008. *Tricks of the Trade: How to Think About Your Research While You're Doing It*. Chicago: University of Chicago Press.

Benner, M., and Geschwind, L. 2016. Svenska universitetsstyrelser och politisk styrning – 40 års erfarenheter. Forskningspolitikk. http://fpol.no/svenska-universitetsstyrelser-och-politisk-styrning-40-ars-erfarenheter/.

Benneworth, Paul, and Ben W. Jongbloed. 2010. Who Matters to Universities? A Stakeholder Perspective on Humanities, Arts and Social Sciences Valorisation. *Higher Education* 59 (5): 567–588.

Berg, Laila Nordstrand, and Romulo Pinheiro. 2016. Handling Different Institutional Logics in the Public Sector: Comparing Management in Norwegian Higher Education and Hospital. In *Towards a Comparative Institutionalism? Forms, Dynamics and Logics Across Health and Higher Education Fields*, ed. Romulo Pinheiro, F. Ramirez, Karsten Vrangbæk, and Lars Geschwind, 145–168. Bingley: Emerald.

Cantwell, Brendan, and Barrett Taylor. 2013. Global Status, Intra-Institutional Stratification and Organizational Segmentation: A Time-Dynamic Tobit Analysis of ARWU Position Among U.S. Universities. *Minerva* 51: 195–223.

Carvalho, Teresa, and Rui Santiago. 2016. Transforming Professional Bureaucracies in Hospitals and Higher Education Institutions. In *Towards a Comparative Institutionalism: Forms, Dynamics and Logics Across the Organizational Fields of Health Care and Higher Education*, ed. Romulo Pinheiro, Lars Geschwind, Francisco O. Ramirez, and Karsten Vrangbæk, 243–269. Bingley: Emerald.

Christensen, Tom, and Per Lægreid. 2011. *The Ashgate Research Companion to New Public Management*. Farnham: Ashgate.

Christensen, Tom, Per Lægreid, and Inger Marie Stigen. 2007. Performance Management and Public Sector Reform: The Norwegian Hospital Reform. *International Public Management Journal* 9 (2): 113–139.

Deem, Rosemary. 1998. 'New Managerialism' and Higher Education: The Management of Performances and Cultures in Universities in the United Kingdom. *International Studies in Sociology of Education* 8 (1): 47–70.

Deem, Rosemary, and Kevin J. Brehony. 2005. Management as Ideology: The Case of 'New Managerialism' in Higher Education. *Oxford Review of Education* 31 (2): 217–235.

Degn, Lise. 2018. Academic Sensemaking and Behavioural Responses – Exploring How Academics Perceive and Respond to Identity Threats in Times of Turmoil. *Studies in Higher Education* 43 (2): 305–321. https://doi.org/10.1080/03075079.2016.1168796.

Degn, Lise, and Mads P. Sørensen. 2015. From Collegial Governance to Conduct of Conduct: Danish Universities Set Free in the Service of the State. *Higher Education* 69 (6): 931–946.

Dougherty, K., and V. Reddy. 2011. *The Impact of State Performance Funding Systems in Higher Education Institutions: Research Literature Review and Policy Recommendations*. CCRC Working Paper No. 37. New York, NY: Teachers College, Colombia University.

Ekman, Marianne, Monica Lindgren, and Johann Packendorff. 2017. Universities Need Leadership, Academics Need Management: Discursive Tensions and Voids in the Deregulation of Swedish Higher Education Legislation. *Higher Education* 75 (2): 299–321.

Engwall, Lars. 2014. The Recruitment of University Top Leaders: Politics, Communities and Markets in Interaction. *Scandinavian Journal of Management* 30 (3): 332–343. https://doi.org/10.1016/j.scaman.2013.12.005.

Flynn, Rob. 2002. Managerialism, Professionalism and Quasi-markets. In *Professionals and the New Managerialism in the Public Sector*, ed. Mark Exworthy and Susan Halford. Buckingham, Philadelphia: Open University Press.

Freidson, Eliot. 1994. *Professionalism Reborn: Theory, Prophecy, and Policy*. Chicago: University of Chicago Press.

Goodall, Amanda H. 2009. *Socrates in the Boardroom: Why Research Universities Should Be Led by Top Scholars*. Princeton and Oxford: Princeton University Press.

Gornitzka, Åse, and Invild Marheim Larsen. 2004. Towards Professionalization? Restructuring of Administrative Work Force in Universities. *Higher Education* 47: 455–471.

Greenwood, Royston, Mia Raynard, Farah Kodeih, Evelyn R. Micelotta, and Michael Lounsbury. 2011. Institutional Complexity and Organizational Responses. *The Academy of Management Annals* 5 (1): 317–371. https://doi.org/10.1080/19416520.2011.590299.

Haake, Ulrika. 2004. *Ledarskapande i akademin: om prefekters diskursiva identitetsutveckling*. [Leadership Making in the Academy: On the Discursive Identity Development of Departmental Heads]. PhD diss Umeå University.

Hansson, Finn, and Mette Mønsted. 2008. Research Leadership as Entrepreneurial Organizing for Research. *Higher Education* 55 (6): 651–670.

Hvidman, Ulrik, and Simon Calmar Andersen. 2013. Impact of Performance Management in Public and Private Organizations. *Journal of Public Administration Research and Theory* 24: 35–58.

Karlsson, Sara, and Malin Ryttberg. 2016. Those Who Walk the Talk: The Role of Administrative Professionals in Transforming Universities into Strategic Actors. *Nordic Journal of Studies in Educational Policy* 2016 (2–3): 315–337. https://doi.org/10.3402/nstep.v2.31537.

Krücken, Georg, Albrecht Blümel, and Katharina Kloke. 2013. The Managerial Turn in Higher Education? On the Interplay of Organizational and Occupational Change in German Academia. *Minerva* 51 (4): 417–442. https://doi.org/10.1007/s11024-013-9240-z.

Krücken, Georg, and Frank Meier. 2006. Turning the University into an Organizational Actor. In *Globalization and Organization: World Society and Organizational Change*, ed. Gili S. Drori, John W. Meyer, and Hokyu Hwang, 241–257. Oxford: Oxford university press.

Ladegård, Gro, and Signy Irene Vabo. 2010. Ledelse og styring: - teoretisk rammeverk. [Leadership and Management: Theoretical Framework]. In *Ledelse og styring*, ed. Gro Ladegård and Signy Irene Vabo, S.15–S.38. Bergen: Fagbokforlaget.

Lind, Jonas Krog, and Kaare Aagaard. 2017. Danske universiteter efter reformbølgen: fra makro-reformer til intra-organisatorisk forandring. In *Styring Og Evaluering I Den Offentlige Sektor*, ed. Eva Moll Ghin, Caroline Howard Grøn, and Mads Kristiansen, 99–120. Copenhagen: Hans Reitzel.

Meek, V. Lynn, Leo Goedegebuure, Rui Santiago, and Teresa Carvalho, eds. 2010. *The Changing Dynamics of Higher Education Middle Management*. Vol. 33. Dordrecht: Springer Science & Business Media.

Melnyk, Steven A., Douglas M. Stewart, and Morgan Swink. 2004. Metrics and Performance Measurement in Operations Management: Dealing with the Metrics Maze. *Journal of Operations Management* 22 (3): 209–218.
Nybom, Thorsten. 2007. A Rule-Governed Community of Scholars: The Humboldt Vision in the History of the European University. In *University Dynamics and European Integration*, ed. Peter A.M. Maassen and Johan P. Olsen, 55–80. Dordrecht: Springer.
O'Reilly, Dermot, and Mike Reed. 2010. 'Leaderism': An Evolution of Managerialism in UK Public Service Reform. *Public Administration* 88 (4): 960–978.
———. 2012. 'Leaderism' and the Discourse of Leadership in the Reformation of UK Public Services. In *Leadership in the Public Sector. Promises and Pitfalls*, ed. Christine Teelken, Ewan Ferlie, and Mike Dent, 21–43. London, New York: Routledge.
Opstrup, Niels. 2014. *Causes and Consequences of Performance Management at Danish University Departments*. PhD diss Syddansk Universitet. Det Samfundsvidenskabelige Fakultet.
Paradeise, Catherine, Emanuela Reale, Ivar Bleiklie, and Ewan Ferlie. 2009. *University Governance*. Dordrecht: Springer.
Pechar, Hans. 2010. Academic Middle Managers Under the New Governance Regime at Austrian Universities. In *The Changing Dynamics of Higher Education Middle Management*, ed. Lynn V. Meek, Leo Goedegebuure, Rui Santiago, and Teresa Carvalho, 15–30. Dordrecht: Springer.
Pollitt, Christopher, and Geert Bouckaert. 2011. *Public Management Reform: A Comparative Analysis-New Public Management, Governance, and the Neo-Weberian State*. Oxford: Oxford University Press.
Rost, Joseph C. 1993. *Leadership for the Twenty-First Century*. Westport: Greenwood Publishing Group, Inc.
Sahlin, Kerstin, and Ulla Eriksson-Zetterquist. 2016. Collegiality in Modern Universities—The Composition of Governance Ideals and Practices. *Nordic Journal of Studies in Educational Policy* 2016 (2–3): 33640.
SOU 2015:92. *Utvecklad ledning av universitet och högskolor. Statens offentliga utredningar*. Stockholm: Wolters Kluwer.
Stensaker, Bjørn. 2014. Troublesome Institutional Autonomy: Governance and the Distribution of Authority in Norwegian Universities. In *International Trends in University Governance: Autonomy, Self-Government and the Distribution of Authority*, ed. Michael Shattock, 34–48. New York: Routledge.
St meld nr 27. 2000–2001. *The Quality Reform*. The Norwegian Ministry of Education.
Stryker, Sheldon, and Peter J. Burke. 2000. The Past, Present, and Future of an Identity Theory. *Social Psychology Quarterly* 63: 284–297.

Thoenig, Jean-Claude, and Catherine Paradeise. 2016. Strategic Capacity and Organisational Capabilities: A Challenge for Universities. *Minerva* 54 (3): 293–324. https://doi.org/10.1007/s11024-016-9297-6.

Thornton, Patricia, William Ocasio, and Michael Lounsbury. 2012. *The Institutional Logics Perspective: A New Approach to Culture, Structure, and Process.* Oxford: Oxford University Press.

Torjesen, Dag Olaf, Hanne Foss Hansen, Romulo Pinheiro, and Karsten Vrangbæk. 2017. The Scandinavian Model in Healthcare and Higher Education – Recentralising, Decentralising or Both? *Scandinavian Journal of Public Administration* 21 (1): 57–80.

Witte, Johanna Katharina. 2006. *Change of Degrees and Degrees of Change: Comparing Adaptations of European Higher Education Systems in the Context of the Bologna Process.* PhD Diss, University of Twente.

Open Access This chapter is licensed under the terms of the Creative Commons Attribution 4.0 International License (http://creativecommons.org/licenses/by/4.0/), which permits use, sharing, adaptation, distribution and reproduction in any medium or format, as long as you give appropriate credit to the original author(s) and the source, provide a link to the Creative Commons licence and indicate if changes were made.

The images or other third party material in this chapter are included in the chapter's Creative Commons licence, unless indicated otherwise in a credit line to the material. If material is not included in the chapter's Creative Commons licence and your intended use is not permitted by statutory regulation or exceeds the permitted use, you will need to obtain permission directly from the copyright holder.

CHAPTER 7

Strategy as Dialogue and Engagement

Timo Aarrevaara, Rómulo Pinheiro, and Johan Söderlind

INTRODUCTION

Interest in organisational strategy spans more than half a century and is a central topic in the business management and organisational literature (Miles et al. 1978; Chandler 2003). Within the organisational field of higher education, particularly in Northern Europe, strategic planning has only emerged in the last two decades or so, as a result of governmental reforms inspired by 'new public management' (Mouwen 2000; Rip 2004; Salminen 2003), leading to the rise of strategic science regimes. Strategy could be broadly defined as pertaining to 'a deliberate conscious set of guidelines that determines decisions into the future' (Mintzberg 1978,

---

T. Aarrevaara (✉)
Faculty of Social Sciences, University of Lapland, Rovaniemi, Finland
e-mail: timo.aarrevaara@ulapland.fi

R. Pinheiro
Department of Political Science & Management, University of Agder, Kristiansand, Norway
e-mail: romulo.m.pinheiro@uia.no

J. Söderlind
School of Industrial Engineering and Management, KTH Royal Institute of Technology, Stockholm, Sweden
e-mail: johanso2@kth.se

© The Author(s) 2019
R. Pinheiro et al. (eds.), *Reforms, Organizational Change and Performance in Higher Education*,
https://doi.org/10.1007/978-3-030-11738-2_7

935). Mintzberg makes an important conceptual distinction between 'intended' (the aim and goals) and 'realised' (the means used and the results) strategy and refers to the strategy formulation process as 'a pattern in a stream of decisions' (Mintzberg 1978, 935).

In other words, strategies are instruments of change, and within higher education institutions, the responsibility of academic leaders who carry them out is to maintain the operation, but at the same time, to embrace change opportunities. Strategies are also flexible tools for dealing with a range of requirements and threats and are related to how universities focus on funds allocation, financial stability, management structure, central operation units, and operational monitoring (Uslu 2018). It is important to ensure the wide support of key stakeholders because the implementation of strategies requires dialogue and compromise (Whittington 2006). Academic staff, in particular, might find that the strategies adopted clash with their own strategic interests and motivations and that they are of low relevance to their performance (Elena-Pérez et al. 2011). The highly dynamic and competitive environment in which universities and other higher education institutions operate places emphasis on the need to adopt strategic focus areas, increase the diversity of the funding base, identify and engage with a multiplicity of internal and external stakeholders, and prepare operational alternatives for performance management (Aarrevaara 2015). Given the traditionally high levels of structural (and cultural) decoupling within universities (Birnbaum 1988), academic subunits and individuals tend to resist attempts to set strategic management priorities at the level of the central administration (Pinheiro and Stensaker 2013). Recent developments suggest that, as a result of managerialism, centralisation is on the rise within universities/subunits (Deem et al. 2007), and that the strategic management of people, resources, and values is one such manifestation (Fumasoli et al. 2015).

This chapter sheds light on two key aspects:

1. Who gets involved in strategic processes in Nordic universities?
2. To what extent do strategies affect academic and managerial behaviour?

To answer these questions, we have developed a conceptual framework that includes several theoretical perspectives on how to interpret strategy work within universities. The data for this chapter were drawn from interviews[1] and a survey with academics, managers, and administrators based at public universities in Finland, Norway, and Sweden. This was part of a much larger project focusing on the performance effects related to changes in leadership and managerial structures of Nordic universities in recent times (consult the introduction to this volume). Their views constitute their perceptions about the key starting points and identification of the strategy, the importance of basic tasks, changes in strategic management, engagement in the processes around a strategy, and the importance of strategies for performance.

Most Nordic universities have a strategic platform, one composed of aims, ambitions, and key priorities in the realms of teaching, research, and the third mission (Pinheiro and Stensaker 2014; Pinheiro et al. 2016). Yet, the importance of strategies only became a key factor in universities' activities around the late 1990s. Since then, the importance of university structures has risen alongside the academic aspects of university performance (Amaral et al. 2003). Strategies and structures are related in the sense that aims and priorities result in new forms of resource allocation and the redefinition of internal tasks, roles, and responsibilities. In the Nordic countries, this trend has been reflected in the strengthening of institutional autonomy in legislation, while at the same time, the emphasis of strategies has been on performance management (Gornitzka et al. 2004). Because of these elements, strategies have a central role in defining the performance that is desired in Nordic universities.

Perspectives on Strategy

This chapter focuses on what a strategy is and how is it defined, paying particular attention to the multi-level approach of organisational design (Frost et al. 2016). Thus, we first look at strategy from the point of view of the *structure*, whereby the meaning of the strategy is a constructive organisational form. The starting point is then the shared commitment to the implementation of the strategy and an element of organisational development. From the perspective of the university structure, strategy is an arena that aggregates diverse interests into common goals.

From a structural perspective, university strategy formulation appears to be a rational process, meaning a series of predetermined decisions about

[1] Interviews were held at six case institutions, two per country: one classic 'flagship' university and another with a more 'regional' character.

how to reach specific ends by resorting to a set of means, what March and Olsen term 'the logic of consequences' (March and Olsen 2006). Universities, however, also carry out a wider social agenda, and in the Nordic countries, their funding and mission are closely linked to wider public interest (Pinheiro et al. 2016). Therefore, universities' strategies are not purely rational practices, but their creation and implementation also involve political choices and limitations (Pfeffer and Salancik 1974). These factors of political choices and limited rational practices do not necessarily optimise performance. Universities have unprofitable activities and/or disciplines that may be unreliable from the point of view of the university's internal performance. For example, costly educational programmes can be an effective public policy instrument for reasoning, such as analysis based on income, gender, or place of residence, and unprofitable performance can be valuable from the perspectives of regional development strategies and socio-economic regeneration programmes (Habibov and Cheung 2017; Lebeau and Bennion 2014).

A second perspective of the strategy is based on *processes* that either change or maintain the activity. From this point of view, the strategies appear in analytical and logical constructions, whereby the consequences of the strategy are understandable to the intra-organisational practitioners and extra-organisational actors (Whittington 2006). The processes that form the strategy are based on a dialogue that broadly considers stakeholders' views and aspirations. Strategic processes reinforce the elements of negotiation and compromise but, at the same time, reduce institutional-level solutions (Aarrevaara and Dobson 2013; Pinheiro 2015). If the strategy is largely based on compromise, elements such as transformation may remain weak in the strategy. This is why universities' ability to undertake reform and organisational change, as well as significant new opportunities for focusing, as a part of their strategy is important.

Our third perspective is based on the *outputs* that the strategy seeks to influence. We interpret the output as an agreement between the internal and external actors of the university, whereby the strategy identifies the organisational goals and the instruments to reach them. From this point of view, university strategies might move universities towards complex and competitive knowledge marketplaces (Pucciarelli and Kaplan 2016). The outputs defined in the university strategies will modify the university's power relations and produce engagement with organisational values. Further, university strategies are arenas within which to interact with external stakeholders and cope with societal contingencies (Aarrevaara et al. 2017; Fumasoli et al. 2015). Strategies can determine which disciplines or cross-disciplinary research themes are at the heart of the strategy so that they can be focused on strategy-based resources. The key to this strategy is that resources (and resource redistribution) generate change and results in focused areas (Covaleski and Dirsmith 1988).

In this chapter, we aim to analyse the data by applying the theoretical and conceptual framework for strategy formulation. This will be done by discussing the literature on strategy as practice and analysing the interviews and survey results as discussed in the first chapter of this volume.

Engagement in the Strategy Process

Our starting point for analysing strategy formulation is to draw a distinction between strategy engagement and strategy as dialogue. Both questions were asked as part of the semi-structured interviews and the survey. Engagement refers to *who* the key players in strategy formulation are. Strategy as dialogue, in turn, refers to the process and content of the strategy, as well as the ways in which actors are engaged with, and committed to, strategy formulation. In previous reporting of FINNUT[2] project data, attention has been paid to the fact that Finnish professors, as the most senior academic staff, have a wider opportunity to influence strategic processes than they have regarding resource allocations (Pekkola et al. 2017). The early engagement of the strategy is, therefore, much more the work of senior research and teaching staff and those in management and administrative positions than those in other academic posts. In addition, Pekkola et al. (2017) have demonstrated that professors in management positions have experience in preparing for strategy, which is similar to the responses of administrative managers. Above all, senior academics also enjoy relatively more professional autonomy regarding the strategy process (Kivistö et al. 2017).

The FINNUT data clearly indicate that participation in strategy formulation is greater at the academic unit level (departments or equivalent) and lowest at the level of the university (see Fig. 7.1). In Sweden, nearly 60% of the respondents reported that they actively participated, whereas in Norway, only about 40% did so, with Finland in between. The data reveal that in practice, and unsurprisingly, engagement in strategy formulation is most common amongst administrative staff and academic managers and lowest amongst academics. Except for Norway, the countries reported

---

[2] FINNUT is a long-term programme for research and innovation in the educational sector under the auspices of the Norwegian Research Council. The programme funds research on a wide spectrum from early childhood education and care to higher education and adult learning.

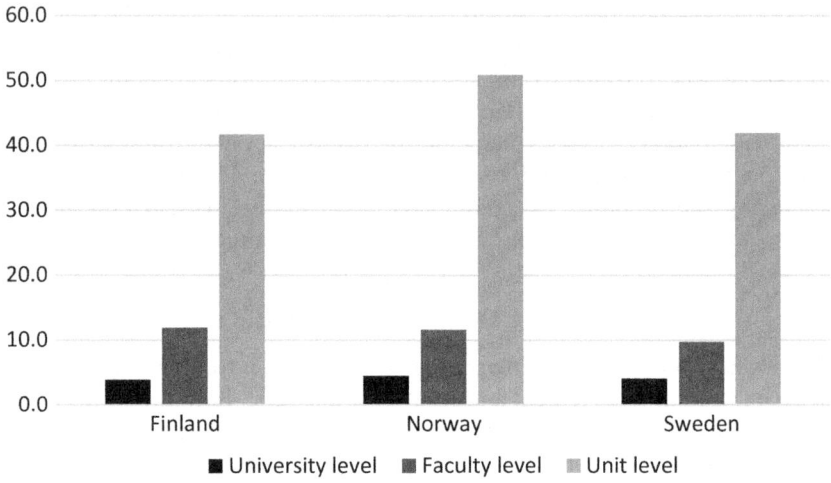

Fig. 7.1 Participation in strategy formulation (percentage of those academics who agreed with values 4 and 5; scale ranged from 1 (*no participation*) to 5 (*strong participation*))

greater levels of participation with unit-level strategy formulation amongst professors when compared with other academic groups (associate professors, assistant professors, senior lecturers, etc.).

Also, from the Finnish interviews, we can verify that the engagement of professors who have only academic responsibilities is different from their engagement in strategy formation (see Pekkola et al. 2017). Early engagement is typical for professors with managerial responsibilities, such as deans or the equivalent. However, the roles for research and teaching professors with no managerial responsibilities are different. It is evident that the role of university strategies is understood in a range of ways. Some informants see the strategies as beacons for everyday activities at the unit level, while the rest of the interviewees connected the strategies with institutional views on the universities' core functions.

> For me, the strategy is that we are doing high-level international research, so it is not so much about the university strategy that we're dealing with. (Academic, flagship, FI)

> We write an annual report, so we write to the Ministry and, there, the [strategic] thematic efforts will also be reflected in what we report. The univer-

sity board is very close and asking for continuous updates, and it is very clear that they want to see that the strategy is reflected in all the work that is happening in the organisation. Then, at the next university board meeting, there is a separate discussion about the implementation of strategies. (Manager, regional, NO)

I like the idea of living a strategy. So, when you make all these everyday decisions, you have to ask yourself, does this contribute to an increase in the number of publications, increased internationalisation, and increased external funding? (Regional, Manager, SE)

The preparatory committees for strategy processes are appointed by those who are attached to administrative and academic leadership professions. Membership in these committees is not merely formal but is related to local practices (Johnson et al. 2007). Even if the strategy of early engagement is launched on the basis of the importance of academic units, commitment amongst other staff may be weak. Such a situation arises particularly when academic staff should be the ones empowered to implement a strategy that has already been decided on (Kotter 1996). This creates the need for a specific strategy to be deployed at later stages. However, those who do not have administrative duties in academic positions are not necessarily obligated to commit themselves to the management and management policies.

Participation in strategy formulation at the university level and across all three countries is very low (5% for all categories), and at the faculty level, the involvement in strategy also remains low (overall, 12%). This indicates that in the academic units engagement is low, especially regarding university-level strategies. As expected, academic staff engage more in strategy making at the unit level, ranging between 25% and 50%. Professors score the lowest, with only 25% being involved in strategy formulation. Associate professors are the most involved at the university, faculty, and unit levels. What is more, associate professors also indicate that they have the greatest influence on strategy formulation at all levels when compared to their more senior and junior counterparts. That said, overall influence over strategic matters remains quite low at all levels, except for almost half of associate professors at the unit level and about one-third of 'other' at the unit level. Professors also scored the lowest at the unit level, with only about one-quarter of respondents reporting that they can influence strategy formulation.

Turning now to the qualitative data, some of those interviewed indicated that strategies are primarily formulated to please external stakeholders and enhance the accountability of universities to the government, as the main funding source. In some interviews, the universities were also found to be successful organisations before the introduction of institutional strategies. The following responses from the interviews are concerned with internationalisation and core functions such as teaching and research.

> The performance reflects government policy, and our main funding source is the Ministry of Education and Culture. I have to report [to our staff] on the policy of the Ministry. That is how we try to anticipate the changing of the operational environment. In this way, we are able to adapt strategies and operational programmes for funding. (Academic, regional, FI)

> Sometimes we have experienced that it is a little difficult to find a connection between strategy and what we see as our opportunities. For example, we are now very ambitious on internationalisation, but we are not aware of priorities and resource usage and so on. (Manager, flagship, NO)

However, other informants were doubtful of the relevance of university strategies for the practical work of teachers and researchers. From this perspective, academics as internal stakeholders are not necessarily motivated by the content of university strategies per se, although their motivations may coincide with the strategies.

> The staff and student bodies and also our other stakeholder groups [participated in the strategy formulation process], and it was applicable to them. On the other hand, a certain amount of work was done [in strategy preparation] by a rather large group [of administrators]. But in any case, they studied the earlier work of actors, and as a result, the draft was a little more focused. Finally, we have reached the stage that we are now at. This is an inclusive project, and of course, in practice, the decisions of the academic unit leadership, dean, and rectors of the university will close the case. (Academic, regional, FI)

> So, if the deans and the Rector say that we should have a commitment and that we agree with it, so there are expectations that we put off and that we have strategic funds. So, I have ... not very much, but I have some strategic funds that I use in the faculty.... So I can allocate these on the basis of quality, but also, for example, around the [strategic] thematic area ... I have strategic space [room to manoeuvre] for it. (Manager, flagship, NO)

> The question is whether [the goals in the strategy] would have been part of my work anyway, because I consider them important. (Academic, regional, SE)

Returning to the survey data, assistant professors are the staff category with the perceived least input on decision-making processes. Academic staff seem to be most responsive to unit strategies: the evaluation of around 60% of assistant professors, associate professors, and professors was that they align their academic behaviour to meet the goals in the unit strategies. Over 30% of the assistant professors, professors, and 'other' also responded that they align their academic behaviour to meet faculty strategies, while associate professors scored slightly lower, at 29%. Also slightly lower was the perceived alignment of academic behaviour with university strategies (average 30%). It seems that academics with managerial roles are more responsive to the strategies than the academics in general. The majority of the academic managers (85%) responded that they align their managerial behaviour to meet the goals of unit strategies, 62% to meet the goals of faculty strategies, and 47% to meet the goals of university strategies. On average, 87% of professors with managerial responsibilities reported that they follow strategies.

Strategies at different levels (university, faculty, and academic unit) were familiar to the managers at distinct hierarchic levels in the universities. In general, members of the academic staff were not as familiar with these, but some recognised that strategies provide frames for academic work, while others thought these were just formalities that are disconnected or decoupled from daily work. An academic from the latter group remarked that he could have used the strategies more strategically to clarify his research and when applying for research funding. Unsurprisingly, managers and administrators were found to be more dependent on the strategies to guide them in their daily work priorities. The dialogue between managers and academics is seldom based on consensus, as illustrated below.

> My wish is to think that I can take into account different perspectives. And even though the administration seems to be trying to streamline our activities, in practice, sometimes it means doubling the workload. Then you need a person who can say that you know how this really is the [way the] process [should be] going. (Academic, regional, FI)

> Yes, it [the strategy] is important because it provides a frame for what should be prioritised and what we should have as the main focus. (Manager, flagship, NO)

So I guess it is good both for those who are motivated and those who think that the university is moving in the wrong direction because they are also becoming sharper in this process. (Manager, flagship, SE)

As for the process of decision-making and developing strategies, for the most part, it is described by interviewees as democratic and open. That said, it is still seen as a top-down process. Suggestions for strategies were made at the highest level and developed down the line in the hierarchy. In this regard, the data reveal significant differences between the engagement practices across Nordic universities. For example, at the department level in the Norwegian cases, a broad range of academics were involved, and they reported open discussions amongst staff. In Finland and Sweden, discussion and involvement at the department or equivalent academic unit level was greater than in other areas. Some pointed to the importance of collegial and informal structures. In all three countries, the stakeholders in the local community were also invited to participate in the strategy formulation process.

Dialogue as Practice

The so-called practice turn in the approach to creating strategy has shifted the focus of debate from an individualist to a more broadly societist perspective, with task dynamics, open information, and influence (Whittington 2006; Pacheco and Newell 2018). This also means a more integrated understanding of the practice of strategy within organisations. The broader meanings of the strategy are embedded in the work of the practitioners so that the perspective can be simultaneously viewed from intra-organisational and extra-organisational perspectives (Whittington 2006). This is of great importance in how practitioners of the strategy produce concepts of strategies. The 'linguistic turn' in this approach to strategy brings the opportunity to unleash the strategy and its instruments without needing to follow cultural and historical practices. In this way, the strategy as practice perspective provides the opportunity to build and implement a strategy without organisational memory and, instead, focuses on what the local actors are actually doing (Jarzabkowski and Spee 2009).

The linguistic turn has questioned the meaning of the strategy as a form of rational planning by emphasising the importance of strategising the dialogue between practitioners. According to this perspective, the dialogue allows practitioners to contribute to the organisations and stakeholders to a greater extent than their original planning would have done (Harisalo and Aarrevaara 2015). Dialogue is especially necessary when actors can engage in the strategy formulation at an early stage. However, the FINNUT data clearly show that the dialogue is inadequate. In practice, most commonly, it is the senior academic and administrative executives who influence the dialogue at the faculty and university levels, with academic engagement declining as one moves up the organisational ladder. Moreover, based on the interviews, it is clear that the majority of those in academic posts only very rarely have a stake in the strategy formulation process. Thus, in the case of Nordic universities, the dialogue does not seem to work, at least in the early stages of the strategy formulation process, as a convergence of different personnel groups and strategic interests and as predicted in the literature (Whittington 2006; Lebeau and Bennion 2014).

Figure 7.2 shows that strategy formulation can be implemented through dialogue at the academic unit level. On the other hand, the numbers of actors at the faculty and university levels are substantially reduced. That said, there are significant variations amongst the three countries. Unit-level influence is highest in Sweden and Finland and lower in Norway. At the faculty level, Finnish and Swedish academics reported greater levels of influence when compared with Norway. Finally, at the level of the university as a whole, Finland and Sweden lead the pack, with Norway lowest overall. In Finland and Sweden only, over two-thirds of the respondents believe that they engage in the strategy process at some level.

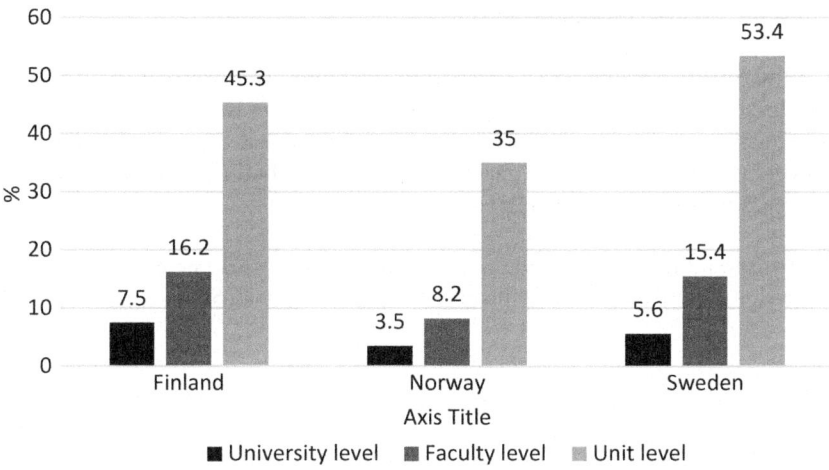

Fig. 7.2 Influence in strategy formulation (percentage of those who agreed with values of influence in strategy formulation, where 4 is *some influence* and 5 is *strong influence*)

More typical for Finnish interviewees was the emphasis on funding mechanisms and financial influence in societal interaction and university governance. Most of the interviewees recognised the role of external stakeholders and their influence on university governance.

> Of course, the fact is that there are external non-university members on the university board. No doubt, they are influenced by the government in their views. And this is also the case regarding donations, and they often determine whether to use donations or benefit from the interest on donations. (Manager, flagship, FI)

In the case of Norway, strategic work emerges from the interplay between many actors within the university as well as key external stakeholders. Compromise seems to be reflected in the generic nature of the goals being adopted, in line with the traditional democratic model of universities. In open dialogue, informal structures and collegial bodies are thought to play a key role.

> It is first and foremost the dean who has both pulled the [strategy] process and has had an influence in that round, I would like to say. But we have had the opportunity to have an input. I was involved in a working group that looked at one of the educational areas. So that way, you can say that I have had some opportunity to influence. What will come out of it, that's another matter. (Manager, flagship, NO)

One Swedish manager suggests that strategies are formulated primarily to please external stakeholders and for enhancing the accountability of universities. This manager downplayed the practical use of strategies for university actors by noting that the university has had considerable success during a period when no strategy existed.

> If you want to see what came out of it [the strategy work] here at the local level, it simply became documents. (Academic, regional, SE)

Strategy as Practice

Strategy as practice examines the evolution of strategies by studying their formulation, planning, and implementation. Attention is not so much on the consequences of the strategy, such as the economic and organisational effects. Instead, strategy as a practice draws attention to practical work as praxis episodes in formal meetings or informal episodes. From this perspective, practical work is either relevant or does not fit the focus of the strategy. Similarly, individuals can determine their position by combining work practices to understand the various domains of human activity and their interrelation to strategies. In this chapter, and following the interview and survey data from the FINNUT project, strategy as practice focuses on the social dimension and social interactions occurring at different levels of the university. Thus, strategy formation and implementation are not key factors, but staff, management, and stakeholder relations are.

However, it has been noted that strategy work is intermittent. The benefits of strategy work provide only temporary revitalisations of the discussions of organisational objectives, which are quickly forgotten once the strategy has been decided upon. The meaning of strategy was unclear for many of the Finnish interviewees, but some emphasised benefits of a strategy. Surprisingly, this was not necessarily dependent on the interviewees' position or rank. Some interviewees were critical of the whole strategy process. The problem, as raised in the Finnish interviews, is the poor connection between strategies and core functions. Thus, for the Finnish interviewees, the top-down process of strategy management or the discussion at different levels has not been a key problem. The main concern is how the strategy links to university performance, as revealed by the following comments.

> We implement the strategy, because excellent research is part of the University strategy. And really, social impact is certainly a matter, and it is part of my own strategy. When we publish the research outcomes, or discuss with scholarly community or patient organisations, we are implementing University strategy. (Academic, flagship, FI)

> The problem with strategic plans is that, at first, we worked hard on it for a year, then it was decided upon, and then it was kind of added to the files. (Manager, flagship, SE)

The accounts from Norway reveal that social relations are aligned with the notion of the university as a more unified, strategic actor rather than a collection of individual units and diverging strategic interests.

> So we work on many levels. And then we try to get it together [coherent whole], so the strategic education committee coordinates this, and then we

get it a little bit, and then we get the faculties to help each other out [based on] what they are good at, so they borrow from each other a little. So we try to build a form to work inside and content such that we are as strategic and coordinated as possible and that we make the most of both time and money. (Manager, regional, NO)

Changing Purpose of the Strategy

From a rational-instrumental theoretical perspective (Christensen et al. 2007), strategy documents are considered to be instruments to reach organisational goals, and actors are expected to align their behaviour to match them. Table 7.1 shows the extent to which academic staff and managers state that they align their behaviour with the goals presented in the strategies. It shows that, to a large extent, managers align their behaviour with unit- and faculty-level strategies, but only to some extent with university-level strategies. This confirms the message from the interviews that, for actors in departments or equivalent academic units, the university-level strategies are mostly symbolic rather than core components of their daily working strategy. The survey data reveal that academic departments' strategies are more strongly based on engagement and dialogue than are university-level strategies.

Table 7.1 also shows that academics, in general, align their behaviour to strategy goals to a lesser degree than do managers. Still, more than 80% of academics in the three countries stated that their behaviour was aligned to goals in unit strategies, compared to about one-third in the case of university strategies. When it comes to academics, country differences are less than those seen in relation to managers. However, academics in Finland, Norway, and Sweden have loyalty towards hierarchically lower-level strategies. In Table 7.2, it can be seen that managers reported their behaviours clearly meeting their goals more often than academics at all university levels.

Respondents across the sample indicated that strategies have become increasingly prominent since the early 2000s, particularly in the last decade. Competition and the need to coordinate and orchestrate activities across the board, as well as assess performance, come to the fore as key purposes for strategic exercises, which, on the whole, have also become more top-down and central to university life.

> For me personally, performance in teaching means that, above all, the process to bring the message—so to say that students will learn—is the most

Table 7.1 Academics' views to meeting goals of strategies (percentage of those who agreed with values 4 and 5)

	Finland	Norway	Sweden
I align my academic behaviour to meet goals in university strategies.	31.8	29.9	28.2
I align my academic behaviour to meet goals in faculty strategies.	41.0	34.9	36.8
I align my academic behaviour to meet goals in unit strategies.	64.2	60.5	66.5

Table 7.2 Administrators' views to meet goals of strategies (percentage of those who agreed with values 4 and 5)

	Finland	Norway	Sweden
I align my management behaviour to meet goals in university strategies.	49.5	46.7	46.5
I align my management behaviour to meet goals in faculty strategies.	69.7	61.6	60.6
I align my management behaviour to meet goals in unit strategies.	86.9	84.1	85.6

important result. In research, the most important issue is publishing. (Academic, regional, FI)

There is not much strategy on teaching … it's a good idea to give good candidates and teaching and such things. And of course, it should be relevant that the students should experience what is relevant … So, yes, you cannot just decide to get so and so many research projects; it's absolutely impossible then. (Academic, flagship, NO)

This proves that the researchers and the departments know what to do as a teacher and researcher. We know what to do, and we struggle, and we are successful during a period, and then perhaps we may stagnate for a period. (Manager, flagship, SE)

Institutional Strategies and Actors

This section deals with a theme that focuses on strategy at the university level and on the university as a strategic actor. University strategies are essential tools for determining how institution-level goals are enforced in academic units. The alternative is traditional federalist university governance, through which the definition of essential and meaningful work is defined at the level of academic units (Balbachevsky and Schwartzman 2011). The key strategy implementation of this determination is resource allocation. The data presented in this section provide an explanation of how strategy setting and allocation of resources can result in a strong institution at the faculty and academic unit levels. This phenomenon is apparent in the respondents' perceptions of how strategic goals affect the allocation of resources at the university, faculty, and academic unit levels (Fig. 7.3).

The data show slight variations in the ways in which strategic goals affect the allocation of resources. In Finland and Norway, strategies are more geared towards university-level initiatives, such as strategic research areas and the establishment of central level units, such as for research, internationalisation, and other activities. In contrast, the data for Sweden suggest that strategic resource allocations are more prominent at the faculty level. Accounts from the interviews show that managers play a critically important role in implementing strategies and assessing strategic results and that there is an increasing tendency for the coupling of core activities and resources with high-level/strategic goals at the university and faculty levels.

The data suggest that in one way or another (i.e. directly or indirectly) university-level strategies have a tendency to dominate over academic unit

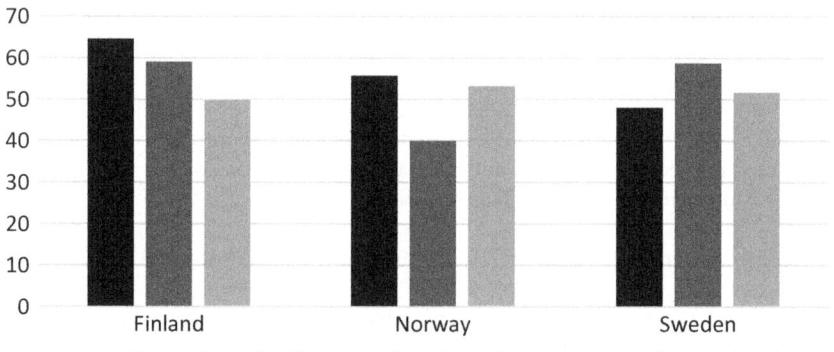

Fig. 7.3 Respondents' views on how strategies affect resource allocation (percentage of those who agreed with values 4 and 5)

strategies, suggesting that the relationship between strategies and organisational life has become more top down (hierarchical) than was the case before. In some interviews, there was discussion about how well university-level strategies take into account academic units' strategic priorities (specialisation areas) and assets (teaching and research excellence).

> We have a new strategy developed by the faculty that will largely follow the university's strategy, support it and, will participate in certain sections where our expertise is best targeted. In these [focus] areas, it is the implementation of the [university] strategy, as well as research and education strategies. And, of course, it also controls the research, that is, especially the strategic funding. (Academic, regional, FI)

Strategies are thought by some, mostly administrators, to be critical tools in processes of change and transformation ('modernisation'), as in the case of mergers. There is also evidence of strategic behaviour by faculties in gaining access to strategic resources, but with them acting as though it is business as usual (decoupling).

> Now, I've been in this position for just 2.5 years, as long as we've had this [change process], but I've never … in any other roles worked so closely on a strategy, and I think it's really necessary when we're now merging. It is so necessary to know where we want to go and that we will all go after the same thing, so I think that in merger processes in particular, [a clear strategy of clear leadership] becomes more important than ever. (Manager, regional, NO)

It should also be emphasised that discussions are thought to be beneficial for people who disagree with the final strategy formulations, as it provides opportunities to develop alternative arguments about the overall direction of the organisation.

> It may not be the strategy documents themselves, but rather the process of getting there and the discussions you have. (Manager, flagship, SE)

Conclusions

The remit of this chapter was to illuminate two critical aspects underpinning university life in the Nordic countries: who gets involved with strategic processes, and to what extent these processes affect behaviour across the organisation. The results based on the FINNUT survey and our interview data indicate that university-level strategies at Nordic universities lack legitimacy. This is because strategy formulation at these universities is based on the complex relationship between the academic departments and the university. These relationships are governed by the setting of objectives, focusing on research and education, as well as on the role of the strategy in allocating the resources required for implementation. Participation in strategy work was found to be unstable, which in turn further weakens the legitimacy of the strategy. The comparative data show that some academic staff are not involved in the strategy process at all, and hence do not relate their daily tasks to the goals and/or values expressed in the strategy.

It seems that in the Nordic countries examined, universities have quite traditional and rational assumptions regarding strategies and strategic work. Academics do not often share this view, as their adherence to the preparation and implementation of the institutional strategies is often accidental. Based on the cross-country data, it can be argued that a strategy has meaning for practitioners and actors in strategy formulation when it is useful to those practitioners. This is particularly apparent in strategy formulation, in which participation is significantly reduced the closer the strategy moves towards the university level. In the three Nordic countries, less than 10% of respondents reported participating in strategy formulation at the university level, and about half of the academic staff reported participating in strategy formulation at the unit level. For administrators, strategy process and strategy implementation are a more natural part of their work. These findings are aligned with the evidence (both within and outside the Nordic region) that recent reform processes aimed at transforming universities into more coherent, strategic actors (Pinheiro and Stensaker 2013; Ramirez 2006) have resulted in a growing gap regarding the values, practices, and priorities of university managers as compared to those of the academic heartland (Berg and Pinheiro 2016; Pekkola et al. 2017).

The factors highlighted above make it possible to rebuild universities' power relationships, engagement, and organisational values in the preparation and implementation of a strategy (cf. Fumasoli et al. 2015). These factors, in turn, define the directions of a university's future and also legitimise the university's position as an organisation (Deephouse et al. 2008). When academic staff define a strategy for the benefit of individuals or units, there is no common understanding of what the strategy is in any of the three Nordic countries. For example, in the Finnish responses, it is typical to criticise the priorities or the profile-based development of the strategy. Some of the respondents remain distanced from the strategy and do not follow the goals or meanings of the strategy in their work.

It is difficult to define the extent to which the strategies enacted in recent years have affected performance in the realms of teaching and research. That said, the so-called strategic turn seems to be associated (goes hand in hand) with a new culture of performativity and accountability (Hansen et al. 2019). However, it is reasonable to conclude that behaviour changes as internal actors (at different levels) align their activities and strategic aspirations with key thematic (strategic) areas to secure additional resources, both people and funding. In this respect, recent reform processes attest to the importance of resource dependencies (Pfeffer and Salancik 2003) in enacting change and transformation within the Nordic university sectors. That being said, there is also evidence of decoupling (Oliver 1991) once academic communities tap into strategic resources; hence, it is difficult to assess the extent to which strategic priorities are in fact guiding academic behaviour.

As regards strategic processes within universities, the FINNUT data sets show that assistant professors and lecturers are the least influential actors in decision-making processes for institutional strategies. Instead, they play a significant role in unit-level strategy work and especially in the grass-roots implementation, or 'localization' (Wedlin and Sahlin 2008), of institutional strategies. Therefore, and on the basis of survey results and interviews, the main observation made is that no single group is fully dominant in strategy formulation despite the increasing role played by certain local agents such as university managers. Similarly, there seems to be no common arena in strategy work where the dialogue takes place. Engagement in university strategy is formed in a dialogue where different groups have different roles and participate at different times according to their social standings within the university (Battilana 2006). If and when the dialogue is successful, the different actors' roles may turn out to be good practices that the university can emulate or institutionalise over time. In those cases in which the dialogue is unsatisfactory and/or it results in inaction or resistance, there is evidence for the belief that academics tend to deny the importance attributed to strategy formulation at the university level.

The data also indicate that without a dialogue and engagement role, the content of strategies is not relevant to Nordic universities. The fact is that different types of staff are not involved in the strategy process. In providing similar access for engagement and dialogue, strategy as practice can take place in different contexts for personnel groups and thus produce a strategic process for the university in which internal and external stakeholders become actively engaged. There is a need for scholarly research about the methods and practices through which strategy practitioners can support the engagement of university staff in the process. There is a lack of this knowledge, especially at the university level, where dialogue seems to be weakest. Based on the results outlined in this chapter, academic staff do not accept the university as a strategy-defining actor, and through the interviews and surveys, an interesting question arises as to how performance management practices can support engagement in the strategy formulation process.

Acknowledgements The data presented in the current volume and individual chapters emanate from a comparative study funded by the Norwegian Research Council under its FINNUT flagship program, a long-term program for research and innovation in the educational sector program. The project number was 237782, and the project was titled 'Does it matter? Assessing the performance effects of changes in leadership and management structures in Nordic Higher Education'.

References

Aarrevaara, Timo. 2015. The Finnish Academic Profession in Health-Related Sciences and Social Services. In *Professionalism, Managerialism and Reform in Higher Education and the Health Services: The European Welfare State and the Rise of the Knowledge Society*, ed. Teresa Carvalho and Rui Santiago, 64–78. London: Palgrave Macmillan.

Aarrevaara, Timo, and Ian R. Dobson. 2013. Movers and Shakers: Do Academics Control Their Own Work? In *The Work Situation of the Academic Profession in Europe: Findings of a Survey in Twelve Countries*, ed. Ulrich Teichler and Ester Ava Höhle, 159–182. Dordrecht, Germany: Springer.

Aarrevaara, Timo, Janne Wikström, and Peter Maassen. 2017. External Stakeholders and Internal Practices in Departments of Teacher Education at European Universities. *Higher Education Quarterly* 71 (3): 251–262.

Amaral, Alberto, V. Lynn Meek, and Ingvild M. Larsen, eds. 2003. *The Higher Education Managerial Revolution?* Dordrecht, Germany: Springer.

Balbachevsky, Elizabeth, and Simon Schwartzman. 2011. Brazil: Diverse Experiences in Institutional Governance in the Public and Private Sectors. In *Changing Governance and Management in Higher Education: The Perspectives of the Academy*, ed. William Locke, William K. Cummings, and Donald Fisher, 35–56. Dordrecht, Germany: Springer.

Battilana, Julie. 2006. Agency and Institutions: The Enabling Role of Individuals' Social Position. *Organization* 13 (5): 653–676.

Berg, Laila Nordstrand, and Rómulo Pinheiro. 2016. Handling Different Institutional Logics in the Public Sector: Comparing Management in Norwegian Universities and Hospitals. In *Towards a Comparative Institutionalism: Forms, Dynamics and Logics Across the Organizational Fields of Health Care and Higher Education*, ed. Rómulo Pinheiro, Lars Geschwind, Francisco O. Ramirez, and Karsten Vrangbæk, 145–168. Bingley, UK: Emerald Group Publishing.

Birnbaum, Robert. 1988. *How Colleges Work: The Cybernetics of Academic Organization and Leadership*. San Francisco: Jossey-Bass Inc.

Chandler, Alfred D. 2003. *Strategy and Structure: Chapters in the History of the American Industrial Enterprise*. Washington, DC: Beard Books.

Christensen, Tom, Per Lægreid, Paul G. Roness, and Kjell Arne Røvik. 2007. *Organization Theory and the Public Sector: Instrument, Culture and Myth*. Milton Park, UK: Taylor & Francis.

Covaleski, Mark A., and Mark W. Dirsmith. 1988. An Institutional Perspective on the Rise, Social Transformation, and Fall of a University Budget Category. *Administrative Science Quarterly* 33 (4): 562–587.

Deem, Rosemary, Sam Hillyard, and Mike Reed. 2007. *Knowledge, Higher Education, and the New Managerialism: The Changing Management of UK Universities*. Oxford, UK: Oxford University Press.

Deephouse, David L., Jonathan Bundy, Leigh Plunkett Tost, and Mark C. Suchman. 2008. Organizational Legitimacy: Six Key Questions. In *The SAGE Handbook of Organizational Institutionalism*, ed. Royston Greenwood, Christine Oliver, Thomas B. Lawrence, and Renate E. Meyer, 49–77. London: SAGE Publications.

Elena-Pérez, Susana, Ozcan Saritas, Katja Pook, and Campbell Warden. 2011. 'Ready for the Future? Universities' Capabilities to Strategically Manage Their Intellectual Capital. *Foresight* 13 (2): 31–42.

Frost, Jetta, Fabian Hattke, and Markus Reihlen. 2016. *Multi-Level Governance in Universities: Strategy, Structure, Control*. Basel, Switzerland: Springer.

Fumasoli, Tatiana, Rómulo Pinheiro, and Bjørn Stensaker. 2015. Handling Uncertainty of Strategic Ambitions—The Use of Organizational Identity as a Risk-Reducing Device. *International Journal of Public Administration* 38 (13–14): 1030–1040. https://doi.org/10.1080/01900692.2014.988868.

Gornitzka, Åse, Bjørn Stensaker, Jens-Christian Smeby, and Harry De Boer. 2004. Contract Arrangements in the Nordic Countries—Solving the Efficiency/Effectiveness Dilemma? *Higher Education in Europe* 29 (1): 87–101. https://doi.org/10.1080/03797720410001673319.

Habibov, Nazim, and Alex Cheung. 2017. The Role of University Education in Selecting Active Strategies for Coping with the 2007 Global Crisis in 28 Transnational Countries. *International Journal of Educational Development* 57: 65–72.

Hansen, H.F., L. Geschwind, J. Kivistö, E. Pekkola, R. Pinheiro, and K. Pulkkinen. 2019. Balancing Accountability and Trust: Higher Education Reforms in the Nordic Countries. Higher Education. Online First. https://doi.org/10.1007/s10734-019-0358-2.

Harisalo, Risto, and Timo Aarrevaara. 2015. *Katalyyttinen puhe lautakunnissa – Tutkimus kuuden suurimman kaupungin lautakunnista*. Tampere, Finland: Tampere University Press.

Jarzabkowski, Paula, and Paul Spee. 2009. Strategy-as-Practice: A Review and Future Directions for the Field. *International Journal of Management Reviews* 11 (1): 69–95.

Johnson, Gerry, Ann Langley, Leif Melin, and Richard Whittington. 2007. *Strategy as Practice: Research Directions and Resources*. Cambridge, UK: Cambridge University Press.

Kivistö, Jussi, Elias Pekkola, and Anu Lyytinen. 2017. The Influence of Performance-Based Management on Teaching and Research Performance of Finnish Senior Academics. *Tertiary Education and Management* 23 (3): 260–275. https://doi.org/10.1080/13583883.2017.1328529.

Kotter, John P. 1996. *Leading Change*. Boston: Harvard Business School Press.

Lebeau, Yann, and Alice Bennion. 2014. Forms of Embeddedness and Discourses of Engagement: A Case Study of Universities in Their Local Environment. *Studies in Higher Education* 39 (2): 278–293. https://doi.org/10.1080/03075079.2012.709491.

March, James G., and Johan P. Olsen. 2006. The Logic of Appropriateness. In *The Oxford Handbook of Public Policy*, ed. Michael Moran, Martin Rein, and Robert E. Goodin, 689–708. Oxford: Oxford University Press.

Miles, Raymond E., Charles C. Snow, Alan D. Meyer, and Henry J. Coleman. 1978. Organizational Strategy, Structure, and Process. *Academy of Management Review* 3 (3): 546–562. https://www.jstor.org/stable/257544.

Mintzberg, Henry. 1978. Patterns in Strategy Formation. *Management Science* 24 (9): 934–948.

Mouwen, Kees. 2000. Strategy, Structure and Culture of the Hybrid University: Towards the University of the 21st Century. *Tertiary Education and Management* 6 (1): 47–56.

Oliver, Christine. 1991. Strategic Responses to Institutional Processes. *Academy of Management Review* 16 (1): 145–179.

Pacheco, Matheus M., and Karl M. Newell. 2018. Search Strategies in Practice: Influence of Information and Task Constraints. *Acta Psychologica* 182: 9–20.

Pekkola, Elias, Taru Siekkinen, Jussi Kivistö, and Anu Lyytinen. 2017. Management and Academic Profession: Comparing the Finnish Professors with and Without Management Positions. *Studies in Higher Education*. https://doi.org/10.1080/03075079.2017.1294578.

Pfeffer, Jeffrey, and Gerald R. Salancik. 1974. Organizational Decision Making as a Political Process: The Case of a University Budget. *Administrative Science Quarterly* 19 (2): 135–151.

———. 2003. *The External Control of Organizations: A Resource Dependence Perspective*. Stanford, CA: Stanford Business Books.

Pinheiro, Rómulo. 2015. The Role of Internal and External Stakeholders. In *Higher Education in the BRICS Countries: Investigating the Pact Between Higher Education and Society*, ed. Simon Schwartzman, Rómulo Pinheiro, and Pundy Pillay, 43–58. Dordrecht, Germany: Springer.

Pinheiro, Rómulo, and Bjørn Stensaker. 2013. Designing the Entrepreneurial University: The Interpretation of a Global Idea. *Public Organization Review* 14 (4): 1–20.

———. 2014. Strategic Actor-Hood and Internal Transformation: The Rise of the 'Quadruple-Helix University'? In *Global Challenges, Local Responses in Higher Education: The Contemporary Issues in National and Comparative Perspective*, ed. Jelena Branković, Manja Klemenčič, Predrag Lažetić, and Pavel Zgaga, 171–189. Rotterdam, the Netherlands: Sense Publishers.

Pinheiro, Rómulo, Lars Geschwind, and Timo Aarrevaara. 2016. A World Full of Mergers: The Nordic Countries in a Global Context. In *Mergers in Higher Education: The Experience from Northern Europe*, ed. Rómulo Pinheiro, Lars Geschwind, and Timo Aarrevaara, 3–28. Dordrecht, Germany: Springer.

Pucciarelli, Francesca, and Andreas Kaplan. 2016. Competition and Strategy in Higher Education: Managing Complexity and Uncertainty. *Business Horizons* 59: 311–320.

Ramirez, Francisco O. 2006. The Rationalization of Universities. In *Transnational Governance: Institutional Dynamics of Regulation*, ed. Marie-Laure Djelic and Kerstin Sahlin-Andersson, 225–244. Cambridge: Cambridge University Press.

Rip, Arie. 2004. Strategic Research, Post-Modern Universities and Research Training. *Higher Education Policy* 17 (2): 153–166.

Salminen, Ari. 2003. New Public Management and Finnish Public Sector Organisations: The Case of Universities. In *The Higher Education Managerial Revolution?* ed. Alberto Amaral, V. Lynn Meek, and Ingvild M. Larsen, 55–75. Dordrecht, Germany: Springer.

Uslu, Baris. 2018. Strategic Actions and Strategy Changes in European Universities: Clues from Institutional Evaluation Reports of the European University Association. *European Journal of Higher Education* 8 (2): 215–229. https://doi.org/10.1080/21568235.2018.1432370.

Wedlin, Linda, and Kerstin Sahlin. 2008. The Imitation and Translation of Management Ideas. In *The SAGE Handbook of Organizational Institutionalism*, ed. Royston Greenwood, Christine Oliver, Thomas B. Lawrence, and Renate E. Meyer, 218–242. London: SAGE Publications.

Whittington, Richard. 2006. Completing the Practice Turn in Strategy Research. *Organization Studies* 27 (5): 613–634.

Open Access This chapter is licensed under the terms of the Creative Commons Attribution 4.0 International License (http://creativecommons.org/licenses/by/4.0/), which permits use, sharing, adaptation, distribution and reproduction in any medium or format, as long as you give appropriate credit to the original author(s) and the source, provide a link to the Creative Commons licence and indicate if changes were made.

The images or other third party material in this chapter are included in the chapter's Creative Commons licence, unless indicated otherwise in a credit line to the material. If material is not included in the chapter's Creative Commons licence and your intended use is not permitted by statutory regulation or exceeds the permitted use, you will need to obtain permission directly from the copyright holder.

CHAPTER 8

Evaluation Practices and Impact: Overload?

Hanne Foss Hansen, Timo Aarrevaara, Lars Geschwind, and Bjørn Stensaker

Introduction

We live in an era when all policy fields and organisations are expected to evaluate their activities (Dahler-Larsen 2012). Not least in universities, multiple evaluation practices have become integrated parts of everyday life. Academic peer review aimed at assessing the quality of publications and the competencies of scholars has been supplemented by other forms of evaluation practices related to accreditation systems and

H. F. Hansen (✉)
Department of Political Science, University of Copenhagen,
Copenhagen, Denmark
e-mail: hfh@ifs.ku.dk

T. Aarrevaara
Faculty of Social Sciences, University of Lapland, Rovaniemi, Finland
e-mail: timo.aarrevaara@ulapland.fi

L. Geschwind
School of Industrial Engineering and Management, KTH Royal Institute of Technology, Stockholm, Sweden
e-mail: larsges@kth.se

B. Stensaker
Department of Education, University of Oslo, Oslo, Norway
e-mail: bjorn.stensaker@iped.uio.no

performance-based funding systems, as well as rankings imposed on universities from the universities' external environments (Stensaker and Maassen 2015). Actors at the European level, for example, related to the Bologna process, and actors at national levels are both drivers in developing these practices. Other types of evaluation practices, such as student assessments of courses, peer-review evaluation of departments and individual performance assessments, are initiated by the universities themselves (Karlsson et al. 2014).

In this chapter, we analyse the evaluation practices in and around the universities in Denmark, Finland, Norway and Sweden as an approach to better understanding the ongoing changes in the governance of the higher education sector in the region. As in many other regions around the world, the public sector in the Nordic countries has been exposed to a range of reforms in which the state has changed its governance approach, allowing for more institutional autonomy. At the same time, the reforms have introduced and changed other policy instruments in the sector, exposing the sector to strengthened demands for accountability on aspects such as quality, relevance, impact, effectiveness and efficiency (Verhoest et al. 2004; Stensaker and Harvey 2011).

Evaluation is a procedure for assessing how public organisations perform on these aspects (Vedung 2010). It can have different purposes and roles associated with changed governance, ranging from being an instrument of control to being a measure for stimulating formative improvement (Hansen 2005). Disclosing the configuration of the evaluative design present in a given country can accordingly inform us about underlying rationales and logic in the emergent governance of higher education in the Nordic countries. In this chapter, two research questions are addressed: (1) What are the major similarities and differences of evaluation practices across the Nordic countries? (2) What are the experiences of these practices from the points of view of academics and managers? The latter issue is of interest as input to our understanding of the meaningfulness and impact of the evaluative practices implemented. Our focus is on institutionalised evaluation routines. Ad hoc evaluations, for example, following up on implementation of reforms, are not included in the analysis.

The analysis takes a comprehensive approach to evaluation practices. By doing so, it adds to the analyses in the other chapters in Part II of this book. Whereas those chapters delve thoroughly into funding dynamics, managerialism and strategy work, this chapter is an attempt to link these aspects together.

The rest of this chapter is structured in four sections. In the section 'Conceptual Framework and Methodology', a conceptual framework of different types of evaluation models is presented. The framework is used for analysing the types of evaluation practices implemented. Further, this section briefly presents the methodology for analysis. In the section 'Mapping Evaluation Practices', evaluation practices in the four countries are mapped and compared. In the section 'Experiences of Evaluation Practices', academics' and managers' views on evaluation are presented and discussed comparatively. The section 'Discussion and Conclusion' holds the conclusion as well as a discussion on further perspectives.

Conceptual Framework and Methodology

Within public sector management, there is an increasing interest in how public governance can and should be constructed in more complex and internationally dependent societies (Treib et al. 2007). In general, the concept of governance has implied a change in public management in which the state may allow for private sector actors to have or take a role; a range of instruments, including rules and regulations, voluntary agreements, standardisation and information are applied; and coordination rather than regulation characterises the operating mode (Levi-Faur 2014).

The changing forms of governance often include the following three elements: (1) increased emphasis on institutional autonomy, which is meant to stimulate a stronger organisational actor-hood and improved management (Verhoest et al. 2004; Seeber et al. 2015); (2) more emphasis on institutional accountability in terms of quality, relevance and overall performance (Stensaker and Harvey 2011); and (3) the introduction of various evaluative measures to inform, control or stimulate both autonomy and accountability (Levi-Faur 2014).

As such, it is possible to argue that evaluation is a key measure in the new emergent governance patterns in higher education. As discussed in Chap. 2, the literature on evaluation is rich in discussions on how to define the concept. As mentioned earlier, we define *evaluation* as procedures for assessing aspects such as the effectiveness and quality of public organisations' activities, among others (Vedung 2010). Evaluation can be performed by both public and private actors, and it can have both 'hard' and 'soft' consequences. Consequences are hard if organisations are sanctioned if they do not meet evaluation criteria; consequences are soft if evaluation routines are implemented as support for learning and quality development

(Weiss 1998). Further, evaluation can be policy driven, managerial or academic in its design (Hansen 2005). Performance-based national funding schemes are examples of policy-driven evaluation. University-driven systems assessing student satisfaction are examples of managerial-driven evaluation, and peer review–based appointment routines are examples of academically driven evaluations. As suggested, evaluations can be conducted at different levels of the higher education system (Stensaker and Harvey 2011), ranging from national systems of quality assurance to evaluation processes that concern universities and their performance or programmes. With *programme*, we refer to an 'organized, planned, and usually ongoing effort designed to ameliorate a social problem or improve social conditions' (Rossi et al. 2004: 29), in our case, educational programmes. However, the levels at which evaluations are conducted are indications of where autonomy is found within the system, what this autonomy is used for and the accountability demands associated with it.

Evaluation processes can be anchored in a number of evaluation models which stipulate the question in focus and specify how to set up criteria for assessment. Table 8.1 presents a typology of evaluation models drawn

Table 8.1 A typology of evaluation models

Evaluation models	*Questions addressed*	*Evaluation criteria*
Result models		
(a) Goal-attainment	Have goals been realised?	Derived from goals
(b) Effect	Which effects can be uncovered?	Open. All types of effects
Process models		
(a) Implementation	Are there implementation problems?	Assess links from the idea about an intervention to decisions about design, implementation, addressee responses and effects
(b) Activity	Are activity levels increasing/decreasing?	Improvement
Actor models		
(a) Users	Are users satisfied?	Formulated by users
(b) Stakeholders	Are stakeholders satisfied?	Formulated by stakeholders
(c) Peers	How do peers assess quality?	Formulated by peers

from the literature on organisational effectiveness (Cameron 1986), the literature on programme evaluation (Scriven 2003) and the literature covering both types of evaluands (Vedung 1997). The typology is a slightly revised and simplified version of the typology discussed in Hansen (2005).

The evaluation models in the typology are ideal types falling into three categories. The result models are summative. In the classical goal-attainment model, results are assessed according to predetermined goals. In the effect model, the scope is broader, as all types of effects, intended/unintended as well as anticipated/unanticipated, are assessed in principle. The process models are formative and explanatory, and the actor models are anchored in the different actors' own evaluation criteria.

All models can be said to represent different modes of governance, where result models in general are associated with more traditional hierarchical governance, process models are often associated with more horizontal and community-oriented governance modes and actor models are more related to market and user-type governance approaches (Treib et al. 2007). Of course, in practice, evaluation designs may often be hybrid phenomena drawing on several models. However, analytically, the models are fruitful tools for uncovering the regulatory logic behind the evaluation routines (Levi-Faur 2014). As such, they are used later for a comparative analysis of the country practices.

The analysis of the evaluation practices is based on several types of data. The mapping of the practices is based on official documentary material such as governmental reports, as well as on available scholarly analyses. The analysis of the experiences of evaluation practices are based on survey as well as interview data collected as part of the FINNUT-PERFACAD project (see Chap. 1 for a more elaborated presentation).[1] In this chapter, we use survey data for the comparative analysis of academics' experiences with evaluation practices and then use interview data in a supplementary and illustrative way to shed light on the dynamics and experienced impacts of evaluation practices of both academics and managers.

Mapping Evaluation Practices

In this section, evaluation practices are mapped by country in order to shed light on similarities and differences across countries. In the mapping of the practices, we use the distinctions discussed earlier: policy-driven,

---

[1] The survey data included in this chapter has been used also in an analysis of accountability relationships (Hansen et al. 2019).

managerial-driven and academic-driven practices. Further, we map evaluation practices related to education activities, research activities and other types of evaluands. In the comparison across countries, we use the typology of evaluation models to address the discussion on similarities and differences.

Denmark

There are eight universities in Denmark. Although the universities are very different regarding age, size, profile and structure, the policy-driven external evaluation practices they are confronted with are very much alike. However, the universities have considerable leeway regarding how to implement external evaluation practices in organisational routines and how to initiate and implement internal evaluation practices. The overall pattern of evaluation practices at Danish universities is presented in Table 8.2.

Policy-driven evaluation practices in Denmark are first and foremost related to performance-based funding streams. Such systems evaluate performance using indicators. When indicators have been decided on, such systems are implemented rather mechanically. In relation to education, nearly all resources have been linked to performance, concrete to the number of students passing exams, since the 1980s. Since 2009, this measure has been combined with bonuses given if students accomplish their studies in timely fashion (DEA 2011). Bonuses constitute nearly 10% of the total amount of funding for educational purposes.

Recently, the funding formula has been further developed, as the Parliament has decided on a new formula for 2019 which, besides student throughput, includes employability, goal attainment (according to contracts negotiated between the government and the individual university) and quality aspects. The quality aspects in the formula have yet to be decided, with student and graduate satisfaction and maybe teacher assessment of quality as dimensions being considered. The performance-based funding formula is, thus, becoming increasingly complex, and it seems more tightly politically governed.

In relation to research, approximately 20% of the total amount of ordinary funding is distributed according to a performance-based formula that includes the number of graduates from master's and PhD programmes, the ability to attract external funding and the number of published research publications. The future plan of the government is to distribute resources

Table 8.2 Overall pattern of evaluation practices at Danish universities

Evaluand	Evaluation 'owners'		
	Policy driven	Managerial driven	Academic driven
Education	• Funding formula emphasising student throughput, employability, goal attainment according to contracts and quality • Pre-evaluation and approval of new programmes • Accreditation of quality assurance systems and programmes • National database including information about students' assessment of quality and graduates' assessment of relevance, among other things	• Students' satisfaction evaluation systems • Stakeholder curriculum dialogue with focus on relevance	• Classroom evaluation dialogue with students • Examination of students
Research	• Partly performance-based funding based on several criteria including bibliometrics	• Appointment and promotion decisions • Peer-review exercises (department level)	• Classic peer review (especially publication and funding and, to some extent, appointments)
Other evaluands	• Development contracts laying down institutional goals and followed up by goal-attainment evaluation • Since 2017, an annual report on HE- and research performance	• Human resource initiatives (systems for evaluation of managers, routine manager-individual staff dialogue)	• Other scholarly qualifications such as third-stream activities in relation to appointments

on the basis of a new formula emphasising quality over quantity, but how to do this has not yet been decided.

According to the principle stated in the university law that universities are self-governing institutions, resources are distributed to the universities as lump sums. This implies that the university boards are responsible for the internal distribution and the principles for use of the resources. This again means that the individual university has leeway in deciding on the budget model and, thus, is able to strongly influence whether and how the incentives in the funding formulae are implemented onwards in the organisation.

Further, in relation to education, the universities are confronted with evaluation practices built into accreditation requirements. In 2007, an accreditation scheme aiming at approving all bachelor's and master's programmes—new ones as well as existing ones—was established. When implemented, the system was criticised for being very bureaucratic. In 2013, it was decided to turn the accreditation regime into a system for improving the quality assurance systems at the universities, emphasising both programme quality and relevance. This regime transformation is still ongoing. In Denmark, the evaluation of PhD programmes is not included in the accreditation system but is handled in a more ad hoc fashion.

Both performance-based funding formulae and the accreditation system are laid down in political agreements, accreditation being a national political response to the Bologna process. However, considering both funding formulae and accreditation as evaluation practices, it becomes obvious that these represent hybrid evaluation models. Whereas the most recent teaching funding formulae combine different types of result models (e.g. goal-attainment, related to contracts, and effect, related to employability, combined with a user model—probably student satisfaction), the research funding formula combines a result model (graduates) more or less indirectly with peer review (external funding and publications). Finally, the accreditation scheme combines a user model, including both students and labour market representatives, with a peer-review model.

In recent years, a national database for comparison across educational programmes, UddannelsesZOOM, has been developed. The database holds information about study elements and dropout rates, for example, but also includes data on students' assessments of quality and graduates' assessments of relevance.

Development contracts have, for many years, been a political steering instrument. The contracts do lay down both national goals and individual university goals, and goal fulfilment has been monitored. Funding has not previously been a part of the contract regime, but as mentioned earlier, this will be the case in the future.

The development contracts are also used as *managerial-driven evaluation practices*, as faculties and departments are asked to deliver into goal fulfilment. Besides this, managerial evaluation practices are first and foremost related to education. Student satisfaction evaluation is a routine exercise. Evaluations of educational programmes by graduates and stakeholders in light of the labour market requirements are carried out in a more ad hoc fashion.

From time to time, some universities conduct research evaluations of departments by flying in international peers. The peers produce an assessment report which may provide input on, for example, strategy processes, but in some situations seems to be more symbolic, legitimising ongoing activities. At the individual level, managers are obliged to conduct what are called 'staff development conversations' on an annual basis. Some managers use this occasion to evaluate staff performance related to publication activities and activities aiming at attracting external funding. In recent years, recruitment and promotion procedures related to academic staff have been changed. Traditional peer review is still part of these processes, but, today, heads of departments and deans have much more influence on these evaluation processes, as well as on the subsequent decisions.

Thus, the importance of *academic-driven evaluation practices* in relation to recruitment and promotion has been challenged. Collegial processes as well as collegial bodies have become advisory and not, as before, decision-making bodies. In the case of evaluation activities related to key academic activities, teaching and research, academic-driven evaluation practices are, however, very important. Examination processes related to learning outcomes have become more structured. The same goes for PhD programmes and the monitoring and evaluation of PhD students' activities. In research, peer review constitutes the core of evaluation related to publishing and funding decisions.

Finland

There are 15 universities in Finland, 14 of which are under the Ministry of Education and Culture, and the direct government core funding they receive is about half of their total funding. For these 14 universities, the evaluation practices are generally based on legislation, but the universities also influence the evaluation practices themselves. The overall pattern of evaluation practices at the Finnish universities are presented in Table 8.3.

Common *policy-driven evaluation practices* have been developing since the 1990s in which the idea of Finnish universities accepting responsibility for the quality of their research and education has gained ground. A common Universities Act in 1997 replaced separate University Acts that had regulated each university in earlier years. This was the starting point for a

Table 8.3 Overall pattern of evaluation practices at Finnish universities

Evaluand	Evaluation 'owners'		
	Policy driven	Managerial driven	Academic driven
Education	• Funding formula emphasising focus areas, employability and national duties • Field-specific funding and external funding for specialisation studies and non-degree programmes • Quality assurance	• Contracting, performance agreements, demand for relevance, student credits, student mobility	• Traditional quality assurance, graduates' employment, student feedback after bachelor's degree
Research	• Policy initiatives as the government's key projects and reforms, including direct government funding for strategic development for national education and science policy aims	• Performance agreements (internal and external), corporate funding	• Scholarly publications (JuFo), international and domestic competitive research funding
Other evaluands	• State of Scientific Research in Finland (report)	• Human resource management	• Regulation-based university evaluation of research

university system in which evaluation could be a system-guiding and economic factor. Since 2005, the Finnish universities have been implementing the European principles of quality assurance at institutions and at the national level. The Finnish universities apply quality as a key element in evaluating higher education. The Universities Act (2009) obliges universities to participate in the evaluation of their operations and quality systems, but the universities also decide on their quality systems. The Finnish system is based on the idea of developing quality systems (enhancement-led evaluations) that correspond to the European principles of quality assurance (FINEEC 2016).

The role of the Finnish Education Evaluation Centre (FINEEC) is crucial in these institutional audits. FINEEC is a semi-independent institution funded by the Ministry of Education and Culture, and it produces the information for knowledge-based decision-making in the development of education. The process is based on enhancement-led principles to reach universities' strategic goals. The final results of the university audits are decided by the Higher Education Evaluation Committee of FINEEC.

Further, the Ministry of Education and Culture conducts performance negotiations with each university annually, and indicators defined in the funding formula since 1998 play a key role in these negotiations (Hicks 2012). Even as recently as the early 2000s, these indicators were mostly quantitative, but the quality factor has been emphasised more in recent years. The significance of 'quality' in the Ministry's 2017 funding formula has a strong correlation with key performance indicators: education is 39%, research is 33% and other education and science policy considerations are 28% of the total government core funding.

The field-specific funding emphasises art, engineering, natural sciences, medicine, dentistry and veterinary medicine. Ten percent of the funding depends on the number of students who complete 55 study points a year. This is to improve performance by reducing the time spent in formal study. Two percent of funding is based on the number of employed graduates, and 3% is based on student feedback. All in all, the Finnish development reflects the international story of university quality assurance in the 2000s being about impact, quality and internationalisation and governments accordingly changing funding formulae (Jongbloed and Vossensteyn 2016).

In research, quality determines 9% of the total core funding. The model includes indicators for competitive research funding and corporate funding. The funding formula also includes other education and science policy matters covering strategy development, field-specific funding and national duties. These indicators in institutional negotiations are partly quality and partly impact and internationalisation.

Based on regulation, the Finnish Academy is responsible for the evaluation of research in Finland. A report, 'The State of Scientific Research in Finland', is launched every second year, aiming to strengthen knowledge-based policymaking in science policy. The report contains analyses of research personnel, funding, scientific impact, bibliometric analysis and co-publications. There are also comparisons with the most important reference countries.

The policy basis described earlier applies to the internal funding allocation of universities. However, *managerial-driven evaluation practices* are varied. Some universities follow the indicator of external financing as closely as possible. For some other universities, however, the internal allocation model is based primarily on historical allocations. The role of quality in performance management is strong for the universities that follow external funding indicators in their internal allocations (Aarrevaara et al. 2018). University tools for the implementation of internal allocation in education include performance-based negotiation or the determination of block grants on a historical basis through a performance contract or a combination of these models (Pruvot et al. 2015).

Performance management and quality assurance started to be accepted almost simultaneously at Finnish universities in the 2000s. These two factors have strengthened the role of universities as autonomous institutions. However, *academic-driven evaluation practices*, academic traditions and collegial practices are still strong factors in elements of quality management. Some of the funding formula indicators relate to a publication forum, JuFo, classifying publications at three qualitative levels. The publication forum is a system maintained by scholarly communities. The importance of degree qualifications, academic evaluation and, in particular, peer-review practices are central to the university system. The Universities Act (2009) obliges universities to evaluate these practices regularly every year in negotiations between the universities and the Ministry of Education and Culture.

Norway

There are currently ten universities in Norway. These universities are very different according to age, size, profile and structure, but the policy-driven external evaluation practices they are confronted with are very similar. The universities still have considerable autonomy concerning their own internal evaluation practices, although some types of evaluations are required by law (Stensaker 2014).

The overall pattern of evaluation practices at Norwegian universities is presented in Table 8.4.

Policy-driven evaluation practices in Norway are first and foremost related to performance-based funding streams. The number of credit points taken determines 25% of the total budget. This system was introduced as part of a major reform in 2003 intended to strengthen the quality, relevance and efficiency of Norwegian higher education (Stensaker 2014). Due to increased criticism of credit points as the key indicator for educational performance, recent changes include the introduction of a new indicator related to study programme completion. However, this indicator has so far only been linked to a small amount of the performance-based funding. A further expansion of possible indicators included in the

Table 8.4 Overall pattern of evaluation practices at Norwegian universities

Evaluand	Evaluation 'owners'		
	Policy driven	Managerial driven	Academic driven
Education	• Partly performance-based funding (25% of total budget) emphasising student credits taken • Institutional accreditation of all universities • Accreditation of study programmes in university colleges at MSc and PhD level • National student satisfaction survey (mandatory for institutions to participate in)	• Institutional QA systems, including routine reviews of study programmes • Stakeholder forum where institutions and representatives of employers discuss relevance of educational offerings (mandatory)	• Student evaluation of teaching (mandatory to conduct, but autonomy is given regarding design) • External examination system administered decentrally by the individual institution (mandatory)
Research	• Partly performance-based funding (15% of the total budget) • A national system for bibliometric registration of research output (used as input to performance-based funding) • National evaluations of disciplines (rotating system)	• The development of performance reports on research output	• Classic peer review regarding external funding of projects, publications and academic appointments (mandatory)
Other evaluands	• Development contracts currently piloted in some institutions • A national database containing key performance indicators on a range of dimensions enable the possibility for institutional benchmarking • An annual report on R&D, innovation and HE performance, indicators etc.	• Human resource initiatives (systems for evaluation of managers, routine manager-individual staff dialogues)	

performance-based funding system is likely, though it might be in relation to recent experiments with developmental contracts between the Ministry of Education and individual institutions. In relation to research, approximately 15% of the total amount of ordinary funding is distributed according to a performance-based formula for research output regarding the number of publications, external funding from the EU and so on. The research-output funding of research is based on input from a national database for academic publishing called Cristin.

A national system of institutional accreditation is also an important element in the policy-driven education practices in Norway. This system accredits all public and private higher education institutions (HEIs), and accreditations determine the degree of institutional autonomy provided. For example, being given the status of a university implies full autonomy concerning the establishment of new study programmes at all levels. In Norway, PhD programmes are included in the accreditation system—with respect to both the institutional accreditation system and when university colleges without the independent right to establish PhD programmes apply to the national quality assurance agency for specific recognition.

It should be noted that a considerable portion of these resources is distributed to universities in the form of lump-sum funding (60%), allowing the institutions significant autonomy concerning their strategic development. Formally, university boards are responsible for the internal distribution and the principles for using economic resources, and the boards also have full autonomy regarding how the university should be internally organised. This again means that the individual university has considerable leeway in deciding on the budget model and, thus, is able to influence whether and how the incentives in the funding formulae are implemented onwards within the organisation.

Additional policy-driven forms of evaluation play an important role in the Norwegian higher education system. First, the Research Council conducts—on a rotating basis—their independent national assessments of specific disciplines, a practice that tends to have implications for how later external research funding schemes and programmes directed at these disciplines are designed. Partly linked to these evaluation processes, the Council also produces an annual report on R&D outputs, staff, performance, innovation and so on for the entire Norwegian higher education system.

More recent policy-initiated evaluations include a national student satisfaction survey conducted by the national QA agency, in addition to experiments with national exams in particular disciplines aimed at establishing and upholding national academic standards.

Compared to the relatively high number of policy-driven evaluations, there are relatively few *managerial-driven evaluation practices* in Norway. Perhaps the most influential of these is the institutional QA system, mandatory for every university and college to establish, in which issues such as management, formal responsibilities and evaluation are central (Stensaker 2014). These QA systems have been a central element of the national accreditation system in place since 2004 and are tightly linked to the external checks conducted by the national QA agency at an institutional level every sixth year. In some institutions, this QA system has been expanded to the area of research and has become more integrated into the regular steering of the institutions.

Every higher education institution in Norway is also required to establish a formal forum where institutional representatives and representatives from employers evaluate and advise the institutions about the relevance of the educational offerings. Finally, several formal evaluations related to an expanding and more professional administration and the perceived need for more data and knowledge in the area of human resources management have been developed administratively within universities.

Academic-driven evaluation practices have become a more common phenomenon in Norway since World War II. However, an external examiner system had already been institutionalised decades earlier. Also, student evaluation of teaching has a relatively long history in Norway, although these activities were later incorporated into the institutional QA systems. While it is mandatory for institutions to conduct student evaluations of teaching according to national regulations, there is significant room for individual autonomy concerning how these systems are designed and implemented.

As in many other Nordic countries, a considerable number of evaluation activities are conducted as part of the daily running of the universities, including academics' involvement in evaluating the possibility of being granted externally funded research projects, evaluations in relation to academic appointments and so on. While universities have started to change the ways in which academic staff is recruited, there is still significant focus put on the traditional peer-review procedure in Norwegian higher education.

Sweden

There are 15 public and 2 private universities in Sweden. In addition, there are more than 30 university colleges providing higher education. There are many differences across the sector when it comes to size, scientific scope and relation between teaching and research. All universities report to the government, and their operations are regulated by the laws and statutes that apply to the higher education sector. They are nationally evaluated by the Higher Education Authority (UKÄ). In addition, they have the responsibility of initiating and undertaking their own evaluations (Table 8.5).

The *policy-driven evaluation practices* in Sweden are partially based on metrics. In education, a funding system based on the input and output of students was introduced in 1993. Approximately half of the money is allocated upon student admission, the other half when students complete their studies. This system does not include any evaluation component but,

Table 8.5 Overall pattern of evaluation practices at Swedish universities

Evaluand	Evaluation 'owners'		
	Policy driven	Managerial driven	Academic driven
Education	• Higher Education Authority (UKÄ): accreditation, institutional audits, reviews of subjects and programmes	• HEI-initiated educational assessment exercises, institutional standardised systems for course evaluation	• Collegial bodies' decisions on new courses and programmes, teacher-driven evaluation of courses, assessment and examination of students
Research	• Bibliometrics: publications, citations and external funding; national evaluations of subjects and programmes (like centres of excellence)	• HEI-initiated research assessment exercises, performance indicators; ad hoc benchmarking within networks	• Classic peer review (funding, publication, appointments)
Other evaluands		• Human resources initiatives (systems for evaluation of managers, routine manager-individual staff dialogue)	

rather, is mechanical in character. However, the assessment of students' performances indirectly affects the outcome. This system has, at times, been criticised and is currently once again under review. The critical remarks are related to quality; the argument put forward has been that academic staff become pressured to lower standards in order to get students through educational programmes. This has been particularly prevalent in areas and institutions where student admissions have been less competitive.

The national evaluation of higher education is under the authority of the UKÄ, which undertakes accreditations of new programmes, subject and programme reviews, thematic evaluations and institutional audits. It evaluates education at all three levels. The focus of the evaluation system has varied over time but has always comprised control, enhancement and information as the three main aims, currently with more emphasis on enhancement-driven institutional audits as compared with the previous, more control-oriented subject and programme reviews.

In research, a performance-based funding system was introduced in 2009 based on indicators: external funding, citations and publications. This was a major shift in Swedish research policy and part and parcel of a larger reform agenda. Over time, 10–20% of the total funding has been allocated on the basis of these indicators. Until then, the direct state funding was allocated entirely based on the size and number of academic staff, sometimes referred to as 'historical principles'.

Managerial-driven evaluation practices are also in place. In addition to the national systems, there have been a number of initiatives at the institutional level, both in education and research. The national policy-driven systems described earlier have, to varying degrees, 'trickled down' to the universities (Hammarfelt et al. 2016). The first research assessment exercise at the institutional level was launched at Uppsala University in 2007 (called Quality and Renewal), which was subsequently followed by a number of similar exercises at other institutions. They have all used peer-review panels and bibliometrics as standard procedure. Some of the Swedish universities have repeated the exercises more than once, usually with a slightly altered methodology (Bomark 2016). They have, for instance, put more focus on research environments (Quality and Renewal, Uppsala University 2017) or societal impact (RAE, KTH Royal Institute of Technology). The outcomes of the evaluations have been used in various ways: for funding allocations (e.g. in the case of bonuses), for further support (for less-than-excellent environments) or simply for recognition (Karlsson 2017).

Similar initiatives from the HEI management have been taken on the educational side. This was particularly the case during a period when some leading universities, in light of more formal autonomy and a criticised national evaluation system, decided to instigate their own subject and programme reviews (Karlsson et al. 2014). The variation in aims and methodology was even larger than in the case of research. These reviews were also affected by the research assessments, contributing to a general feeling of evaluation fatigue in Swedish higher education. The current national system puts much emphasis on the universities' own responsibility for assuring and enhancing quality. This might indicate more management-led evaluations in the near future, both in the form of large-scale, comprehensive exercises like the ones mentioned earlier and by introducing more formalised quality assurance cycles and processes on an annual basis.

Although both policy- and managerial-driven evaluation practices have been intensified, *academic-driven evaluation practices* do not seem to have decreased, either in number or in importance. Many of them are intertwined with managerial practices, such as the hiring of academic staff and promotion decisions. The relation between the collegial bodies at Swedish universities and the line management has been discussed quite frequently in the last decade. As a consequence of the autonomy reform in 2011, collegial bodies have, like in Denmark, become more advisory than decision-making. However, all major decisions regarding academic core activities shall still be made by academically qualified staff, according to the Higher Education ordinance.

Evaluation practices regarding academic activities start with the assessment of students. This is an area in which academic judgement is key, and traditionally, this has been under the discretion of academic staff themselves with few guidelines. Increasingly, the assessment of students has become more structured and more related to intended learning outcomes, a development fuelled by the Bologna process. This development is intended to increase the transparency of the assessment process. Furthermore, doctoral education has also become rationalised and structured, moving away from the traditional master-apprentice model to becoming an education based on a curriculum, structured supervision, occasional mentoring and individual study plans to be followed up at least once annually.

In the research realm, peer-review activities seem to grow continuously due to an increasing number of publications, journals, book publishers and conferences. Official reports from the Swedish Research Council show that Swedish researchers are indeed very productive in terms of publications but also that their papers are not as cited as the other top nations (Vetenskapsrådet 2017).

Closely related to both policy-driven and managerial practices are the evaluations performed in research councils and private foundations that inform decisions on funding. Typically, leading professors form peer-review panels who grade research applications. Since a large portion (55%) of Swedish public research funding is external and competitive, these activities are important (Geschwind 2017).

Comparison

The mapping of evaluation practices in the Nordic countries has revealed both similarities and differences across countries. In this respect, our findings are in line with former studies focussing more narrowly on national evaluation systems related to education (Hansen 2014; Schmidt 2017). In all four countries, policy- and managerial-driven evaluation practices are widespread. And these types of evaluations have become more important compared to academic-driven practices. Further, policy-driven evaluation practices seem to include more performance elements across time as still more indicators and measures are developed and included in evaluation practices.

The process can be observed in relation to both education and research evaluation. In evaluation practices related to education, student activity measures have become supplemented with measures focussing on timely student throughput, student satisfaction and employability. And in evaluation practices related to research, classical academic peer-review routines have been supplemented with bibliometric measures in the form of publication and citation counting, as well as with an attention to impact. This development has raised discussions on whether the performance-based funding systems have promoted quantity more than quality. In recent years, there seems to have been a turn towards giving more weight to quality.

There are, however, differences across countries regarding which new measures to adopt and when to adopt them. The Nordic countries seem to monitor each other's evaluation practices as well as those of other northern European countries, thereby seeking inspiration for further developing their own practices. Differences across countries are also seen in how they have responded to the evaluation demands implemented according to the Bologna process. In Denmark, the accreditation system, although now in transformation, has constituted a hard regulation system stating that every educational programme has to be accredited. In Norway and Sweden, universities have more authority to establish new programmes. In Finland, a softer, enhancement-led quality assurance approach, rather than an accreditation approach, has been adopted, and in Sweden, institutional audits have now become the main feature of the national system, evaluating the quality assurance systems rather than the quality itself.

Further, performance-based research funding schemes are anchored in different approaches. Denmark, Finland and Norway have schemes focussing on counting publications, while Sweden's scheme centres on assessing the number of citations. Although the publication counting schemes look similar at first sight, emphasising scholarly publications and competitive funding, there are important differences. For example, the transparency in the Norwegian system is much stronger than in the Danish system. This fact probably makes it much easier to use the performance information in the system for other purposes than the official purpose related to the redistribution of resources at the national level.

In Norway and Finland, national research evaluation systems driven by the Norwegian Research Council and the Finnish Academy have been developed, whereas the approaches in Sweden and Denmark have been university led or faculty anchored.

Table 8.6 summarises our findings on evaluation models; result models, process models and actor models are in use.

Overall, similar evaluation models have been implemented across the Nordic countries. We find result, process and actor models in use in all four countries. At the same time, however, there are many differences in the details. For example, activity-based educational funding formulae are used in one way or another in all four Nordic countries. In Denmark and Norway, the number of credit points taken are important; in Sweden, the number of completed degrees is prioritised. In Denmark and Norway, the emphasis on timely student throughputs is more intense than in Finland and Sweden.

Activity- and effect-based funding formulae are also in use in the allocation of resources to research. Research funding formulae, however, also differ across countries. For example, Sweden is the only country that includes effect indicators in the form of citation counts.

In all the countries, we also find examples of policy-driven indicators reflected in managerial practices at both the organisational and individual

Table 8.6 Evaluation models in use

Evaluation models	Used in evaluation procedures	Country
Result models		
• Goal attainment	• Contract steering	• DK, FI, NO
• Effect	• Employability focus	• DK, FI
	• Ability to attract external funding, influence funding for research	• DK, FI, NO, SWE
	• Citation patterns influence funding for research	• SWE
Process models		
• Activity	• Funding formula education	• DK, FI, NO, SWE
	• Formula including student throughput	• DK, NO
	• Funding formula research (publications)	• DK, FI, NO, SWE
Actor models		
• Users	• Student surveys	• DK, FI, NO. Gaining importance at the national level
• Stakeholders	• Relevance in education	• DK, NO
• Peers	• Research evaluation	• All countries. Classic use in relation to publishing and funding decisions. Challenged in relation to appointment and promotion decisions

employers' level, as some universities implement national indicators in internal resource allocation, hiring and firing procedures and decisions concerning individuals' reward-based salaries. However, universities apply these practices in very different ways.

Experiences of Evaluation Practices

The previous section mapped and compared evaluation practices across the Nordic countries. In this section, the focus is on how academics experience these practices. Key questions on this aspect include: Do they find it legitimate and meaningful? How do they experience its impacts?

Academics' Views on Evaluation: Meaningful?

The survey data (Table 8.7) show that Nordic academics perceive evaluation as a fairly legitimate task. However, there seems to be some misalignment between the personal opinions regarding academic performance and measured academic performance. Evaluation is experienced most negatively in Denmark. In particular, there is a striking difference between Denmark and the other Nordic countries in perceiving measurement as a sign of mistrust.

Many interviewees reflected upon the meaning of the growing number of evaluations. An interviewee from Sweden described how policy-driven evaluations fuel managerial-driven evaluations, as some universities undertake their own evaluations to prepare for the national reviews carried out by the UKÄ:

> There are, like, so many evaluations. Before UKÄ, there are also a couple of internal evaluations, etc. (Flagship, Social science)

A department head from Denmark (flagship, natural science) gave voice to an experience of evaluation overload. This person felt that too much evaluation is conducted, with some evaluation procedures being principles without specific purposes. Further, the same individual had experienced evaluation procedures taking a lot of time but seldom producing new knowledge.

Various evaluations on research, teaching, university activities and the innovation system in Finland have also caused a lot of work for the interviewees. Although various evaluations produce legitimacy according to

Table 8.7 Respondents' views on the legitimacy of evaluation and measurement (percentage of those who answered 4 (*agree*) and 5 (*strongly agree*))

	Denmark (%)	Finland (%)	Norway (%)	Sweden (%)
Control and evaluation of my work is a legitimate task	42	46	49	51
Internal procedures for measuring academic performance are in accordance with my understanding of academic performance	18	25	22	23
In my opinion, performance measurements are signs of mistrust	47	23	36	28

the survey results, the knowledge base of these evaluations is subject to much criticism. The main argument of the criticism is that the information used does not sufficiently support the academic tasks. One of the leaders of an academic unit stated:

> I feel that our own observations, development work, monitoring and student feedback, locally, and our general evaluation are more useful compared to the management system, even at the faculty level. (Regional, academic leader, sciences)

One of the Swedish interviewees belonging to the social sciences reflected upon the implications of changes in evaluation practices and experienced them as mistrust:

> I think it used to be part of the profession to be able to … just like teachers, and there has been a deprofessionalisation, that's for sure. […] Well, they (academic assessments) have been replaced by these quantitative evaluation systems rather than showing confidence in those who are educated to the assessments themselves. (Flagship, social sciences)

When asked about the degree of changes regarding evaluation and accountability issues in the last decade, all the groups reported an increased focus on this. In Norway, an administrator stated:

> […] as management, we are required to have a little more accountability by our owner, KD [Ministry of Education], than we were 10 years ago […] But we are working hard to fulfil what we think are the orders we have received. Also, in other areas as well, I feel that we must be more responsible for the good management of human resources […] We have had financial problems. There is more focus [now] on having proper management and control processes. It must be quality assured … We got a quality assurance system from Bologna. So, yes, I really feel that it has become more [focus on evaluation]. (Flagship, administrator)

Still, there were large variations in how meaningful this development was. Some found evaluation meaningful:

> I am stimulated by the demand for higher performance. I want to do more. I get motivated to do more when people around me appreciate what I am doing and give feedback. (Regional, manager, sciences)

Others were more detached and did not pay attention to this regime, while some were more critical, questioning the role of universities as independent institutions if they were met by such indicators and questioning the impact from New Public Management.

Academics' Views on Impacts of Evaluation

Table 8.8 shows that academics from all the countries are quite pessimistic about the positive impacts of measurement and evaluation, with respect to both performance and the atmosphere at work, regardless of the fact that they consider evaluation a rather legitimate activity. This observation holds true for both research and teaching tasks. Denmark differs most from the other three countries, particularly concerning research rather than teaching. In the perceptions of impacts of research performance measurement on work atmosphere specifically, the Danish figures are considerably lower than the figures for Sweden, especially, but also for Norway.

The interview data illustrate a range of different impacts of *educational evaluation*, from non-positive to positive. A Danish academic (flagship, natural science) characterised the teaching team to which he belonged as anarchistic. They routinely conduct student evaluations using surveys.

Table 8.8 Respondents' views on the impact of evaluation and measurement (percentage of those who answered 4 (*agree*) and 5 (*strongly agree*))

	Denmark (%)	Finland (%)	Norway (%)	Sweden (%)
Measurements increase my performance in teaching	13	16	18	18
Measurements increase my performance in research	16	26	26	28
Teaching performance measurements have a positive impact on the atmosphere surrounding academic work	11	12	16	19
Research performance measurements have a positive impact on the atmosphere surrounding academic work	11	15	19	26
Control and evaluation of my work has a positive impact on my teaching performance	16	20	23	29
Control and evaluation of my work has a positive impact on my research performance	14	23	22	26

These results are read, and sometimes colleagues have fun doing that, but in his experience, the evaluations do not influence practice.

Others, however, characterised the routine student evaluations as a kind of fire alarm. If an evaluation uncovered problems, action was necessary. Sometimes, not-so-good evaluations also had the consequence of the responsible programme leader having to explain upwards in the hierarchy: 'Up to father and over the knee', as one (flagship, academic, social science) phrased it. In this way, evaluation routines can be seen as enhancing accountability.

Some of the Swedish interviewees also reflected upon the positive impacts of the external educational evaluations carried out by the UKÄ. They saw the evaluations as opportunities to work with quality development at the organisational level:

> And actually then, there has been good quality work as a consequence. Although nobody thinks this last evaluation system has been particularly good, the result has been good ... You got an opportunity to reflect and go through the education holistically and scrutinise this with successive progression and coherence, etc. (Flagship, Social Sciences)

If a programme faces a negative outcome in an external evaluation, this seems to lead to extensive internal activity, as reputation could be threatened:

> Well, of course, that we made it the first round was considered kind of good. I know my colleague at the XX programme, the programme director, when they failed the first round, they had a huge amount of work inwards in the organization. (Flagship, Social Sciences)

Also, if national evaluations are linked to funding, and good performance is rewarded with extra money, impact was thought to increase:

> Well, when there was talk about linking funding to evaluation, then people really got busy. (Regional, Social Sciences)

Further, some interviewees also reflected upon the impact of educational evaluations at the system level. Here, the experience was that evaluations have led to a greater awareness of who is good and who is less good. This is particularly the case in evaluations where grading is used:

> One can only see that we had this [name of evaluation]; it led to an increased awareness of: they are good, they are less good. Even if it's not exactly a competition, I think it leads in that direction. (Flagship, Regional)

As for the Norwegian academics, they are also performing student evaluations of the different subjects, but the impact of the evaluations varies:

> What comes out of the evaluations depends—here, I am very arrogant—it depends on which students are showing up during the evaluation. (Regional, Academic, Sciences)

Most of them emphasised that the feedback from students was of high importance for them; however, the informal system through the daily contact with students was of higher importance than the institutionalised evaluation systems, as illustrated here:

> Well, I have a strong focus on the student feedback. But not through the formal system. I organise it myself. Informal and self-organised. (Flagship, Academic, Social Sciences)

In relation to *research evaluation*, the Danish interview data show that managers who 'own' evaluations are positive regarding the impact on performance. For example, a former and a present dean at different universities (both social sciences) who had introduced performance-based research funding had both experienced a positive impact on research performance. However, they were also aware that undesirable side effects could occur, and, when such effects were recognised, the evaluation practices had been changed.

The interviews clearly indicate that evaluations also have an impact on the atmosphere of the academic units. The evaluations' consequences for the atmosphere of academic life are not necessarily constant, because the competitive situations are temporary in character. These situations, especially before an evaluation, highlight the contradiction between unit-based interests and collegiality. A leader of a Finnish academic unit stated:

> Every time, a little depends on our situation, and if we are evaluated, we cannot truly be collegial. Frankly, the academic leaders of the large units somehow have their own interest. (Regional, academic leader, sciences)

From the Norwegian data, we can read that the impact of evaluations is more closely connected to research than teaching. This is seen through the employment process but also through the allocation of funds. The metric system for publications is of particular importance for allocations at both the individual level (e.g. allocation of funds for daily operating activities, conferences and sabbaticals) and the institutional level (e.g. getting PhD students). There are critical voices that question whether this focus in the evaluations is of importance, but they also question this emphasis on research over teaching. A statement from a manager regarding the hiring procedures illustrates this:

> Research is what comes first in the review of the competences of applicants … The evaluation from the review committee contains 14 pages related to research, and then there might be a couple of sentences at the end, summing up: "The applicant has been teaching for ten years, so he must be competent." So, we are also focussed on highlighting development projects on the teaching side. (Regional, Manager, Social sciences)

Although the overall survey data indicate that academics are quite pessimistic about the direct impacts of evaluation and measurement, the interview data show that there may be, indirectly, more positive dynamics following these activities.

DISCUSSION AND CONCLUSION

The analysis in this chapter has drawn on a broad conceptualisation of the concept of evaluation. *Evaluation* has been defined as 'procedures for assessing the effectiveness and quality of public organisations'. This broad conceptualisation has made it possible to bridge the analyses in the other chapters in Part II of this book. While those chapters have gone thoroughly into the dynamics and influence of evaluation-based funding systems, managerialism and strategy work, this chapter has given the broader picture of how these themes are interrelated.

The analysis has shown that there are different evaluation practices within the Nordic region, though the ideas behind developing evaluation practices are similar; they aim at improving performance on a wide range of aspects, such as quality, effectiveness and, in some contexts, especially in recent years, internationalisation, impact and employability. But looking into the specific practices, evaluation systems are varied. In relation to education, the Nordic countries adopt slightly different compared to the evaluation requirements in the Bologna process, and they include slightly different indicators in their performance-based funding systems. In relation to research, Finland and Norway have developed national evaluation systems: in Finland, driven by the Finnish Academy, and in Norway by the research council. In Denmark and Sweden, there are no national systems as such. Here, the universities have more autonomy to organise evaluations themselves. Also, performance-based funding systems related to research include different indicators and are organised differently. Internationally popular governance and evaluation ideas are, thus, translated into national policy agendas and administrative cultures. We find convergence in policy talk but less convergence in practices (Pollitt 2002).

Even though quality enhancement has been an important topic on the national agendas, a discussion is ongoing on whether evaluation practices and indicators related to both research and education have caused the focus to move from quality to quantity. This has raised an agenda about how to develop systems and practices focussing more on 'real' quality. Future studies should look into how this agenda develops and how the initiatives implemented influence university performance.

A general pattern across the four countries is that policy-driven evaluation schemes have been institutionalised and expanded, and management-oriented schemes—sometimes mirroring the national systems—have gained importance. Last but not least, the academic-driven evaluations have proliferated in systems with fierce competition for recognition and rewards. Given the public nature and the long tradition of public sector steering in the Nordic region, the national policy-driven initiatives are still seen as quite legitimate by the academic staff. As seen in these case studies, the growth of policy- and managerial-driven schemes have not meant a reduction in academic forms of evaluations, resulting in an overall growth of evaluations in the system. There are, however, signs that academic forms of evaluation are changing, as indicators used in the policy-driven evaluation systems are finding their way into academic evaluation practices, just as academic evaluation is becoming a stepping stone for managerialism.

Although the policy-driven evaluation schemes in all the countries seem to carry some legitimacy, academic staff throughout the Nordic region do not consider these very effective as tools for improving performance, either in research or in education. It seems that evaluation criteria in policy- and managerial-driven evaluation schemes often do not match academic definitions of what constitutes and supports good performance. Danish academics, in particular, were found to be quite negative towards the potential performative impact of evaluations. Why Denmark stands out is not easy to identify through our data, but one possible explanation is that evaluations have perhaps been perceived as more 'intrusive' when compared to those implemented in the other Nordic countries. A related explanation is that Denmark also seems to have more expansion in managerial-driven evaluations than the other countries, which may have contributed to the negative atmosphere. It is also possible that the negative perceptions identified among the Danish academics are an indicator of 'evaluation fatigue'. Maybe evaluation has been overdone, and a proper balance between higher education policy initiatives, managerial initiatives and academic duties has not yet been found.

Returning to some of the concepts introduced in our analytical framework, it could be argued that evaluations have taken up a central role in the changed governance of higher education in all four countries. Given the historical forms of governance of higher education found in the Nordic region, it is striking that the growth of evaluation schemes, to a large extent, is policy driven and, as such, under the supervision of the national authorities. While the state has delegated a substantial number of evaluations to intermediate bodies and agencies, the governance of the sector is still very much a public affair in all the countries. This pattern reflects the intensified accountability demands due to the growth of the higher education sectors and the corresponding increases in tax-financed resources spent. It also shows that decentralisation in the form of increased institutional autonomy occurs in tandem with centralisation initiatives, a pattern also known from the hospital sectors in some of the countries (Torjesen et al. 2017).

One can, however, also argue that the new element found in the region is not so much the dominant position taken by the state but, rather, that many of the evaluation schemes introduced are summative and result-oriented with elements of user and stakeholder orientation. What we see, therefore, is that the nation states are strengthening competition in the sectors and developing more market-like governance structures while still holding on to the Nordic universal welfare model.

Acknowledgements The data presented in the current volume and individual chapters emanate from a comparative study funded by the Norwegian Research Council under its FINNUT flagship program, a long-term program for research and innovation in the educational sector program. The project number was 237782, and the project was titled 'Does it matter? Assessing the performance effects of changes in leadership and management structures in Nordic Higher Education'.

References

Aarrevaara, T., L. Wahlfors, and I.R. Dobson. 2018. The Higher Education Systems and Institutions, Finland. In *Encyclopedia of International Higher Education Systems and Institutions*, ed. J.C. Shin and P. Teixeira. Berlin: Springer.

Bomark, N. 2016. *Drawing Lines in the Sand: Organizational Responses to Evaluations in a Swedish University*. PhD diss., Uppsala University.

Cameron, K.S. 1986. Effectiveness as Paradox: Consensus and Conflict in Conceptions of Organizational Effectiveness. *Management Science* 32 (5): 539–553.

Dahler-Larsen, P. 2012. *The Evaluation Society*. Stanford: Stanford University Press.

DEA. 2011. *Taxametersystemet under lup (The Taxi-Meter System Investigated)*. Copenhagen: DEA.

FINEEC. 2016. *National Plan for Education Evaluation 2016–2019*. Helsinki: The Finnish Education Evaluation Centre.

Geschwind, L. 2017. Higher Education Systems and Institutions, Sweden. In *Encyclopedia of International Higher Education Systems and Institutions*, ed. Jung Cheol Shin and Pedro Nuno Teixeira. Dordrecht: Springer.

Hammarfelt, B., G. Nelhans, P. Eklund, and F. Åström. 2016. The Heterogeneous Landscape of Bibliometric Indicators: Evaluating Models for Allocating Resources at Swedish Universities. *Research Evaluation* 25 (3): 292–305.

Hansen, H.F. 2005. Choosing Evaluation Models. *Evaluation* 11: 447–462.

———. 2014. 'Quality Agencies': The Development of Regulating and Mediating Organizations in Scandinavian Higher Education. In *Building the Knowledge Economy in Europe: New Constellations in European Research and Higher Education Governance*, ed. C. Meng-Hsuan and Å. Gornitzka, 188–218. Cheltenham: Edward Elgar Publishing.

Hansen, H.F., L. Geschwind, J. Kivisto, E. Pekkola, R. Pinheiro, and K. Pulkkinen. 2019. Balancing Accountability and Trust: Higher Education Reforms in the Nordic Countries. Higher Education. Published online 21 January. https://doi.org/10.1007/s10734-019-0358-2.

Hicks, D. 2012. Performance-Based University Research Funding Systems. *Research Policy* 41: 251–261.

Jongbloed, B., and H. Vossensteyn. 2016. University Funding and Student Funding: International Comparisons. *Oxford Review of Economic Policy* 32 (4): 576–595.

Karlsson, S. 2017. Evaluation as a Travelling Idea: Assessing the Consequences of Research Assessment Exercises. *Research Evaluation* 26 (2): 55–65.

Karlsson, S., K. Fogelberg, Å. Kettis, S. Lindgren, M. Sandoff, and L. Geschwind. 2014. Not Just Another Evaluation – A Comparative Study of Four Educational

Quality Projects at Swedish Universities. *Tertiary Education and Management* 20 (3): 239–251.

Levi-Faur, D. 2014. The Welfare State: A Regulatory Perspective. *Public Administration* 92 (3): 599–614.

Pollitt, C. 2002. Clarifying Convergence: Striking Similarities and Durable Difference in Public Management Reform. *Public Management Review* 4 (1): 471–492.

Pruvot, E.B., A.-L. Claeys-Kulik, and T. Estermann. 2015. Strategies for Efficient Funding of Universities in Europe. In *The European Higher Education Area – Between Critical Reflections and Future Policies*, ed. A. Curaj et al., 153–168. Heidelberg: Springer.

Rossi, P.H., H.E. Freeman, and M.W. Lipsey. 2004. *Evaluation: A Systematic Approach.* 7th ed. Thousand Oaks, CA: Sage.

Schmidt, E.K. 2017. Quality Assurance Policies and Practices in Scandinavian Higher Education Systems: Convergence or Different Paths? *Journal of Higher Education Policy and Management* 39 (3): 247–265.

Scriven, M. 2003. Evaluation Theory and Metatheory. In *International Handbook of Educational Evaluation*, ed. T. Kellaghan, D.L. Stufflebeam, and L.A. Wingte, 15–30. Dordrecht: Kluwer Academic Publishers.

Seeber, M., B. Lepori, M. Montauti, J. Enders, H. de Boer, E. Weyer, I. Bleiklie, K.L. Hope, S. Michelsen, G. Nyhagen Mathisen, et al. 2015. European Universities as Complete Organizations? Understanding Identity, Hierarchy and Rationality in Public Organizations. *Public Management Review* 17 (10): 1444–1474.

Stensaker, B. 2014. Troublesome Institutional Autonomy: The Governance and Distribution of Authority in Norwegian Higher Education. In *International Trends in University Governance: Autonomy, Self-Government, and the Distribution of Authority*, ed. M. Shattock, 34–48. New York: Routledge.

Stensaker, B., and L. Harvey, eds. 2011. *Accountability in Higher Education: Global Perspectives on Trust and Power.* New York: Routledge.

Stensaker, B., and P. Maassen. 2015. A Conceptualization of Available Trust-Building Mechanisms for International Quality Assurance of Higher Education. *Journal of Higher Education Policy and Management* 37 (1): 30–40.

Torjesen, D.O., H.F. Hansen, R. Pinheiro, and K. Vrangbæk. 2017. The Scandinavian Model in Healthcare and Higher Education: Recentralising, Decentralising or Both? *Scandinavian Journal of Public Administration* 21 (1): 57–80.

Treib, O., H. Bähr, and G. Falkner. 2007. Modes of Governance: Towards a Conceptual Clarification. *Journal of European Public Policy* 14 (1): 1–20.

Vedung, E. 1997. *Public Policy and Program Evaluation.* New Brunswick, NJ: Transaction Publishers.

———. 2010. Four Waves of Evaluation Diffusion. *Evaluation* 16 (3): 263–277.

Verhoest, K., B.G. Peters, G. Bouckaert, and B. Verschure. 2004. The Study of Organizational Autonomy: A Conceptual Review. *Public Administration and Development* 24 (1): 101–118.

Vetenskapsrådet. 2017. *The Swedish Research Barometer 2017*. Stockholm: Vetenskapsrådet.

Weiss, C.H. 1998. Have We Learned Anything New About the Use of Evaluation? *American Journal of Evaluation* 19 (1): 21–33.

Open Access This chapter is licensed under the terms of the Creative Commons Attribution 4.0 International License (http://creativecommons.org/licenses/by/4.0/), which permits use, sharing, adaptation, distribution and reproduction in any medium or format, as long as you give appropriate credit to the original author(s) and the source, provide a link to the Creative Commons licence and indicate if changes were made.

The images or other third party material in this chapter are included in the chapter's Creative Commons licence, unless indicated otherwise in a credit line to the material. If material is not included in the chapter's Creative Commons licence and your intended use is not permitted by statutory regulation or exceeds the permitted use, you will need to obtain permission directly from the copyright holder.

Taking Stock and Moving Forward

CHAPTER 9

Governing Performance in the Nordic Universities: Where Are We Heading and What Have We Learned?

Lars Geschwind, Hanne Foss Hansen, Rómulo Pinheiro, and Kirsi Pulkkinen

---

L. Geschwind (✉)
School of Industrial Engineering and Management, KTH Royal Institute of Technology, Stockholm, Sweden
e-mail: larsges@kth.se

H. F. Hansen
Department of Political Science, University of Copenhagen, Copenhagen, Denmark
e-mail: hfh@ifs.ku.dk

R. Pinheiro
Department of Political Science & Management, University of Agder, Kristiansand, Norway
e-mail: romulo.m.pinheiro@uia.no

K. Pulkkinen
Faculty of Social Sciences, University of Lapland, Rovaniemi, Finland
e-mail: kirsi.pulkkinen@ulapland.fi

© The Author(s) 2019
R. Pinheiro et al. (eds.), *Reforms, Organizational Change and Performance in Higher Education*,
https://doi.org/10.1007/978-3-030-11738-2_9

Introduction

In this last chapter, we will summarize the main findings from this extensive comparative study, draw some conclusions, and discuss possible implications for research, policy, and practice. The starting point for the project FINNUT-PERFACAD (consult Chap. 1 of the current volume for details) was that the conditions of the environment under which Nordic higher education institutions (HEI) operate have changed dramatically during the last decade. Policy efforts aimed at modernizing the sector have paid considerable attention to the way in which public universities operate. A privileged focus has been attributed to aspects such as efficiency, effectiveness, and accountability (Fägerlind and Strömqvist 2004; Gornitzka and Larsen 2004). In addition to managing their internal operations in a more cost-efficient manner, public universities in the Nordic countries and elsewhere are increasingly expected to respond adequately to the needs of various external stakeholder groups (Jongbloed et al. 2008; Neave 2002). One of the mechanisms being used to achieve these goals lies in enhancing the rationalization of internal structures and activities (Ramirez 2006, 2010) by, inter alia, promoting professional management (Amaral et al. 2003; Paradeise et al. 2009). As a result, most Nordic universities have developed extended administrative structures (at central and unit levels) capable of strategically supporting their primary activities (cf. Aarrevaara et al. 2014), and some have introduced recent changes in the nomination of formal leaders, such as filling the positions by appointment rather than election (Hansen 2017).

Yet, in spite of these trends, few studies have investigated, in a systematic fashion and comparative manner, the effects such types of strategic measures are having on the actual performance of individual institutions. This study has addressed this knowledge gap by investigating the impact of the rationalization processes—with a focus on the rise of professional management (managerialism) and the strengthening of leadership structures—on the teaching and research performance of public universities in Norway, Finland, Denmark, and Sweden in the period 2003–2013. The research problem driving the project is the following:

- *To what extent are changes in leadership and management structures related to shifts in teaching and research performance in public universities across the Nordic countries in the last decade?*

In order to address this query, we focused on three key dimensions: drivers, actors, and effects. The study adopted a mixed-methods design based on desktop research (comparative database) and a survey questionnaire along with interviews with staff of selected public universities (for details consult Chap. 1 of the current volume).

Before moving on to discussing the main findings of the project, a selection of previously undertaken studies of the Nordic higher education systems, as well as the conceptual backdrop, will be revisited.

The PERFACAD Project in Context: Earlier Studies on Nordic Higher Education

In many contexts, in particular from the outside, the Nordic countries are discussed as *one* system. This volume also contributes to that discussion with its explicit comparative approach. Over the years, the Nordic higher education system has been in focus in a number of studies. A decade and a half ago, Fägerlind and Strömqvist (2004) published an edited volume with contributions from all Nordic countries: *Reforming higher education in the Nordic countries. Studies of change in Denmark, Finland, Iceland, Norway and Sweden.* They write in their concluding chapter that the global economy has had a substantial influence on higher education in the Nordic countries, where the social function of education has changed from welfare state social engineering to globalized market features. Further, they conclude that the academic oligarchy has lost power and that the role of the state is not as straightforward as it used to be before these reforms. During the 1990s, all Nordic countries increased their student participation rates, in particular, Finland. All countries have had traditions of strict centralization of higher education systems. However, recent decentralization reforms have changed systems from normative legislation to funding and evaluation systems and by appointing external members to university boards. Performance-based funding systems were in place in all systems based on the number of students and their achievements in the form of degrees or credits. By the early 2000s, all five Nordic countries had introduced a management by results governance model. HEIs have been given more autonomy with respect to programmes, internal organization, and economy. In all countries, designated organizations were created for the evaluation of higher education, and in all cases except Sweden, the organizations are somewhat autonomous from the Ministry.

At the beginning of the volume, Fägerlind and Strömqvist also ask the question whether the Nordic countries are similar or different. The answer they give is that it is "complex." On the one hand, all countries share the fact that they have become increasingly similar due to, for instance, the Bologna system, globalization, and governance trends. They were also distinct regarding the organization of the tertiary education landscape, where Finland, in particular, had chosen the most explicit binary sector, Norway was a front runner in the implementation of the Bologna degree structure, and Sweden's higher education system was considered by the authors as too uniform and based on an ideology of "sameness."

In a comparative project between the United Kingdom, Norway, and Sweden from the 1990s, a number of similar conclusions are made. The final volume (Kogan et al. 2000) summarizes, "We noted how all three governments urged universities to adopt explicit quality assurance practices, market behaviour, stronger vocational missions and public accountability, but the policies came out differently" (200). The United Kingdom and Sweden were basically the opposite, where Sweden's tradition of state planning gave way to self-regulation at the university level. Norway was hesitant to "insinuate nationally devised practices." The researchers also identified different national policy styles, where the English were described as "heroic," the Norwegian as "incremental," and the Swedish as "adversarial."

A more recent study of the Nordic countries was undertaken by Ahola et al. (2014). Regarding governance, they concluded that all national systems have strengthened institutional autonomy, and a new governance regime had been introduced, based on delegation of state authority to HEIs by the use of performance-based funding and evaluations. Managerial forms of governance have largely replaced collegial modes. This is particularly the case in Denmark and Finland, where there are the most "extreme" versions of reforms and where universities have become more autonomous institutions. Other organizational aspects mentioned include the introduction of tuition fees, centres of excellence, doctoral schools, and mergers within and between universities. The authors interpret this as a transformation of the Nordic model of higher education as part of the larger transition from welfare state to welfare society, where "the state no longer solely takes the role as a protector, while to a greater extent expecting the higher education institutions to operate as entrepreneurs in a global market" (Ahola et al. 2014, 8).

Recently, based on research evidence from 12 European flagship universities, including the Nordic countries, Maassen (2017) discussed why the outcomes of reforms in general are not in line with reform intentions. One explanation for this "governance paradox" would be the neglect of institutional trajectories of universities, what is commonly known as "path dependencies" (cf. Krücken 2003), as one of modern society's oldest but still existing organizations.

The comparative analyses mentioned above not only tell us something about the individual country, but they also shed light on historical development in relation to other, neighbouring countries. Our results build upon these empirical and theoretical insights about the Nordic higher education systems. Before we discuss the findings, we will briefly revisit the theoretical backdrop and the methodology used in the project.

Revisiting the Conceptual Backdrop

The theoretical approach taken in this project, discussed at some length in Chap. 1, was inspired by a typology developed by Norwegian scholar Johan P. Olsen (2007). This typology focused on various aspects of governance of universities and also stressed the ability of universities—as institutions—to resist, adapt, and respond to change initiatives from external and internal actors. It emphasizes the resilience of universities and their capacity to fight back against unwanted and perceived intrusive policy and management initiatives. Olsen suggested four visions, or typologies (along two dimensions, autonomy vs. conflict), for the modern university based on different assumptions about what the university is for as well as the circumstances under which it will operate appropriately. At the heart of Olsen's inquiry is the question, *what type of university and for what type of society?*

Olsen's neo-institutional model (Table 9.1) captures various dimensions of modern universities: external–internal, change–stability, market–collegiality–bureaucracy. Universities are highly institutionalized organizations laden with rules, norms, and regulations. Traditionally, they have been described as loosely coupled and bottom-heavy (Clark 1983), with an impressive capacity to resist, delay, and simply not do what is expected of them by external stakeholders. This picture has changed in the last decades, and present-day universities are increasingly described as "strategic actors" (Krücken and Meier 2006), more tightly coupled, rational, and even "complete" organizations (Seeber et al. 2015), yet still

Table 9.1 Visions of the European university

Autonomy: / *Conflict:*	University operations and dynamics are governed by internal factors	University operations and dynamics are governed by environmental factors
Actors have *shared* norms and objectives	**The University is a self-governing community of scholars** Constitutive logic: Free inquiry, truth finding, rationality and expertise. Criteria of assessment: Scientific quality. Reasons for autonomy: Constitutive principle of the University as an institution: authority to the best qualified. Change: Driven by the internal dynamics of science. Slow reinterpretation of institutional identity. Rapid and radical change only with performance crises.	**The University is an instrument for national political agendas** Constitutive logic: Administrative: Implementing predetermined political objectives. Criteria of assessment: Effective and efficient achievement of national purposes. Reasons for autonomy: Delegated and based on relative efficiency. Change: Political decisions, priorities, designs as a function of elections, coalition formation and breakdowns and changing political leadership.
Actors have *conflicting* norms and objectives	**The University is a representative democracy** Constitutive logic: Interest representation, elections, bargaining and majority decisions. Criteria of assessment: Who gets what: Accommodating internal interests. Reasons for autonomy: Mixed (work-place democracy, functional competence, *realpolitik*). Change: Depends on bargaining and conflict resolution and changes in power, interests, and alliances.	**The University is a service enterprise embedded in competitive markets** Constitutive logic: Community service. Part of a system of market exchange and price systems. Criteria of assessment: Meeting community demands. Economy, efficiency, flexibility, survival. Reasons for autonomy: Responsiveness to "stakeholders" and external exigencies, survival. Change: Competitive selection or rational learning. Entrepreneurship and adapting to changing circumstances and sovereign customers.

Source: Olsen (2007, 30) [Official permissions secured from Springer]

heavily dependent on the external environment for resources, legitimacy, and power (Bleiklie et al. 2015). Bleiklie and colleagues have recently introduced the concept of "penetrated hierarchies" for understanding universities as organizations. The authors stress the introduction of more hierarchical bureaucratic governance of universities, the conflict between leadership and academic staff, and the relationship between members of the organization and key external audiences who penetrate their organization by influencing the legitimacy of control models and resource decisions.

As outlined in Chap. 1 of this volume, the theoretical framework being adopted resulted in an operationalization comprising six organizational/management mechanisms, listed below and related to organizational performance:

- Strategy
- Decision-making structures
- Organizational structures
- Accountability measures
- Funding arrangements
- Cultural climate

These mechanisms were further operationalized in a number of themes in the interviews and survey discussed in Chap. 1. We also formulated a few basic assumptions in light of the research problem and following on Olsen's work:

Strategy

- H0: An overarching and penetrating institutional strategy boosts performance.
- H1: An overarching and penetrating institutional strategy alienates staff and negatively affects performance.
- H2: Strategies that are developed through participation boost performance.

Decision-Making Structures

- H0: More hierarchical decision-making structures stimulate increased performance.

- H1: More hierarchical decision-making structures negatively affect performance.
- H2: Participatory decision-making structures stimulate increased performance.

Organizational Structure

- H0: Larger, more interdisciplinary structures boost performance.
- H1: Larger, more interdisciplinary structures negatively affect performance.
- H2: Diverse structures are best fitted to the diversity found in universities, and diversity boosts performance.

Accountability Measures

- H0: More systematic and regular (intense) reporting boosts performance.
- H1: More systematic and regular (intense) reporting negatively affects performance.
- H2: It is the way and form of reporting that affects performance.

Funding Arrangements

- H0: More incentives and results-oriented funding boost performance.
- H1: More incentives and results-oriented funding negatively affect performance.
- H2: A mixed funding arrangement is the best way to boost performance.

Cultural Climate

- H0: Systematic training and competence building in the organization boost performance.
- H1: Systematic training and competence building (which takes time away from primary activities) negatively affect performance.
- H2: Cultural change through participatory and trust-based processes drives performance.

As mentioned in Chap. 1, these hypotheses have not been tested in each chapter, but they have been instrumental in the operationalization of the study. We will now return to these mechanisms, themes, and assumptions and discuss them in relation to results presented in the empirical chapters composing Part II of the current volume.

COMPARATIVE THEMATIC FINDINGS

Strategy

Starting out with the thematic strategies, earlier research has shown how they have become part and parcel of modern universities for planning and steering and also for organizational identity formation (Fumasoli et al. 2015). Chapter 7, in particular, sheds light on two critical aspects of strategies: *who* gets involved with strategic processes and *to what extent* these processes affect behaviour across the organization. The results show that participation in strategy work varies across cases, and many times, participation is low, which in turn affects the legitimacy of the strategic process, per se. The data show that some academic staff are not involved in strategic processes at all, which alienates them from their own institutional goals and values. Furthermore, the authors show that strategies at lower levels are considered more relevant to academic staff, and whereas less than 10% of survey respondents were involved at the university level, around half of the academic staff reported participation at the unit level.

These findings suggest that there is a growing gap between values, practices, and priorities, as expressed in strategies, held by university managers and administrators as compared with those of floor-level academics (Pinheiro and Stensaker 2014; Ramirez 2010). Thus, when we talk about universities as strategic actors, not all employees are necessarily included, but rather, only a small portion of the total staff (Pekkola et al. 2017). Strategies have the capacity to rebuild the university's power relationships, engagement, legitimacy, and organizational values. However, where academic staff define a strategy for the benefit of individuals or units, there is no common understanding of what the strategy is within or among any of the four Nordic countries.

It is difficult to assess how strategies have affected performance in teaching and research. That said, the so-called strategic turn seems to be associated with a new culture of performativity and accountability (Hansen et al. 2019). Our data show that assistant professors and lecturers are least influential in decision-making processes for institutional strategies. Instead, they play a significant role in unit-level strategy work and especially in the grass-roots implementation, or localization or translation (Sahlin and Wedlin 2008), of institutional strategies. On the basis of survey results and interviews, the main observation made is that no single group is fully dominant in strategy formulation, and there seems to be no common arena where the strategy dialogue takes place (Battilana 2006). The findings regarding strategy also indicate that the process is as important as the outcome. Without dialogue and buy-in from internal stakeholders, the content of the strategies will remain irrelevant and the effects minimal.

Decision-Making and Organizational Structures

Regarding decision-making and organizational structures, some important changes have taken place in the Nordic countries. External stakeholders have become members of advisory councils and university boards. A corporate-like governance structure, including boards with a majority of external members and a chairman who is politically approved, has been introduced (Benner and Geschwind 2016). In Denmark, this corporate-like governance structure has been mandatory for all universities since 2003, while political approval of board chairs has only recently been introduced. Here, the former autonomy of universities has been restricted. In Denmark and Finland, the formerly elected leaders have been replaced by appointed leaders. The new Universities Act that went into effect in 2010 in Finland changed the legal status of universities from being part of the state administration to independent legal entities. Legislative regulation on central aspects such as staffing policies (in particular, regulation on qualifications of the staff, recruitment, and remuneration) and internal governance of universities were significantly changed; currently, Finnish universities enjoy a relatively high level of autonomy compared to many other European countries (see Pruvot and Estermann 2017).

In Norway, the managerial structures have been changed through the "Quality reform" of 2003–2004, with an effort made to enhance political and social accountability by including politically appointed stakeholders on the boards of the universities. The Ministry of Education introduced a model where the board appointed their chair and also appointed the rector. This model replaced the traditional one where the rector was elected by the university and also chaired the board (Gornitzka and Larsen 2004).

Still, despite the Ministerial preference for the appointment model, institutions can voluntarily choose which model to follow (or they can follow a combination of the two). This has resulted in a hybrid version in many universities, with both appointed and elected leaders in key roles of the institutions. The aim in giving universities the possibility of choosing their own governing model was twofold: to increase autonomy (Stensaker 2014), on the one hand, and to respect the traditions of universities as collegial entities, on the other hand (Olsen 2007).

The decision-making structures in Sweden have changed during the last two decades. The country has a long tradition of central state governance based on planning. However, this changed during the 1980s and 1990s across many sectors, higher education included. During the 1990s, following a groundbreaking reform in 1993, the higher education sector was fundamentally deregulated through a reduction in central laws and ordinances and an increased formal autonomy for HEIs. Although most universities remained state agencies, the autonomy (or freedom) reformed two HEIs, Jönköping University and Chalmers University of Technology, which became private foundations upon applications to the government. The main differences were regarding the internal organization and the regulations around the hiring of academic staff. Academic positions had to that point been centrally regulated, but from that point on, professorships could be initiated by each HEI. In 2011, another autonomy reform was implemented deregulating the internal organization of HEIs and academic positions. However, an even more far-reaching autonomy bill suggesting Swedish HEIs become private foundations was rejected by the sector a couple of years later (Geschwind 2017).

In Chap. 6, academic leadership is in focus. The pre–New Public Management (NPM) state-regulated system meant detailed centralized decision-making about, for instance, hiring of professors and the introduction of new educational programmes. The findings from the survey and interviews reveal that the roles of academic leaders are changing, most dramatically in Denmark and Finland, but also in Norway and Sweden, which have been the target of more evolutionary reforms. The perceived decision-making power of leaders differs significantly between countries, with Danish managers reporting the lowest degree of power. This finding is, in itself, rather interesting since the rationale for implementing NPM-inspired unitary management models (with centralization of decision-making) is to empower specific (formal managers) individuals (Berg and Pinheiro 2016). Thus, it should be reflected in the views of academic staff in interviews, stressing what they perceived as increasing managerial power.

The traditional professional, collegial academic leadership that is based on rotating systems, election among peers, and collegial decision-making has been complemented with, and in some places replaced by, a "managerial logic" (cf. Deem and Brehony 2005) substantiated on order-giving, performance measurement, and appointed managers as a new academic profession (*managerialism*). A related identified trend is the greater focus on individual leaders and managers (*leaderism*) (Ekman et al. 2017). This development is met with different opinions by HEI employees, ranging from deep concern in Denmark to moderate appreciation in Finland and Norway and occasional frustration expressed by Swedish managers with regard to the power of external stakeholder influence. Hence, as in the other themes, reforms have not been implemented to the same depth and at the same pace across and within universities. The ability and willingness to follow a strict, more corporate-like management style are unevenly distributed.

Accountability Measures

As public organizations dependent on the support of several stakeholders (Benneworth and Jongbloed 2010), universities in the Nordic countries meet with a number of accountability requests. In recent decades, a number of reforms have been implemented in order to increase the accountability of universities (Hazelkorn et al. 2018; Hansen et al. 2019). *Professional accountability* is important in relation to the quality of educational programmes and particularly the quality of research. However, professional accountability has, in all countries to some extent, been challenged or at least complemented by political and social accountability. *Political accountability* has been enhanced through the introduction of New Public Management instruments such as performance-based funding, contract governing, and evaluation "machines" (Dahler-Larsen 2012).

This has kept political expectations, and thus, also political accountability, at a high level. Higher education in general and universities in particular continue to be at the core of educational policies, and therefore, political interests. At the concrete level, this has been evident in the government programmes and action plans of past ruling cabinets, but also in the prominent role of the European Commission ("modernization agenda") and the importance of skills and research to the Europe of Knowledge, more generally (Maassen and Stensaker 2011; Pinheiro

2015). At the same time, important stakeholders such as several trade unions, student unions, employer organizations (such as the Confederation of Finnish Industries) have continued to keep universities and higher education at the forefront of their political agendas (Klemenčič 2018).

Professional accountability in Finland has remained strong alongside the other forms of accountability. For instance, various scientific associations operating under the Federation of the Finnish Learned Societies are actively exercising their gatekeeping role, especially in publishing. Scientific associations are often responsible for publishing scientific journals and other publications and appoint the editorial boards and editors for these journals. Also, the various trade unions, such as the Finnish Union of University Professors and the Finnish Union of University Researchers and Teachers, continue to play a critical role in upholding and safeguarding professional norms and values of the Finnish academic profession.

The majority of Norwegian HEIs are state owned, but private institutions are granted the same state funding as the public ones. As for professional autonomy, there has been an increased focus on the quality of teaching and alignment in educational programmes, but also on research quality as well as quantity. This increased focus on quality and quantity associated with a bureaucratic and political form of accountability is challenging the professional autonomy of academics. That being said, professional accountability remains strong, both as a stand-alone aspect of academic work and as intertwined in political accountability. As in Finland, university teachers and researchers' unions are strong voices for the Norwegian academic profession. Peer review is an ever-growing activity, for example, in conferences, research proposals, academic publications, and hiring and promotion of academic staff, and senior academics spend a significant amount of time assessing colleagues.

One specific aspect of accountability measures is evaluation, highlighted in some detail in Chap. 8. Evaluative procedures have become widespread in Nordic higher education since the 1990s.

As shown in Table 9.2, there are different evaluation practices within the Nordic region, although the ideas behind developing evaluation practices are similar. In relation to educational tasks, the Nordic countries adopt slightly different approaches than those of the Bologna process, including different indicators for their performance-based funding systems. In relation to research, Finland and Norway have developed national evaluation systems that are driven by the Finnish Academy and the research council, respectively. In Denmark and Sweden, there are no

Table 9.2 Evaluation models and procedures

Evaluation models	Used in evaluation procedures	Country
Result models		
• Goal attainment	Contract steering	DK, FI, NO
• Effect	Employability focus	DK, FI
	Ability to attract external funding influences funding for research	DK, FI, NO, SWE
	Citation patterns influence funding for research	SWE
Process models		
• Activity	Funding-formula education	DK, FI, NO, SWE
	Formula including student throughput	DK, NO
	Funding-formula research (publications)	DK, FI, NO, SWE
Actor models		
• Users	Student surveys	DK, FI, NO. Gaining importance at the national level
• Stakeholders	Relevance in education	DK, NO.
• Peers	Research evaluation	All countries. Classic use in relation to publishing and funding decisions. Challenged in relation to appointment and promotion decisions.

Source: Chap. 8 of this volume

national systems, and the universities have more autonomy to organize evaluations themselves. Hence, with regards to evaluations, we find evidence of yet another case of policy convergence combined with diversity when it comes to implementation (Pollitt 2002; Maassen 2017).

A general pattern across the Nordic countries is that policy-driven evaluations have been institutionalized and expanded, and management-oriented schemes—sometimes mirroring the national systems—have gained importance. Last but not least, the academically driven evaluations have proliferated as well. Our findings indicate that evaluations with similar *evaluands* lack coordination. This has created a feeling of evaluation overload among academics, although, generally speaking, many academics still regard national evaluations as legitimate tasks.

Another important finding concerns the usefulness of evaluations. Although the policy-driven evaluation schemes in all the Nordic countries seem to be largely accepted, academic staff do not consider these effective as tools for improving performance, either in research or in education. There seems to be a mismatch between academic and managerial conceptions of what constitutes and supports quality and performance. This is particularly the case in Denmark, where domestic academics stand out as the most negative. Explanations that are discussed in Chap. 8 include the fact that the evaluations have been perceived as intrusive managerial instruments adding extra workloads without tangible returns or rewards for academic staff.

Evaluations have taken up a central role in the changed governance of higher education in all four countries, which in itself reflects intensified accountability demands due to the growth of the higher education sectors and the corresponding increases in the public resources being allocated to the sector (see Chap. 3). It also shows that decentralization, in the form of increased institutional autonomy, occurs in tandem with centralization initiatives (managerialism and leaderism), as detected in earlier studies in the Nordics (Torjesen et al. 2017).

Performance Measurement and Management

The empirical evidence provided throughout this volume shows that performance measurement and management have become important, and growing in importance, principles in higher education governance in the Nordic countries. There are many common features in the actions taken by the respective governments, but also important differences. Performance management has been criticized for encouraging quantity on behalf of quality, and the criticism has recently been followed by a political request to incorporate quality criteria in the performance management approaches. Already, in the 1980s and 1990s, performance management was introduced in educational funding in Denmark and Sweden, and in today's system, educational programmes are funded solely according to a performance principle, where funding is based on the number of students passing exams as well as on bonuses given if students accomplish their studies in due time. In Denmark, it has been decided to further develop the funding system to include employability criteria as well as quality aspects possibly linked to student assessments. Since 2009, an increasing part of the funding for basic research, in recent years amounting to 20%, has been performance based. The formula includes the number of graduates from master's and PhD programmes, the ability to attract external funding, and the counting of publications. A quality aspect is included in counting publications as publication channels are divided into two groups, one releasing more points and resources than the other. Universities also negotiate performance contracts with the Ministry. Hitherto, contracts have not been related to funding, but the institutions have to document goal attainment, and recently, it has been decided to link goal attainment to funding, starting in 2019. In Denmark, salaries are rather marginally linked to performance, although this is increasingly gaining importance.

In Finland, after the reform of 2010 making universities legally independent from the state hierarchy, the university sector can be considered one of the administrative sectors governed/financed by the state, where the ideals of NPM are most comprehensively applied (Kauko and Diogo 2012). Some of the recent empirical studies have also proven the effectiveness of using performance-based funding in increasing the performance of Finnish universities (see Seuri and Vartiainen 2018). Although the execution of performance management on behalf of the Finnish Ministry of Education and Culture has been highly structured, its further application in individual universities within their own internal management and strategies is not controlled by the Ministry. As a matter of fact, individual universities, and in many cases also their subunits, like faculties, have developed their own internal variations of performance management (Kallio and Kallio 2014). The extensiveness of performance-based funding in providing resources to universities, professionalization of academic and administrative management positions, the use of contractual arrangements (performance agreements), outsourcing and centralization of support and administrative services in universities, and the use of various types of competitive funding are examples where the influence of performance management is most visible. One important aspect of performance measurement is the salary system for university personnel. Since 2008, the salary system at universities encompassing both academic and administrative staff has been based on performance measurements, where a maximum of one-third of the salary is performance based. Even though the salary or other performance-based financial incentives have not proven to be the main motivation of Finnish academics to work harder (see Kivistö et al. 2017), they are applied as a means to impose system and institutional level incentives on the individual level, and thereby draw attention to what is considered valuable.

The funding system in Norway provides a more stable budget than the Danish and Finnish systems, as 70% of the funding is in the form of a block grant. Still, the 30% of performance-based indicators increasingly function as a policy tool used to stimulate improvement in both teaching and research, but also as a managerial tool at the institutions. Teaching indicators constitute the largest share (24%), focusing on throughput of students and internalization. As for research indicators (the remaining 6%), these are related to throughput of PhD students, external funding of research (e.g. from the EU and the Norwegian Research Council), and lastly, from the metrics related to publications. The Norwegian Publication Indicator was introduced in 2004 as a system to measure publication activities. As a policy and performance management tool, such indicators from research are meant to stimulate excellence and productivity, but also to increase the accountability of public research. Another important aspect is to align research with societal and economic needs (Aagaard et al. 2015). Despite the broad objectives, the financial role of the Indicator is marginal as it only distributes 2% of the funding to the sector (ibid.). This funding system based on metrics and a market model has, on the one hand, increased autonomy within the universities as the boards are responsible for prioritizing within the allocated financial frames and for aligning their activities to meet the goals for the sector. On the other hand, ex-post control has increased, and the contractual relationships between universities and the state based on performance metrics are replacing the trust-based foundational pact (Stensaker 2014). The increased autonomy is counteracted by controlling instruments, reporting systems, and the financial incentive systems following students and research activities (Christensen 2011).

In Sweden, as well, performance measurement has become more important over time (Geschwind 2017). As mentioned above, one of the most dramatic changes in Swedish higher education was the introduction of performance-based funding in education, based on the inflow of students and throughput. The previous system was criticized for being too rigid, based on central planning, and not driving quality enough. The latter argument has also been used against the current system. Since funding is so closely related to student success, there have been discussions about decreased demands for passing students. The system is based on the idea that different educational areas bear different costs. A student in the humanities is supposed to cost far less than an engineering student, for instance. Another effect of this system has been increased marketing activity by HEIs. An important aspect of the system is the use of a "ceiling" for the number of students recruited. Allocation of funds has a limit, linked to a maximum number of students. Throughput of students has been a controversial quality indicator, and whereas there have been occasional discussions on the risks of lowering demands on students, there are also examples where student throughput has been linked to incentives. Generally speaking, though, this has not affected the individual academic but rather organizational units and HEIs.

In research, the traditional model was block-funding based on historical principles rather than performance. Direct state funding was the bulk of the total funding of research. Lately, there has been a development towards more competitive external funding rather than direct state funding, and as of 2018, the external funding makes up slightly more than half of the total funding. A milestone in Swedish research policy was the introduction, in 2009, of performance-based funding as part of the direct state funding. Since its introduction, 10–20% of the total funding has been allocated to HEIs based on performance, as shown in publications and external funding.

The national systems of performance measurement and management are described in Table 9.3. So what can be said about the actual effects of these systems, both for universities and for individual academics? The in-depth empirical studies in this volume (Chaps. 4 and 5) focus on research rather than education, which is no coincidence. The performance management systems are primarily used for research, albeit other academic activities are also discussed to varying degrees in terms of performance. Following Dahler-Larsen (2014), it can be concluded that research performance measurement has had the greatest constitutive effects on academic staff.

The results discussed in these two chapters show that performance-based research funding systems have had notable effects on Nordic universities. Performance indicators are implemented for resource allocation and decision-making in a way that impacts how university actors understand and perceive research activities. Not only do they contribute to a rationalization of formal university structures (Ramirez and Christensen 2013), but they also subtly contribute to an institutionalization and consolidation of research metrics as organizing principles of research (Geschwind and Pinheiro 2017). Even though there are concerns within universities, metrics are generally accepted and even appreciated as a means of enhancing transparency and for assisting university leaders in their efforts to set priorities and improve performance. From the perspective of incentives, publication practices are heavily influential in all countries. Researchers are

Table 9.3 Main components of the performance-related research funding systems in Denmark, Sweden, Finland, and Norway

	Sweden	Norway	Denmark	Finland
Introduced	2009	2005	2010	2010
Size	20% of institutional research funding and annual additions	6% of total institutional funding	19% of institutional research funding and increasing every year	33% of total institutional funding
Indicators	• Publications • Citations • External research funding	• Publications • External research funding • EU research funding • PhD production	• Publications • External research funding • PhD production • Student throughput	• Publications • External research funding • PhD production

Source: Chap. 4 of this volume

considering the implications of where to publish as defined by performance measures. Most important are "reputational factors" (Kwiek 2016) rather than the introduction of remunerative incentives such as bonuses and direct salary consequences. However, at some universities in Finland and Denmark, the remunerative incentives have become very important tools, putting pressure on academics to publish high-quality research. The use of metrics is important nevertheless, and the establishment of national metrics in research also influences how success is communicated internally in universities. The technical legitimacy of the measures is generally high, meaning that metrics are perceived as accurately assessing research performance. There are some interesting differences between the countries, however, with more criticism aimed at the crudeness of measures in Norway, Denmark, and Finland, where publications are categorized on a scale with few levels. This is even seen as a threat to high-quality research as it might prompt the production of more publications of lesser quality. The institutionalization of performance measures was also found to vary across scientific fields and institutions. The results from this study show that in the social sciences as well, which have been later to adopt bibliometrics, researchers now act in accordance with measures. An interesting aspect is also the reconstitution of research as a result of performance measurement; the importance of the publication outlet affects how researchers make sense of research. Again, in the three countries of Denmark, Finland, and Norway, with their respective systems of publication levels, this is clearly evident, whereas in Sweden, this was not discussed.

Funding Arrangements

Among all OECD countries, the Nordic countries are, year after year, in the group of countries with the highest levels of public expenditures (compared to GDP) on HEIs. Compared with other countries in the Western world, the four countries' respective higher education and research sectors studied here have remained largely unaffected by the latest financial crisis. An issue affecting the role of higher education in Nordic societies has been the introduction of fees for non-EU students in Denmark in 2006, and in 2011, Sweden followed suit. However, that is an issue beyond the scope of the empirical studies of this volume. Another topic being recently discussed in the Nordic countries is the relationship between external and internal funding for research and, in turn, its consequences for performance. In an often-cited report, Swedish scholars Öquist and Benner (2012) argued that systems with more direct state funding perform better in research. One of the benchmarks in this study was Denmark (the others were the Netherlands and Switzerland). This has led to a political debate in Sweden on the balance between direct state funding and competitive external funding (Öquist and Benner 2012). As shown in Fig. 9.1, there are significant differences between the Nordic countries regarding this issue. In Norway, only about 30% of total research funding is external, whereas the same number in Sweden and Finland is over 50%.

The relationship between internal and external funding also has influence over power relations within HEIs. Chapter 5 includes a discussion about how the increasing proportion of external funding affects authority relations surrounding research activities (Whitley 2011; Whitley and Gläser 2014). It is concluded that authority over research has decreased for managers and increased for funders as a result of these developments. In addition, successful researchers (i.e. those who win grants) receive more freedom in relation to their managers. This is also discussed in Chap. 6.

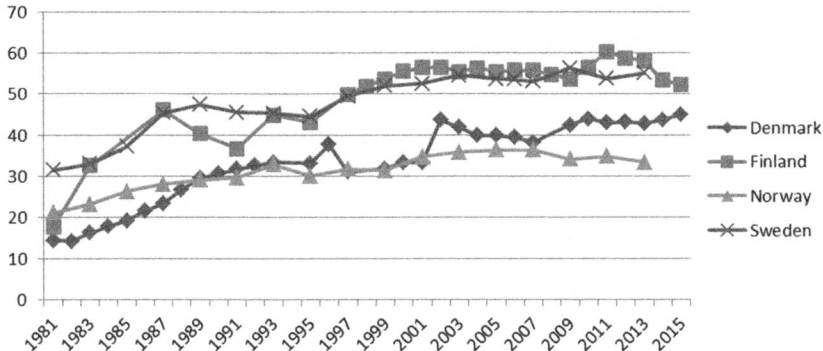

Fig. 9.1 Development in external funding as a percentage of total funding for research at Nordic HEIs. Source: Chap. 5 in this volume

Concluding Discussion

Having exposed here the main findings across the core categories and themes being investigated in the study, a critical question remains—how does this volume contribute to our knowledge about performance, leadership reforms, and universities as organizations? The richness of data and our comparative approach have made a number of conclusions possible. This was thematically discussed above, although admittedly, the initial project question on the relationship between leadership reforms and actual performance in all its crudeness turned out to be more complicated to assess than initially anticipated, not least of all due to challenges we faced in finding appropriate indicators for comparison, not to mention the different definitions (e.g. what counts as student or staff categories) across the Nordic countries. In fact, one of the major conclusions made by the research team is that there are, indeed, four distinct Nordic higher education systems, each with its own dynamics and peculiarities as well as sets of interrelated (nested) variables, which makes any comparative or causality assessment a challenging task. That being said, and guided by Olsen's visions of the European university, we can unequivocally conclude that the conditions of the environments under which Nordic HEIs operate have changed dramatically during the last decade. With reference to our initial hypotheses, it can be concluded that the H0s, based on a generally rationalist view of universities, have guided the policies and reforms in the Nordic countries. However, our survey and interview data reveal more nuanced and multifaceted experiences, more closely related to the H1s and H2s, emanating from an institutionalist view of universities.

Policy efforts aimed at modernizing the sector have paid considerable attention to the way in which public universities operate. A privileged focus has been given to aspects such as efficiency, effectiveness, and accountability. Most Nordic universities have developed extended administrative structures (central and unit levels) capable of strategically supporting their primary activities, and some have introduced recent changes in the nomination of formal leaders, moving to appointed positions rather than elected ones. Here is a clear distinction between Denmark and Finland, on the one hand, and Norway and Sweden, on the other. The more radical reforms in the former two countries have brought with them a development towards managerialism and leaderism that can be traced in the other two countries as well, albeit not to the same degree. As expected, it is, indeed, apparent that aspects of all four Olsen visions appear in the findings. As a general conclusion, though, we find signs of movement towards universities becoming more hierarchical, bureaucratic organizations where the modus operandi associated with the "community of scholars" has gradually been replaced by a market-driven logic substantiated on entities that are, formally speaking, more "autonomous" but also highly dependent on the external environment (Sahlin 2012). There are also signs of change in what Olsen calls a "representative democracy," where the role of elective collegial bodies has gradually changed. We therefore find the concept of "penetrated hierarchies" introduced by Bleiklie et al. (2015) to be useful for unpacking and explaining the complex structures of Nordic universities. The authors identify a new institutional template for organizational control, stressing the virtues of a hierarchical bureaucratic model that creates pressures within universities. These pressures are mediated by actors at different levels of the organizational field. This conclusion is, indeed, also valid in our analysis. Furthermore, we found empirical support for the second main conclusion of Bleiklie et al. (2015); namely, that control models are associated with ongoing power struggles between leadership and professionals, which in turn, are partly contingent on their respective control of external resources. Stated differently, our findings reveal that social standing (Battilana 2006), legitimacy (Deephouse and Suchman 2008), and resource dependencies (Pfeffer and Salancik 2003) do matter within the context of change dynamics in universities as modern organizations. What is more, these dimensions reinforce (and are tightly nested in) one another, thus making any causal claims with respect to the link between structural change and performance a daunting task.

Following ongoing evidence of the transformation of universities as strategic actors (Whitley 2008), another important conclusion arising from this research project is that universities are *active* entities, not only through the collective efforts of their employees but also as organizations. Contrary to what was the case in the past, it has become rather important for university actors (at multiple levels) to initiate and show activity (Karlsson 2016; Geschwind 2018). One explanation for this is found in the need for legitimacy in the view of external stakeholders and, further on, with taxpayers (Suchman 1995). The formulation of strategies (Chap. 7) is one such example. The launch of evaluations (Chap. 8) is another example, and the introduction of management and measurement systems (Chap. 6) is a third one. Yet, another is the pressure from governmental agencies to respond to demands for accountability, efficiency, and effectiveness (cf. Hazelkorn et al. 2018). In combination with more ambitious professional leaders and managers, this has created a sector packed with initiatives, some of which are aligned, some overlapping, some co-existing, and some conflicting (Geschwind 2018). Evaluation provides an interesting example in this regard, where there is now a combination of policy-initiated, managerial, and professional evaluations that make up a wide array of initiatives.

It is also clear that reforms have similar aims and primary rationales across the Nordic countries. The close collaboration between the countries and the "travelling of ideas" (Sahlin and Wedlin 2008) between the countries has created conversion at the policy level, similar to trends found elsewhere in Europe (Witte 2008). That said, it is worth pointing to the fact that the operationalization of these ideas—such as stronger, professionalized management; the use of metrics and strategies; and the roles of external stakeholders like funding bodies and others—differs significantly, and there is plenty of manoeuvre room for governments and university leaders to navigate in. One distinctive difference between the four countries is the introduction of increased formal autonomy for universities in Denmark and Finland and the changes in recruitment and appointment of academic managers. Another distinct difference is the use of publication points in all countries except Sweden. The discussion about "level 1" or "level 2" publication seems to have become institutionalized in all three countries and has been found to have effects on researchers' behaviour, although the effects are deeper in some scientific fields than others.

Performance measurement and management have proliferated as well, albeit with important differences. First, it should be noted that performance is discussed more in relation to research than education. The metrics used deeply affect researchers in all countries, but particularly so in Denmark, Finland, and Norway, where each publication is marked with a number and thus made easily measurable. This has also complemented other available metrics, such as the h-index, impact factor, and discipline-specific lists of prestigious journals that are still the most common ways to measure excellence in some scientific areas. Although performance-based funding has been used in education in all countries, with slight variations, the performance measures—basically input/output—are less directly related (or even questionably so) to quality and performance. This, in turn, might have consequences for the quality of education, which is an issue that needs further research.

Publication statistics show that performance has been high in the Nordic countries and also that performance is, today, more transparent, measurable, and comparable. However, there is also a growing critical discussion on the concept of performance and its relationship to quality and impact of research. Some of the findings in this project indicate that performance management systems encourage researchers to publish too much and that researchers are more eager to apply various strategies in order to add "points" to their résumé than they are to pose challenging and meaningful research questions (Seeber et al. 2019). Not least in the social sciences, this has been increasingly debated (Alvesson et al. 2017). Future studies should look into how this agenda develops and how initiatives implemented influence university performance in relation to researcher behaviour. A similar effect is found in applications for competitive grants, in particular in systems such as in the Nordic countries, where external funding is an important part of the incentives, becoming a goal in itself rather than a means. Both HEIs and individual academics apply for ever more research grants, not only to sustain a perceived optimal level but also for merit, leading to growth at all levels and casualization of academic staff.

As mentioned earlier, national differences and similarities have appeared in our project. Our case universities included both flagship universities and so-called regional universities. Not least of all, the latter term is controversial, and our impression is that it is considered pejorative and not necessarily used (at least in Denmark and Sweden). Being linked to the region is important, but "being regional" is less attractive, as identified in earlier inquiries (Pinheiro 2012). We have found few differences between these two types of universities. Some trends worth exploring in future studies include the relatively greater importance of education (and thus its stakeholders) and the more managerial type of steering, with appointed managers even in Norway and Sweden. We also selected soft and hard scientific fields in order to control for differences across the sciences. Also there, we found few significant differences. Worth mentioning, however, is the greater dependence on external funding and more acceptance of the use of metrics for measuring quality in the hard sciences.

Performance measurement and management have, indeed, created different universities than those before the implementation of NPM. For many senior academics who experienced academic life prior to NPM reforms, the changes have been rather dramatic. Some of these voices have been heard in this project. In contrast, for younger academics, this world of performance indicators is part and parcel of being an academic in the twenty-first century. The development over time and generational shifts are important. Further (longitudinal) studies of early career researchers' perceptions of current developments within universities are necessary. Finally, we need to continuously discuss how evaluation, measurement, and management systems affect academic life and its core activities of research and education. We surely hope this volume has encouraged our fellow colleagues across the social sciences to pursue these and other related inquiries in the near future.

Acknowledgements The data presented in the current volume and individual chapters emanate from a comparative study funded by the Norwegian Research Council under its FINNUT flagship program, a long-term program for research and innovation in the educational sector program. The project number was 237782, and the project was titled 'Does it matter? Assessing the performance effects of changes in leadership and management structures in Nordic Higher Education'.

REFERENCES

Aagaard, Kaare, Carter Bloch, and Jesper W. Schneider. 2015. Impacts of Performance-Based Research Funding Systems: The Case of the Norwegian Publication Indicator. *Research Evaluation* 24 (2): 106–117.
Aarrevaara, Timo, Ian R. Dobson, and Liisa Postareff. 2014. The Scholarly Question in Finland: To Teach or Not to Teach. In *Teaching and Research in Contemporary Higher Education: Systems, Activities and Rewards*, ed. Jung

Cheol Shin, Akira Arimoto, William K. Cummings, and Ulrich Teichler, 135–152. Dordrecht, The Netherlands: Springer.

Ahola, Sakari, Tina Hedmo, Jens-Peter Thomsen, and Agnete Vabø. 2014. *Organisational Features of Higher Education: Denmark, Finland, Norway & Sweden*. Oslo: NIFU.

Alvesson, Mats, Yiannis Gabriel, and Roland Paulsen. 2017. *Return to Meaning: A Social Science with Something to Say*. Oxford: Oxford University Press.

Amaral, Alberto, V. Lynn Meek, and Ingvild M. Larsen, eds. 2003. *The Higher Education Managerial Revolution?* Dordrecht, The Netherlands: Kluwer Academic Publishers.

Battilana, Julie. 2006. Agency and Institutions: The Enabling Role of Individuals' Social Position. *Organization* 13 (5): 653–676.

Benner, Mats, and Lars Geschwind. 2016. Svenska universitetsstyrelser och politisk styrning—40 års erfarenheter. *Forskningspolitikk*. http://fpol.no/svenska-universitetsstyrelser-och-politisk-styrning-40-ars-erfarenheter/.

Benneworth, Paul, and Ben W. Jongbloed. 2010. Who Matters to Universities? A Stakeholder Perspective on Humanities, Arts and Social Sciences Valorisation. *Higher Education* 59 (5): 567–588. https://doi.org/10.1007/s10734-009-9265-2.

Berg, Laila Nordstrand, and Rómulo Pinheiro. 2016. Handling Different Institutional Logics in the Public Sector: Comparing Management in Norwegian Universities and Hospitals. In *Towards a Comparative Institutionalism: Forms, Dynamics and Logics Across the Organizational Fields of Health Care and Higher Education*, ed. Rómulo Pinheiro, Lars Geschwind, Francisco O. Ramirez, Karsten Vrangbæk, and L. Geschwind, 145–168. Bingley, UK: Emerald Group Publishing.

Bleiklie, Ivar, Jürgen Enders, and Benedetto Lepori. 2015. Organizations as Penetrated Hierarchies: Environmental Pressures and Control in Professional Organizations. *Organization Studies* 36 (7): 1–24.

Christensen, Tom. 2011. University Governance Reforms: Potential Problems of More Autonomy? *Higher Education* 62 (4): 503–517.

Clark, Burton R. 1983. *The Higher Education System: Academic Organization in Cross-National Perspective*. Berkeley, CA: University of California Press.

Dahler-Larsen, Peter. 2012. *The Evaluation Society*. Palo Alto, CA: Stanford University Press.

———. 2014. Constitutive Effects of Performance Indicators: Getting Beyond Unintended Consequences. *Public Management Review* 16 (7): 969–986.

Deem, Rosemary, and Kevin J. Brehony. 2005. Management as Ideology: The Case of 'New Managerialism' in Higher Education. *Oxford Review of Education* 31 (2): 217–235. https://doi.org/10.1080/03054980500117827.

Deephouse, David L., and Mark Suchman. 2008. Legitimacy in Organizational Institutionalism. In *The SAGE Handbook of Organizational Institutionalism*, ed. Royston Greenwood, Christine Oliver, Kerstin Sahlin, and Roy Suddaby, 49–77. London and Thousand Oaks: Sage Publications.

Ekman, Marianne, Monica Lindgren, and Johann Packendorff. 2017. Universities Need Leadership, Academics Need Management: Discursive Tensions and Voids in the Deregulation of Swedish Higher Education Legislation. *Higher Education* 75 (2): 299–321. https://doi.org/10.1007/s10734-017-0140-2.

Fägerlind, Ingemar, and Gorel Strömqvist, eds. 2004. *Reforming Higher Education in the Nordic Countries: Studies of Change in Denmark, Finland, Iceland, Norway and Sweden.* Paris: International Institute for Educational Planning.

Fumasoli, Tatiana, Romulo Pinheiro, and Bjørn Stensaker. 2015. Handling Uncertainty of Strategic Ambitions—The Use of Organizational Identity as a Risk-Reducing Device. *International Journal of Public Administration* 38 (13–14): 1030–1040. https://doi.org/10.1080/01900692.2014.988868.

Geschwind, Lars. 2017. Higher Education Systems and Institutions, Sweden. In *Encyclopedia of International Higher Education Systems and Institutions*, ed. Jung Cheol Shin and Pedro Nuno Teixeira. Dordrecht, The Netherlands: Springer.

———. 2018. Legitimizing Change in Higher Education: Exploring the Rationales Behind Major Organizational Restructuring. *Higher Education Policy*: 1–15. https://doi.org/10.1057/s41307-018-0088-6.

Geschwind, Lars, and Rómulo M. Pinheiro. 2017. Raising the Summit or Flattening the Agora? The Elitist Turn in Science Policy in Northern Europe. *Journal of Baltic Studies* 48 (4): 513–528. https://doi.org/10.1080/01629778.2017.1305178.

Gornitzka, Åse, and Ingvild Marheim Larsen. 2004. Towards Professionalisation? Restructuring of Administrative Work Force in Universities. *Higher Education* 47 (4): 455–471.

Hansen, Hanne Foss. 2017. Higher Education Systems and Institutions, Denmark. In *Encyclopedia of International Higher Education Systems and Institutions*, ed. Jung Cheol Shin and Pedro Nuno Teixeira. Dordrecht, The Netherlands: Springer.

Hansen, Hanne Foss, Lars Geschwind, Jussi Kivistö, Elias Pekkola, Rómulo Pinheiro, and Kirsi Pulkkinen. 2019. *Balancing Accountability and Trust: University Reforms in the Nordic Countries*. Higher Education. Online First. https://doi.org/10.1007/s10734-019-0358-2.

Hazelkorn, Ellen, Hamish Coates, and Alexander C. McCormick, eds. 2018. *Research Handbook on Quality, Performance and Accountability in Higher Education*. Cheltenham, UK: Edward Elgar Publishing.

Jongbloed, Ben, Jürgen Enders, and Carlo Salerno. 2008. Higher Education and Its Communities: Interconnections, Interdependencies and a Research Agenda. *Higher Education* 56 (3): 303–324.

Kallio, Kirsi-Mari, and Tomi J. Kallio. 2014. Management-by-Results and Performance Measurement in Universities – Implications for Work Motivation. *Studies in Higher Education* 39 (4): 574–589.

Karlsson, Sara. 2016. *The Active University: Studies of Contemporary Swedish Higher Education*. Doctoral diss., KTH Royal Institute of Technology.

Kauko, Jaakko, and Sara Diogo. 2012. Comparing Higher Education Reforms in Finland and Portugal: Different Contexts, Same Solutions? *Higher Education Management and Policy* 23 (3): 1–20.

Kivistö, Jussi, Elias Pekkola, and Anu Lyytinen. 2017. The Influence of Performance-Based Management on Teaching and Research Performance of Finnish Senior Academics. *Tertiary Education and Management* 23 (3): 260–275. https://doi.org/10.1080/13583883.2017.1328529.

Klemenčič, Manja. 2018. The Student Voice in Quality Assessment and Improvement. In *Research Handbook on Quality, Performance and Accountability in Higher Education*, ed. Ellen Hazelkorn, Hamish Coates, and Alexander C. McCormick, 332–343. Cheltenham, UK: Edward Elgar Publishing.

Kogan, Maurice, Marianne Bauer, Ivar Bleiklie, and Mary Henkel. 2000. *Transforming Higher Education: A Comparative Study*. London: Jessica Kingsley.

Krücken, Georg. 2003. Learning the 'New, New Thing': On the Role of Path Dependency in University Structures. *Higher Education* 46 (3): 315–339. https://doi.org/10.1023/a:1025344413682.

Krücken, Georg, and Frank Meier. 2006. Turning the University into an Organizational Actor. In *Globalization and Organization: World Society and Organizational Change*, ed. Gili S. Drori, John W. Meyer, and Hokyu Hwang, 241–257. Oxford: Oxford University Press.

Kwiek, Marek. 2016. The European Research Elite: A Cross-National Study of Highly Productive Academics in 11 Countries. *Higher Education* 71 (3): 379–397.

Maassen, Peter. 2017. The University's Governance Paradox. *Higher Education Quarterly* 71 (3): 290–298.

Maassen, Peter, and Bjørn Stensaker. 2011. The Knowledge Triangle, European Higher Education Policy Logics and Policy Implications. *Higher Education* 61 (6): 757–769. https://doi.org/10.1007/s10734-010-9360-4.

Neave, G. 2002. The Stakeholder Perspective Historically Explored. In *Higher Education in a Globalising World: International Trends and Mutual*

Observations: A Festschrift in Honour of Ulrich Teichler, ed. Jürgen Enders and Oliver Fulton, 17–37. Berlin: Springer.

Olsen, Johan P. 2007. The Institutional Dynamics of the European University. In *University Dynamics and European Integration*, ed. Peter Maassen and Johan P. Olsen, 25–54. Dordrecht, The Netherlands: Springer.

Öquist, Gunnar, and Mats Benner. 2012. *Fostering Breakthrough Research*. Stockholm: The Royal Swedish Academy of Sciences.

Paradeise, Catherine, Emanuela Reale, Ivan Bleiklie, and Ewan Ferlie. 2009. *University Governance: Western European Comparative Perspectives*. Dordrecht, NL: Springer.

Pekkola, Elias, Taru Siekkinen, Jussi Kivistö, and Anu Lyytinen. 2017. Management and Academic Profession: Comparing the Finnish Professors with and Without Management Positions. *Studies in Higher Education*: 1–15. https://doi.org/1 0.1080/03075079.2017.1294578.

Pfeffer, Jeffrey, and Gerald R. Salancik. 2003. *The External Control of Organizations: A Resource Dependence Perspective*. Stanford, CA: Stanford Business Books.

Pinheiro, Romulo. 2012. *In the Region, For the Region? A Comparative Study of the Institutionalisation of the Regional Mission of Universities*. PhD diss., Faculty of Education, University of Oslo.

Pinheiro, Rómulo. 2015. Citius, Altius, Fortius: Mobilising the University for the 'Europe of Knowledge'. In *New Voices in Higher Education Research and Scholarship*, ed. Filipa M. Robeiro, Yurgos Politis, and Bojana Culum, 1–17. Hershey, PA: IGI-Global.

Pinheiro, Rómulo, and Bjørn Stensaker. 2014. Designing the Entrepreneurial University: The Interpretation of a Global Idea. *Public Organization Review* 14 (4): 497–516.

Pollitt, Christopher. 2002. Clarifying Convergence: Striking Similarities and Durable Differences in Public Management Reform. *Public Management Review* 4 (1): 471–492. https://doi.org/10.1080/14616670110071847.

Pruvot, Enora Bennetot, and Thomas Estermann. 2017. *University Autonomy in Europe III: The Scorecard 2017*. Brussels: European University Association (EUA).

Ramirez, Francisco O. 2006. The Rationalization of Universities. In *Transnational Governance: Institutional Dynamics of Regulation*, ed. Marie-Laure Djelic and Kerstin Sahlin-Andersson, 225–244. Cambridge: Cambridge University Press.

———. 2010. Accounting for Excellence: Transforming Universities into Organizational Actors. In *Higher Education, Policy, and the Global Competition Phenomenon*, ed. V. Rust, Laura M. Portnoi, Val D. Rust, and Sylvia S. Bagley, 43–58. Basingstoke, UK: Palgrave Macmillan.

Ramirez, Francisco O., and Tom Christensen. 2013. The Formalization of the University: Rules, Roots, and Routes. *Higher Education* 65 (6): 695–708.

Sahlin, Kerstin. 2012. The Interplay of Organizing Models in Higher Education Institutions: What Room Is There for Collegiality in Universities Characterized by Bounded Autonomy? In *Managing Reform in Universities: The Dynamics of Culture, Identity and Organisational Change*, ed. Bjørn Stensaker, Jussi Välimaa, and Clàdia Sarrico, 198–221. Basingstoke, UK: Palgrave Macmillan.

Sahlin, Kerstin, and Linda Wedlin. 2008. Circulating Ideas: Imitation, Translation and Editing. In *The SAGE Handbook of Organizational Institutionalism*, ed. Royston Greenwood, Christine Oliver, Kerstin Sahlin, and Roy Suddaby, 218–242. London: Sage.

Seeber, Marco, Benedetto Lepori, Martina Montauti, Jürgen Enders, Harry de Boer, Elke Weyer, Ivar Bleiklie, et al. 2015. European Universities as Complete Organizations? Understanding Identity, Hierarchy and Rationality in Public Organizations. *Public Management Review* 17 (10): 1444–1474. https://doi.org/10.1080/14719037.2014.943268.

Seeber, Marco, Mattia Cattaneo, Michele Meoli, and Paolo Malighetti. 2019. Self-Citations as Strategic Response to the Use of Metrics for Career Decisions. *Research Policy* 48 (2): 478–491. https://doi.org/10.1016/j.respol.2017.12.004.

Seuri, Allan, and Hannu Vartiainen. 2018. *Yliopistojen rahoitus, kannustimet ja rakennekehitys*. Helsinki: Talouspolitiikan arviointineuvosto. https://www.talouspolitiikanarviointineuvosto.fi/wordpress/wp-content/uploads/2018/01/Seuri_Vartiainen_2018-1.pdf.

Stensaker, Bjørn. 2014. Troublesome Institutional Autonomy: Governance and the Distribution of Authority in Norwegian Universities. In *International Trends in University Governance: Autonomy, Self-Government and the Distribution of Authority*, ed. Michael Shattock, 34–48. New York: Routledge.

Suchman, Mark C. 1995. Managing Legitimacy: Strategic and Institutional Approaches. *Academy of Management Review* 20 (3): 571–610.

Torjesen, Dag Olaf, Hanne Foss Hansen, Rómulo Pinheiro, and Karsten Vrangbaek. 2017. The Scandinavian Model in Healthcare and Higher Education—Recentralising, Decentralising or Both? *Scandinavian Journal of Public Administration* 21 (1): 57–80.

Whitley, Richard. 2008. Constructing Universities as Strategic Actors: Limitations and Variations. In *The University in the Market: Proceedings from a Symposium Held in Stockholm 1–3 November 2007*, ed. Lars Engwall and Denis Weaire. London: Portland Press Ltd.

———. 2011. Changing Governance and Authority Relations in the Public Sciences. *Minerva* 49 (4): 359–385. https://doi.org/10.1007/s11024-011-9182-2.

Whitley, Richard, and Jochen Gläser. 2014. The Impact of Institutional Reforms on the Nature of Universities as Organisations. In *Organizational Transformation and Scientific Change: The Impact of Institutional Restructuring on Universities and Intellectual Innovation (Research in the Sociology of Organizations, Volume 42)*, 19–49. Bingley: Emerald Insight. https://doi.org/10.1108/S0733-558X20140000042000.

Witte, Johanna. 2008. Aspired Convergence, Cherished Diversity: Dealing with the Contradictions of Bologna. *Tertiary Education and Management* 14 (2): 81–93. https://doi.org/10.1080/13583880802051840.

Open Access This chapter is licensed under the terms of the Creative Commons Attribution 4.0 International License (http://creativecommons.org/licenses/by/4.0/), which permits use, sharing, adaptation, distribution and reproduction in any medium or format, as long as you give appropriate credit to the original author(s) and the source, provide a link to the Creative Commons licence and indicate if changes were made.

The images or other third party material in this chapter are included in the chapter's Creative Commons licence, unless indicated otherwise in a credit line to the material. If material is not included in the chapter's Creative Commons licence and your intended use is not permitted by statutory regulation or exceeds the permitted use, you will need to obtain permission directly from the copyright holder.

Appendix A: FINNUT Interview Guide
English

Topic		Academics	Academics	Managers	Managers	Administrators	Administrators
		main questions	sub/support questions	main questions	sub/support questions	main questions	sub/support questions
Topic 1: Goal specificity, degree of autonomy	1	What does performance mean to you?		What does performance mean to you?		What does performance mean to you?	
	2	How much freedom do you have to decide what you do when it comes to teaching? What about research (eg. What projects you participate in)?		How much freedom does the staff in your unit have when it comes to teaching? What about research (eg. what projects they participate in)?		How much freedom do you have to decide what you do?	
	3	Do you teach in the areas where you have research expertise?	Are the tasks linked to each other when it comes to goals and performance?	Is there coherence between a staff member's teaching and research?	Are the tasks linked to each other when it comes to goals and performance?	To what extent are your tasks coherent with those of academic staff?	Are they linked to each other when it comes to goals and performance?
	4	Do you experience conflicting demands for academic work? (eg. From managers, academic staff, research groups)	Are performance targets pre-set or negotiated?	Do you think there are conflicting demands for academic work? (eg. From managers, academic staff, research groups)	Are performance targets pre-set or negotiated?	Do you experience conflicting demands for administrative work? (eg. From managers, academic staff)	Are performance targets pre-set or negotiated?

APPENDIX A: FINNUT INTERVIEW GUIDE ENGLISH

Topic 2: Decision-making and strategy	5	How familiar are you with the content of strategies at different levels in your university?	Are the strategies aligned?	How familiar are you with the content of strategies at different levels in your university?	Are the strategies aligned?	How familiar are you with the content of strategies at different levels of your university?	Are the strategies aligned?
Strategy refers to a formal, written document.	6	How important is strategy for your behaviour in teaching? What about research?	To what extent does quality play a role?	How important is strategy for decision-making in your unit (eg. the ways in which you work with teaching and research related issues)?	To what extent does quality play a role?	How important is strategy for your work?	
	7	Has there been change in the role or content of strategy in the past decade?	In what way?	Has there been change in the role or content of strategy in the past decade?	In what way?	Has there been change in the role or content of strategy in the past decade?	In what way?
Decision-making refers to formal structures but also to the informal ones that are considered to have a real effect.	8			To what extend are you free to make strategic choices on the research/education profile of the department/unit?	What are the most important factors that hamper/boost your freedom? (eg. Upper management, internal distribution, external funding, national steering, academics)		
	9	Who gets involved in strategy formulation? Who has influence in the process?	How does the consultation work (formal, informal, written, dialogue)?	Who gets involved in strategy formulation? Who has influence in the process?	How does the consultation work (formal, informal, written, dialogue)?	Who gets involved in strategy formulation? Who has influence in the process?	How does the consultation work (formal, informal, written, dialogue)?
	10	To what extent are strategic goals linked to performance targets on teaching and research?	Are there differences between teaching and research?	To what extent are strategic goals linked to performance targets on teaching and research?	Are there differences between teaching and research?	To what extent are strategic goals linked to performance targets on administrative tasks?	What about teaching and research?

APPENDIX A: FINNUT INTERVIEW GUIDE ENGLISH

Topic 3: Control and evaluation	11	Are personal performance targets formulated for your teaching? What about research?	Is a quality dimension included?	Are personal performance targets formulated for teaching? What about research?	Is a quality dimension included?	Are personal performance targets formulated for your work? Are they somehow linked to teaching and research activities?	Is a quality dimension included?
Formal vs informal - This refers to universities' internal systems, not external ones from eg. the Ministry	12	Who ascertains whether these targets are met?	Who has the power to decide?	Who ascertains whether these targets are met?	Who has the power to decide?	Who ascertains whether these targets are met?	Who has the power to decide?
	13	How is your performance measured in teaching? And research?	Who has influence on how the measuring is done? (Formal and/or informal channels?)	How is your performance measured in managerial aspects? What role to evaluation results play in this?	Has there been change in the emphasis of evaluations during the past decade?	How is your performance measured?	
	14	To what extent is performance data useful for improving your academic work?	If it is, how?	To what extent is performance data useful for improving academic work?	If it is, how?	To what extent is performance information used for improving administrative work?	Eg. How administrative work is structured or offered.
	15			What kind of rewards are high performing units and individuals provided with? Are sanctions posed on low performing ones?		What kind of rewards are high performing units and individuals provided with? Are sanctions posed on low performing ones?	

Topic 4: Support structures	16	How would you describe the administrative support you receive, related to your teaching? What about research?		How would you describe the administrative support you receive?		How well do you think the existing support structures provide support for academic performance?	
Research office, educational development, quality assurance etc.	17	To what extent do you get the help you need? Can you given an example on how support structures have helped you reach your academic performance targets?	What kind of help is missing or particularly useful?	What types of support structures and services do you find important with regard to teaching performance? What about research performance?		In your experience, what types of support structures do you think the academic staff need?	
Not part of the academic structure, separate but there to support the academic work	18			To what extent has there been an emphasis on developing support structures?	Have they become more sophisticated in the last decade?	To what extent has there been an emphasis on developing support structures?	Have they become more sophisticated in the last decade?

Topic 5: External stakeholders	19	To what extent do you cooperate with external stakeholders (outside academia)?	How, and why, is contact with external stakeholders established?	To what extent do you cooperate with external stakeholders?	How, and why, is contact with external stakeholders established?	To what extent do external stakeholders have an impact on university rules and regulations, procedures and resource allocation?
	20	Do external stakeholders have an impact on your academic work (research/teaching)?		What kind of impact do external stakeholders have on the academic work of your unit?		What kind of impact do external stakeholders have on academic staff?
Reference to actors outside of the university and scientific community (policy-makers, funders, industry etc.)	21	In what ways do external stakeholders affect the internal relations within the university?		In what ways do external stakeholders affect the internal relations within the university?		In what ways do external stakeholder affect the internal relations within the university?
	22	To what extent do external stakeholders influence your time schedules or priorities?	Do these choices have an effect on teaching and research performance?	To what extent do external stakeholders influence your time schedules or priorities?		To what extent do external stakeholders influence your time schedules or priorities?
	23	How well do the demands from management, external stakeholders and academic colleagues align?	Can you provide examples?	How well do the demands of management and external stakeholders align with the needs of academic staff?	Can you provide examples?	Seen from your point of view, how well do the demands of management and external stakeholders align with the needs of administrative staff?

Topic 6: Trust /accountability Reference to being responsible for something in relation to others; transparency and documentation of action	24	Who do you feel you are accountable to?	Please elaborate on how and why?	Who do you feel accountable to?	Please elaborate on how and why?	Who do you feel accountable to?	Please elaborate on how and why?
	25	Who are you formally accountable to?	(If there is a difference), why do you think these differ?	Who are you formally accountable to?	(If there is a difference), why do you think these differ?	Who are you formally accountable to?	(If there is a difference), why do you think these differ?
	26	Has there been change, in the last decade, in the importance attributed to accountability by the university?	If so, to what extent and how?	Has there been a change (last decade) in the importance attributed to accountability by the university?	If so, to what extent and how?	Has there been change, in the last decade, in the importance attributed to accountability by the university?	If so, to what extent and how?
	27	Can, and do, you freely express your views on the ways in which your university is run or with regard to teaching and research, in your working environment?	Are there situations where you feel your freedom is constrained or enhanced?	Can, and do, you freely express your views on the ways in which your university is run or with regard to teaching and research, in your working environment?	Are there situations where you feel your freedom is constrained or enhanced?	Can, and do, you freely express your views on the ways in which your university is run in your working environment?	Are there situations where you feel your freedom is constrained or enhanced?
Trust / control is a mediating mechanism leading to incentives for higher/lower performance.	28	To what extent is your behavior influenced by performance demands?	Reference to eg. Plans, evaluations, bibliometrics	To what extent is your behavior influenced by performance demands?	Reference to eg. Plans, evaluations, bibliometrics	To what extent is your behavior influenced by performance demands?	What about the academic staff?
	29	Is the culture in your unit better described by collegialism or individualism?	Is the environment competitive and hampering internal cooperation, or generous and supportive of cooperation?	Is the culture in your unit better described by collegialism or individualism?	Is the environment competitive and hampering internal cooperation, or generous and supportive of cooperation?	Is the culture in your unit better described by collegialism or individualism?	
	30	How important are meritocratic criteria for promotion in your unit?		How important are meritocratic criteria for promotion in your unit?		What issues or merits do you feel play an important role in the atmosphere of your working unit?	

Topic 7: Incentives / recognition (career, HR, dialogue)

#	Question	Options	Question	Options	Question	Options
31	Which types of recognition do you find important? [Note: after the general question, go through the list on the right for the parts not mentioned in the open answer.]	o peer recognition o publication points o student feedback o management recognition o financial o media attention	Which types of recognition do you find important for the performance of your unit?	o peer recognition o publication points o student feedback o management recognition o financial o media attention	Which types of recognition do you find important from a (academic) performance perspective?	o peer recognition o publication points o student feedback o management recognition o financial o media attention
32	Does your salary have a performance-dimension (eg. % of salary)?	If so, to what extent does that affect your daily tasks and priorities? Can you provide an example?	Does your salary have a performance-dimension (eg. % of salary)?	If so, to what extent does that affect your daily tasks and priorities? Can you provide an example?	Do you have a performance dimension in your salary (eg. %)?	If so, to what extent does it affect your daily tasks and priorities?
33			Does the university have promotion schemes in place (eg. tenure track)?	If so, is it linked to performance? How?	Does the university have promotion schemes in place (eg. tenure track)?	If so, is it linked to performance? How?
34	Do incentives have an effect on your overall academic performance?		Do incentives have and effect on the overall performance of your unit?		In your opinion, does recognition have an effect on your performance? What about overall academic performance?	
35	Has there been change in your teaching loads in the past 10 years? What about publishing?	If so, has this had an impact (positive/negative) on research productivity? What about quality?	Has there been change in your managerial work loads in the past 10 years?	If so, has this had an impact (positive/negative) on research productivity? What about quality?	If you think about the past decade, has there been change in the administrative work loads?	
36	What do you think are the key accomplishments that will secure your academic career?	Formally? What about informally?	What do you think are the key accomplishments that will secure an academic career?	Formally? What about informally?		
37	Who treats you with courtesy?	Eg. Academic staff, managers, administrative staff, external stakeholders?	Who treats you with courtesy?	Eg. Academic staff, managers, administrative staff, external stakeholders?	Who treats you with courtesy?	Eg. Academic staff, managers, administrative staff, external stakeholders?

APPENDIX A: FINNUT INTERVIEW GUIDE ENGLISH

Round up			
38	How would you describe the overall tendencies and development of university policy and management during the last decade?	For example: - More/less autonomy? - More/less competition?	
39	Is there something you would like to add which hasn't been covered in the questions before?		
40	Can we use the answers from this interview in other related projects and for educational purposes, if we find it useful?		
	A consent form will be provided for the interviewees to sign.		

Appendix B: FINNUT Survey Questions

FINNUT-PERFECT

Dear scholar,

How is your daily life as a teacher/researcher/manager in higher education affected by:

- strategic work at different levels;
- evaluations of teaching and research;
- resource allocation?

In this study, funded by the Norwegian Research Council, the aim is to investigate the relationship between changes in leadership and managerial structures, and shifts in teaching and research performance. Little is known about this, and the results will be relevant for employees, policy makers, managers and those involved with higher education issues.

There are 20 scholars engaged in the research consortium and the study compares higher education institutions across the Nordic region. The study follows ethical guidelines in the respective countries to assure anonymity.

For more information on the project:
http://www.uia.no/om-uia/fakultet/fakultet-for-samfunnsvitenskap/institutt-for-statsvitenskap-og-ledelsesfag/effects-of-changes-in-leadership-and-management-structures-in-nordic-higher-education

The survey takes about 20 minutes and begins by asking questions of background information.

The survey closes on 15th October 2015.

Your participation is truly appreciated, and we thank you in advance!

Background information

Please write your birth year (e.g. 1968)?

_____

Gender:
- ☐ Female
- ☐ Male
- ☐ Other

The country in which you work (for your primary job):
- ☐ Denmark
- ☐ Finland
- ☐ Norway
- ☐ Sweden
- ☐ Other, please specify_____

Please select your nationality.
- ☐ Danish
- ☐ Finnish
- ☐ Norwegian
- ☐ Swedish
- ☐ European (outside of Scandinavia)
- ☐ Other, please specify_____

Levels of employment

Universities in the Nordic countries are organised in different ways. When we ask questions related to your employment, we distinguish between three formal levels at which there is a separate tier of management:

1. University level (level 1);
2. Faculty level/level above departments (e.g. schools) (level 2);
3. Department level/equivalent (e.g. research centre/group, institute, groups with a formal structure and official manager) (level 3).

Please select your university.
- ☐ Aalto University
- ☐ Hanken School of Economics
- ☐ Lappeenranta University of Technology
- ☐ Tampere University of Technology
- ☐ University of Helsinki
- ☐ University of Eastern Finland
- ☐ University of the Arts Helsinki
- ☐ University of Jyväskylä
- ☐ University of Lapland

APPENDIX B: FINNUT SURVEY QUESTIONS

Side 3 av 17

☐ University of Oulu
☐ University of Tampere
☐ University of Turku
☐ University of Vaasa
☐ Åbo Akademi University

Please select your university.
☐ Norwegian School of Economics
☐ Norwegian University of Life Sciences
☐ Norwegian University of Science and Technology
☐ University of Agder
☐ University of Bergen
☐ University of Nordland
☐ University of Oslo
☐ University of Stavanger
☐ University of Tromsø - The Norwegian arctic university

Please select your university.
☐ Chalmers University of Technology
☐ Karlstad University
☐ Karolinska Institutet
☐ KTH Royal Institute of Technology
☐ Linköping University
☐ Linnaeus University
☐ Luleå University of Technology
☐ Lund University
☐ Mid Sweden University
☐ Stockholm School of Economics
☐ Stockholm University
☐ Swedish University of Agricultural Sciences
☐ Umeå University
☐ University of Gothenburg
☐ Uppsala University
☐ Örebro University

Please select your university.
☐ Aalborg University
☐ Aarhus University
☐ Copenhagen Business School
☐ IT University Denmark
☐ Roskilde University
☐ Technical University Denmark

Side 4 av 17

☐ University of Copenhagen
☐ University of Southern Denmark

Are you affiliated to more than one official academic unit (department, research centre/institute/school, or equivalent)?
☐ Yes
☐ No

In international statistics, universities are classified by "Field of Education" or "Field of Science". Please select the category under which your teaching (your academic degree programme) falls, and the broad category under which your research and publications **primarily** fall.

For more information about the field of education, follow the link:
http://edutechwiki.unige.ch/en/Fields_of_science_and_technology_classifications

For more information about the field of science, follow the link:
http://egracons.eu/sites/default/files/Isced%202013%20fields%20of%20education%20code%20list.pdf

My teaching/field of education is classified as:
☐ 00. Generic programmes and qualifications
☐ 01. Education
☐ 02. Arts and humanities
☐ 03. Social sciences, journalism and informations
☐ 04. Business, administration and law
☐ 05. Natural sciences, mathematics and statistics
☐ 06. Information and communication technologies
☐ 07. Engineering, manufacturing and construction
☐ 08. Agriculture, forestry, fisheries and veterinary
☐ 09. Health and welfare
☐ 10. Services
☐ 99. Other, please specify _____

My research/field of science is classified as:
☐ 01. Natural Sciences

314 APPENDIX B: FINNUT SURVEY QUESTIONS

☐ 02. Engineering and Technology
☐ 03. Medical and Health Sciences
☐ 04. Agricultural Sciences
☐ 05. Social Sciences
☐ 06. Humanities
☐ 99. Other, please specify

Please select your employment level.

☐ Assistant professor: (universitetslektor)
☐ Associate professor: (førsteamanuensis, førstelektor, post doc)
☐ Professor (professor, dosent)
☐ Other, please specify

Please select your employment level.

☐ Lecturer (adjunkt)
☐ Assistant professor (meriteringsanställning)
☐ Associate professor (lektor)
☐ Professor (professor)
☐ Other, please specify

Please select your employment level.

☐ Yliopistonlehtori (urapornastaso/level III)
☐ Yliopistotutkija (urapornastaso/level III)
☐ Erikoistutkija (urapornastaso/level III)
☐ Kliininen opettaja (urapornastaso/level III)
☐ Akatemiatutkija (urapornastaso/level III)
☐ Professori (urapornastaso/level IV)
☐ Akatemiaprofessori (urapornastaso/level IV)
☐ Tutkimusprofessori (urapornastaso/level IV)
☐ Tutkimusjohtaja (urapornastaso/level IV)
☐ Other, please specify

Please select your employment level.

☐ Assistant professor (adjunkt, forsker)
☐ Associate professor (lektor, klinisk lektor, senior forsker)
☐ Professor (professor, professor MSO, klinisk professor)
☐ Other, please specify

Do you have a PhD?

☐ Yes
☐ No

What type of employment contract do you have?

☐ Permanent position
☐ Tenure track
☐ Temporary teaching and/or research position
☐ Temporary management position
☐ Other, please specify

Is this a full time (100%) position?

☐ Yes
☐ No
☐ I don't know/not applicable

Please state what per-centage (of fulltime hours) you are contracted to work.

How long have you worked in the higher education sector?

☐ 0-5 years
☐ 6-10 years
☐ 11-15 years
☐ 16-20 years
☐ 21-30 years
☐ More than 30 years

Do you have an official management position at university, faculty- or department level (e.g. head or deputy head of an official unit)?

☐ Yes
☐ No

My management position is

☐ Rector
☐ Vice-rector

APPENDIX B: FINNUT SURVEY QUESTIONS

☐ Dean
☐ Vice-dean
☐ Head of department
☐ Deputy-Head of department
☐ Other, please specify _____

Does your current position include decision making on the areas stated below?

	1 to a low degree	2	3	4	5 to a high degree	I don't know/not applicable
Budgetary matters	☐	☐	☐	☐	☐	☐
Staff recruitment	☐	☐	☐	☐	☐	☐
Strategies	☐	☐	☐	☐	☐	☐
Performance indicators	☐	☐	☐	☐	☐	☐

How long have you been an academic manager?

☐ 0-5 years
☐ 6-10 years
☐ 11-15 years
☐ 16-20 years
☐ 21-30 years
☐ More than 30 years

Based on your contract/approved work plan, and in an average week, how is your working time divided (please write numbers, add up to 100%):

Teaching _____
Research _____
Administration/management _____
Other _____

Based on your average week; what percentage of time do you actually spend on (please write numbers, add up to 100%):?

Teaching _____
Research _____
Administration/management _____
Other _____

How many hours do you work in an average week? _____

Organisational structures

How many people are employed in your unit?

☐ 1-5
☐ 6-15
☐ 16-30
☐ 31-50
☐ 51-100
☐ More than 100

We offer:
☐ Bachelor's programmes
☐ Master's programmes
☐ PhD-programmes

I am a member of a research group.
☐ Yes
☐ No
☐ I don't know/not applicable

Participation in decision-making and strategy

I participate in:

	1 no participation	2	3	4	5 strong participation	I don't know/not applicable
Strategy formulation at university level	☐	☐	☐	☐	☐	☐
Strategy formulation at faculty level	☐	☐	☐	☐	☐	☐
Strategy formulation at unit level	☐	☐	☐	☐	☐	☐
Resource allocation at university level	☐	☐	☐	☐	☐	☐
Resource allocation at faculty level	☐	☐	☐	☐	☐	☐
Resource allocation at unit level	☐	☐	☐	☐	☐	☐

I have influence on:

	1 no influence	2	3	4	5 strong influence	I don't know/not applicable
Strategy formulation at university level	☐	☐	☐	☐	☐	☐

APPENDIX B: FINNUT SURVEY QUESTIONS

Strategy formulation at faculty level
Strategy formulation at unit level
Resource allocation at university level
Resource allocation at faculty level
Resource allocation at unit level

I align my academic behavior to meet the goals in the strategies:

	1 strongly disagree	2	3	4	5 strongly agree	I don't know/not applicable
University strategies (level 1)	☐	☐	☐	☐	☐	☐
Faculty strategies (level 2)	☐	☐	☐	☐	☐	☐
Unit strategies (level 3)	☐	☐	☐	☐	☐	☐

I align my managerial behavior to meet the goals in the strategies:

	1 strongly disagree	2	3	4	5 strongly agree	I don't know/not applicable
University strategies (level 1)	☐	☐	☐	☐	☐	☐
Faculty strategies (level 2)	☐	☐	☐	☐	☐	☐
Unit strategies (level 3)	☐	☐	☐	☐	☐	☐

The following actors have influence on the development of educational programmes (e.g. bachelor programmes):

	1 no influence	2	3	4	5 strong influence	I don't know/not applicable
University board	☐	☐	☐	☐	☐	☐
Faculty board	☐	☐	☐	☐	☐	☐
Study board	☐	☐	☐	☐	☐	☐
Department council/equivalent	☐	☐	☐	☐	☐	☐
Academic staff collectively	☐	☐	☐	☐	☐	☐
Academic staff individually	☐	☐	☐	☐	☐	☐

The following actors have influence on the content of educational programmes (e.g. bachelor programmes):

	1 no influence	2	3	4	5 strong influence	I don't know/not applicable
University board	☐	☐	☐	☐	☐	☐
Faculty board	☐	☐	☐	☐	☐	☐
Study board	☐	☐	☐	☐	☐	☐
Department council/equivalent	☐	☐	☐	☐	☐	☐
Academic staff collectively	☐	☐	☐	☐	☐	☐
Academic staff individually	☐	☐	☐	☐	☐	☐

Performance management

Compared with other units in the university:

	1 below average	2	3 average	4	5 above average	I don't know/not applicable
My unit's teaching performance is	☐	☐	☐	☐	☐	☐
My unit's research performance is	☐	☐	☐	☐	☐	☐

Compared with colleagues within my unit:

	1 below average	2	3 average	4	5 above average	I don't know/not applicable
My teaching performance is	☐	☐	☐	☐	☐	☐
My research performance is	☐	☐	☐	☐	☐	☐

Performance is a significant factor in internal resource allocation at faculty level:

	1 strongly disagree	2	3	4	5 strongly agree	I don't know/not applicable
Teaching performance	☐	☐	☐	☐	☐	☐
Research performance	☐	☐	☐	☐	☐	☐

Performance is a significant factor in internal resource allocation at unit level:

	1 strongly disagree	2	3	4	5 strongly agree	I don't know/not applicable
Teaching performance	☐	☐	☐	☐	☐	☐
Research performance	☐	☐	☐	☐	☐	☐

Incentives/motivations/encouragements

What motivates you as a manager?

	1 of no importance	2	3	4	5 of high importance	I don't know/not applicable
Acknowledgement from the university/faculty/unit-management	☐	☐	☐	☐	☐	☐
Acknowledgement from the academic staff in my unit	☐	☐	☐	☐	☐	☐
Acknowledgement from external colleagues	☐	☐	☐	☐	☐	☐
Acknowledgement from external stakeholders	☐	☐	☐	☐	☐	☐
Acknowledgement from students	☐	☐	☐	☐	☐	☐

APPENDIX B: FINNUT SURVEY QUESTIONS 317

Financial incentives
Media attention

What do you think motivates academics in your unit?

	1 of no importance	2	3	4	5 of high importance	I don't know/not applicable
Acknowledgement from the university-/faculty-/unit-management	☐	☐	☐	☐	☐	☐
Acknowledgement from me as their unit manager	☐	☐	☐	☐	☐	☐
Acknowledgement from academic staff in the unit	☐	☐	☐	☐	☐	☐
Acknowledgement from external colleagues	☐	☐	☐	☐	☐	☐
Acknowledgement from external stakeholders	☐	☐	☐	☐	☐	☐
Acknowledgement from students	☐	☐	☐	☐	☐	☐
Financial incentives	☐	☐	☐	☐	☐	☐
Media attention	☐	☐	☐	☐	☐	☐

What motivates you as an academic?

	1 of no importance	2	3	4	5 of high importance	I don't know/not applicable
Acknowledgement from the university-/faculty-/unit-management	☐	☐	☐	☐	☐	☐
Acknowledgement from my unit manager	☐	☐	☐	☐	☐	☐
Acknowledgement from the academic staff in my unit	☐	☐	☐	☐	☐	☐
Acknowledgement from external colleagues	☐	☐	☐	☐	☐	☐
Acknowledgement from external stakeholders	☐	☐	☐	☐	☐	☐
Acknowledgement from students	☐	☐	☐	☐	☐	☐
Financial incentives	☐	☐	☐	☐	☐	☐
Media attention	☐	☐	☐	☐	☐	☐

Measurements increase my performance in:

	1 Strongly disagree	2	3	4	5 Strongly agree	I don't know/not applicable
Teaching	☐	☐	☐	☐	☐	☐
Research	☐	☐	☐	☐	☐	☐

Performance measurements have a positive impact on the atmosphere surrounding academic work.

I have regular dialogue with my manager regarding my career progression.

	1 Strongly disagree	2	3	4	5 Strongly agree	I don't know/not applicable
Teaching	☐	☐	☐	☐	☐	☐
Research	☐	☐	☐	☐	☐	☐

I have regular dialogue with my staff regarding their career progression.

1 disagree	2	3	4	5 agree	I don't know/not applicable
☐	☐	☐	☐	☐	☐

Compared with colleagues in similar positions in my unit, in the last three years I have

	1 strongly disagree	2	3	4	5 strongly agree	I don't know/not applicable
Published more	☐	☐	☐	☐	☐	☐
Had more teaching	☐	☐	☐	☐	☐	☐
Supervised more Master's/PhD students	☐	☐	☐	☐	☐	☐

Funding arrangements

The funding my unit receives from the university is based on:

	1 low degree	2	3	4	5 high degree	I don't know/not applicable
Annual negotiations	☐	☐	☐	☐	☐	☐
Previous budgets	☐	☐	☐	☐	☐	☐
Measured performance	☐	☐	☐	☐	☐	☐
Earmarked funding	☐	☐	☐	☐	☐	☐
Other, please specify	☐	☐	☐	☐	☐	☐

My unit has:

	1 low degree	2	3	4	5 high degree	I don't know/not applicable
External funding for teaching	☐	☐	☐	☐	☐	☐
External funding for research	☐	☐	☐	☐	☐	☐
Extraordinary funding from the university/faculty	☐	☐	☐	☐	☐	☐

318   APPENDIX B: FINNUT SURVEY QUESTIONS

My unit decides on its own resource allocation model.

1 not at all   2   3   4   5 to a large extent   I don't know/not applicable

Strategic goals affect the allocation of resources:

	1 not at all	2	3	4	5 to a large extent	I don't know/not applicable
At university level						
At faculty level						
At unit level						

The study programmes at my unit have:

1 low level of applicants   2   3   4   5 high level of applicants   I don't know/not applicable

In the last five years, the number of applicants to my unit's study programmes have:

1 decreased   2   3   4   5 increased   I don't know/not applicable

Support services

It is easy to get access to support services:

	1 strongly disagree	2	3	4	5 strongly agree	I don't know/not applicable
Teaching support						
Research support						
Administrative support/secretarial support						

Support services have a positive effect on my:

	1 strongly disagree	2	3	4	5 strongly agree	I don't know/not applicable
Teaching performance						
Research performance						
Administrative/managerial work						

Autonomy and control

Evaluation and quality assurance procedures at my university have a positive impact on:

	1 strongly disagree	2	3	4	5 strongly agree	I don't know/not applicable
My unit's teaching performance						
My unit's research performance						
My own teaching performance						
My own research performance						

I have autonomy in the following areas:

	1 strongly disagree	2	3	4	5 strongly agree	I don't know/not applicable
Teaching content						
Pedagogical approach in teaching						
Learning outcomes of my teaching						
Research topic						
Research methods						
Partners in research projects						

There is a tension between managerial priorities and academic autonomy.

1 strongly disagree   2   3   4   5 strongly agree   I don't know/not applicable

These tensions negatively affect:

	1 strongly disagree	2	3	4	5 strongly agree	I don't know/not applicable
My teaching performance						
My research performance						

These tensions negatively affect:

	1 strongly disagree	2	3	4	5 strongly agree	I don't know/not applicable
My teaching performance						
My research performance						
My managerial performance						

I experience a high level of expectations from my unit's manager regarding:

	1 strongly disagree	2	3	4	5 strongly agree	I don't know/not applicable
Teaching performance						
Research performance						

APPENDIX B: FINNUT SURVEY QUESTIONS

I experience a high level of expectations from my academic colleagues regarding:

	1 strongly disagree	2	3	4	5 strongly agree	I don't know/not applicable
Teaching performance	□	□	□	□	□	□
Research performance	□	□	□	□	□	□

Control and evaluation of my work:

	1 strongly disagree	2	3	4	5 strongly agree	I don't know/not applicable
Is a legitimate task	□	□	□	□	□	□
Has a positive impact on my teaching performance	□	□	□	□	□	□
Has a positive impact on my research performance	□	□	□	□	□	□

Internal procedures for measuring academic performance:

	1 strongly disagree	2	3	4	5 strongly agree	I don't know/not applicable
Are in accordance with my understanding of academic performance	□	□	□	□	□	□
Have an impact on my decisions regarding academic work	□	□	□	□	□	□

In my opinion:

	1 strongly disagree	2	3	4	5 strongly agree	I don't know/not applicable
Performance measurements are signs of mistrust	□	□	□	□	□	□
Performance measurements increase transparency and fairness	□	□	□	□	□	□

Local atmosphere, unit level (level 3)

In my academic unit:

	1 strongly disagree	2	3	4	5 strongly agree	I don't know/not applicable
My manager is fair	□	□	□	□	□	□
Gender balance is recognized	□	□	□	□	□	□
Excellence in teaching is recognised	□	□	□	□	□	□
Excellence in research is recognised	□	□	□	□	□	□
High quality of publications is recognised	□	□	□	□	□	□
Academic freedom is recognised	□	□	□	□	□	□

	1 strongly disagree	2	3	4	5 strongly agree	I don't know/not applicable
Societal relevance and outreach is recognised	□	□	□	□	□	□
Hard work is recognised	□	□	□	□	□	□
Acquisition of external funding is recognised	□	□	□	□	□	□

In my academic unit:

	1 strongly disagree	2	3	4	5 strongly agree	I don't know/not applicable
The roles and responsibilities are clear	□	□	□	□	□	□
The division of labour is fair	□	□	□	□	□	□
I can influence decision-making	□	□	□	□	□	□
Performance measurements contributes to work overload	□	□	□	□	□	□

In my academic unit:

	1 strongly disagree	2	3	4	5 strongly agree	I don't know/not applicable
Individuals are rewarded	□	□	□	□	□	□
Groups are rewarded	□	□	□	□	□	□
Collaboration between groups within the unit is rewarded	□	□	□	□	□	□
Collaboration amongst different units in the university is rewarded	□	□	□	□	□	□
Collaboration with individuals from other universities is rewarded	□	□	□	□	□	□

My unit has:

	1 strongly disagree	2	3	4	5 strongly agree	I don't know/not applicable
A friendly and supportive atmosphere	□	□	□	□	□	□
An open and constructive climate	□	□	□	□	□	□
A low degree of conflict	□	□	□	□	□	□
A culture of sharing information amongst academic staff	□	□	□	□	□	□
An inclusive culture	□	□	□	□	□	□
A multidisciplinary nature	□	□	□	□	□	□
A culture of talking negatively about absent colleagues	□	□	□	□	□	□

The relationship between academic and administrative staff in my unit is:

1 very bad	2	3	4	5 very good	I don't know
□	□	□	□	□	□

Index[1]

A

Academic autonomy/freedom, 155–157, 173
Academic norms, 171
Academics, 7, 10, 11, 13, 16, 20, 24–29, 38, 40, 43, 44, 46, 48, 49, 51, 53, 55–58, 74, 80, 85, 88, 91, 94, 95, 99, 104, 112, 113, 116, 118, 119, 126–136, 138, 139, 141, 146, 147, 149–151, 153, 156, 158, 161–169, 171, 181–206, 212, 213, 215–221, 224–230, 236–239, 243, 246, 248, 249, 251–253, 255–263, 271, 275, 277, 279–284, 286, 287, 291–293
Academics' perceptions, 118, 119, 263
Accountability, 4, 5, 7, 18, 20, 21, 23, 24, 38–52, 56, 58, 59, 70, 92, 96, 112, 114, 128, 129, 134, 138, 146, 182–186, 218, 222, 229, 236–238, 239n1, 257, 259, 263, 270, 272, 275–278, 280–288, 290, 291
Authority relations, 146–177, 288
Autonomy, 8, 14, 16–19, 29, 40–44, 53, 56, 57, 59, 74, 77, 82, 91, 101, 150, 155, 156, 171, 176, 183, 184, 186–188, 203, 215, 237, 238, 246, 248, 249, 252, 262, 271, 273, 278, 279, 281, 282, 285
See also Formal autonomy; Living autonomy

B

Benchmark, 288
Bibliometrics, 49, 51, 75, 76, 78, 117, 121–125, 129, 131, 132, 138–140, 192, 202, 245, 251, 253, 287
Budget-maximisation logic, 169, 175, 177

---

[1] Note: Page numbers followed by 'n' refer to notes.

C

Centralisation/centralization, 11, 49, 55, 188, 194, 203, 204, 212, 263, 271, 279, 283, 284
Collegiality, 102, 162, 183, 184, 187, 189, 190, 193, 196, 201, 204, 205, 220, 222, 243, 246, 252, 260, 272, 279, 280, 290
Competence building, 23, 276
Conflict, 14, 16, 184, 186, 197, 273, 275, 291
Contracts, 7, 17, 41, 53, 55, 71, 73, 74, 76, 77, 120, 158n4, 195, 240, 242, 246, 248, 280, 284
Control, 11, 14, 17, 19, 45, 49, 50, 55, 56, 77, 112, 133, 134, 141, 146, 148, 158, 164, 167, 175, 183, 185, 186, 191, 192, 205, 227, 236, 237, 251, 257, 275, 284, 285, 290, 293
Convergence, 5, 6, 58–60, 70, 95, 205, 221, 262
Cultural change, 23, 276
Culture, 5, 6, 20, 55, 58, 59, 119, 132, 190, 229, 262, 277

D

Decentralisation/decentralization, 11, 81, 154, 183, 263, 271, 283
Decision-making, 11, 21, 22, 84, 115, 135, 136, 181–206, 219, 220, 229, 243, 252, 275, 276, 278–280, 286
Decoupling, 212, 227, 229

E

Effectiveness, 7, 17, 39, 40, 45, 48, 52, 55, 78, 100, 121, 187, 195, 236, 237, 239, 261, 270, 284, 290, 291
Efficiency, 7, 17, 38, 39, 48, 53, 70, 71, 78, 86, 90, 95, 96, 100, 104, 112, 121, 140, 185, 187, 236, 246, 270, 290, 291
Engagement, 211–230, 277
Enrollments, 70, 72, 88, 100
European Union, 83
Evaluation, 4, 38, 39, 44–48, 51, 52, 58, 73, 74, 84, 85, 92, 93, 95, 100, 104, 121, 122, 131, 137, 158, 183, 186, 188, 194, 219, 235–263, 271, 272, 280–283, 291, 293
Evaluation experiences, 46
Evaluation impacts, 258, 260, 262
Evaluation models, 237–240, 242, 254, 255, 282
Evaluation practices, 29, 46, 235–263, 281
Excellence, 56, 70, 76, 95, 96, 103, 104, 116, 154, 227, 272, 285, 292
External research funding, 53, 76, 83, 94, 121, 125, 146–177, 248
External stakeholders, 7, 14, 16, 19, 41, 44, 183, 186, 188, 192, 197, 212, 214, 218, 222, 230, 270, 273, 278, 280, 291

F

Flagship university, 26, 126, 130, 139, 186, 190–192, 201, 203, 205, 213n1, 273, 292
Formal autonomy, 19, 44, 182, 188, 203, 252, 279, 291
Funding, 5, 7–9, 17, 18, 23, 29, 38, 41–44, 46, 48–51, 53–59, 70, 71, 73, 75–78, 82–86, 88, 90, 91, 93–95, 99–104, 140–141,

146–177, 187, 188, 191, 192, 197–202, 204, 205, 212, 214, 217–219, 222, 227, 229, 236, 238, 240, 242–246, 248–251, 253, 254, 259–261, 271, 275, 276, 281, 283–288, 291–293
Funding agencies, 12, 49, 146, 191
Funding allocations, 55, 76, 77, 176, 245, 251
Funding regimes, 41, 242

G

Governance, 4–6, 14, 21, 24, 40–43, 54, 55, 58–60, 71, 73–75, 77, 80–82, 91, 98–101, 104, 112, 147, 148, 181, 187–189, 222, 226, 236, 237, 239, 262, 263, 271–273, 275, 278, 279, 283

H

Historical overview, 78–79, 86–87, 96
Human resources, 84, 127, 139, 249, 257

I

Impact, 5, 6, 47, 85, 115, 116, 122, 125, 128, 130, 140, 154, 165, 167, 168, 171, 194, 197, 235–263, 270, 286, 292
Incentives, 4, 17, 23, 48, 52, 53, 56–58, 78, 85, 91, 92, 95, 104, 114, 115, 121, 123–129, 134, 136, 138–141, 166, 171, 186, 192–194, 197, 198, 242, 248, 276, 284–287, 292
Institutional autonomy, 41, 92, 187, 213, 236, 237, 248, 263, 272, 283
Institutional theory, 148
Isomorphism, 4, 58

L

Leaderism, 184, 203, 280, 290
Leadership, 4–30, 74, 91, 127, 132, 165, 182–184, 188, 189, 193, 196, 199–201, 204, 205, 213, 217, 218, 227, 275, 279, 280, 289, 290
Leadership structures, 4–30, 270
Legitimacy, 13, 21n1, 39, 114–118, 120, 130–134, 138, 139, 141, 163, 195, 228, 256, 262, 275, 277, 287, 290, 291
Living autonomy, 176

M

Management, 38, 46, 51–58, 73, 76, 84, 91, 100, 112, 126, 127, 134, 139, 141, 146, 148, 152, 159–161, 168, 170, 174, 181–189, 191–194, 196, 199–201, 203–205, 211–213, 215, 217, 223, 237, 246, 249, 252, 257, 270, 271, 273, 275, 279, 280, 283–288, 291–293
See also Management systems
Management systems, 18, 194, 257, 286, 292, 293
Managerialism, 10, 71, 183–186, 194, 203, 205, 212, 236, 261, 262, 270, 280, 290
Managers, 13, 16, 26, 29, 46, 52, 53, 114, 119, 127, 128, 130–132, 137, 139, 146–149, 155, 155n3, 156, 158–177, 182, 185–206, 213, 215, 219, 224, 226, 228, 229, 236, 237, 239, 243, 260, 277, 279, 280, 288, 291, 293
Measurement, 52, 53, 55, 56, 60, 115–117, 130, 132, 133, 135, 137, 140, 203, 256, 258, 261, 291, 293

Mergers, 41, 72–77, 95, 153, 227, 272
Metrics, 48, 56, 71, 112–119, 125–141, 185, 192, 198, 250, 261, 285–287, 291–293
Mixed methods, 24, 271
Modernisation agenda/modernization agenda, 5, 58, 59, 280

N
New Public Management (NPM), 4–6, 8, 13, 21, 41, 55, 58–60, 70, 112, 132, 182, 183, 197, 203, 211, 258, 280, 284, 293
Nordic countries, 5–8, 10, 28, 29, 38, 41–51, 53–60, 70, 71, 94, 112–113, 120, 140, 153–155, 162, 164, 172, 203, 204, 213, 214, 227–229, 236, 249, 253–256, 261, 263, 270–273, 277, 278, 280–283, 288, 289, 291, 292
Nordic higher education, 4–30, 70–105, 271–273, 281, 289
Nordic universities, 5, 7, 59, 114, 118, 119, 136, 146, 155, 175, 212, 213, 220, 221, 228, 229, 270–293

O
Organisational change, 214
Organisational goals, 52, 214, 224
Organisational structures, 23, 88, 133
Organisational values, 214, 228

P
Path dependencies, 273
Perceived effects, 116, 118, 126, 132, 138, 165, 219, 263

Performance-based funding, 6, 41–44, 46, 48, 49, 51, 53–55, 57, 60, 80, 84, 112–141, 160, 185, 191, 236, 240, 242, 246, 248, 251, 253, 261, 262, 271, 272, 280, 281, 284–286, 292
Performance management, 146, 160, 187, 191–194, 205, 212, 213, 230, 245, 246, 283, 284
Performance measurement, 26, 38, 45, 51–58, 112, 134, 139, 203–205, 258, 280, 283–288, 292, 293
Policy convergence, 5, 6, 38, 58–60, 71, 104, 282
Policy initiatives, 18, 24, 76–79, 87, 95, 96, 105, 263
Power, 13, 18, 39, 78, 97, 119, 131, 137, 147, 148, 171, 176, 181–206, 271, 275, 280, 290
Power relations, 183, 214, 228, 277, 288
Professionalisation/professionalization, 38, 55, 284
Publications, 28, 43, 44, 49–51, 53, 54, 56, 58, 76, 85, 100, 103, 115, 117, 121–123, 125–132, 135, 136, 138–140, 161, 192–194, 198, 202, 205, 217, 235, 240, 242–244, 246, 248, 251–254, 261, 281, 284–288, 291, 292

Q
Quality agencies, 248, 249
Quality of education, 49, 73, 292
Quality of research, 41, 49, 50, 123, 130, 174, 280
Quality procedures, 237, 261

INDEX

R

Rationalisation/rationalization, 4–8, 10–13, 27, 58, 270, 286
Recruitment, 42, 95, 99, 162, 164, 189, 190, 193, 196, 198, 199, 243, 278, 291
Reforms, 4, 6–8, 12, 13, 16, 17, 19, 21, 29, 41–44, 51, 55, 58–60, 70–105, 112, 146, 152, 154, 176, 183, 185–190, 193, 203–205, 211, 214, 228, 229, 236, 244, 246, 251, 252, 271–273, 279, 280, 284, 289–291, 293
Reform trajectories, 70–105
Regional university, 26, 27, 119, 126, 130, 134, 137–139, 141, 186, 190–192, 205, 292
Relevance, 5, 14, 17, 50, 59, 73, 79, 121, 153, 212, 218, 236, 237, 241, 242, 244, 246, 247, 249
Reporting, 23, 26, 39, 47, 56, 57, 100, 183, 197, 204, 215, 217, 276, 279, 285
Research evaluation, 48, 137, 243, 253–255, 260, 282
Research freedom, 149, 158
Research funding, 29, 49, 53, 76, 83, 86, 90, 93, 94, 100, 101, 112, 120, 121, 123–125, 146–177, 219, 242, 244, 245, 248, 253, 254, 287, 288
Research indicator, 56, 122, 135, 136, 285
Research performance, 7, 10, 29, 53, 93, 122, 129, 131, 132, 134, 136, 138, 139, 192, 241, 258, 260, 270, 286, 287
Resource dependencies, 229, 290
Resources, 6, 19, 39, 40, 54, 55, 60, 73, 75–79, 82, 84, 89, 98, 100, 103, 112, 113, 115, 117, 120, 121, 123, 124, 126, 127, 129, 137–140, 148, 154, 162, 164, 166, 168, 174, 175, 182, 185, 191, 194, 200, 204, 212, 213, 215, 218, 226–229, 240, 241, 244, 247–250, 254, 255, 257, 263, 275, 283, 284, 286, 290
Results-oriented funding, 23, 276
Roles, 8, 10–14, 17–19, 22, 29, 38, 42, 43, 45, 46, 48, 50, 56, 60, 70, 82, 87, 89, 103, 114–119, 132, 136–141, 152, 157, 160–162, 165, 173, 176, 181–206, 213, 216, 219, 222, 226–229, 236, 237, 244–246, 248, 258, 263, 271, 272, 278–281, 283, 285, 288, 290, 291

S

Strategic actorhood, 18
Strategic actors, 19, 74, 77, 182, 223, 225, 228, 273, 277, 291
Strategic goals, 196, 226, 245
Strategic planning, 82, 211
Strategy, 19, 21, 22, 24, 28, 52, 55, 95, 151, 155, 163, 165, 166, 168–170, 172, 175, 183, 185, 186, 189, 191, 192, 194–198, 211–230, 236, 243, 245, 261, 275, 277–278, 284, 291, 292
  See also Strategy as practice
Strategy as practice, 215, 220, 222–224, 230

T

Teaching indicators, 56, 122, 285
Teaching performance, 125, 129, 258

Tight coupling, 273
Trust, 8, 28, 40, 71, 114, 131, 141, 184, 186

U
Universities as strategic actors, 277, 291
University as institutions, 16, 18, 19, 88
University as organisations, 17, 139
University governance, 14, 24, 112, 187, 222, 226
University responses, 11

V
Visions of the university, 14–16

The manufacturer's authorised representative in the EU is Springer Nature Customer Service Centre GmbH, Europaplatz 3, 69115 Heidelberg, Germany. If you have any concerns regarding our products, please contact ProductSafety@springernature.com

Printed and bound by CPI Group (UK) Ltd, Croydon, CR0 4YY
23/03/2026
02076667-0009